3DS MAX 4 FUNDAMENTALS

By Ted Boardman

New Riders

201 West 103rd Street, Indianapolis Indiana 46290

3ds max 4 Fundamentals

Copyright © 2001 by New Riders Publishing

International Standard Book Number: 0-7357-1066-X

Library of Congress Catalog Card Number: 00-109346

Printed in the United States of America

First Printing: April 2001

05   04   03   02   01   7   6   5   4   3   2

Interpretation of the printing code: The rightmost double-digit number is the year of the book's printing; the rightmost single-digit number is the number of the book's printing. For example, the printing code 01-1 shows that the first printing of the book occurred in 2001.

Publisher
David Dwyer

Associate Publisher
Al Valvano

Executive Editor
Steve Weiss

Product Marketing Manager
Kathy Malmloff

Managing Editor
Sarah Kearns

Acquisitions Editor
Linda Anne Bump

Development Editors
Laura Frey
Linda Seifert

Project Editor
Linda Seifert

Copy Editor
Joy Dean Lee

Technical Editors
Eric Schuck
Jeff Solenberg

Cover Designer
Andrew Risch

Interior Designer
Kim Scott

Compositor
Gina Rexrode

Proofreader
Marcia Deboy

Indexer
Cheryl Lenser

Software Development Specialist
Jay Payne

Trademarks

All terms mentioned in this book that are known to be trademarks or service marks have been appropriately capitalized. New Riders Publishing cannot attest to the accuracy of this information. Use of a term in this book should not be regarded as affecting the validity of any trademark or service mark.

Warning and Disclaimer

Every effort has been made to make this book as complete and as accurate as possible, but no warranty of fitness is implied. The information provided is on an "as is" basis. The authors and the publisher shall have neither liability nor responsibility to any person or entity with respect to any loss or damages arising from the information contained in this book or from the use of the CD or programs accompanying it.

Contents at a Glance

Table of Contents

About the Author

Ted Boardman came to 3ds max in a rather unorthodox way. He didn't attend any well-known art institute or design school. Rather, because of his interest in architecture born of his European travels and work experiences, Ted began an architectural design firm. Beginning in 1983, he introduced AutoCAD to his business and became an AutoCAD trainer in the mid-1980s. Over time Ted converted his business to presentation and animation services. In fact, since 1991, most of his work has centered on 3D presentations and animations created using 3D Studio, 3D Studio VIZ, MAX, and other PC software.

Ted is one of twelve carefully chosen Discreet Authorized Training Specialists. As such, he is an independent trainer of 3ds max and 3D Studio VIZ for individuals and corporations around the world. He has developed training methods to increase the productivity of MAX clients in disciplines as varied as architecture, aerospace, television, advertising, Web design, and computer gaming. Ted's training sessions, like this book, focus on how to work efficiently and effectively.

The founder of the Boston Area 3D Studio User Group, Ted is very active in the 3ds max community. You can find him lecturing, demonstrating MAX, or sharing his ideas at training programs and conventions around the world. He has also written *Inside 3D Studio MAX 2 Volume 2: Modeling and Materials; Inside 3D Studio MAX 3: Materials, Modeling, and Rendering; Inside 3d Studio VIZ;* and a bimonthly column in *Cadence Magazine*.

About the Technical Editors

Eric Schuck, a graduate of Purdue University's Technical Graphics program, has been working in 3D environments for six years. During that time, he has taught 3D computer graphics at both ITT Technical Institute and Indiana University/Purdue University at Indianapolis. Eric has also designed several computer graphics course curricula for all campuses of ITT Technical Institute across the country. In addition to his work in the educational setting, Eric currently serves as the 3D Visualization Director at Outside Source Design Studio in Indianapolis.

Jeff Solenberg, a veteran 3ds max technical editor, has a degree in CAD Drafting and Computer Visualization. A 3ds max user since the release of 3D Studio R4 for DOS, Jeff is a freelance modeler/animator and teaches courses on 3ds max through the Computer Graphics department at ITT Technical Institute in Indianapolis. He has also served as an officer in the Indianapolis 3D User Group.

Dedication

To my late father, Carl G. Boardman, Jr.

Acknowledgments

This book would not have been possible without the support and professional advice and help from the staff at New Riders. The author gets more credit than deserved as the folks behind the scenes pull everything together into a coherent work.

My sincerest thanks to those at New Riders who have made *3ds max 4 Fundamentals* the book that it is:

Linda Bump, Senior Acquisitions Editor

Laura Frey, Development Editor

Linda Seifert, Development and Project Editor

Jennifer Eberhardt, Senior Development Editor

Jeff Solenburg, Technical Editor

Eric Schuck, Technical Editor

Jay Payne, Software Specialist

A Message from New Riders

As the reader of this book, you are our most important critic and commentator. We value your opinion and want to know what we're doing right, what we could do better, in what areas you'd like to see us publish, and any other words of wisdom you're willing to pass our way.

As Executive Editor at New Riders, I welcome your comments. You can fax, email, or write me directly to let me know what you did or didn't like about this book—as well as what we can do to make our books better. When you write, please be sure to include this book's title, ISBN, and author, as well as your name and phone or fax number. I will carefully review your comments and share them with the authors and editors who worked on the book.

Please note that I cannot help you with technical problems related to the topic of this book, and that due to the high volume of email I receive, I might not be able to reply to every message.

Email: steve.weiss@newriders.com

Mail: Steve Weiss
         Executive Editor
         New Riders Publishing
         201 West 103rd Street
         Indianapolis, IN 46290 USA

Visit Our Web Site: www.newriders.com

On our Web site, you'll find information about our other books, the authors we partner with, book updates and file downloads, promotions, discussion boards for online interaction with other users and with technology experts, and a calendar of trade shows and other professional events with which we'll be involved. We hope to see you around.

Email Us from Our Web Site

Go to www.newriders.com and click on the Contact link if you

- Have comments or questions about this book.
- Want to report errors that you have found in this book.
- Have a book proposal or are interested in writing for New Riders.

- Would like us to send you one of our author kits.

- Are an expert in a computer topic or technology and are interested in being a reviewer or technical editor.

- Want to find a distributor for our titles in your area.

- Are an educator/instructor who wants to preview New Riders' books for classroom use. In the body/comments area, include your name, school, department, address, phone number, office days/hours, text currently in use, and enrollment in your department, along with your request for either desk/examination copies or additional information.

Call Us or Fax Us

You can reach us toll-free at (800) 571-5840 + 9 + 3567 (ask for New Riders). If outside the U.S., please call 1-317-581-3500 and ask for New Riders. If you prefer, you can fax us at 1-317-581-4663, Attention: New Riders.

note

Technical Support for This Book Although we encourage entry-level users to get as much as they can out of our books, keep in mind that our books are written assuming a non-beginner level of user-knowledge of the technology. This assumption is reflected in the brevity and shorthand nature of some of the tutorials.

New Riders will continually work to create clearly written, thoroughly tested and reviewed technology books of the highest educational caliber and creative design. We value our customers more than anything—that's why we're in this business—but we cannot guarantee to each of the thousands of you who buy and use our books that we will be able to work individually with you through tutorials or content with which you may have questions. We urge readers who need help in working through exercises or other material in our books—and who need this assistance immediately—to use as many of the resources that our technology and technical communities can provide, especially the many online user groups and list servers available.

Introduction

Whether you are a new user to 3ds max 4 or are upgrading from an earlier version, *3ds max 4 Fundamentals* will have techniques and methods of working that will help you be more productive and efficient at many levels of 3D scene creation.

As a 3ds max 4 instructor who provides training sessions for individuals and corporations from around the world, I am always surprised to find that although 3ds max users are creating beautiful 3D stills and animations, they are working much too hard to get the results.

The Concepts

In the first part of this book, I walk you through some of the traditional concepts that have been used throughout the ages to create art that emotionally connects the viewer with the work. This kind of connection can convey the goals of your story and presentation. Everything you do in 3ds max 4 is art, not technology, and being aware of traditional art concepts will give you the edge on the competition and make your scenes more aesthetically pleasing.

The basic concepts that are important to the way 3ds max functions are also discussed to help you understand why you should take a certain approach to modeling, materials, lighting, or animation to get the most from the software.

The Fundamentals

The discussions and exercises contained in this book will walk you through the concepts and work methods that, while fundamental, are essential to an understanding of how 3ds max 4 functions. You will also learn how to apply the basic knowledge into a workflow that will make you productive.

You will learn important fundamentals such as these:

- Using the Reference Coordinate systems in 3ds max 4 that allow you to manipulate objects in 3D space efficiently.

- Working in 2D to set up complex 3D objects that can be edited quickly and easily.

- Reducing scene overhead to get the most out of the hardware you have available.

- Using efficient materials to simulate complex geometry to increase rendering speed.

- Applying lighting to scenes that is both cost-effective and convincing to the viewer.

- Gaining control of your animations to make editing easier and more enjoyable.

As new users or users anxious to dive into the new features introduced in 3ds max 4, you will want to get stunning results as soon a possible from your new purchase.

Take the time to get a good grounding in these fundamental issues and the fancy work will come much more naturally to you as you dig deeper into the software.

Many of the basic concepts and methods you will learn in this book are not topics that are covered well, if at all, in the manuals or more advanced books. You need this information.

The Exercises

The exercises in the book illustrate the point of the topics being introduced rather than teach you how to build a diner or a roller coaster. Concentrate on the concepts of the process more than the individual steps involved. Read the exercise through, and then perform the steps, stopping and thinking along the way about how you might apply the lessons to work that is more pertinent to your needs.

Use the lessons learned from each exercise to come up with scenes of your own, incorporating the techniques and methods until you understand the process. Start with simple scenes that will allow you to focus on understanding the concepts and the fundamentals will quickly become part of your daily routine.

It is not my intention for you to learn to read from the exercises, but to learn to think and apply the methods as naturally as you brush your teeth.

The Files and Content

The files that are included on the CD-ROM that ships with the book include the files necessary for the exercises. The CD-ROM also includes other files that are either more complete versions of the basic exercise files, such as the diner scene, or totally unrelated files, such as the bug scene.

Open all the files in the book and analyze how the objects were modeled, how the lights were placed, and how the materials and animation were created. Play with those scenes to come up with other approaches to improving them. Try to learn something new every day you work with 3ds max 4. This book is just the beginning.

The New Features

The third part of the book introduces new and upgrade users to some of the exciting new features introduced in 3ds max 4. Many of these new features build on the fundamentals to make it much easier for you to create complex scenes in as short a time with as much flexibility as possible. Some of the new features are not fundamental in concept or use, but the treatment here is to ease you into using them in your work.

The Source

The exercises and concepts are all from actual professional-level classes that I teach for all disciplines of 3ds max 4 users. The exercises are derived from solutions to common problems that arise among new and experienced users alike.

Take this information and build your career upon it. Wherever 3ds max 4 may take you, good luck and have fun.

PART I

3D Graphics Concepts

Graphics Concepts: Learning from the Masters

In This Chapter

Computer graphics is just that, *graphics*. It is a 2D representation of a 3D scene created to cause the viewer to have some intended emotional response.

There have been countless resources poured into determining what makes effective graphics, from primitive cave drawings, to painting and drawing, photography and film, and now, to 3D computer graphics.

The 3D part of 3D graphics is only evident during the development phase. The end result, except in a very few 3D viewing methods, is ultimately presented as a 2D static or moving image. You must still be aware of the principles of what has been accepted, or at least promoted, as good design over the years and apply those same principles to your development of 3D scenes.

It is not the intent of this chapter to teach you the principles of good design but to bring your attention to some of the topics you should be prepared to learn more about to help you become a better 3D artist.

Read the descriptions in the chapter, play with the examples, and check out the bibliography for books on the various subjects. Then try to condition yourself to look with a critical eye at magazine images, television and movies, and other animators' work to see what strikes you as relevant and what is not.

You do not want to directly copy techniques and methods, but you do want to use the fundamental principles to develop a style of your own. Your work will then become art and not just a lucky guess, or worse, a yucky mess.

Good art is often about bending the rules to come up with something that really makes the viewer sit up and take notice at first glance. That is the emotional response you should be striving for. However, you cannot bend the rules, until you know what the rules are.

Some of the principles and concepts you will learn to look for include:

- **Storyboarding**   You will learn the importance of storyboarding to firm up the scene development cycle.

- **Scene development**   You will learn to think about traditional basics of scene composition and layout and about how camera angles can affect the mood of the scene

- **Color and lighting**   There are both physical and psychological sides of color. Traditional art forms have long recognized the effect of color on human emotions. You will look at some of the fundamentals of color as it pertains to a scene and the lighting within the scene.

- **Animation and movement**   In this section you will learn to look for the fundamentals of techniques used in film and video both with camera and object movement in a scene and editing between clips.

- **Application of 3D in the real world**   You will learn some of the opportunities available if you are new to 3D and want to make a career of it.

If you have a chance to take a watercolor or oil painting class, or a film or video class, it is well worth it. The more contact you can manage for hands-on or, at least, art appreciation sessions, the more comfortable you will be with incorporating the fundamental principles into your own work.

In working with 3ds max 4, especially for new users, it is very easy to get absorbed by the technology of creating 3D scenes. You must remember that, no matter how technical the presentation will be, the end result is still art. You are trying to extract an emotional response from the viewer.

Key Terms

Composition   The composition of an image is the layout of foreground and background elements in a picture that forms the relationships between the elements.

Complementary color   In a traditional color wheel, the complementary color is the mix of primary colors opposite any other primary color in the wheel.

Light temperature   Measured in degrees Kelvin, light temperature affects the color attributes of light. Low color temperatures are the warm red hues, while high temperatures are cool blues hues. The color temperature can affect the perceived mood of an image.

Line of action   In the film world, the line of action, or 180-degree rule, is an imaginary line between two characters or elements in a scene over which a camera very seldom crosses.

Storyboarding

A storyboard is nothing more than an outline, usually in graphical form, of what the project will contain and how the scenes will be laid out.

It can be as simple as a few quick sketches on a pad of paper or as complex as an airbrushed comic book style description of the story. The purpose of the storyboard is to organize your thoughts and portray them in a manner so that your client and coworkers will know what the plan is and how it will be executed.

Often the individual panels of a storyboard will cover the action at the key frame of an animation. Other times it will include information about the composition and color information of the scene as well.

While animations can probably benefit more from a good storyboard, still images should also be planned and sketched to show color information, lighting and camera angles, highlight locations, or cropping information. See Figure 1.1 for a quick-and-dirty storyboard sketch of four panels to show the build-up of a scene for an architectural presentation.

No matter how simple the storyboard is, do not take it for granted. Get into the habit early of creating a storyboard for every project, no matter how small.

In tight production schedules, working out a comprehensive storyboard and getting all parties to sign off before any 3D work starts is a process that will save you countless hours of wasted time and talent down the road.

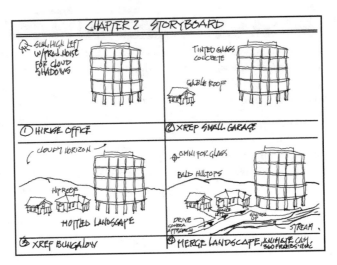

Figure 1.1   A simple storyboard for an architectural presentation.

Scene Development

Scene development must start the minute you conceive a project. It will be an integral part of the storyboard process in which you will sketch the major components of the scene. You have undoubtedly seen the movie director looking through a square made with the thumb and first finger of each hand. He is checking the composition of the scene as it relates to the width/height aspect ratio of the film he is shooting on.

In this section you will have a look at two concepts of screen development that sort of go hand in hand.

- **Scene composition**   Scene composition is the blocking of the scene and the placement and attitude of the objects within that blocking.
- **Camera angles**   Camera angles are critical to the mood of the scene and just a few degrees of change can result in a totally different feel to the scene.

Review the concepts presented here and use the Web or the local library to dig further into the subject. Again, these are concepts you want to become familiar with and then try to apply them to your scenes to see what difference changes make.

Scene Composition

The blocking out of the scene can be adjusted to create different moods that will indicate to the viewer a feeling of rest or movement. Composition can also be used to draw the viewer's eye to the part of the scene that you deem most important while detracting the viewer from less important areas. You will look at a few of the basic composition styles that relate to many art forms but are primarily borrowed from painting techniques. You will look at several of the fundamental layouts with an explanation of the principles involved. Learn to train your eye to see these compositions in nature and you will develop a feel for how to incorporate them into your 3D work. Some of the fundamental forms of composition include:

- Quadrant
- Sequential
- Asymmetrical or dynamic balance
- Symmetrical
- Golden mean
- Rule of Thirds

A short explanation and example of each follows. Again, try to envision how you might plan your scenes during the storyboard process to utilize these techniques in your work.

Quadrant

A composition of a quadrant of light and dark areas with a balance in size and position of objects in the scene. The amounts of the values, either lightness or darkness or size, do not have to be equal on all sides of the quadrant. The mood is often quiet and balanced. See Figure 1.2 for a quadrant composition.

Sequential

A sequential composition depends on a rhythm of sizes and values in the scene that leads the viewer's gaze across the image. It forces the viewer to begin at one side or the other rather than focusing on just that part of the image. Elements in the scene cause the viewer to want to see what is progressively farther in the image. A moving object could be used to draw the viewer's attention, but the scene layout should support that movement (see Figure 1.3).

Asymmetrical or Dynamic Balance

Asymmetrical composition creates a balance between the two sides of a scene. One side could be empty space, which in itself can be a powerful element of a scene. The other elements lead the viewer's gaze from the empty space and over the larger elements to the smaller elements. This type of composition usually indicates movement and action (see Figure 1.4).

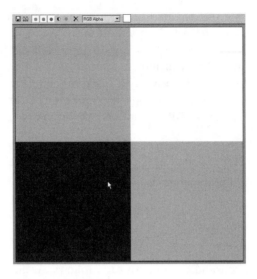

Figure 1.2   Quadrant composition.

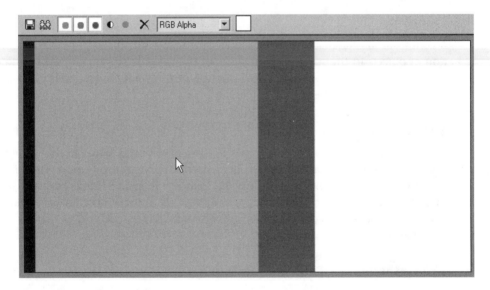

Figure 1.3   Sequential composition.

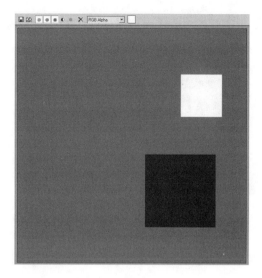

Figure 1.4   Asymmetrical composition.

Symmetrical

A symmetrical composition is in perfect balance promoting peacefulness and rest. You have to be careful with symmetrical composition. When used judiciously, it can be very effective, but in the wrong circumstances, it can be very boring (see Figure 1.5).

Golden Mean or Fibonacci Sequence

Tradition artists have long used the Golden Mean to add a sense of balance and grace to a scene, a sculpture, or a building. It is a mathematical formula based on a ratio of 1 to 1.618 and is found often recurring in nature in seashells and the pattern of sunflower seeds in the flower, for example (see Figure 1.6).

Rule of Thirds Composition

The Rule of Thirds style of composition is not really equal thirds, but a scene divided into areas: foreground, middle ground, and background. It can be either horizontal, vertical, or both and can be representative of rest or action depending on the proportions and size and attitude of objects in the areas (see Figure 1.7).

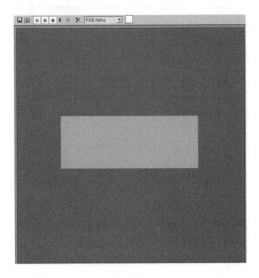

Figure 1.5   Symmetrical composition.

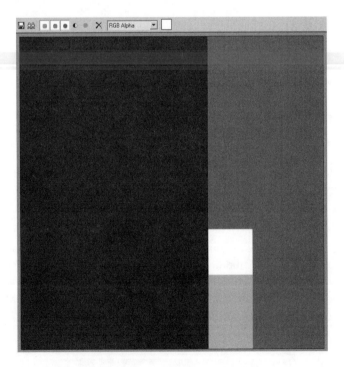

Figure 1.6   Golden Mean or Fibonacci Sequence composition.

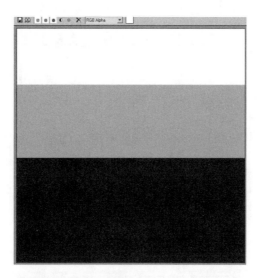

Figure 1.7   Rule of Thirds composition.

Forms Within a Composition

Another factor is how the shapes and forms are developed within the composition. It is not necessarily the form of the objects themselves in the scene, but can also be the layout of the objects within the scene that defines the forms. For example, a straight row of blocks is very static, but you may have a curved row of blocks in a scene that meanders from the front left to the back right that gives the scene an entirely different feel. Both scenes are made of blocks, however.

Three basic forms that are often used in composition are as follows:

- **Rectilinear**   A rectilinear layout is static and heavy. It promotes a peaceful, or perhaps brooding, feeling in the scene (see Figure 1.8).

- **Curved**   A curved layout tends to be peaceful as well, but with a sense of slow movement that can draw the viewer's eye from one element in the scene to another without jolting the viewer's senses. Curves can be used to lead the viewer into discovering new elements in the scene (see Figure 1.9).

- **Diagonal**   A diagonal element added to a scene denotes fast movement and draws the viewer's eye quickly across the composition. The angle and scale can heighten or diminish the effect. It can be used to create a sense of the drama (see Figure 1.10).

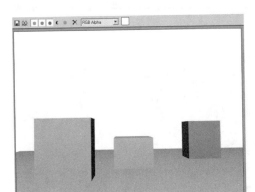

Figure 1.8   Rectilinear forms or composition.

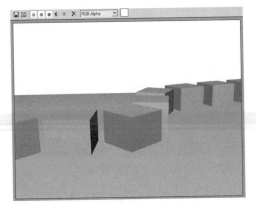

Figure 1.9   Curved composition.

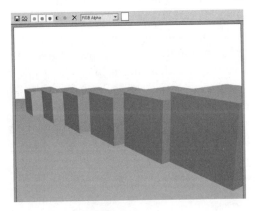

Figure 1.10   Diagonal composition in compound planes.

Horizon Position

The position of the horizon in a scene can have an effect on the overall mood of the image. This is especially true when using the Rule of Thirds basic composition.

When the horizon is directly in the middle of a scene, the effect is that of a calm, quiet mood. Again, it usually makes a scene so symmetrical and quiet that the image tends to be boring. It is generally better to place your horizon near one of the horizontal third's lines.

Dropping the horizon in the bottom third of the image would be more appropriate if the sky in our image is of greater importance. Perhaps you want to foster the illusion of a free spirit with nothing to stop forward progress. Spaciousness is added to the feeling.

Raising the horizon nearer to the top of the image, thereby exposing more water, could lend itself to a scene that requires the illusion of stability and closeness.

For scenes with characters, the main character's eyes should be near the top-third line to command attention from the viewer. With the main character's eyes at the lower-third line the viewer would be looking over the character's head, giving the character less weight in the scene.

See Figure 1.11 for an example of the scene with the horizon near the middle, near the bottom third, and near the upper third.

As mentioned earlier, the Rule of Thirds is both a horizontal and vertical composition method and the sailboat scene can benefit from applying the rule more completely. See Figure 1.12 for an example of the sailboat being positioned near one of the vertical thirds and the sun has been repositioned into the upper-right third's zone.

Figure 1.11   Using the horizontal Rule of Thirds composition can affect the mood of the scene. The horizon in the center should be avoided. A low horizon alludes to spaciousness, and a horizon nearer the top helps the illusion of closeness.

Figure 1.12   Using both horizontal and vertical Rule of Thirds composition, the sailboat has been positioned near the lower-left third's area and the sun is in the upper-right third's area.

tip   The horizon discussed in this section is not necessarily a physical horizon as seen in the ocean images. The horizon is any horizontal element of the image the draws the viewer's eye into the distance. It could be the edge of a table in a still-life scene or the base of buildings in an outdoor scene.

Camera Angles

Camera angles are a very important part of a photographer's or filmmaker's repertoire of tools to set the mood of a scene. Camera angles include both the angle at which the camera is held in relationship to the main characters in the scene and the camera lens angle, whether the shot is wide-angle or telephoto. See Figure 1.13 for an example of the sailboat from a low camera angle with a wide-angle lens.

Figure 1.13   A low camera angle to the subject combined with a wide-angle lens can add to the drama in an image.

To illustrate the principle of composition of form, Figure 1.14 departs from the recti-linear forms in the previous sailboat images and adds a diagonal element. Even though the sailboat is not really moving in any of the images, this diagonal form certainly suggests motion. The diagonal formed by the hull draws the viewer's attention to the horizon while the diagonal formed by the mast indicates toward the sun, making it a more important element in the scene.

Color and Lighting

Color and lighting are two powerful tools that will help you set the mode of a scene to enhance the mood established by the composition and camera and character angles. Again, this discussion is on color and lighting as they have been traditionally used in art thought the years.

Light is what images are all about in the first place. Anything we view is the result of light being bounced off a surface to our eyes.

Color is a quality of the light returned from the surface based on what range of lightwave frequencies can escape from the surface.

note

A viewer can often be tricked by composition techniques into making assumptions about an image that are not really indicated in the scene. Did you think about the fact that the water does not show enough ripples to get the sailboat moving as fast as it appears to be? Maybe it is just sinking!

Figure 1.14   Adding diagonal elements to the scene draws attention to the horizon and to the sun while giving the image an illusion of motion.

Lighting

Lighting here refers not only to the light that comes from a light sources, such as the sun or a light bulb, but also to the relationships between the light areas and the dark areas in a scene.

Artists spend many hours studying the relationships. Monet did studies of haystacks and the Rouen Cathedral in France to portray the "transformation of a subject" due to the effect of light itself. George Surat used different methods of painting dots of color to represent light in outdoor scenes. The illusion of light was created by using color, not by actually lighting the scene.

Light areas in the scene come forward while dark areas recede. This is a technique developed by the Old Masters painters, Rembrandt being one of the more famous, who used this concept in painting to focus the viewer's eye into important areas of the image. This method can be applied to computer-generated images just as effectively.

There is also a school of painting style known as the Luminists in which very bright light is often the center of attention and it influences everything in the scene to a noticeable degree. Some notable Luminist painters are Sidney Wildersmith, J.M.W. Turner, George Curtis, and, perhaps, Thomas Kinkade. Search for the painters on the Internet for examples of how they gave the illusion of bright light and how it affected the overall mood. See Figure 1.15 to see how a Luminist painter might have approached the sailboat scene.

Figure 1.15   View of the sailboat scene with quasi-Luminist school of painting techniques applied.

Color

As you can see from the figures in this book, color is an element that can be important to any image. While some very important artists in the past, Ansel Adams and Alfred Hitchcock for example, have produced some spectacular works in grayscale images, they relied on composition, form, and camera angle to enhance the story each was trying to tell.

note

Open a file on the CD-ROM called Luminist Boat.png to see a colored version of the image.

Even subtle color changes can effect dramatic changes to scenes in both the mood and the 3D depth illusion.

Complementary Colors

An important factor in color theory is that of complementary colors, complementary being derived from complete. First, it is important to know that the complementary colors are derived from the primary colors, and in the case of computer renderings, the primary colors are red, green, and blue.

note

Painter's primary colors are red, blue, and yellow but some of the practical information such as the affect one color has on another can be transferred from paint to light.

When the primary colors are mixed in equal amounts the results are these:

- red + green = yellow
- red + blue = magenta
- blue + green = cyan

The complementary colors are those diametrically opposed in the color wheel. Figure 1.16 shows a color wheel and the arrow shows that the complementary color of blue is yellow.

In Figure 1.17, you will see two dark rectangles with two lighter rectangles in the center of each. The dark patch on the left is a slightly purple shade of blue, and the dark patch on the right is pure blue. Both the small rectangles are the same color yellow. In the grayscale image in the book, you may be able to see a difference in the shading of the small rectangles, but if you open the file on the CD called COMP_COLOR_RECTANGLES.PNG you will see a noticeable difference in the two yellow rectangles. The one on the right, paired with its complementary color, is much brighter and more vibrant.

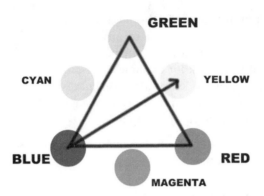

Figure 1.16   The standard color wheel showing that yellow is the complementary color of blue.

Figure 1.17   Complementary colors are shown in action. The large rectangle on the left is a purplish blue while the large rectangle on the right is pure blue. Both small rectangles are the same yellow color. The yellow, paired with its complement color, blue, is more vibrant and clean.

You can also see Figure 1.18 for a more practical example of using the yellow with the pure blue. Three lemons are depicted on a velvety blue drape. Open the image called LEMONS.PNG on the CD-ROM for the color version of the image.

Figure 1.18 This scene applies the complementary color theory in a more practical setting.

More Lighting

Lighting as an art form here refers more to photography and film, of course, than to painting, but not the technical aspects of when to put what light bulb shining on which objects.

There are two broad areas of lighting concepts from history that you should look into to improve your overall lighting skills.

- Temperature of light
- Placement of light

The temperature of light is a purely technical aspect of lighting that can affect the mood of your scenes, and the placement of lights has been used to generate an overall mood of scenes since the very early days of photography and film.

Temperature of Light

Essentially the temperature of light is a physical aspect of the light source that affects the color of the light. It is not the same as the color of the objects, however, nor the same as using colored filters over lights to generate color. Light temperature is given in degrees Kelvin (K).

What you should be looking at in light temperature is whether it lends a warm or cool feeling to the scene.

In photography, warm lighting is lighting with temperatures below 4000K. The colors tend to run to the yellow and red ranges. Warm colors lend a balance and peacefulness to a scene. These are examples of warm lighting and the corresponding temperatures:

- **Candlelight** Candlelight is very warm and has a temperature of around 1900K and has a red-orange hue. The mood generated by candlelight is legendary.

- **Incandescent** Regular household lightbulbs are incandescent and cast a yellowish-red light at a temperature of around 2800K. The feeling is close and warm in such light.

- **Floodlights** Running a bit cooler at around 3200K and up, floodlight effects work well for exterior night scenes where you want to open the scene up and make it slightly less comfortable to the viewer.

On the cool side of the equation, as you get into the higher light temperatures, the scene becomes more harsh and dramatic. The viewer is not lulled into such a sense of well-being and comfort. These are examples of cool light:

- **Daylight** At around 5200K direct sunlight is still somewhat yellow. The mood generated is not uncomfortable, but is more open and expansive.

- **Strobe light** Strobe lighting is definitely moving into the realm of cold and somewhat threatening light temperatures. Most strobes are in the range of 6000K and can be used to heighten the tension in a scene.

- **Skylight** Skylight is the light bounced back from the water and particles in the northern sky where it picks up a decidedly cold effect with a temperature of around 11000K. It can be bright and very harsh.

Consider incorporating the effects of changing light temperatures in your computer rendering to set the viewer on edge or to calm the viewer as your needs arise. Using varying lighting temperatures has traditionally been a very effective tool in both films and television. Study movies to see where the lighting temperature changes to change to mood.

Placement of Light

One of the most noticeable detractions in a film or computer-generated image is of flat lighting, a scene with no differentiation between the foreground lighting and the background lighting. Having a range of lighting through the depth of the scene heightens the feeling of 3D quality.

Overall light placement and the quality of the light can play a large role in how the audience reacts to an image or scene. Again, this is not the placement of individual lights in a given setting, but the juxtaposition of light and dark.

- **Foreground lighting**   Lighting the foreground brighter than the background tends to compress the scene somewhat. Foreground lighting does not work the same as flat lighting, but in a way that puts the viewer into the scene. It does not have to be a dramatic change in value from light to dark to be effective.

- **Background lighting**   When the background is lit brighter than the foreground, the user becomes detached from the action and the tension in increased. The greater the difference in the light intensity is, the more anonymity the viewer feels from the action.

- **Soft or hard light**   This softness or hardness of light and shadows is projected into the perception of the viewer, either making the viewer more at ease or at odds with the scene. The contrast between the dimmest and brightest lights can enhance or diminish the effect.

- **Backlighting**   Backlighting, used almost constantly and very prominently in film and television seems to be ignored often in computer rendering. Strong backlighting on characters and objects in a scene separates them from the background and focuses the viewer's attention on them.

Watch film and television with the preceding topics in mind. We have grown accustomed to seeing the effects on a day-to-day basis and do not even notice them. When you begin looking for foreground lighting or backlighting, for example, you will be amazed that you took it for granted all these years. You cannot incorporate the effects into your work until you become aware of how they might be used, and experience is often the best teacher.

Motion and Movement

You can and should refer to current or past techniques utilized in more established art forms for cues to making your moving presentations and animations elicit a emotional response from the viewer to support and reinforce the color and composition elements.

In this section you will be introduced to several areas you will want to study that will help increase the impact of the message you are trying to convey with your scenes. You will learn about topics such as:

- Object movement
- Camera movement
- Content editing
- Effects

Review the fundamental concepts presented in this section, and then investigate the topics further on the Internet or try courses that might be offered in your local area that are not necessarily aimed at computer animation, but at the more traditional fields of film, video, and photography.

Object Movement

Objects moving in your scenes should be kept to a minimum. Objects should not move just because they can, but as an integral part of the story you are trying to tell.

Unnecessary movement, especially at the edges of the main action, can distract the viewer from the point being stressed in the story. Again, as you learned in the composition discussions, the main character should not often be in the center of the frame but should be composed according to the Rule of Thirds or the Golden Mean.

Moving objects, especially human or animal characters, should appear to have weight and a specific center of gravity that influences their movement. It is much better to have limited movement reinforced by gestures that show the character's weight, as shifting of the hips or arm movement to keep the balance. The viewer will read a lot more into the gestures than in having the character moving all over the frame.

Taking cues from theater and movies, exaggeration in movement to make sure the viewer has gotten the point being made, is an effective tool. This works with inanimate objects that are moving as well. For example, if a rubber ball rolls in front of the viewer and stops, a slight skewing of the objects in the direction of travel upon stopping and a spring backward will reinforce the weight and movement of the ball. This is methodology that you can learn from traditional cartoon artists.

Camera Movement

Camera movement is a very delicate balancing act within film and video fields. You want to let the viewer know that movement has taken place, but you do not want to tamper with the viewer's equilibrium, except in very rare dramatic cases such as car chases or climbing cliffs.

You will look at four basic camera moves that are used in the film and video industry for the vast majority of scenes.

- **Zoom**   Zooming is, of course, accomplished by changing the focal length of the lens, for example, from a wide-angle far shot to a telephoto close-up shot. The effect is a very steady movement with changes in perspective that can accentuate the fact that you are closer or farther away from the subject.

- **Dolly**   Dollying the camera physically moves the camera while leaving the perspective intact. It is best used for indicating the first person character moving in the scene. There is a camera method called vertigo (from the Alfred Hitchcock film that first introduced it to Hollywood) in which the camera is dollied in and zoomed out at the same time. Although very tricky to accomplish, this can be very dramatic.

- **Pan or crab**   With this method the camera is physically moved sideways to the scene. It must be done very slowly to hold the viewer's orientation.

- **Hand held**   A relatively new camera move to replicate a light hand-held camera being walked or run through the scene. Overdone, this method is very disconcerting to most viewers, but in moderation, can add impact to the action.

Turning a camera on a point is very, very seldom done. For example, standing in one spot and turning around while pointing the camera straight ahead. Without peripheral vision, the turning motion is extremely uncomfortable, even for a few degrees. Try to avoid turning the camera at all costs.

 tip   An effective method of getting quick results from computer scenes is to borrow from the Ken Burns' television series on the Civil War or from traditional cartoon methods. Use a large image and pan or crab the camera across the image to create the illusion of movement. It is quick, easy, and effective.

Editing

Traditionally, movies are made or ruined in the editing room. Short scenes are stitched together by the editors into a coherent stream with very smooth transitions that give the illusion of a seamless story.

You must incorporate some of these fundamental techniques into your work to make the viewer comfortable with the presentation, whether you are working on an entertainment feature or trying to sell a client on a new idea for a machine.

Editing techniques to be aware of include:

- **Cut**   In a cut the scenes change abruptly from one scene to the next. This is by far the most common technique used in film and television today. Timing of the cut is of utmost importance to make it seamless to the viewer.

- **Fade or dissolve**   The transition from one scene to the next is blended with the first fading out as the next fades in. It must be done quickly to avoid the distraction of half of one scene bleeding through the next. Fades and dissolves usually indicate a shift of time or distance between two scenes, from an exterior shot to an interior shot, for example.

- **Wipe**   A wipe transition is similar to a fade, but there is a clear line of demarcation between one scene and the other. It could be a circle that grows or a page turn, for example, and is used to indicate a greater time or distance span than the fade or dissolve.

- **Cutaway**   In a cutaway transition the viewer is shown something else in the scene during the transition. For example, in a conversation between two characters, the camera could leave one character, pan to the horizon, and then back to the second character. It indicates a distraction in the story flow.

Miscellaneous Subjects

There are a couple of other issues with film and video techniques worth familiarizing yourself with. Using either or both can enhance the power of your message without the viewer being necessarily aware of the fact you have used the technique.

- **Line of action**   This very important fundamental of film is often ignored by computer animators. The viewer may not realize what is wrong but knows that something is missing. The line of action is a line drawn between the two main characters or objects is the scene. The camera seldom should cross over this sacred line as it throws the viewer's sense of stability out the window. If two characters are talking face to face, the line runs through their faces. When the camera switches back and forth from one character to the next, the camera always stays on the same side of the line. Crossing the line and moving up, over, or behind a character is very disconcerting to the viewer's sense of place.

- **Blurring effects**   This is usually not something intentional, but the effect of film being a sequence of individual frames being played back over time. Objects in motion are blurred when moving rapidly because the image spans two or more frames. This can greatly enhance the feeling of movement. You have all grown up with the effect in film and video and miss it if it is not in the scene.

These topics are a few of the types of things that, when you are aware that the effects or methods exist, can be used to add much impact at a low time cost to your presentation whether it entertainment or technical in nature. Everyone appreciates being entertained rather that threatened or made seasick by a viewing experience.

Real World Applications and Uses of 3D Imagery

In this section of the chapter, you will review some of the places where opportunities exist for those of you looking for positions in the 3D world of today. Some of them may be very apparent, and others you may not have thought of.

The design and creation of 3D scenes is still relatively new. Some have tried to incorporate 3D into areas that have failed for one reason or another, while other areas are currently successful in implementing 3D scenarios.

Whatever the reasons for success or failure, cost effectiveness of the process is key to sustained success in any field. No matter to which discipline you decide to apply your talents in 3D, if it does not represent a cost-effective solution to a problem, its chances of success are limited.

This book is intended to help you over the initial hurdle of making the process cost-effective and efficient. Apply the lessons learned and strike out into the world to find your niche in 3D. Be flexible and ready to move on into new fields when the opportunity arise.

Some of the fields currently implementing 3D with success include:

- **Architecture and engineering**   From the preliminary design phases and product development to approval processes and marketing products, both architecture and engineering fields are finding 3D presentations to be invaluable to getting the point across to the client. Civil engineering tends to be lagging slightly, probably due to the very large systems needed to keep up with huge data sets, but that is changing rapidly.

- **Advertising**   You can see, or not see, depending on how convincingly the process is executed, 3D in very much of the television advertising today. The work tends to be fast paced and creative, and the pay scales are among the highest.

- **Computer games**   This is often the intended field of choice for people to get into the field of 3D scene creation in the first place. The medium is ideal for the delivery of games, and with the advent of shared gaming over the Internet, this is an exciting path to embark upon. The hours can be long and stressful, but the rewards can also be great.

- **Forensics**   The use of 3D stills and animations to clarify legal issues is a slow-growing field with great possibilities. The techniques have to be developed carefully to keep impartiality in focus, but the impact can be the difference between life and death.

- **Education**   From preschool to grad school, more and more 3D graphics are being used to simulate or reinforce many more traditional learning methods. This is a field that appears to have few fixed boundaries and should prove very interesting as more young computer-savvy teachers enter the field.

- **Web site development**   With the increase in bandwidth for Internet access, more and more Web sites are adding 3D content to enhance the experience and information flow to the viewer. This is another field that should have a lucrative future in the use and application of 3D.

- **Retail**   Online shopping and catalogs are a booming business now and growing rapidly. Many products sold would benefit greatly from giving the viewer control over moving and disassembling the products they would like to purchase. 3ds max 4 ships with demo information on preparing 3D objects for Web and retail presentations.

- **Film and television**   From feature-length space films to logos introducing the local news on television, 3D graphics in these industries is here to stay. With the eventual adoption of digital films and televisions, the transfer of scenes will become much easier, more than likely increasing the use of 3D media in the process.

- **Fine arts**   The use of 3D in the world of fine arts is still very much in the experimental stages. Many aficionados are still struggling with the concept of traditional photography as a fine art, so computer-generated fine art will have to pay its dues. Over time, however, the expression of ideas in 3D will take on a life of its own with new ways of defining fine art. The career opportunities, of course, are a very individual thing and something that would make your guidance counselor or parents cringe at the thought.

There is probably no field that is immune to incorporating 3D images. Because 3D graphics is relatively new, there will still be successes and failures, not because of the 3D itself, but because it is not implemented in a cost-effective and appropriate manner.

The lessons you learn in this book will give you the fundamental information to start you on a career in 3D that will help make decisions toward making the process cost-effective and fun at the same time.

Chapter Summary

The intent of this chapter is not so much to teach you specific topics but to make you aware of the many aspects that have been historically proven to enhance a viewing experience. The topics for you to investigate further include:

- **Storyboarding**   You have learned of the importance of storyboarding to firm up the scene development cycle. A good storyboard clarifies the thought process and sets the stage for good workflow.

- **Scene development**   Learning to think about traditional basics of scene composition and layout and how camera angles can affect the mood of the scene is essential to making scenes that draw the appropriate response from the viewer and make the best use of valuable screen real estate for the greatest impact.

- **Color and lighting**   There are both physical and psychological sides of color. Traditional art forms have long recognized the effect of color on human emotions. You have been introduced to some of the fundamentals of color as it pertains to a scene and the lighting within the scene.

- **Animation and movement**   In this section you learned to look for the fundamentals of techniques used in film and video, both with object and camera movement in a scene as well as some of the issues involved in editing story segments into a coherent story.

Not in the same vein as the topics listed here, but as an aid to anyone planning a career move into the broad arena of 3D scene creation, you have been introduced to a few of the areas in which 3D is becoming a viable option.

Bibliography

This a short compilation of books related to the topics covered in this chapter for to study the subjects and concepts further. The Internet is your best resource for more investigation as your time and interests permit.

Drawing Figures

- Blair, Preston. *Cartoon Animation*. Walter Foster Publishing. ISBN: 1560100842

- Culhane, Shamus. *Animation from Script to Screen*. St. Martins Press. ISBN: 0312050526

- Fagin, Gary. *The Artist's Complete Guide to Facial Expression*. Watson-Guptill Publishing. ISBN: 0823016285

- Hogarth, Burne. *Dynamic Figure Drawing*. Watson-Guptill Publishing. ISBN: 0823015777
- Katz, Stephen. *Film Directing Shot by Shot*. Focal Press. ISBN: 0941188108
- Staake, Bob. *The Complete Book of Caricature*. North Light Books. ISBN: 0891343679

Art History

- Berger, John. *Ways of Seeing*. Viking Press. ISBN: 0140135154
- Fleming, William. *Arts and Ideas*. HBJ College and School Division. ISBN: 0155011049

Anatomy

- Feher, Gyorgy, and Andras Szunyoghy (Illustrator). *Cyclopedia Anatomicae*. Black Dog and Leventhal Press. ISBN: 1884822878
- Gray, Henry. *Gray's Anatomy*. Running Press. ISBN: 0914294083

Animation

- Lutz, Edwin George. *Animated Cartoons: How They Are Made, Their Origin and Development*. Applewood Books. ISBN: 1557094748
- Thomas, Frank, and Ollie Johnston. *The Illusion of Life: Disney Animation*. Hyperion. ISBN: 0786860707
- White, Tony. *The Animators Workbook*. Watson-Guptill Publishing. ISBN: 0823002292

Color Theory

- Lamb, Trevor, and Janine Bourriau. *Colour Art and Science*. Cambridge University Press. ISBN: 0521499631
- Walch, Margaret, and Augustine Hope. *Living Colors : The Definitive Guide to Color Palettes Through the Ages*. Chronicle Books. ISBN: 0811805581

Lighting and Rendering

- Birn, Jeremy. *Digital Lighting & Rendering*. New Riders Publishing ISBN: 1562059548
- Cameron, Stephen G., and Stuart Simms. *Advanced Courseware: Lighting Module*. Autodesk Inc. ISBN: 1564440036

3ds max 4 Concepts: The Fundamentals

In This Chapter

In Chapter 1, "Graphics Concepts: Learning from the Masters," you learned about the concepts helpful in presenting graphics in any form—traditional media or computer generated—for the maximum impact on the intended audience.

In this chapter, you will learn concepts specific to 3ds max 4. These concepts are important to you, the new user, to help make sense of the intentions of the designers and programmers of max 4 and to fully exploit the functionality of the software. 3ds max 4 is a program where just learning the correct buttons to push is not going to make you a productive artist. You must develop a feel for the toolset and an understanding of the underlying concepts to combine tools and work methods in efficient and productive ways.

While subsequent chapters in this book will walk you through processes step by step, this chapter is a broad discussion with some examples to highlight important concepts. Becoming familiar with these concepts will give you a basis for the later tutorials.

It is often heard that tutorials will certainly teach the reader how to push buttons to get a specific result, but that the reader doesn't know why one particular method is used over another. A goal of *3ds max 4 Fundamentals* will be to help you understand the "why" as well as the "how" of working with max 4, keeping in mind, of course, that two or three methods of accomplishing any given task usually exist.

Some of the concepts in this chapter may seem quite complex, especially because many of you have not yet worked with 3ds max 4. Do not be discouraged, however, as complex as they seem they are still fundamental to understanding max 4.

Read through the description of each concept and absorb what you can from it. Place a bookmark at the beginning of the chapter and refer to it when you encounter applications of the concept later in the exercises.

Once you know *what* topic to look for, referring to this chapter or using the 3ds max 4 online User Reference from the pull-down menu will be much easier. Making you aware that a concept exists is the main theme of this chapter. These concepts, along with the glossaries provided with the exercises in Part II, "3ds max 4 Basics," and Part III, "New and Updated max 4 Features," of this book, should make your introduction to the world of 3D more enjoyable.

In Chapter 2 you will learn concepts important to the understanding of how 3ds max 4 functions, including:

- Object naming standards
- Understanding compound shapes
- Cloning objects
- Applying modifiers
- Using the Modifier Stack
- Sub-object level editing
- Materials and maps
- Lighting
- Keyframe animation
- Mathematical accuracy

Object Naming Standards

When first working with 3ds max 4, assigning names to objects as you create them does not seem like an important task. However, to be productive you must get into the habit of typing in a name (that makes sense to you and your coworkers) for each new object. Developing object naming standards for your office should be a priority.

As each 2D or 3D object is created in 3ds max 4, the software automatically assigns a name to that object. The name is usually derived from the type of object with a sequential number added to the end of the name, for example, Box01, Line01, Torus433, and so on.

After applying only a few modifications to the object it quickly bears no resemblance to its name and no clue exists as to what Box01 might refer to when searching a list of named objects. For example, it would be entirely possible to open a file containing a landscape with a pond and trees, looking at listing of all the objects and seeing Plane01 trough Plane236 and Cylinder01 through Cylinder1021. The result is a long search and selection process to pick any specific object in the scene. Renaming objects in the beginning with logical names would speed the selection process when editing the file.

Figure 2.1 shows a simple scene with objects that have their original automatically assigned names. It might be difficult to determine which of the objects was an ellipse.

Figure 2.2 shows the same scene but with the object names edited to be more relevant to what the object is actually representing. The properly named objects are easier to choose in the Select Objects dialog and the object name that appears in the Modifier list better identifies the selected object.

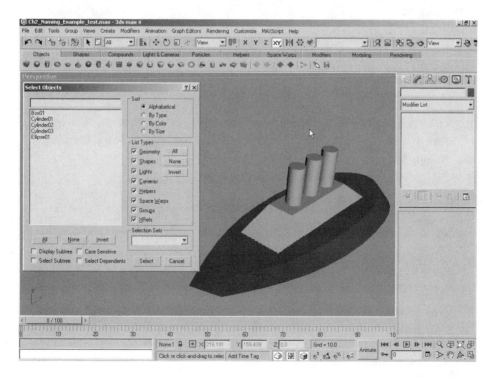

Figure 2.1   A simple ship with original object names in the Select Objects dialog.

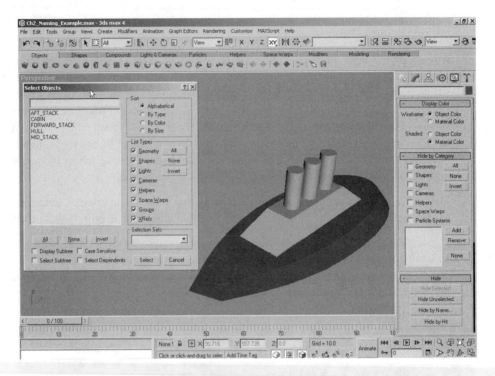

Figure 2.2   A simple ship with logical object names in the Select Objects dialog.

Objects may be renamed at the time of object creation in the Create panel or at anytime by selecting the object, highlighting the name in the Modifier List, and overwriting the text with a new name.

Setting Up a Naming Standard

It would be helpful in any company using 3ds max 4 to develop a set of naming standards for everyone in the company to use as reference. If enforced, this standard enables everyone to recognize and find objects much more quickly in a scene and allows the use of sorting techniques in the Select Objects dialog. A simple naming standard example is shown in the following list:

- **MAJOR ACTORS**   Use all caps to name major objects or characters. Caps make the objects easier to identify and cause the name to be sorted at the top of the Select by Name list when the Case Sensitive option is checked at the bottom of the dialog (see Figure 2.3).

- **Minor Actors**   Objects with less importance or background objects can begin with caps with the rest of the letters being lowercase. This separates them from the more frequently selected main objects, but indicates a 3D background object.

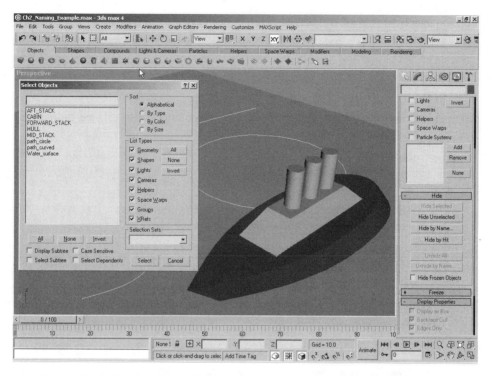

Figure 2.3   To sort, check the Case Sensitive option in the Select Objects dialog.

- **2D objects and shapes**   2D objects and 2D shapes used in the scene as motion paths can be named with all lowercase letters. These lowercase names migrate toward the bottom of the Select by Name list when the Case Sensitive option is checked.

Another possibility would be to start all object names with 2D- or 3D- to distinguish them in the Select by Name list.

In short, object naming is not something you can just leave to 3ds max 4 and then expect to work productively. The little time you spend up front on developing a naming scheme and typing the name when you create objects will be rewarded many times over.

When you have many objects in your scene and you find yourself scrolling through the Select by Name dialog even with a logical naming scheme, you can edit the names of objects by starting the name with a number 1. This forces those objects to the top of the list for the current editing session when Case Sensitive is checked. Delete the 1 when you are finished with that group of objects.

Naming and Notation Other than at Object Level

Assigning logical names to 2D and 3D objects is the most important initial standard you should develop for 3ds max 4, but there are other areas of the program where names can be assigned for clarity. The following list indicates a few of the places where logical names can be helpful:

- **Graph editors**   Track Views and Schematic Views can be named for later recall (see Figure 2.4).

- **Modifiers**   Names of modifiers can be changed or appended by right-clicking the name in the Modifier Stack and choosing Rename in the menu (see Figure 2.5).

- **Named selection sets**   Multiple selected objects can be given a common name to make reselection easier (see Figure 2.6).

- **Groups**   The Group command combines multiple objects into a single logical entity for editing (see Figure 2.7). Group names appear in brackets [SHIP] in Select by Name lists.

Get into the habit early of using short, concise names throughout 3ds max 4 and set a naming standard for your office for increased productivity and ease of use.

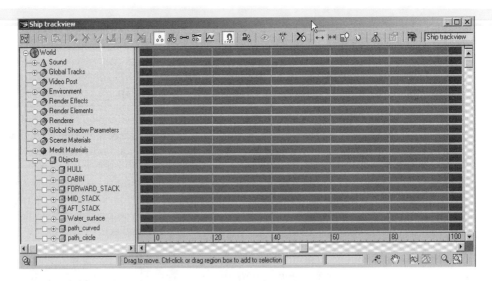

Figure 2.4   A Track View with unique name in the upper-right corner.

Understanding Compound Shapes

2D objects in 3ds max 4 are known collectively as shapes. There is a simple concept of compound shapes that you should be aware of from the start when using max 4. Much of the power of converting 2D shapes into 3D objects in max 4 requires you to understand how using compound shapes will affect the end result of the model. It is a simple, yet important concept.

Shapes are composed of sub-object level entities, vertices, segments, and splines. You will learn more about vertices and segments in subsequent chapters, but splines are an important part of compound shapes. A *spline* is a type of curve that is interpolated between two endpoints and two or more tangent vectors.

In 3ds max 4 shapes have names and, when created, are assigned a color in the viewports. Each shape is made up of one spline by definition. For example, a Circle 2D primitive is a shape containing one spline, as is a complex curving Line primitive. A Donut primitive is a shape composed of two splines: concentric circles. The Donut has a single name and both circles are the same color in the viewport (see Figure 2.8).

If two concentric circles are converted to 3D objects, with the Extrude modifier for example, the result is two cylinders of the same height, one inside the other. If a Donut compound shape is extruded the result is a cylinder with a hole through the center. In Figure 2.9, you will notice that the concentric circles on the left share faces on the top (and bottom) when extruded, which can make editing and material appli-

Figure 2.5
A Bend modifier in a Modifier Stack with notation added.

cation difficult. The Donut compound shape, consisting of two splines, results in a radically different object. max 4 builds a solid from the outside spline until it encounters a closed "island" spline where it creates a void.

Understanding compound shapes can aid you in creating objects as varied as building elevations with window openings to a splined collar for a machine (see Figure 2.10).

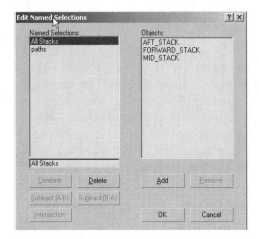

Figure 2.6   The Edit Named Selections dialog.

Compound shapes can be created by two methods: one at creation time and the other while editing. The methods are

- Using the Start New Shape button
- Using the Attach option to attach two or more Editable Splines

If, after creating a primitive 2D shape, you uncheck the Start New Shape option in the Create panel, any subsequent shapes will be added as new splines to the original (see Figure 2.11). If you convert any shape to an Editable Spline, and then use the Attach option, you can add any valid shape as a new spline (see Figure 2.12).

Figure 2.7
The Group command pull-down menu.

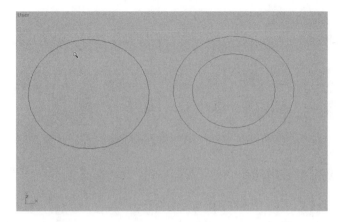

Figure 2.8   Perspective viewport with a simple circle shape on the left and a compound donut shape on the right.

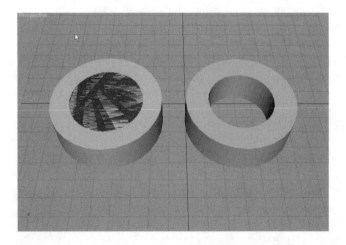

Figure 2.9   3D objects created from extruding two circle shapes on the left and a compound shape Donut on the right.

note   Most new users would attempt to create the objects shown in Figure 2.10 by using the 3D Boolean operations available in the Create panel. While it would be possible to use Boolean operations with similar end results, the mathematical overhead would be significant, slowing the system, and the chances of complex Boolean operations failing is fairly high, requiring adjustments and experimentation to accomplish the task.

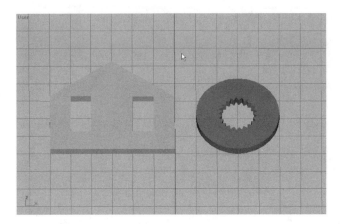

Figure 2.10   Two examples of extruded compound shapes.

Again, the concept of compound shapes may seem confusing to you until you have a chance to use them in context during a project. However, reading through this part of the chapter will introduce you to the concept and you will more readily recognize the importance of compound shapes and how to deal with them when you get into chapters that make use of them in the exercises.

tip

Conversely, single or multiple splines that are part of a compound shape can be selected and detached to create new simple or compound shapes.

Cloning Objects

The process of copying objects to create new objects in 3ds max 4 is known as cloning. Making a Copy clone is just one option of cloning along with Instance and Reference clones.

You can use cloning in max 4 to give flexible editing capabilities to your objects, which can increase productivity enormously.

Primarily, cloning of objects is accomplished by *transforming* an object while holding down the Shift key.

Transforming an object while holding down the Shift key calls up a Clone Options dialog (see Figure 2.13) with three primary options available:

Figure 2.11

Clear the Start New Shape check box after creating the first shape to create new splines added to the shape.

- **Copy**   A Copy clone looks exactly the same as the original object, but there is no connection between the two. Editing one has no effect on the other.

- **Instance**   An Instance clone has a two-way connection between any modifications to either object. Edit the original and the Instance clone is also edited and edit the Instance clone and the original changes, as well.

- **Reference**   A Reference clone has a one-way connection, from the original object to the reference object, but not from the Reference to the original. Edit the original object and the Reference object also changes. Edit the Reference object and no changes are passed to the original.

> **note**
>
> *Transform* is a collective term in 3ds max 4 for any of three actions: Move, Rotate, or Scale.

tip

An additional benefit of using Instance or Reference clones is that their memory footprint is considerably smaller than the original object or Copy clone. This increases the efficiency of your scene for better system performance and faster rendering.

By using cloning effectively in 3ds max 4 you can set up editing options that offer high flexibility and control over similar objects. Several typical scenarios might be

- **Multiple Instance Clones**   You create one column for a building and clone it many times using the Instance option. With the two-way connection you can then select one of the Instance columns, modify it, and all the other Instances will change accordingly.

- **Multiple Reference Clones**   Create one bolt and clone it many times with the Reference option. The one-way Reference connection passes changes from the original to the Reference but not from Reference to original. Select the original and modify it, all References change. Select any Reference, modify it, and none of the others are affected.

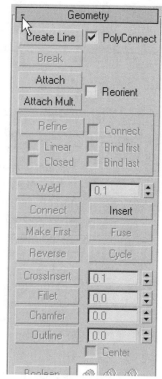

Figure 2.12

Convert a shape to an Editable Spline and use Attach to add splines to a compound shape.

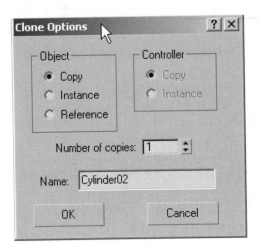

Figure 2.13   The Clone Options dialog.

■ **References of References**   Clone an original window in a building as a Reference. Select the Reference and clone it as a Reference. Select the new Reference and clone it as a Reference. Repeat this process until you have, say, 10 windows. Select the original, modify it, and all the References change. Select any Reference, modify it, and only the References downstream are affected.

■ **References with Instances**   Create a 2D compound shape that is a computer back panel with cutouts. Create a Reference clone of the 2D shape. Apply an Extrude modifier to the Reference to make it a 3D object. The Extrude information does not get passed to the original. Clone the Reference again as multiple Instances. Select the original 2D shape, modify it, and all 3D Instances are modified accordingly. This is an extremely efficient and flexible method to control multiple 3D objects. An example would be a 2D cross section shape of a wall building element, clone it as a Reference, and add an Extrude modifier. The Reference shape becomes a 3D wall. Clone the 3D wall as Instance to make 10 stories. Now when you modify the 2D cross section, all 10 stories reflect those changes.

Some tools within 3ds max 4 offer Instance as one of the creation methods. The Loft command (extruding one or more 2D shapes along a 2D path) defaults to Instance when you choose a 2D shape as the Loft cross section (see Figure 2.14). This allows you to modify the original 2D cross section to affect the complex 3D lofted object. For example, say you use Loft to create an object like a hose by lofting a circle along a curved spline. You can add an Edit Spline modifier to the circle shape and watch the loft object change as you change the shape of the circle by manipulating the vertices on the original circle shape.

Other Cloning Options

So far, all discussions of cloning have been in reference to modifications to the physical objects. However, cloning can also take place at the Animation controller level. (Animation controllers will be discussed in more detail later in this chapter.)

It is possible to animate an object moving through space, for example, and copy the animation controller to a Clipboard buffer in the Track View Graph Editor. You then select another object and paste the controller from the original as a Copy or Instance clone as shown in Figure 2.15. This replicates the movement on the new object with or without the two-way connection.

Some of the other tools and commands with cloning options are

- Mirror command
- Snapshot command
- Array command
- Nurbs surface option
- Clone command in Edit pull-down menu
- Virtual Frame Buffer cloning
- ActiveShade Floater or Viewport cloning
- Slice modifier

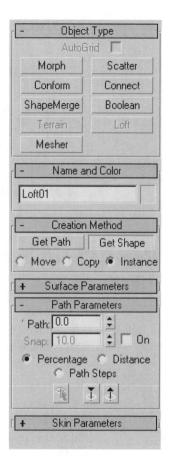

Figure 2.14
Instance option selected as default on loft cross section.

As you can easily see, the concept of cloning is a far-reaching, integral part of 3ds max 4. Learning what the concept is about is simple, applying the concept efficiently in production work requires a little practice and planning. As with all aspects of 3ds max 4, start with simple examples and work your way into more complex situations to develop a feel for how a tool or concept works.

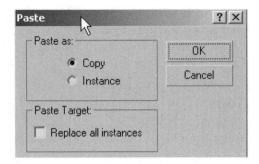

Figure 2.15   Pasting an animation controller as Copy or Instance.

Applying Modifiers

Building models in 3ds max 4 is essentially a two-step process, *create* and *modify*. First you create a basic 2D or 3D object then you modify it into its final form.

One of the primary forms of modifying objects in 3ds max 4 is the core of its power and flexibility, the capability to add discrete modifiers to objects. The modifiers are generally independent of each other and of the base object, which allows you to change, add, or remove modifiers at any point in the construction history without affecting any modifications made before or after that point in time.

There are many modifiers available, some work with only 2D shapes, others only with 3D objects, many with both 2D and 3D objects. Several modifiers are called World Space modifiers and actually alter the space that an object occupies, so when the object is moved through space the modifier affects it. Object Space modifiers, on the other hand, act on the object itself and move with the object as it travels. See Figure 2.16 for a list of modifiers that can be applied to 2D or 3D objects and see Figure 2.17 for modifiers that affect only 3D objects.

The order in which modifiers are applied to objects often has a profound effect on the end result. For example, if you apply a Bend modifier, followed by a Taper modifier to a cylinder and make adjustments the result is very different from applying the Taper modifier and then the Bend modifier with the same settings. See Figure 2.18 for a cylinder with Bend followed by Taper modifier. See Figure 2.19 for the same cylinder with the Taper placed before the Bend.

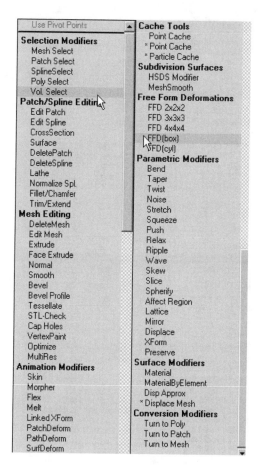

Figure 2.16   The Modifier list with a 2D shape selected.

Learning to use the modifiers with their variety of adjustments should be a high priority in your quest to master 3ds max 4. Once you are comfortable with individual modifiers, experiment with combinations of modifiers to achieve your modeling requirements. Use your imagination to apply even the most unlikely sounding combinations of modifiers and you will soon develop a feeling for what works for your particular situation.

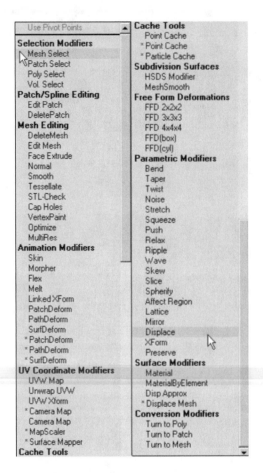

Figure 2.17   The Modifier list with a 3D object selected.

The Modifier Stack

As you apply modifiers to objects in 3ds max 4 the program keeps track of order in the Modifier Stack. Think of the Modifier Stack as the history of editing your object (see Figure 2.20).

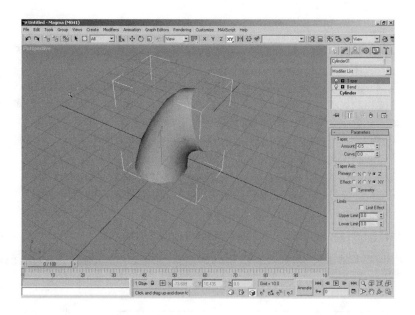

Figure 2.18   A cylinder with Bend modifier, then Taper modifier.

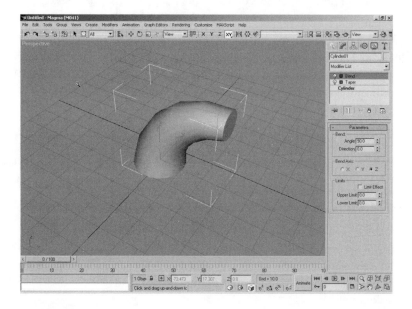

Figure 2.19   The same cylinder with Taper modifier, then Bend modifier.

It is generally possible to select a modifier in the stack and make changes to the modifier without affecting modifiers above or below that point in the stack. This allows a freedom to design and experiment with your models unfound in most other software packages. Dropping to the Cylinder level gives you access to the base parameters of the cylinder such as radius, height, and number of segments, again without affecting the modifiers higher in the stack.

Modifiers may be repositioned in the stack by dragging and dropping up or down the stack or modifiers may be completely removed from the stack.

New right-click menus in 3ds max 4 allow you to perform various operations to modifiers such as Cut and Paste to new locations in the stack or to other objects in the scene (see Figure 2.21).

Figure 2.20
The Modifier Stack for a cylinder with four modifiers applied.

> **note**
> The new right-click menus in the Modifier List replace the Edit Stack dialog found in previous releases of 3D Studio MAX.

With the right-click menu, you can also rename modifiers to add notation as mentioned earlier in this chapter and you can collapse the stack to "bake" the modifications into the model and clear the stack. The mesh now has no modifiers that you can access, but new modifiers may still be added. Modifiers may also be disabled in the viewports or the renderer or both. This is a great tool for analyzing 3ds max 4 models with modifiers that you obtain from other sources and you need to edit the object or just want to see how it was built.

In 3ds max 4 you can expand the modifiers in the stack to access sub-object level editing options. Figure 2.22 shows an example of an expanded FFD 4×4×4 modifier with access to its Control Points, Lattice, and Set Volume controls.

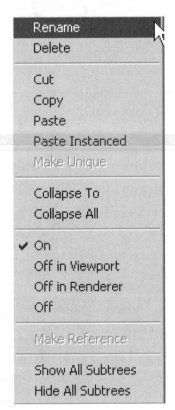

Figure 2.21
The new right-click menu for the Modifier Stack in 3ds max 4.

In the exercises in Part II and Part III of this book, you will learn to apply modifiers to 2D and 3D objects to build complex models of real-world objects. You will learn to navigate and edit the Modifier List to make changes to your models.

Figure 2.22

Expanded FFD 4×4×4 modifier with access to sub-object controls.

Becoming comfortable with all aspects of the Modifier List will be an essential part of working with 3ds max 4. The full depth of its possibilities is beyond the scope of this fundamental book. But if you use the information you learn here as a basis from which to work, and you experiment with new combinations and permutations, you will quickly learn your way around and develop your own style of modeling.

Sub-Object Level Editing

Up to this point in our discussions you have heard about working with objects, both 2D and 3D, in a 3ds max 4 scene. Primitive objects are created and then modified at the object level by applying and adjusting modifiers.

Another whole world of control exists in 3ds max 4 at what is known as sub-object level. The most common sub-object level editing that you will do is on 2D or 3D objects to gain access to the fundamental building blocks that make up the objects.

In order to access the sub-object levels of a 3D mesh, you must either convert the Primitive, a Box or Cylinder for example, to an Editable Mesh or apply a modifier like Edit Mesh that has options to select at the sub-object level. The sub-object levels associated with a 3D mesh are

- **Face** Faces are the triangular flat planes that define the surface of a model and can be selected as faces, the triangles themselves, or polygons, groups of faces defined by solid edges. Another form of face selection is by Element, which is group of faces defined as an entity.

- **Edge** Edges are the boundaries of each triangular face and may be visible or invisible. Visible edges can be selected and edited in many ways.

- **Vertex** Vertices are the nondimensional points at the apex of each triangular face. Vertices may be selected and edited like faces or edges.

The selection tools built into 3ds max 4 can be used to select a set of faces, for example, and then edit that selection set with the options available in the Modifier List as shown in Figure 2.23.

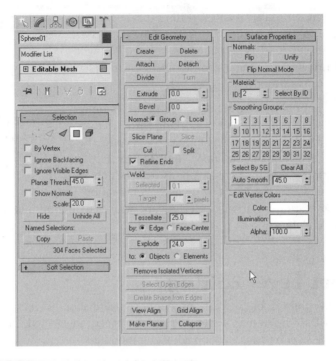

Figure 2.23   Sub-object face editing options in the Modifier List.

As an alternative, most any modifier can be applied directly to the selection set of faces and will affect only those faces. An example would be to select only faces on the top half of a cylinder, applying a Bend modifier to those faces, and adjusting the modifier controls. The result is a cylinder bent only on the top half rather than the whole cylinder as seen Figure 2.24.

Just as 3D mesh objects have sub-object level editing capabilities, so do 2D shapes. The sub-object levels associated with 2D shapes are

- **Spline**   Splines are sub-object level entities that are formed by clearing the Start New Shape button at creation or by attaching two or more shapes together as discussed earlier in this chapter.

- **Segment**   Segments are the visible 2D connectors between the vertices.

- **Vertex**   Vertices are the nondimensional points at each end of a segment.

Like a mesh object, the sub-object levels of 2D shapes can be accessed by converting them to an Editable Spline or by applying a modifier that allows access to the sub-object level. As an example, Figure 2.25 shows the Spline sub-object level editing options of an Editable Spline.

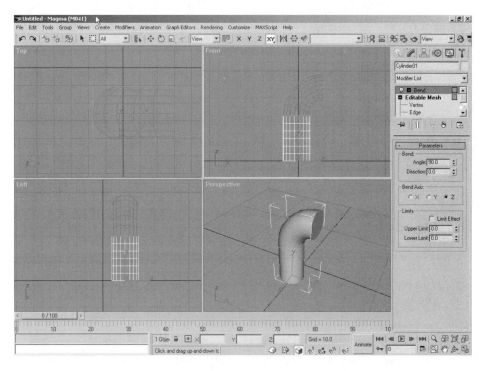

Figure 2.24 A Bend modifier applied to a Face sub-object selection.

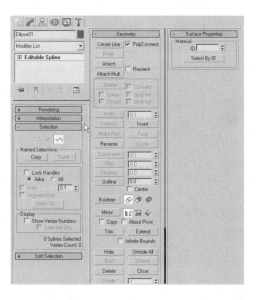

Figure 2.25 The sub-object Spline level editing options of an Editable
Spline 2D shape.

There are even special modifiers whose primary function is only to create sub-object level selection sets. Other modifiers are then applied above those selections in the Modifier List to create highly editable entities. Those modifiers include:

- MeshSelect
- SplineSelect
- PolySelect
- PatchSelect
- Vol.Select (volume select)

caution

> Once you have applied modifiers at the sub-object level that change the topology of the mesh—delete or add faces for example—you can usually not drop below that point in the Modifier List without causing problems with the object. 3ds max 4 issues a warning that there could be potential problems.

Sub-object modes can be found in many areas of 3ds max 4 other than 2D and 3D objects, including:

- **Modifiers**   Many modifiers have sub-object editing capabilities such as Gizmo or Center for the Bend modifier or Axis for the Lathe modifiers

- **Animation keys**   If you select, and then right-click most types of animation keys in the Track View or the Track Bar, you have sub-object tangency options for the incoming and outgoing side of the key.

- **Materials**   While not called sub-object mode, many materials in 3ds max 4 are made of sub-materials. Multi/Sub-object material is a single material comprised of many materials that can be applied an object.

- **Boolean operations**   3D Boolean operations allow editing of the original operands at sub-object level. For example, if you use Boolean Union to join two 3D objects, you can edit at sub-object level to adjust the position of one of the operands after the Boolean operation.

tip

Use the User Reference option in the pull-down Help menu to search for "sub-object" for other applications. Again, do not be afraid to experiment.

While working in 3ds max 4 you should always be on the lookout for a Sub-object button to gain access to a new level of editing capability.

Materials and Maps

Understanding the concept of materials and maps in 3ds max 4 is fundamental to working with the software. The two terms are used throughout the printed and online documentation and it is assumed that both terms make sense to the new user. Not always so! The efficient use of materials is probably more important than the ability to model well in max 4. For example, it would be entirely possible to have a perfectly modeled scene and make it look terrible with bad materials. Conversely, it would be possible to take a mediocre model and make it look great with good materials. Understanding the basic concepts and differences between materials and maps will help you toward creating good materials more quickly.

Materials

Materials make up the surface information assigned to 3D mesh objects in the scene. This surface information cues the viewer to what an object is supposed to represent in the scene. Certainly the form or shape of an object is a hint as to what it is supposed to be, but the key is to apply a material that convinces the viewer that something may be steel, wood, cloth, or jelly. So, materials are assigned to objects in the scene.

note You will seldom see the terms "realistic" or "realism" used in this book. While many claim to want to make realistic renderings, a more accurate term might be *convincing renderings*. Scenes in the real world are full of distractions that would be very out-of-place in a computer rendered scene. In reality, our brains filter many of these distractions to form our perceptions. If the distractions are included in the computer renderings, they become, well, distractions.

The surface information for even the simplest max 4 materials are generally made up of several components that, when combined, define simulated real-world materials. The components include, but are not limited to:

- Surface color
- Texture
- Shininess
- Highlights
- Transparency
- Reflectivity

Study your surroundings to develop a feel for how various materials appear to your eye and you will be on the path to re-creating those materials in 3ds max 4.

Maps

While materials are surface attributes we see on objects in a scene, maps are the patterns that make up the various components of the materials. Maps are not assigned directly to objects in the scene, but are used in the material definition of color, bumpiness, transparency, and so on. Maps, however, may also be loaded directly as projected images in 3ds max 4 lights or as background images in the viewports or the rendered image. Figure 2.26 shows two Material Editor Sample windows, one with an image loaded as a background or projector map, the other with the same image as the Diffuse Color pattern of a material.

New users are often confused by the terms materials and maps and will try to apply a map created for background or projectors directly to objects in the scene with no results.

As mentioned, maps are used as patterns for the components of a material; like color and reflectivity. In many of the component channels, however, it is not the color information that the material uses, rather the whiteness of each pixel. A good example of this is a Bump map. A material can be used to give the illusion that a surface is bumpy without the need to generate any extra geometry. This is a time- and resource-saving method of creating convincing objects. The white pixels in the map image appear to cause a surface to bump up, while the black pixels do nothing. Gray pixels appear to bump based on their whiteness value. See Figure 2.27 for an example of a bump map called Cellular used in a material and applied to a flat plane. While color maps can be used as bump, opacity, or glossiness maps, for example, and it is often easier to convert them to grayscale images to more easily visualize the effectiveness in a material.

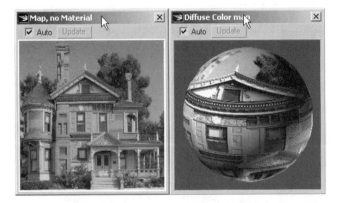

Figure 2.26   Left: Sample Material window is a map only. Right: Sample window is the same map applied as Diffuse Color of a material.

Figure 2.27   A Cellular map used in the bump map slot of a material and applied to a flat plane. The surface texture is an illusion caused by the whiteness values of the pixels in Cellular map.

Mapping Coordinates

Any discussion of materials and maps is not complete without mentioning mapping coordinates. When a map is used in most material components, the user must indicate the placement, orientation, and scale of the pattern within the material. Reflection, refraction, and 3D procedural maps are exceptions.

Objects require that mapping coordinates be applied to describe how the pattern is to be repeated over the surface. It is important to adjust this pattern repetition to give the patterns a more convincing look. Several methods of generating mapping coordinates are available, including:

- **General mapping coordinates**   An option for specific mapping coordinates for primitive objects. These are not adjustable and are only for general use.
- **Apply UVW map modifier**   This modifier has a plethora of adjustments for very accurate map placement and scaling.
- **Special mapping coordinates**   Lofted objects, for example, objects created with cross sections extruded along a path, generate mapping coordinates that follow the curvature of the path. Adjustments for scaling along the length of the object and around the perimeter of the object are available.

Start creating materials with simple map assignments and work your way up to more complexity after you understand the fundamentals. Study the materials that ship with 3ds max 4 to see how they were created and assign them to primitive objects for mapping coordinates. The fundamental concepts of materials and maps can be applied over and over in a material to create complex, deep materials that will make you an artist.

Lighting Concepts

Lighting a scene in 3ds max 4 is one of the most important aspects of achieving the desired end result, but often the part of the process given the least attention by the new users.

Many of us have limited or no training or experience in lighting as an art. Whereas Chapter 1 discussed traditional forms of lighting in art forms such as film or painting, this discussion will be more directly related to 3ds max 4 without getting into the details. Understanding the process of lighting scenes in max 4 will make it easier to learn the specific tools as you encounter them in your work.

Radiosity

A major difference in real-world lighting and default lighting in max 4 is a subject known as radiosity or global lighting, the effects of light bouncing from one object to the next in a scene. Bounced light is a significant influence in how we perceive the real world and, primarily because of the computer resources need to calculate radiosity, it has been left out of max 4.

Radiosity can be simulated in 3ds max 4 by careful placement of extra lights that use the built-in capability of max 4 lights to include or exclude individual objects from the affects of a particular light.

Attenuation

Another aspect of natural lighting is that of attenuation. In the real world, light diminishes in intensity by the inverse square of the distance from the light source. Lights in 3ds max 4, on the contrary, keep the same intensity to infinity. There are several attenuation tools for lights that you can access to control how quickly the light attenuates (see Figure 2.28).

note

There are several third-party radiosity renderers for 3D Studio MAX available on the market. Check current information for max 4 availability.

Shadow Casting

Shadow casting lights can be a source of confusion for new 3ds max 4 users. By default, max 4 lights do not cast shadows, the option must be toggled on in the light parameters. There are two types of shadows that lights can cast:

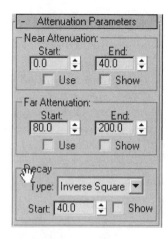

Figure 2.28
In max 4, the Attenuation Parameters rollout is used to control how quickly light dies out from the source.

- **Shadow map**   With mapped shadows, the distance of objects from the light source is calculated relative to each other. A grayscale map is generated based on the coverage of one object in front of another, the map is stored temporarily, then composited onto the image at render time to appear as shadows. A scene with many high-resolution shadow maps can overtax your computer resources and slow rendering to a crawl. Mapped shadows can be adjusted for resolution, moved toward or away from the source, or adjusted for edge softness.

- **Raytrace**   Raytraced shadows are calculated from sample rays of light traced from the object to the light source to the viewer during the render process. This is mathematically more intense, which is often slower than mapped shadow calculations, but uses much less temporary storage resources. There are fewer adjustments and the shadows tend to be very hard-edged.

As a general rule, raytrace shadows are more appropriate for outdoor shadows in bright sun, but you will have to learn to use the controls for each shadow type and adjust for the conditions in your scenes. Good shadows are not so much a science as an art that you will learn through experience.

Both shadow types have density and color control, and both types can have maps assigned that alter the pattern within the shadow area.

In any case, because shadow casting is resource intensive, only use shadows on lights that are absolutely necessary.

Painting with Light

Rather than approaching lighting in 3ds max 4 as you would in lighting a room in the real world, you might think of it as though you are painting the scene with light.

Placing lights to accentuate or draw the viewers' attention from areas of the scene adds to the illusion of 3D depth and promotes a particular mood or drama for the viewer.

Keyframe Animation Concepts

The term *keyframe* comes from traditional animation where a master artist drew key frames of characters to indicate various poses during motion. Junior artists then traced the in-between steps over the key frame drawings on acetate or film to get the character from one pose to the next. When the acetates were photographed and played back in sequence the character came to life in an animation.

3ds max 4 is considered a keyframe animation program because the creation process is similar. You, the master artist, pose objects and characters at points in time to generate a key, recording that position or setting. 3ds max 4 fills in the in-between frames to generate an animation that plays back smoothly. This section of the chapter is not intended to teach you about how the Track View works, but to familiarize you with the concepts of keyframe animation in hopes the Track View will make more sense when you encounter it in the exercises to come in later chapters.

note

The standard frame rate in the U.S. and some other countries is based on NTSC (National Television Standards Committee) playback rate at 30 fps (frames per second). Many other countries around the world use the PAL system, which has a standard playback of 25 fps. Movie film playback is at 24 fps. 3ds max 4 allows you to set animation for these rates or you may set a custom frame rate in the Time Configuration dialog. Check your local system or your client's standard before starting an animation.

Much of the control the user has over animation is controlled in two places, Track View and Track Bar, both of which show the same information, but the Track View is more detailed.

The Track View

See Figure 2.29 for a typical Track View dialog. This shows a hierarchical list of the scene on the left and a graphical representation of the keyframes on the right. Each gray oval key represents an event in time. There are five keys for position changes and two keys for rotation changes for a simple scene of an animated box. The second rotation key is white to indicate it is the selected key.

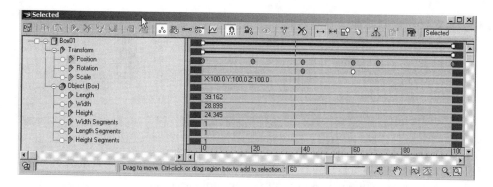

Figure 2.29   Track View for animated Box01. You see a hierarchical list of the scene on left, and individual keys in time on the right.

Individual keys or groups of keys can be selected and moved in time to change the speed of events. The closer together two keys are in the Track View the faster the event because it takes place in less time.

The Track Bar

The Track Bar is an abbreviated view of the Position, Rotation, and Scale keys shown just below the Frame Slider in the display (see Figure 2.30). It contains essentially the same information as the Position, Rotation, and Scale area of the Track View, but is limited to one row of keys in the display. To access the unseen keys, for example there are both Position keys and Rotation keys at frames 40 and 60 for the box in the Track View shown in Figure 2.29, you must right-click on the key in the Track Bar to access a menu listing the keys for that point in time (see Figure 2.31).

Figure 2.30   Track Bar for the same animated box represented in the Track View of Figure 2.29.

Mathematical Accuracy

The mathematical accuracy of 3ds max 4 is not necessarily a concept, but causes enough confusion among new users that it is worth discussing in a chapter on concepts.

First a little background. CAD software and other programs designed primarily for modeling are considered *double precision* math programs. That is, the internal calculations are all evaluated at an accuracy of 64 decimal places. This enables the software to provide accurate detail in scenes ranging from extremely large, like the planet Earth, to very small, like microscopic machine parts with the resources available on today's common PCs and workstations.

Figure 2.31
When two events happen at the same point in time, right-clicking on a key in the Track Bar displays a menu for selecting the appropriate key.

A large portion of the computer's resources in a typical 3ds max 4 scene must go into calculating things like high-resolution bitmaps, shadow and lighting effects, bump mapping, and reflections. To free enough resources to accomplish these tasks quickly enough to be cost-effective, the software designers have used *single precision* math, 32-decimal place internal calculations.

While 32 decimal places may seem like more than you would ever imagine you would need, very large and very small objects use a majority of the available decimal places and rounding errors start to manifest themselves rather quickly.

Typical scenes in which you may experience effects from the mathematical precision issue include:

- **Large scenes** Cityscapes or landscapes that cover more than, perhaps, two miles by two miles.
- **Scene with large and small objects** A large building with areas of detail smaller than, say, two inches.
- **Scenes with objects far from the coordinate system origin** Objects with pivot point absolute coordinates in the hundreds of thousands of units.

Solutions for each scenario would vary, but increasing or decreasing the scale of the object by a factor of 10 or 100, breaking up the scene into low detail and high detail scenes, moving the entire scene close to 0,0,0 absolute coordinate position would be possible solutions for the preceding list of problems.

One guide to potential system accuracy problems can be found in the General Preferences dialog accessed from the Customize menu, Preferences option (see Figure 2.32). For more information use the 3ds max 4 Help file and search for General Preferences.

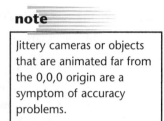

note

Jittery cameras or objects that are animated far from the 0,0,0 origin are a symptom of accuracy problems.

If you are aware that there may be potential rounding errors that will occur during internal calculations in 3ds max 4, it will be easier for you to plan a scene and to fix or work around situations that may arise while you work.

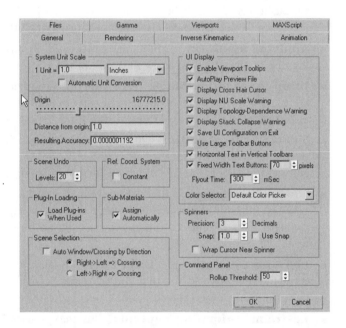

Figure 2.32   The General Preferences dialog showing the decimal accuracy Origin slider. See 3ds max 4 Help for more detail.

Chapter Summary

The topics covered in Chapter 2 will give you a basis of understanding that will help you learn 3ds max 4. New users who are not aware of some of these concepts can certainly learn the software and create beautiful scenes, but perhaps not with the efficiency and control of someone who takes the time to familiarize himself with the concepts. While performing the exercises later in this book refer to this chapter when you recognize some of the topics presented here, including:

- **Object naming standards**   A logical naming scheme makes you much more productive, especially when collaborating with others.

- **Understanding compound shapes**   Compound shapes (shapes containing multiple splines) is an important concept in modeling in 3ds max 4.

- **Cloning objects**   Cloning objects as Copies, Instances, or References allows various levels of linking between modifications for editing control. Instance and Reference clones also have a smaller memory footprint for more efficiency.

- **Applying modifiers**   A fundamental concept in 3ds max 4 is that of applying discrete modifiers to allow flexible editing control.

- **Using the Modifier Stack**   After applying modifiers in max 4, the Modifier Stack allows you to move up and down in the history of modifications for unprecedented freedom to experiment with or change your models.

- **Sub-object level editing**   In addition to editing various types of objects in max 4, be it splines or meshes or modifiers, you also have access to sub-levels of editing on the components of which the object is made.

- **Materials and maps**   Materials make up the surface appearance of objects in your scene and maps are the patterns in material components. You learned the concepts of mapping coordinates to describe position and scale of those patterns.

- **Lighting concepts**   You learned that 3ds max 4 lights are different than those in the real world and that you will paint your scene with light rather than light the scene as you would a room.

- **Keyframe animation concepts**   3ds max 4 uses keys placed in time to record various changes in the scene, then interpolates those changes between the key frames to create a smooth animation.

- **Mathematical accuracy**   The internal mathematics that are essential to describing scenes in 3ds max 4 are limited to 32 decimal places to make max 4 one of the fastest rendering programs available. This accuracy enables you to spot and work around potential issues caused by the accuracy levels.

PART II

3ds max 4 Basics

Workflow/GUI: A Road Map of max 4

In This Chapter

The purpose of this chapter is to give you an overview of the 3ds max 4 interface and to familiarize you will the terminology used in navigating the menus and panels that make up the work environment. The areas of the 3ds max 4 user interface that you will learn about include:

- **Pull-down menus**   These are primarily menu systems of file controls, option settings, and access to other tools. Little of your day-to-day work is done in the pull-down menus.

- **Right-click menus**   Throughout 3ds max 4 you will find that if you click with the right mouse button, you will generally get a menu choice. The menu you get depends on where you click and what type of object is selected in the scene when you click. Experiment by right-clicking everywhere.

- **Toolbar and tab panels**   You will learn about a series of toolbars and tab panels with buttons for groups of commands.

- **Command panels**   You will navigate a set of command panels that allow access to most tools with many options available for creating and modifying scenes.

- **Quad menus**   You will learn how to use a new system of right-click menus allowing quick access to many editing tools for object and sub-object editing.

- **Keyboard shortcuts**   You will learn how to use and modify keyboard shortcuts for one- or two-key access to many commands.

- **Viewport navigation**   You will experience some of the tools necessary to move around and through your scenes and how to make efficient use of viewports.

- **Status bar**   The status bar at the bottom of the display contains a variety of commands and informational fields such as World Coordinate readout of current cursor position, current grid spacing, number of currently selected objects, and text information about the current command. The status bar also contains buttons for snap options and time control functions.

- **Frame slider and Track Bar**   The Frame slider can be dragged to set the current frame of an animation. The Track Bar shows keys created by editing with the Animate button on.

- **Transformation**   Move, Rotate, and Scale are the three transforms in 3ds max 4. You will learn to use these for productivity.

- **Coordinate systems**   Learning the fundamentals of the coordinate systems will give you more control over your scenes.

- **Using grids**   The grid systems are a powerful tool in 3ds max 4.

- **Customizing menus**   You will learn how to access areas for customizing menus and buttons to configure 3ds max 4 to fit your work style more closely.

Certainly a key to being productive in 3ds max 4 is the ability for you to know and have quick access to the myriad of tools available throughout the program.

Key Terms

GUI   Graphical User Interface, what you see in the display.

Command panel   Six user interface panels for accessing most of the modeling and editing tools in 3ds max 4.

Tab panel   A row of tabbed toolbars that can be customized by the user.

Toolbars   A docked or floating collection of command and editing buttons.

Pull-down menus   Menu options at the top of the display that reveal menus when clicked.

Quad menus   A customizable series of menus that appear around the cursor in the display upon right-clicking.

Status bars   An area of controls and informational windows at the bottom of the display.

Time controls   A set of buttons at the lower right of the default display used to

configure and control the creation and playback of animations.

Viewport controls   Navigation tools at the lower right of the display to adjust the viewer's perspective of viewports.

Viewports   A rectangular window to view the 3ds max 4 scene.

Home grids   A grid and work plane that defines the default working planes for 3ds max 4.

MAXScript listener   A window at the lower left of the display with a white and a pink field that is used in conjunction with the MAXScript scripting language.

Keyboard shortcuts   Combinations of keys that, when pressed, call various commands or options in 3ds max 4. They are fully customizable.

Workflow and Graphic User Interface

While the organization of the menu systems is quite intuitive for such a large program, it can be very intimidating to the new user. There is a certain amount of rote memorization necessary for the placement and usage of the various areas within 3ds max 4. Many tools can be found in more than one place, and it is possible that in each place you find a tool, it may have slightly different controls. Discreet is very concerned with consistency throughout the menu options, but some areas are purposely different, and a few have just fallen through the cracks. Fear not, the confusion and intimidation you may feel at first will quickly be left behind for confidence and surefootedness as you get higher on the learning curve.

Many menus in 3ds max 4 are dynamic and will adapt themselves to the task at hand. For example, if you create a box and right-click to access the quad menu you will be presented with a Display and a Transform quad menu. If you choose the

Convert To: Editable Mesh option in the Transform quad menu, the box becomes a Editable Mesh in the shape of a box. Right-click again and you are presented with four quad menus: Display, Transform, Tools 1, and Tools 2. The Tool menus are new options specific to editing Editable Mesh objects. Convert To: Patch option will bring up still other options specific to Patch editing.

Particularly important to the effective use of the user interface and to tools such as Align, Mirror, and Array is the understanding of how the various Coordinate systems function. A surprising number of users who have had MAX for years still do not understand the basic Coordinate systems and are, therefore, missing out on a lot of control and speed. They create wonderful scenes, but are working harder than necessary to get the job done.

Keyboard shortcuts and customized menus are a great boon to productivity. However, using the standard 3ds max 4 layout and menu system while you are learning the software will introduce you to more options that are presented in a more direct manner than many of the shortcuts. After you become comfortable with how the program works and what tools are available, then advance into the shortcut methods of accessing those tools.

Walk through this guided tour of the 3ds max 4 user interface and feel free to drill deeper into the hierarchy of the menu system as you see things that interest or intrigue you. The more you know about the interface the more efficient you will be in production.

When you start 3ds max 4 for the first time, you are presented with the display layout shown in Figure 3.1.

You will now investigate the logical areas of the menu system and will learn how to access options within those areas. The next chapter sections are broken into the main display areas of the default configuration. You will also explore some of the important navigation and workspace tools available.

Pull-Down Menus

The options across the top of the display, File, Edit, Tools, and so forth, are known as the pull-down menus. See Figure 3.2 for the pull-down menu options.

note

The background colors have been changed slightly for better printing in the book.

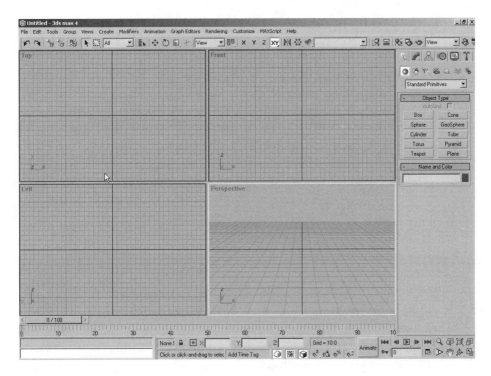

Figure 3.1   This is the standard default display layout as seen when you start 3ds max 4 for the first time.

Moving your cursor over an option and clicking reveals a pull-down menu of choices in several forms, as you see in the Edit menu (see Figure 3.3).

The menus have shading and symbols for various functions as shown in this list:

- **Black text**   Text options with no symbols are direct commands, and when you click, a command is executed immediately. The Hold command is an example that stores the current scene in a disk buffer that may be retrieved with the Fetch command. Often the commands will have the keyboard shortcut indicated on the right side of the pull-down menu.

File   Edit   Tools   Group   Views   Create   Modifiers   Animation   Graph Editors   Rendering   Customize   MAXScript   Help

Figure 3.2   These are the pull-down menu options.

- **Gray text**   This indicates the command is not available at this time. For example, you cannot Undo if you have not yet done anything.

- **Text followed by three dots**   When clicked, these commands call a diaolog with options. Edit Named Selections is an example in the Edit pull-down menu.

- **Text followed by a black arrow**   Clicking this entry calls a sub-menu with new choices. Select By is an example in the Edit pull-down menu.

Figure 3.3
The Edit pull-down menu is a typical pull-down menu option.

Not much of your day-to-day production work will be executed from the pull-down menus. Many of the options found here are setup and file tools and configuration options that you access occasionally as needed.

You can access often-used tools from the pull-down menus, such as Primitive object creation tools and many of the modifiers. However, those options are more readily accessible from the command panels and toolbars, or eventually, the keyboard shortcuts.

Many of the rendering and environment effects are easily accessed from the Rendering pull-down menu, and the RAM Player can be called to view images or animations. But again, those are not commands or options that you tend to use over and over in production.

The most important pull-down menu option for new users is the Help pull-down. You should constantly be using the User Reference in the Help while reading this book and while learning 3ds max 4 (see Figure 3.4). There is information in the User Reference that is not available in the printed manuals, and it is often illustrated with step-by-step tutorials and explanations that will shed light on many of the topics you will encounter.

Take a few minutes to click on the pull-down menu choices and some of the sub-choices to familiarize yourself with the options and workflow of the menus. Many of the options will be unavailable and some will not do anything at this point, but the better you learn where things are located, the easier the tutorials in the rest of the book will be.

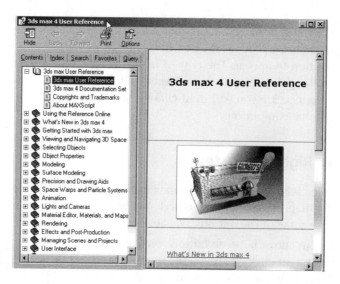

Figure 3.4   Clicking the Help pull-down menu option and choosing User Reference opens a powerful Windows-style Help system.

tip

You can also access the Discreet 3ds max 4 online support community from the Help pull-down menu if the computer is connected to the Internet. This is by far the best place for professional expert advice on all aspects of using 3ds max 4 in a production environment.

It is a professional Web site sponsored and maintained by Discreet. You are required to use your real name and to conduct business in a professional, courteous manner. Post clear and specific messages, and you will have an international response team at your disposal.

Other 3ds max related Web sites that are not directly supported by Discreet, but which are full of useful information can be found by doing a search using any of the popular search engines. For each site you find, there will usually be several links to other sites.

caution

There are commands or options that, when accessed in the Customize pull-down menu, for example, could radically change the viewport and menu layout. If that should happen, just go to the File pull-down menu, click Reset, and reset without saving any changes. This returns you to the default layout.

The Right-Click Menus

There are many areas of 3ds max 4 where you can right-click with the mouse and get a menu option to appear. The type of menu you get is dependent on where in the display you right-click and what objects are selected in the scene when you right-click. In Exercise 3.1 you will right-click in several locations to see several examples of right-click menu options.

Exercise 3.1: Right-Click Menus

1. Open a file called Ch3_Right_Click.max from the CD-ROM. It is a simple scene with a 2D shape and a 3D mesh object. You will perform several right-click operations to see some of the options available.

2. Position your cursor between buttons on the main toolbar and right-click when you see the Pan hand cursor. You will call a pop-up menu with choices to customize the user interface or to toggle the Main Toolbar, Tab Panel, or Command Panel options on or off. The checkmark indicates a panel that is on (see Figure 3.5).

Figure 3.5
Place the cursor between buttons on the main toolbar and right-click when you see the Pan hand cursor to access the pop-up menu.

3. In the pop-up menu, choose Tab Panel option. This displays a new set of tab panels below the main toolbar each with its own set of buttons (see Figure 3.6). You will learn more about tab panels in the next section of this chapter.

4. In the Perspective viewport, right-click anywhere and you will see a Transform and a Display quad menu appear (see Figure 3.7).

5. Move the cursor over the command panel on the right side of the display and right-click to call a menu that will let you navigate the command panel and its rollouts (see Figure 3.8). There will be more information on those later.

Figure 3.6   In the tab panels with the Objects tab panel active, you have buttons for creating 3D geometry.

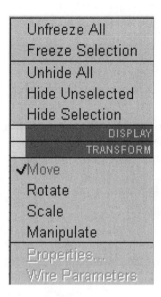

Figure 3.7 Right-click in the Perspective viewport with no objects selected and two quad menus appear, Transform and Display.

Figure 3.8 Right-click on the command panel to access a navigation menu for the command panel and its rollouts.

6. Position the cursor carefully between the top of the command panel and the tab panel. When you see the arrow cursor with a white panel (see Figure 3.9), right-click to access the navigation options plus options to Float or Dock the command panel (see Figure 3.10).

7. In the Perspective viewport, select the Teapot object and right-click. You now have a quad menu similar to the one that appeared when you right-clicked in a viewport with no objects selected. However, several new options appear at the bottom of the Transform menu (see Figure 3.11).

8. In the Transform quad menu, choose the Convert To option to open more menu choices and choose Convert to Editable Mesh. The command panel changes to reflect the new object type.

9. Right-click in Perspective viewport again and you now have four quad menus. Two new Tools quad menus offer tools to edit the Teapot at sub-object level.

tip

If you have a graphics card that supports dual monitors, the floating panels and toolbars can be moved to the second monitor for more working space.

tip

You can also double-click on the Command Panel name at the top of a floating panel to dock it on the right side of the display.

Figure 3.9   Right-click on the command panel to access a navigation menu.

Figure 3.10   Right-click in the area between the top of the command panel and the tab panel for a menu with navigation options plus Float and Dock options for the command panel.

10. In the Perspective viewport, select the hex NGON01 shape, right-click, and then choose Convert To and Convert to Editable Spline. Right-click again and you have new options to edit 2D shapes at sub-object level.

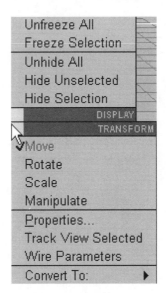

Figure 3.11   Right-click in a viewport when a 3D object is selected and you have additional menu options in the Transform quad menu.

Figure 3.12   Right-click on the Perspective viewport label to access a menu of viewport controls.

11. Right-click on the Perspective viewport label for yet another menu of viewport options (see Figure 3.12).

While you are learning 3ds max 4, get into the habit of right-clicking on everything you encounter or select in the scene. Go to the pull-down Help menu for the User Reference and in the Search tab enter *right-click* to investigate more information on the options.

The Toolbars and Tab Panels

Just below the pull-down menu is the main toolbar (see Figure 3.13).

Figure 3.13   The main toolbar is found just below the pull-down menus.

From here you have groups of buttons that control various aspects of 3ds max 4 that you will be accessing often in production including:

- Undo and Redo commands
- Hierarchical Linking and SpaceWarp Binding commands
- Select options
- Transforms
- Coordinate system options
- Named Selection sets
- Alignment tools
- Rendering options

Much of your day-to-day work is spent accessing the main toolbar to select and transform objects. Learning the options available for selecting objects such as Selection Region types, Select by Name, Window and Crossing Selection modes, and the Selection Lock toggle are good options to investigate further.

tip

To find out what each button is, place the cursor over the button and after a second, a ToolTip appears with the name of the command. Use the Help pull-down, User Reference to find more information about the command.

If you do not see any ToolTips, they can be enabled in the Customize pull-down menu, Preferences dialog, General tab, UI Display area. Just check Enable Viewport Tooltips.

In the default startup display, there are no command options between the toolbar and the viewports. However, in Exercise 3.1, you used right-click menus to open the tab panel in this area of the display. The tab panels often mirror commands found in the command panels and are just another way to access those commands including:

note

Rather that reprint information that is readily available, you will often be directed to the User Reference file for in-depth descriptions of the tools. If there is a lesson you should get from this chapter, it is how to use the built-in Help system.

- **Objects**   These include 3D Primitive and Extended Primitive geometry.
- **Shapes**   2D splines and NURBS curves are types.
- **Compounds**   Boolean, Morph, Connect, Terrain, Conform, Terrain, and Loft tools are found in this tab panel.
- **Lights and Cameras**   You can create lights and cameras from this tab panel. However, you can also find the Light Include/Exclude and Light Lister tools that are not found anywhere else in the program.
- **Particles**   You can access commands to create Particle systems from this tab panel.

- **Helpers** Dummy Helpers, Point Helpers, and the Tape Measure tool are found here along with Gizmos that act as containers for atmospheric effects such as fog and combustion.

- **SpaceWarps** In this tab panel, you can create SpaceWarps that deform 3D space and any objects that are bound to the defined space.

- **Modifiers** A full compliment of 2D and 3D modifiers can be accessed from this panel.

- **Modeling** This is a collection of tools commonly used in modeling objects. It is intended as an example of how you might customize your own panels to give you the tools you most often use.

- **Rendering** The standard rendering options are here, plus access to Environment, Effects, and RAM Player among other commands.

note

When you click on most buttons in the tab panels, the command panel will change to reflect the command being accessed.

You can customize existing panels and build your own panels for a completely different user interface that will increase your productivity by placing the tools you use most readily at hand.

By positioning the cursor over the tab panel label, you can right-click and choose Convert to Toolbar. This floats the tab panel buttons in a separate window that can be repositioned or moved to a second monitor. Right-click in the blue area at the top of the floating toolbar and you have options to dock it to the top or sides of the display or to make it a tab panel again.

All this flexibility seems a little confusing at first, but after you become familiar with 3ds max 4, you can customize the display for your tastes and needs.

The Command Panel

The majority of the tools and controls you will use in production can be found in the command panel, docked on the right side of the display by default. The command panel opens in the Create panel, but has options for the following:

- **Create panel** From here you access tools to create 3D or 2D objects, Particle systems, Patch and NURBS surfaces, and Compound Object options.

caution

Become well-accustomed to the default user interface before customizing it. All the tutorials in this book and most tutorials you will find elsewhere are based on the standard user interface.

- **Modify panel**   When an object is selected in a scene and you enter the Modify panel, you have access to many object and sub-object editing capabilities.

- **Hierarchy panel**   In the Hierarchy panel you can adjust pivot points, Inverse Kinematics options, and object linking controls.

- **Motion panel**   From here you can assign Animation controllers to objects or adjust key settings for existing animations.

- **Display panel**   The Display panel has options for hiding and freezing objects and for displaying various properties of your scene, such as See Through mode, animation Trajectories, and Vertex Ticks, to name a few.

- **Utilities panel**   You have a variety of added utilities that help manipulate your scene. Many times these are features that did not make it into the final release of 3ds max 4 or are added as bonus tools.

The command panels are made up of different methods of accessing information including:

- **Buttons**   Buttons have icons indicating the function of the command. The Create panel has a second row of buttons for different object types, including 3D and 2D Primitives, Lights, Cameras, Helpers, SpaceWarps, and Systems.

- **Lists**   When you click on a list, you have options for new creation methods or lists of modifiers.

- **Rollouts**   Rollouts are indicated by a bar that has a + when rolled up and a – when expanded. You can also access rollouts by right-clicking in the panel. See Chapter 10 for more information on new command panel features for 3ds max 4.

Figure 3.14
Right-click at the top of a command panel to float it. This panel shows the buttons at the top, the list of Create options, and Name and Color rollout of the Teapot object. Right-click in the blue area at the top of the floating panel to dock it.

As mentioned earlier, you can right-click at the very top of a command panel and float it over the viewports. See Figure 3.14 for the Create command panel showing the buttons, lists, and rollout.

Quad Menus

Right-click quad menus are a new feature in 3ds max 4 intended to boost production by placing often-used commands and options close at hand as you are working in production. Hunting through deep hierarchies of menus can add immeasurable time over the course of a day's work. Refer to Chapter 10, "Modeling: Enhancing Productivity," for more information on the new features and customization of quad menus.

Keyboard Shortcuts

Many of the commands and options of 3ds max 4 can be accessed with one to three key combinations on the keyboard. These shortcuts are critical to the efficient use of 3ds max 4. While this book tends to lead you through the menu system so you can visualize more of the options to the various commands, there are a few instances where some of the more common preassigned keyboard shortcuts are used. Examples include H for the Select by Name list, W to minimize or maximize a viewport, or M to call the Material Editor.

The keyboard shortcuts are fully customizable and may be saved as a .kbd file type so the user can carry his or her shortcuts to other computers. In Exercise 3.2 you will perform a few steps to access the area where you can customize keyboard shortcuts and write a custom file.

Exercise 3.2: Accessing Keyboard Shortcut Assignments

1. Open 3ds max 4. In the Customize pull-down menu, choose Customize User Interface (see Figure 3.15).

Figure 3.15   In the Customize pull-down menu, choose Customize User Interface.

Figure 3.16   In the Custom User Interface dialog, click the Keyboard tab
for keyboard shortcut settings.

2. In the Customize User Interface dialog, click the Keyboard tab. This calls a panel
   showing the keyboard shortcuts for the Main UI option. Shortcuts with text in
   the right side of the column have shortcuts assigned; others can have shortcuts
   assigned, but do not by default (see Figure 3.16).

3. At the lower-right corner of the dialog are buttons to Write Keyboard Chart to a
   file, to Load or Save existing charts, or to Reset any changes. Close the dialog.

Viewport Navigation

There are essentially two parts to viewport navigation: viewing the layout of the viewports and manipulating your position in relation to the viewports.

To change the configuration of the viewport layout you can right-click on any
viewport label and choose Configure in the menu. In the Viewport Configuration
dialog, click the Layout tab and you will see the possible layout configurations (see
Figure 3.17).

By right-clicking in any of the viewport areas in the dialog you can access a list of
viewport options (see Figure 3.18).

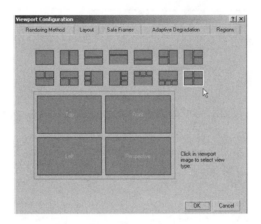

Figure 3.17   Right-click on any viewport label and choose Configure in the menu. In the Viewport Configuration dialog, click the Layout tab to select a new viewport layout.

tip   While you are in an active viewport, as indicated by the yellow border, you can type the first letter of the desired viewport to switch. However, B is for bottom, and K is for back.

The viewport navigation controls are the eight buttons in the lower-right corner of the display. Figure 3.19 shows the navigation buttons for a Perspective viewport. Different viewports have different buttons. If you right-click in the Front viewport to activate it, you will see that the bottom left of the group of eight buttons changes from FOV to Region Zoom.

Try creating several 3D Primitive objects or open the Ch3_Right_Click.max file from the CD-ROM and, using the User Reference file, investigate the many options for viewport navigation.

In the active viewport, typing the first letter of the view you want will switch to that view. For example, typing T will switch to the Top viewport, and G will show the active Grid viewport. The notable exception is that K will get you to the back viewport.

Figure 3.18
Right-click on a viewport image to access the possible viewports to display.

Keyboard shortcuts can be assigned to the viewport navigation tools as well. For example, the I key is Interactive panning that can be used in the middle of many Create commands. The W keyboard shortcut is also a commonly used method of toggling a viewport from maximized to minimized.

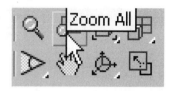

Figure 3.19
The eight buttons in the lower-right corner of the display are the viewport navigation controls. They are dynamic and change according to the type of active viewport.

tip

If you type E, the viewport will switch to Track View. Typing other options do not work at this point. To get out of Track View viewports, place the cursor between buttons in the toolbar for Track View and right-click. If the viewport is maximized to full display, you will have an option to minimize it. After you minimize it, you can right-click between buttons again and choose a new view type from the list.

The Status Bar

The status bar (see Figure 3.20) contains information and buttons that aid in the navigation of the viewports including:

- MAXScript Mini Listener windows
- Selected objects field
- Current command tips
- Selection Lock toggle
- Current World Coordinate cursor position fields
- Grid spacing information
- Time Tag field
- Window/Crossing Selection mode toggle
- Degradation override toggle
- Snap toggles

As you are learning 3ds max 4, always check the current command tips field for tips on how to use the current command.

Figure 3.20   The status bar at the bottom of the display.

tip

> You may enter data directly into the Coordinate field as Absolute or Relative coordinates to transform the current selected object. Absolute coordinates being based on the World 0,0,0 coordinate and Relative coordinates being based on the current World coordinate position of an object's Pivot Point.

Frame Slider and Track Bar

The Frame slider and Track Bar function together to let you view and manipulate keyframes for animation (see Figure 3.21). When the Animate button is toggled on and highlighted red and the Frame slider is set to a frame other than 0, most edits in 3ds max 4 will become animated to that point in time. You will learn more about animation in Chapter 8, "Animation: A Moving Experience".

The keys that appear in the Track Bar when an object is animated represent a change, position, or rotation for example, at a point in time. This is the method 3ds max 4 uses to keep track of animated changes.

By default the Frame slider and Track Bar show 100 frames. However, by using the time configuration controls in the status bar, you can set the total number of frames to anything you wish.

In the Track Bar, you can move keys to change when an event happens in time or by right-clicking on a key, you can change parameters of that key.

If you have a sound file assigned to your animation, the keys and the sound file can be shown together (see Figure 3.22). This is done by right-clicking on the Track Bar and choosing Configure and then Show Sound Track in the menu.

Figure 3.21   The Frame slider is located above the Track Bar.

Figure 3.22   The sound file is shown below the Track Bar.

Transformations

Transforming objects through space is a lot of what you will be doing in the 3ds max 4 interface. The three transformations in 3ds max 4 are Move, Rotate, and Scale.

To increase production by transforming objects quickly and accurately, 3ds max 4 has several features that will aid the process including:

- Transform Gizmos
- Reference Coordinate system
- Grid Helper objects
- Transform Type-in capability

Each can be helpful on its own and when used in combination with each other. You will perform a couple of simple exercises to get a feel for each of these tools, but you should investigate them more thoroughly on your own as you go through the exercises in the other chapters of this book.

The Transform Gizmo

The Transform Gizmo is probably the most noticeable option for the new user. If you create or select any object and click one of the three Transform buttons in the toolbar, the axis tripod for that object will become larger and the x-, y-, and z-axes will change color.

Exercise 3.3: Fundamental Transform Gizmo Functions

1. Open 3ds max 4. You should be in the four viewport default file. In the Create panel on the right side of the display, click on the Teapot button in the Object Type rollout (see Figure 3.23). In the Perspective viewport, click and drag the cursor to create a Teapot that fills about half of the viewport. You will see the axis tripod at the base of the Teapot. The red x- and y- axes indicate the active transform plane. In the middle of the toolbar at the top of the display, you will see the XY button toggled on.

2. In the toolbar, click on the Select and Move transform button. The axis tripod turns multicolored to
indicate it is active (see Figure 3.24). As you move
the cursor over the three Gizmo legs, you will see the
axis letter change to yellow when it is active.

3. Place the cursor over the x-axis leg, click on the leg,
and drag the mouse back and forth. The Teapot is
restricted to movement in the x-axis. Pick on the
other axis and move the Teapot.

4. Notice the colored-corner indicators for each pair of
Transform Gizmo axes. Move the cursor over one of
the corner indicators and both associated Gizmo letters turn yellow. Click and drag the mouse on a corner indicator and the transformations are restricted
to two planes, the x-axis and the y-axis, for example.
Try the other corners.

5. In the pull-down menus, click File, and then click
Save As (see Figure 3.25). Name the file
TEAPOT01.MAX and click the Save button in the
Save File As dialog. This saves the Teapot for use in
later exercises.

Get into the habit of transforming objects with the
Transform Gizmo and your productivity is bound to
increase. Try using Select and Rotate to restrict the
rotation of the Teapot on the various axes.

Figure 3.23
In the Create panel in the
Object Type rollout, click the
Teapot button, and then
click and drag in the
Perspective viewport to
create a Teapot object.

Figure 3.24   With an object selected in the scene, click the Select and
Move transform button. The axis tripod changes to the
Transform Gizmo, a multicolored tripod used to restrict
transformations.

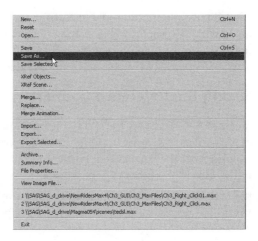

Figure 3.25   In the pull-down menus, click File, and then choose Save As.

> **tip**
>
> Pressing the X key toggles the Transform Gizmo on and off if it should ever get in the way.

> **tip**
>
> While you are transforming objects by picking and dragging with the mouse and before you release the left mouse button to finalize the transform, you can click the right mouse button to cancel the transform operation. If you release the left mouse button before right-clicking, you must use the Undo button to move the object back to its original transform.

Reference Coordinate System

By default you created your Teapot on the World Coordinate grid plane in the Perspective viewport in Exercise 3.3. There are, however, several Coordinate systems of which World is just one option.

To make the best use of many of the editing tools available in 3ds max 4, you will have to take the time to become familiar with the Reference Coordinate systems.

The Reference Coordinate system is set in the main toolbar in a field just to the right of the Transform buttons (see Figure 3.26). In Exercise 3.4 you will learn to set the various Reference Coordinate systems and to experiment with changing the system.

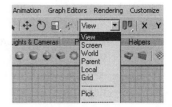

Figure 3.26

This is the list of Reference Coordinate systems from the main toolbar.

The Reference Coordinate system is simple to learn. You just have to apply yourself to become familiar with the variations. Use the User Reference found in the Help pull-down menu to search for help on reference or transform.

Exercise 3.4: Accessing the Reference Coordinate Systems

1. Open the file called TEAPOT01.MAX that you saved in Exercise 3.3. Select the Teapot01 object in the Perspective viewport. Notice the axis tripod. The axis directions correspond with the smaller red, green, and blue World Coordinate system tripod at the lower-left corner of each viewport.

2. Right-click in the Left viewport to activate it and notice the Teapot axis tripod shifts so that it is no longer the same as the World axis tripod. The y-axis points up instead of the z-axis.

3. Right-click in the Top and Front viewports and the Teapot's tripod changes for each viewport. You are using the View Reference Coordinate system. The y-axis points up the viewport in all non-orthographic viewports (User, Perspective, Camera, and Light viewports), the x-axis points right, and the z-axis points out from the viewport toward the viewer.

4. Right-click in the Perspective viewport to make it active. The View Reference Coordinate system corresponds to the World system in non-orthographic viewports.

5. In the main toolbar, click on the View field to the right of the Transform buttons and choose World from the list. Right-click in each viewport to see how the Teapot's tripod corresponds with the World tripod.

6. Change the Reference Coordinate system to Screen and right-click in each viewport to see if you can see how it differs from the others. Use the pull-down Help menu, User Reference to look up what each Reference Coordinate system does.

7. Create teapots in the other viewports, select each one at a time, and right-click in the viewports with the various Reference Coordinate systems set. Try transforming the teapots with different settings in each viewport. Exit 3ds max 4 without saving the new information.

tip

Coincidentally, the World, Local, and Grid all work the same for this particular scene.

By reading the Help files and trying simple experiments in the viewports you will quickly see how the systems work. Without knowledge of the Reference Coordinate systems, tools such as Align, Array, and Mirror will never be productive because their functionality depends on the active viewport and Reference Coordinate system.

Using Grids

Grids are another flexible and powerful system in 3ds max 4 that self-taught users often do not discover until they have been using the software for a while.

Being familiar with grids early in the 3ds max 4 learning curve can help you work faster and more accurately. When you start 3ds max 4 for the first time or whenever you start with the default settings, you have three grid planes active that you can work on, the World plane (as seen in the Perspective and Top viewports) and the Left and Front viewport grids. The planes are visible in each of the viewports, and each plane passes through the 0,0,0 World Absolute coordinate point. The heavy black lines on the visible grid define these planes.

You can also define custom Grid objects that can be transformed in the viewports to represent a plane in space wherever you need a work plane. There are two common methods of creating the custom grid planes:

- Using the Create panel, Helpers panel, Grid command button
- Using AutoGrid to define the plane from a face

The Grid objects are similar to any other object for they can have a name and may be transformed and animated. However, they will never render in the scene. After the new grid is created and active, it is very much like the World grid at startup. You can use the Grid Point and Grid Lines snap options to create objects using the grid as a guide.

Grid Helper Objects

Helper Grid objects are created in a scene and then repositioned to define a plane in space. They are initially created parallel to the currently active grid, whether it is the default World grid or another custom grid. Exercise 3.5 walks you through a simple process of creating a grid, transforming it, and activating it.

Exercise 3.5: Creating a Custom Grid Object

1. Open the file called TEAPOT01.MAX that you created in Exercise 3.3 if it is not still open. Right-click in the Perspective viewport to make sure it is active. When you created the Teapot object, it was created on the World grid plane as defined by the visible grid.

2. In the Create panel, Geometry panel, click on the Helpers button. In the Object Type rollout, click the Grid button (see Figure 3.27).

3. In the Perspective viewport, click behind and left of the Teapot and drag the cursor to the right front of the viewport. This drags out a four-paned Grid object named Grid01.

4. In the main toolbar, click the Select and Rotate button. Right-click on the Select and Rotate button, and in the Rotate Transform Type-In dialog (see Figure 3.28), enter 45 in the Offset:World x-axis field and press Enter. Close the Transform Type-In dialog. The grid should now be rotated 45 degrees as seen in Figure 3.29.

Figure 3.27
In the Create panel, Geometry panel, Helpers panel, click the Grid button.

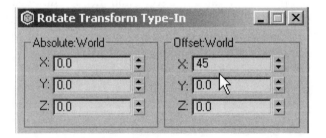

Figure 3.28   Enter 45 in the Offset:World x-axis field of the Rotate Transform Type-In dialog.

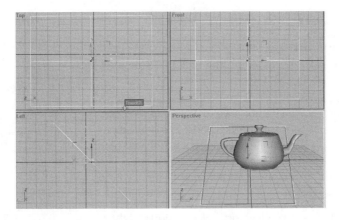

Figure 3.29   After pressing Enter, the grid should be rotated 45 degrees
in the World x-axis.

5. In the main toolbar, click the Select button. In the Perspective viewport, move the
cursor over any edge of the new grid, right-click, and choose Activate Grid from
the Tools1 quad menu (see Figure 3.30). This activates the new grid to become the
working-grid plane.

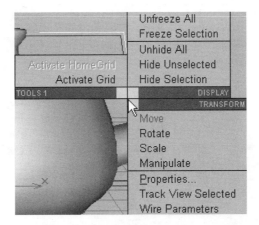

Figure 3.30   With Grid01 selected, move the cursor over the edge of the
grid, right-click, and choose Activate Grid in the Tools1 quad
menu.

6. In the Create panel, Geometry panel, click on the Cylinder button (see Figure 3.31). In the Perspective viewport, click anywhere and drag a small cylinder. The Cylinder is created on the new plane defined by Grid01 (see Figure 3.32).

> **tip** You do not have to work on the visible plane in the viewports. The grid defines an infinite plane in space as the current work plane. The visible grid can be set up to aid in snapping to grid points or grid lines for more control.

7. In the Perspective viewport, select Grid01, right-click on the grid, and choose Activate Home Grid from the quad menu to deactivate the Grid01 object. The default World grid system is now reactivated. Move on to the next exercise without closing 3ds max 4.

You can have as many grids in a scene as you want, but only one can be active at anytime.

> **tip** It is a good idea to rename the Grid objects with logical names if you are going to have more than one or two Grid objects in a scene.

Figure 3.31
In the Create panel, Geometry panel, click the Cylinder button.

Figure 3.32   Click and drag a Cylinder primitive object anywhere in the Perspective viewport.

Using the AutoGrid Option

A faster method of creating Grid objects is using the AutoGrid feature when creating primitive objects. You have the options of using a temporarily defined grid for the creation of that one particular object or of using the grid and simultaneously creating it as a permanent Grid object.

Exercise 3.6 will step you through both processes.

Exercise 3.6: Using AutoGrid to Create Temporary and Permanent Grid Objects

1. You should still have the file open from Exercise 3.5. In the Create panel, Geometry panel, Object Type rollout, click the Box button. Check the AutoGrid option just above and to the right of the Box button (see Figure 3.33).

2. In the Perspective viewport, move the cursor over the surface of the Teapot and the Cylinder in the scene. The cursor reads the Face Normal, a vector projecting perpendicular to the triangular face, and the Transform Gizmo reorients itself to the plane defined by the face.

3. Click and drag the cursor to create a Box primitive on several places on the Teapot and the Cylinder. The Boxes are created in the plane of each face you initially click on when starting the Box. See Figure 3.34 for some example boxes created with this method and a box in the creation process showing the temporary grid. When the new Box is created and you perform another action, the active grid reverts to the default Home grid.

4. Hold the Alt key and click and drag anywhere on the surface of the Teapot to create a new Box primitive. When you finish the Box, the new Grid object is created in place and is set as the permanent active grid. You can continue to work in the plane defined by the new grid until you select the new grid, right-click on it, and set the Home grid or any other grid as active.

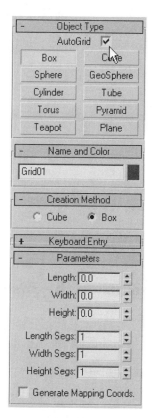

Figure 3.33
In the Create panel, Geometry panel, Object Type rollout, click the Box button, and then check the AutoGrid option.

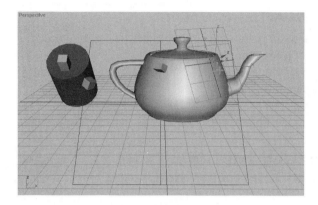

Figure 3.34   Click and drag to create several Box primitives on various locations on the Cylinder and Teapot surfaces. The a temporary grid plane is defined by the face under the cursor.

You may also check the AutoGrid option in the Object Type rollout and create new temporary or permanent grids in the same manner.

5. Close 3ds max 4 without saving any of the information in the file.

Grids in 3ds max 4 are very easy to use and manipulate. The regular use of grids in modeling will increase your productivity noticeably at a minimum cost to computer resources.

Customizing the 3ds max 4 User Interface

Because 3ds max 4 is so comprehensive, the menu hierarchy must be relatively complex and deep to accommodate all the options. This, of course, increases the number of mouse clicks to get a day's work done.

In this chapter you will learn where to find many of the options in 3ds max 4 that will allow you to reconfigure the user interface to your needs and workflow. Some of the customizable areas have been mentioned, such as the ability to float and dock the command panel or the tab menus. Some areas of user interface customization include:

- Resizable viewports
- Expandable command panels
- Rearrange rollout order

- Floating toolbars
- Floating command panels
- Hiding command panels, the main toolbar, tab menus, and the Expert mode
- Create custom toolbars, quad menus, viewport colors, and keyboard shortcuts
- Saving and loading custom user interfaces
- MAXScript language

As mentioned earlier in the chapter, it is a good idea to stick with the default interface while you are learning the fundamentals of 3ds max 4. You will find that most tutorials and most support information will refer to the default configuration.

Resizable Viewports

Resizing the viewports in the display is a simple dragging process. By clicking and dragging between viewports when you see the double- or quad-arrow cursor, you can change viewport sizes on-the-fly at any time (see Figure 3.35). To return to the default layout, position the cursor between the viewports, right-click, and choose Reset Layout.

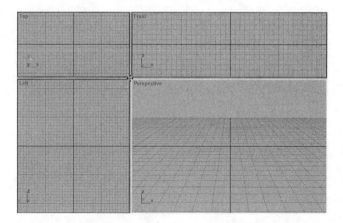

Figure 3.35   Click and drag when you see the arrow cursor between viewports to resize the viewports to your liking. Right-click when you see the arrow cursor between viewports and choose Reset Layout to return to the default layout.

Expandable Command Panel

Some of the command panels in 3ds max 4 are quite long with lots of rollouts. You have already learned that you can scroll through the rollouts or right-click between options and choose rollouts from a list. In 3ds max 4 you can also expand either docked or floating command panels by positioning the cursor on the edge of the panel and dragging in increments as wide as the panels themselves. See Figure 3.36 for an example of the Create Particle System panel expanded to show three panels. Drag them back to return to one panel wide.

note

The expandable panels are especially useful if you have a dual monitor system with the expanded panels on a separate monitor.

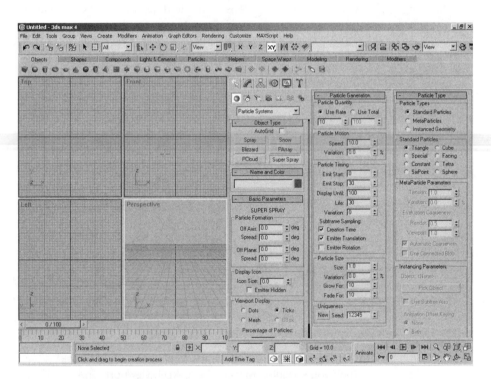

Figure 3.36   The Create Particle Systems panel is expanded to three panels wide.

Rearrange Rollout Order

There are many times when you will find yourself working with long rollouts and having to jump from the top rollout to a rollout way down in the panel.

An example might be that you have converted a circle to an Editable spline and you have to jump back and forth between the Rendering rollout at the top of the panel to the Geometry rollout at the bottom.

You can drag and drop the rollout title bar up and down the panel. A blue line will show where it will be inserted when you release the left mouse button (see Figure 3.37).

To return the rollout order to the default state, right-click in an expanded rollout when you see the hand cursor and choose Reset Rollout Order in the pop-up menu.

Floating Toolbars

Toolbars can be floated in the display by positioning the cursor on the outside edge of the toolbar to show the arrow cursor with rectangles (see Figure 3.38) and then either right-clicking to choose Float from the menu or dragging the toolbar into the viewports.

To dock the floating toolbar, drag it back into position along the edge of the viewports or right-click in the blue title area and choose Dock in the menu.

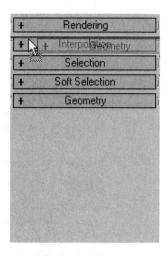

Figure 3.37
Clicking and dragging the rollout title bar allows you to drag and drop the rollout to a new position in the panel. When you are over another rollout title the rollout you are dragging will become transparent and will blur the rollout below it.

Figure 3.38   Position the cursor along the outer edge of the toolbar to display the arrow with rectangle cursor and either right-click and choose Float or drag the toolbar into the viewports.

Floating Command Panel

Command panels can be floated or docked in the
same manner as toolbars. Position the cursor at the
edge until the arrow-with-rectangle cursor appears,
and then either right-click for the menu or drag the
command panel into the viewports. See Figure 3.39
for the right-click menus with docking options.

Hiding the Command Panel, Toolbar, Tab Menus, and Expert Mode

Sometimes it is convenient to work on as large a display area as is possible with your
monitor setup. There are several options in 3ds max 4 that can give you some relief.
The first is to just close the command panel.

Hiding the command panel can be done by right-clicking at the edge of the command panel when you see the arrow-with-rectangle cursor or to the right of the tabs
in the tab menu and clearing the check next to Command Panel in the menu. This
works for the tab menus and the main toolbar as well (see Figure 3.40).

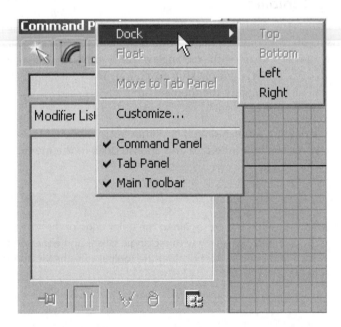

Figure 3.39   Right-click in the blue title area of a floating command panel
or toolbar to find docking options.

You can turn the option back on by right-clicking and checking the appropriate options.

> **tip**
>
> If you hide the main toolbar, tab menu, and command panel, there is nothing to right-click on to enable any of the options. Press the 3 key for the Hide/Unhide Command Panel keyboard shortcut. This will toggle the command panel back on so you can check the appropriate options. Pressing the 2 key toggles the tab menu on and off.

Figure 3.40
Right-click on the edge of the command panel or to the right of the tabs in the tab menu and clear an option in the menu to hide it.

You can clear the display of everything except the pull-down menus, the slider bar, and the Track Bar by clicking Views in the pull-down menu and choosing Expert Mode at the bottom of the menu. To exit Expert Mode you click the Cancel Expert Mode button that appears in the lower-right corner of the display (see Figure 3.41).

Figure 3.41
To exit Expert Mode, click the Cancel Expert Mode button that appears in the lower-right corner of the display.

Create Custom Toolbars, Quad Menus, Viewport Colors, and Keyboard Shortcuts

You can create new or modify existing toolbars, quad menus, keyboard shortcuts, and change display colors all within an easy-to-use Customize User Interface dialog (see Figure 3.42). You can essentially change the entire look and workflow of 3ds max 4 to suit your needs.

The dialog is accessed by right-clicking on the edge of the command panel, toolbar, or tab menu, and choosing Customize in the menu. You can also choose it from the Customize User Interface pull-down menu.

Saving and Loading Custom User Interface Schemes

Complete customized interfaces or each of the components, such as the toolbars can be saved as individual files that you can transport to other computers. This allows you to use your custom interface on someone else's machine without affecting their preferred way of working.

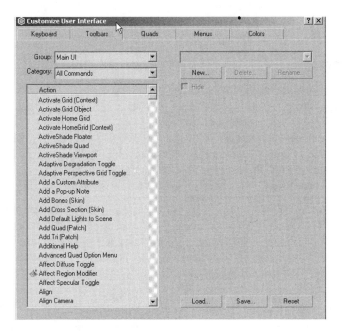

Figure 3.42   Practically all aspects of the user interface can be customized
in the Customize User Interface dialog.

New interface schemes can be loaded from the Customize User Interface pull-down
menu, Load Custom UI Scheme option.

tip

> If you should mess up your interface while customizing it or if you work
> on a machine that has an interface you are not comfortable with, you can
> revert to the default interface by choosing Revert to Startup Layout in the
> Customize User Interface pull-down menu. You can also choose Load Custom UI
> Scheme and load the DefaultUI.cui file found in the UI subdirectory.

You can also lock the current user interface with the Lock UI Layout option listed in
the Customize User Interface pull-down menu (see Figure 3.43).

MAXScript

This fundamentals book will not cover MAXScript, but you should be aware that it is
another option available for very flexible customization of 3ds max 4.

MAXScript is a programming tool that is built into 3ds max 4 that allows the user access to most aspects of the program. Using the scripting language or the Macro Recorder feature in 3ds max 4, you can create anything from custom menu buttons to full-fledged plug-ins for customizing max 4.

The MAXScript language is simple enough that you do not have to be a skilled programmer to learn it or utilize it.

The Help pull-down menu has a dedicated MAXScript Reference to help you learn to program (see Figure 3.44).

MAXScript commands may be entered directly into the MAXScript Mini Listener windows, the pink and white windows at the bottom left of the display.

Learn as much as you can about how and why 3ds max 4 functions and you will be able to create powerful tools that make repetitive steps and complex processes a single-button option in your customized user interface.

Figure 3.43
In the Customize User Interface pull-down menu dialog, select Lock UI Layout.

Figure 3.44
MAXScript help can be found in the Help pull-down menu to get you started in programming with the built-in macro language.

Chapter Summary

In this fundamental introduction of 3ds max 4's Graphical User Interface you have learned some of the basics of navigating the many menu systems, control panels, and viewports. 3ds max 4 allows very flexible customization to help you adjust your tools to be readily at hand to match your workflow.

Many of the commands found in 3ds max 4 can be accessed from several places by default, but rather than presume they know better than you about what layout works, the programmers have left access to most areas of the interface. Some of the areas covered include:

- **Right-click menus** You have learned that it is well worth the trouble of right-clicking on everything from buttons to menus to all the spaces in between.

- **Toolbar and tab panels**   Toolbars and tab panels can be customized and moved to various areas of the display, including a second monitor if your system is so configured.

- **Command panels**   You have learned that the command panel is aptly named. The command panel is a place where you can access the most commonly used commands and options.

- **Quad menus**   You learned how to use a new system of right-click menus allowing quick access to many editing tools for object and sub-object editing. You also learned that they are customizable.

- **Keyboard shortcuts**   Becoming familiar with and creating your own versions of keyboard shortcuts is essential to productive use of 3ds max 4.

- **Viewport navigation**   You experienced some of the tools necessary to move around and through your scenes and learned how to make efficient use of viewports. You also learned to use and create grid planes for more modeling control.

- **Status bar**   Learning to watch and use the status bar at the bottom of the display can increase productivity in day-to-day work. From transforming objects to controlling Snap options, the status bar offers powerful options.

- **Frame slider and Track Bar**   You learned that the Frame slider can be dragged to set the current frame of an animation. The Track Bar shows keys created by editing with the Animate button on, allowing you to edit the time that events take place.

- **Transformations**   Move, Rotate, and Scale are the three transforms in 3ds max 4. You learned to use these for productivity.

- **Coordinate systems**   Knowing the fundamentals of the coordinate systems gives you more control over the Transform tools and many of the alignment tools such as Array, Align, and Mirror.

- **Using grids**   The grid systems are a powerful tool in 3ds max 4. You learned methods of creating new grids or using the AutoGrid tool.

- **Customizing menus**   You learned how to access areas for customizing menus and buttons to configure 3ds max 4 to fit your work style more closely.

- **MAXScript**   You got a brief introduction of the scripting language built into 3ds max 4 that allows new commands to be created by writing them or by using a macro recorder.

2D Modeling: Create Your World

In This Chapter

Chapter 4 is about creating models in 3ds max 4. Starting with fundamental 2D concepts and work methods, you will learn some of the more important basic tools for quickly, and above all, efficiently building 3D worlds.

In the Chapter 4 exercises, you will build many of the elements to create an interior scene of a roadside diner. None of the exercises is extremely complex so that you can focus on the various processes used to reach a goal and not necessarily the goal itself. In a production environment, you will use these fundamental tools over and over to create a variety of 3D objects.

As you perform the exercises, try not to develop the mindset that lofting is the only method to make walls and counters. Nor do you want to assume that walls and counters are the only use for lofting. Use your imagination to project the lessons learned in this chapter, and the rest of the book for that matter, to whatever it is you want to model.

It is beyond the scope of this book to cover all tools and modeling methods available in 3ds max 4. The New Riders 3ds max 4 series of books will cover more of the advance modeling techniques that are specific and in-depth to character modeling or outdoor scenes, for example.

Refer to Chapter 2, "3ds max 4 Concepts: The Fundamentals," for a refresher on the underlying concepts of 3ds max 4 as they are presented in a practical application in this chapter and use the glossary at the beginning of this chapter for further reference. Some of the topics covered in this chapter are

- Setting up a scene
- 2D shapes, the foundation of modeling
- 2D modifiers, editing at the 2D level
- 2D modifiers, turning 2D to 3D
- Rendering 2D shapes

Key Terms

Shape   A shape is an object made up of one or more splines.

Spline   A spline is a collection of vertices and connecting segments that form a line.

Sub-object   Some types of objects let you change to a sub-object level to edit their component parts. For example, editable meshes have Vertex, Edge, Face, Polygon, and Element sub-object levels. NURBS models can have Surface, Curve, Point, Surface CV, Curve CV, and Import sub-object levels. You change the active sub-object level using the Modifier Stack rollout on the Modify panel. The right-click menu provides an alternative way to change the sub-object level.

Vertex   A vertex is a nondimensional point in space. Vertices are found in both 2D and 3D objects.

Segment   A segment is the part of a 2D shape that connects two vertices.

Edge   The edge of a 3D face or patch is the boundary of a triangular face that connects two vertices.

Face   A face is a flat triangular plane that is the building block of mesh surfaces.

Polygon   A polygon is a collection of triangular faces surrounded by visible edges.

Element   An element is a sub-object level collection of faces that is treated as a single entity.

Modifier   A modifier changes an object's geometrical structure, deforming it in some way. When you apply a Taper modifier to the end of a cylinder, for example, the vertices near the end move closer together. Modifiers make changes in the geometry that stay in effect until you adjust or delete the modifier.

Modifier Stack   The Modifier Stack is a hierarchical list of modifiers that represents the history of changes to an object.

2D Fundamentals: Setting a Foundation

Why would you want to work in 2D after having invested so much in a powerful 3D system like 3ds max 4?

Working in 2D in 3ds max 4 is a powerful, efficient method of getting much of the preliminary modeling parameters designed before creating the much more inefficient

3D mesh objects. The 2D information can also be linked to the final 3D mesh objects for easy and flexible editing control.

Throughout the exercises in this chapter you will create many of the objects in the diner scene by first preparing or importing the 2D outlines, and then converting them to 3D mesh objects.

Setting Up the Scene

An important step in being productive with 3ds max 4 is to start off on the right foot for any given project. In this chapter you will be modeling the interior of a diner that is similar to any one you can find strewn across the United States landscape, narrow and basic, and probably built in the 1950s. You will set up the workspace in max 4 to use standard U.S. building units and a work grid that is flexible for a likely range of object sizes. It is not critical that you work with a grid system, but after you understand how grids function your workflow will increase in speed and accuracy.

You will adjust the display units of 3ds max 4 so that all numeric fields display in a typical U.S. architectural format, namely feet and inches with fractions.

The default internal system of units that max 4 uses for all calculations is 1 Unit = 1 Inch. It is important to understand the difference between the system units and the display units. Clicking Customize in the pull-down menu and choosing Preferences can set system units (see Figure 4.1). System units can be set to various U.S. or metric standards.

caution

> Only change the System Units Scale when absolutely necessary and with the knowledge of all parties you are collaborating with.
>
> Having System Units set to Meters and Display Units set to Feet and Inches, for example, will often return unexpected results.

In Exercise 4.1, you will set the Display Units and the Grid Spacing to standards that you will use throughout the exercises in this book. You will save the settings to a prototype file that max 4 will automatically load when you reset the software or when you start a new max 4 file.

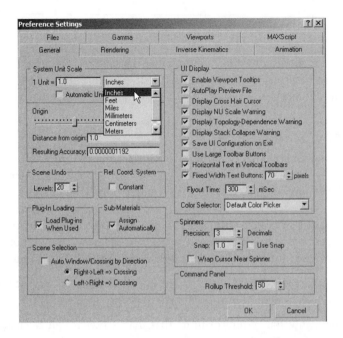

Figure 4.1   The Preference Settings dialog showing System Unit Scale options.

Exercise 4.1: Setting Display Units

1. To set the Display Units to Feet and Inches, click Customize in the pull-down menu and choose Units Setup from the list (see Figure 4.2).

2. In the Units Setup dialog, check US Standard and from the list choose Feet w/Fractional Inches. The default setting of 1/8th rounding is fine, but this may be set as small as 1/100th of an inch if necessary (see Figure 4.3). Click OK to close the dialog. If you move the mouse around the active viewport, the numbers in the Transform Type-in boxes in the status bar are in feet and inches.

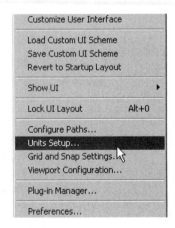

Figure 4.2
Choose Units Setup in the Customize pull-down menu.

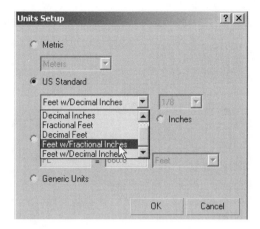

Figure 4.3   Select US Standard and choose Feet w/Fractional Inches in
the list.

---

caution   If work accuracy is important, you should set the rounding amount one
level below the required accuracy. For example, if your work needs to be
accurate to the nearest 1/8th inches, set the rounding amount to 1/16th
to minimize rounding errors.

---

note   The Default Units is set to Feet in the Units Setup dialog. All this means
is that if you type an integer in a numeric field and press Enter, the
number will be in feet. If you want inches, you have to type the inch mark (double
quote). If you want feet and inches you must type both the foot (single quote) and
inch marks.

---

3. In the Customize pull-down menu, choose Grid and Snap Settings. The Grid and
Snap Settings dialog appears showing the Snap setting tab. Click the Home Grid
tab and type 1" in the Grid Spacing field and 12 in the Major Lines every Nth
field as shown in Figure 4.4. Close the dialog.

4. In the File pull-down menu, choose Save As. Check to be sure that the current
subdirectory is /3DSMAX4/Scenes. Type maxstart.max in the File Name field and
click the Save button.

Figure 4.4   Enter 1" (inch) in the Grid Spacing field and 12 in Major Lines every Nth.

> **tip**
>
> Major Lines every Nth serves two purposes. First, it sets the spacing of the heavier grid lines in the display viewports. Every 12th line or at 12 foot spacing is heavier in this case. Secondly, it controls the scaling of the grid as you zoom in and out in a viewport. The current Grid Spacing should be reported as Grid = 1'0" on the status bar. There is a Major Grid line every 12 feet. If you zoom in slowly, the Grid spacing will shift automatically at some point. The status bar will read Grid = 0'1" and the Major lines will be every 12 inches. Zooming out will switch to a Grid of 12 feet, 144 feet, and so on.
>
> By default, the Grid Spacing will not be smaller than the Grid Setting. You must clear the Inhibit Grid Subdivision Below Grid Spacing in the dialog to get a grid of 1/12". Click the Zoom Extents All button to return to the default viewport zoom level, if you have changed it. Grid Spacing and Major Lines settings may be changed at any time for flexible control of the Grid.

5. In the File pull-down menu, choose Reset. Click the Yes button when prompted Do You Really Want to Reset? When max 4 resets to a new scene check to see that the status bar shows Grid = 1'0". If it does, then max 4 has read the maxstart.max file and loaded your settings. If it reads Grid = 10.0, then repeat steps 1–5 of this exercise.

The maxstart.max file will always be loaded on startup of 3ds max 4 or whenever you perform a reset. You can have many settings stored in this file and you could even have objects or lights if your scenes are repetitive.

Shapes and Splines

As mentioned in Chapter 2, a very important concept of 3ds max 4 is that of compound shapes—2D *shapes* containing multiple *splines*.

Shapes are 2D objects that have a name and a display color assigned at creation time. Each shape, by definition, contains at least one spline. But shapes may also contain multiple splines to become compound shapes. The compound shape may contain multiple splines that:

- are closed and nested with no overlapping;
- and/or have Separate splines, closed or open;
- and/or have Overlapping splines, closed or open.

note

To revert to the factory default settings in 3ds max 4 you can simply delete the maxstart.max file or rename it.

caution

It is recommended for most users only to have settings preset in the maxstart.max file. Other objects, especially lights, could cause problems if you forget they are in the file.

caution

Overlapping splines are invalid shapes and, when converted to 3D, will create self-intersecting geometry. This can be a cause of corrupt files that will not load or be recovered.

tip

In the Utilities panel you will find a Shape Check utility. This utility tells you if a shape self-intersects and highlights the area in red in the display (see Figure 4.5).

In Exercises 4.2 and 4.3, you will learn two methods of creating compound shapes, using the Start New Shape option and attaching existing shapes. You will save the shapes to create 3D mesh objects in a later exercise.

In Exercise 4.2, you will create the 2D data needed to extrude a simple 3D wall with a window opening using the Start New Shape option to make the compound shape. You will save the 2D shape to use in a later exercise.

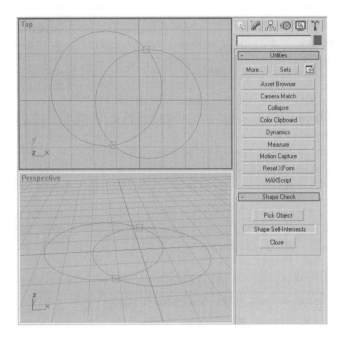

Figure 4.5   An invalid, self-intersecting shape identified with the Shape
Check utility.

Exercise 4.2: Start New Shape Compound Shape Method

1. Start 3ds max 4 or, if you are already in max 4,
    choose File from the pull-down menu, and select
    Reset. If prompted, save or discard your current
    scene, then click Yes when prompted Do You Really
    Want to Reset?

2. Right-click in the Front viewport to activate it and
    type W to maximize the viewport. Click the 3D
    Snap toggle button at the bottom of the display to
    toggle it on. It is set to Grid snap by default.

3. In the Create panel, Shapes panel, click the Rectangle button in the Object Type
    rollout. Click and drag your mouse near the far left of the viewport on a Grid
    intersection on the black horizontal origin line. Drag your mouse up and to the
    right until the Parameters rollout indicates you are snapping to Grid intersections
    to create a Rectangle with Length = 9'0"and Width = 38'0".

tip

You will not be able to
drag the cursor far enough
to the right to be able to
see the Grid intersection
38 feet to the right of
where you initially clicked.

4. In the Object Type rollout, clear the Start New
   Shape check box and click and drag another rectangle that has a Length = 6'0" and a Width = 8'0"
   snapping on the grid one foot below the top of
   the existing rectangle. Click the Zoom Extents
   All button and the Front viewport should look
   similar to Figure 4.6.

5. Click the Select button and type H to open the
   Select by Name dialog. You should only have one
   shape named Rectangle01 in the Select by Name
   list. It is one shape made of two splines. Click the
   Select button to close the dialog.

note

If you have Rectangle01
and Rectangle02 in the
Select by Name list you
have either not cleared the
Start New Shape check
box or have not clicked
the Select button to com-
plete the process.

6. In the Modify panel, highlight Rectangle01 and rename the compound shape
   frontwall. In the File pull-down menu, choose Save As. Name the file Ch4_front-
   wall_shape.max and save it in a directory where it will be available later to convert to a 3D mesh and see the advantages of compound shapes in action.

In Exercise 4.3, you will create a compound shape from two primitive 2D shapes, an
ellipse, and a rectangle and, using the Attach option at sub-object level, you will create a compound shape. You will then clean up the shape to create the profile of a
domed ceiling for the diner. Along the way, you will learn about the importance of
First Vertex and Vertex welding.

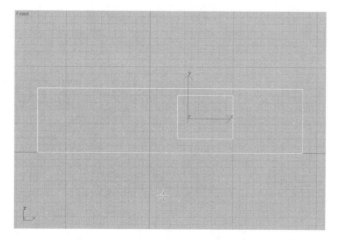

Figure 4.6   A compound shape created by dragging the large rectangle
with the Start New Shape option checked, clearing Start New
Shape, and then creating the smaller rectangle.

Exercise 4.3: Attach Compound Shape Method

1. Start 3ds max 4 or, if you are already in max 4, choose File from the pull-down menu, and select Reset. If prompted, either save your current scene, and then click Yes when prompted Do You Really Want to Reset?

2. Right-click in the Left viewport to activate it and type W to maximize the viewport. Click the 3D Snap toggle button at the bottom of the display to toggle it on. It is set to Grid snap by default.

3. In the Create panel, Shapes panel, click the Rectangle button in the Object Type rollout. Click and drag your mouse near the upper left of the viewport on a Grid intersection. Drag your mouse down and to the right until the Parameters rollout indicates you are snapping to Grid intersections to create a Rectangle with Length = 4'0"and Width = 18'0".

4. In the Shapes panel, click the Ellipse button and click and drag from the upper-left corner to the lower-right corner of Rectangle01. Ellipse01 will be created inside the rectangle as seen in Figure 4.7.

5. Click the Select button and pick on the edge of Rectangle01 or type H, highlight Rectangle01 in the list, and click the Select button. Rectangle01 turns white in the viewport and the pivot axis appears to indicate the rectangle is selected.

6. Move the cursor over the edge of Rectangle01, right-click, move the cursor over Convert To: in the Transform Quad menu. Click Convert to Editable Spline in the new menu (see Figure 4.8).

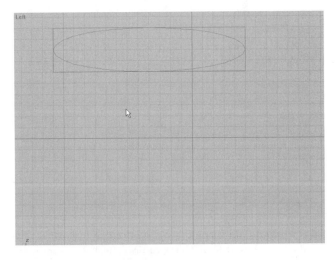

Figure 4.7   Here is Rectangle01 with Ellipse01 inside—two shapes each made of one spline.

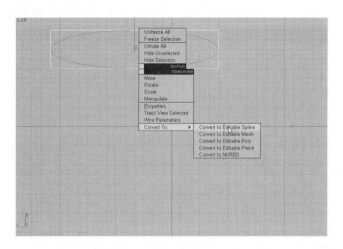

Figure 4.8   Choose Convert to Editable Spline in the new Quad menu.

tip   The Attach option is only available in an Editable Spline or within an Edit Spline modifier. More on that later in this chapter.

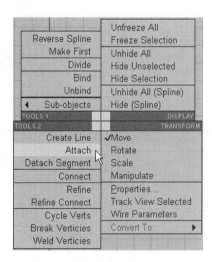

Figure 4.9   Choose Attach in the new Quad menu.

7. Move the cursor over the selected Rectangle01 again and right-click. Choose Attach in the Tools2 Quad menu (see Figure 4.9). Move the cursor over Ellipse01 and click when you see the Attach cursor. The shape is now a compound shape made of two splines.

8. In the Modify panel, Stack View, click the plus sign to the left of Editable Spline in the Modifier Stack view to expand Vertex, Segment, Spline. Choose Spline to highlight it (see Figure 4.10). This gives you access to the sub-object editing tool Trim in the Modify panel.

9. In the Modify panel, Geometry rollout, click the Trim button and, in the left viewport pick the point on the shape indicated in Figure 4.11. You have used two primitive shapes, attached them, and trimmed parts away.

10. In the File pull-down menu, choose Save As and name the file Ch4_ceiling_profile.max. You will have more work to do later in Chapter 5 with this file.

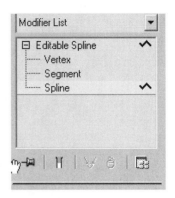

Figure 4.10
Highlight Spline in the expanded Modifier Stack view.

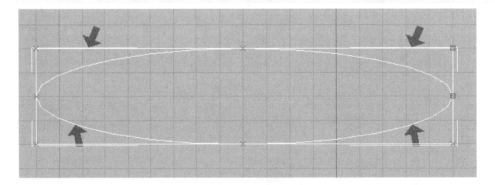

Figure 4.11   With the Trim button selected in Modify panel, pick the four points shown on the compound shape.

Edit Spline Modifier Versus Editable Spline

tip

Refer to Chapter 2 for a discussion on the concepts of sub-object editing, modifiers, and Modifier Stack.

In Exercise 4.3 you used the Convert to Editable Spline to access what is known as sub-object editing.

One issue that can be confusing to the new user and one that is important is the difference between Convert to Editable Spline and applying an Edit Spline modifier. An explanation will require a little knowledge of the Modifier Stack.

The Modifier Stack is the history of editing objects in 3ds max 4.

If you apply an Edit Spline modifier to a 2D shape, you get access to the various sub-object editing levels: vertex, segment, spline.

The Edit Spline modifier is located at a point in the Modifier Stack history to which you can return to make changes. Further, you can drop below the Edit Spline modifier in the Modifier Stack history to make changes to modifiers placed on the shape prior to Edit Spline or to the base parameters of the 2D shape primitive, the Length, Width, and Corner Radius of a Rectangle, for example.

Converting a shape to Editable Spline gives you access to the same sub-object level editing as the Edit Spline modifier, but "bakes in" any base parameter or modifier data applied before the conversion. You can make new edits, but cannot change old edits.

Whichever method you choose for accessing sub-object level editing depends on several factors, workflow, and subjectivity being among them.

- The Edit Spline modifier is more flexible generally because you can choose it in the Modifier Stack. It can also be removed or disabled from the Stack. This option uses more memory because each Edit Spline modifier makes a full copy of the original.

- The Editable Spline is more efficient. No history of edits is kept.

caution

If when using the Edit Spline modifier, you make changes to the topology of the shape, that is, you add or delete a vertex, segment, or spline, dropping below that modifier in the stack will give unexpected results. 3ds max 4 issues a warning to that effect.

tip

The Edit Mesh modifier is generally much more resource intensive because the underlying 3D mesh is more complex. Use Edit Mesh only when necessary.

In Exercise 4.4, you will work with an Editable Spline to create shapes for a window sash and window trim for the front wall. It is an example of working with existing 2D shapes at the sub-object level to extract data to create new shapes. This ensures that the new shapes are sized correctly and in the correct spatial orientation for later use.

Exercise 4.4: Creating New Shapes from Existing Shapes

1. Open 3ds max 4 if you have closed it or choose File, Reset from the pull-down menu to clear the current scene. From the File pull-down menu choose Open and open the file called Ch4_frontwall_shape.max from the CD-ROM that accompanies this book. This file is the two rectangles that you created with the Start New Shape button in Exercise 4.2. You should be in the Front viewport.

2. In the File pull-down, choose Save As. In the File Save As dialog, click the plus sign button to the left of the Save button. This saves the file as a new file named Ch4_frontwall_shape01.max on your hard drive.

> **tip** Using the File Save As option and clicking the plus sign button to save incrementally named files is a good habit to get into during production. It helps ensure that you will be able to retrieve at least partial data if something happens to the working file. In large projects the incremental files can use valuable disk space, so delete or archive them when appropriate.

3. The first step will be to center the window opening rectangle within the wall outline rectangle from left to right so the window opening is in the correct position. Click the Select button and pick on the frontwall shape. In the Modify panel, Stack view, click the plus sign to the left Editable Spline to expand the list. Click Spline in the list.

> **note** You neither added an Edit Spline modifier or Converted to Editable Spline for this shape. The process of using the Start New Shape option automatically created an Editable Spline from the two original rectangles.

4. Pick the smaller window opening spline in the Front viewport. It turns red when selected. Click the Align button in the toolbar. Move the cursor over the outer white rectangle spline in the Front viewport. When you see a small crosshair appear on the Align cursor pick the shape to call the Align Sub-Object Selection dialog.

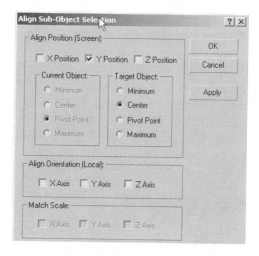

Figure 4.12   Check the X Position option of Align to align the Pivot Point to the center.

5. In the Align Sub-Object Selection dialog, check the X Position option to align the Pivot Point of the small rectangle shape to the center of the large rectangle shape. (see Figure 4.12). Click OK to finish the alignment.

> **caution**
>
> It is imperative that you understand the coordinate system for commands like Align to work properly. In step 5, Align is using the screen coordinate system to determine the orientation of the x-, y-, and z-axes. Refer to Chapter 3, "Workflow/GUI: A Road Map of max 4," for more details on the coordinate system.

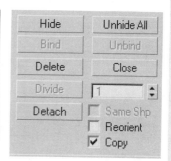

Figure 4.13
Check the Copy check box before clicking the Detach button.

6. Now that the window opening spline is in place, you will detach the spline from the shape as a copy. The new spline will be used for the window trim. At Spline sub-object level, make sure the small rectangle spline is selected and red. Find the Detach option at the bottom of the Modify panel, Geometry rollout (see Figure 4.13). Check the Copy check box. Click the Detach button and name the new shape window_trim in the Detach dialog as shown in Figure 4.14. Click OK. In the Stack view, click at the Editable Spline level to exit Sub-object mode.

7. Click the Select button, type H, and double-click window_trim in the list to select it. In the Stack view, click the plus sign to the left of Editable Spline, and choose Spline in the list. Pick on the rectangle in the Front viewport to select it and highlight it red.

8. In the Modify panel, Geometry rollout, type –6" in the numeric field to the right of the Outline button (see Figure 4.15) and press Enter. This creates a new spline 6" offset from the original. In the Stack view, choose the Editable Spline level to exit sub-object mode. The result is a compound shape made of two splines as shown in Figure 4.16.

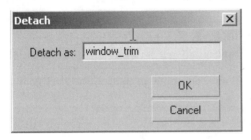

Figure 4.14
Name the new shape window_trim
and click OK to close the dialog.

Figure 4.15
New spline offset 6" from original with Outline command at Spline sub-object level.

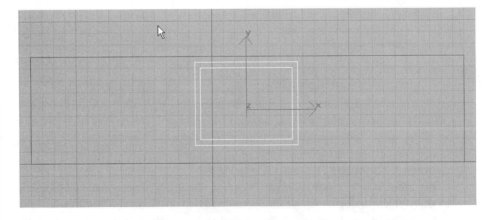

Figure 4.16   Compound shape named window_trim made of two
rectangular splines.

In Exercise 4.5 you will repeat the preceding exercise to create a similar compound shape that will later be used as the window sash.

Exercise 4.5: Creating a 2D Window Sash

1. If you are not still in the file from Exercise 4.4, from the File pull-down menu choose Open and open the file called Ch4_frontwall_shape01.max on the CD-ROM. You should be in the Front viewport.

2. In the File pull-down, choose Save As. In the File Save As dialog, click the plus sign button to the left of the Save button. This saves the file as a new file named Ch4_frontwall_shape02.max on your hard drive.

3. Make sure window_trim shape is selected. You will detach the spline from the shape as a copy. The new spline will be used for the window sash. In the Stack view, expand Editable Spline and choose Spline in the list. The inner rectangle spline should still be selected. If not, click on it to highlight it.

4. Find the Detach option at the bottom of the Modify panel, Geometry rollout. Check the Copy check box. Click the Detach button and name the new shape window_sash in the Detach dialog as shown in Figure 4.17. Click OK. In the Stack view, click at the Editable Spline level to exit Sub-object mode.

5. Click the Select button, type H, and double-click window_sash in the list to select it. In the Stack view, click the plus sign to the left of Editable Spline, and choose Spline in the list. Pick on the rectangle in the Front viewport to select it and highlight it.

6. In the Modify panel, Geometry rollout, type 2" in the numeric field next to the Outline button and press Enter. This creates a new spline 2" offset to the inside from the original. In the Stack view, choose the Editable Spline level to exit Sub-object mode. The result is a compound shape made of two splines.

7. Save the file. It should already be named Ch4_frontwall_shape02.max.

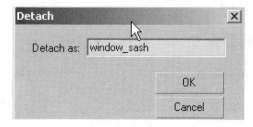

Figure 4.17   Name the detached rectangle window_sash in the Detach dialog.

More on Sub-Object Shape Editing

Sub-object editing at the 2D Shape level is very important to production. It is beyond the scope of this book to cover all the functionality and the possible methods of accessing the tools, but this section will cover a few of the more commonly used Sub-object tools used on shapes. Exercise 4.6 will cover a Sub-object Vertex editing example, in Exercise 4.7 you will learn how to work at the Segment level, and Exercise 4.8 will walk you through Spline examples. The end result of the three exercises will be a 2D shape that you will use later to create the stools at the diner counter.

Do these exercises, then strike out on your own and experiment with the other Sub-object editing options to get a feel how the options work. Use simple examples so you can concentrate on what is happening not how to make beautiful 2D shapes. The ability to make beautiful complex shapes will come after you are comfortable with the basic functionality.

tip

In the first Outline operation, the new spline was created 6" outside the original by entering –6". In this exercise, the new spline was created on the inside with 2". Whether positive numeric entries go outside or inside depends on the direction of the original spline as it was created. If you do not get the desired results the first time, click the Undo button and type the correct number.

In Exercise 4.6 you will create a line and, at Sub-object level, you will modify it to be the profile of a stool that will be used at the counter in the diner scene.

note

This is not necessarily the method you would use to create the stool profile in production. There are a few steps included in this exercise intended to familiarize you with Sub-object editing. Work with max 4 for a while and you will develop your own methods that fit your workflow.

In production you would tend to create a line with curves and straights that roughly fits the final shape and make fewer edits to get it to the end form.

Exercise 4.6: Editing at Vertex Sub-Object Level

1. Open 3ds max 4 to a new scene or perform a File, Reset to clear the current scene. If you have any information that you need to save do so at this time. Save the empty file using File, Save As and call it Ch4_stool_profile.max.

2. Right-click in the Top viewport to activate it and type W to maximize the viewport. Click the 3D Snap button to toggle it on. It should be set to Grid by default. In the Create panel, Shapes panel, click the Line button and, in the Top viewport

pick somewhere on the black horizontal grid line and move the cursor up to snap on the grid intersection 2 feet above it (see Figure 4.18). Pick on the grid intersection and right-click to finish the line.

3. Click the Zoom Extents All or Zoom Extents button to fill the display with the line. In the Modify panel, highlight the name Line01 and rename the shape stool_profile. Click the plus sign left of Line in the Stack view and choose Vertex sub-object level. The line in the viewport now shows two vertices, one at each end, and one segment connecting the two. The bottom vertex has a white box around it indicating First Vertex. That will be important in later exercises.

4. You will now add vertices and move them to start to form the top of the stool. Toggle 3D Snap off and in the Modify panel, Geometry rollout, click the Refine button (see Figure 4.19). Click three times on the line in the upper 75 percent of the line similar to Figure 4.21 to add three new vertices. Click Refine to turn it off.

tip

> Vertex sub-object level has a command similar to Refine called Insert. The difference is that when you Insert a new vertex, the vertex stays connected to the cursor to allow you to move it in the display, when you pick to set it in place you have a new vertex attached to the cursor. Refine tends to be more controllable at first, but Insert can be useful with practice.
>
> Refine can also be found at Segment sub-object level. It works the same as Vertex Refine.

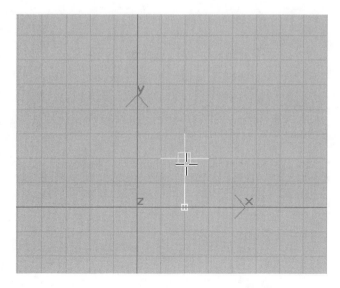

Figure 4.18   Start a line on the black horizontal grid line and move the cursor to snap on the grid intersection 2 feet above it.

note   A line is always similar to an Editable Spline because it has no Base Parameters of its own. If you convert it to Editable Spline there is no change except to the object level name in the Stack view.

5. You will now move the new vertices to form the stool seat. Click, then right-click the 3D Snap toggle and check both Grid Points and Vertex to enable those snap modes (see Figure 4.21). Close the Grid and Snap Settings dialog.

tip   Whenever you snap one object to another both options must be active for snaps to function. Here you use the Vertex snap to pick the vertex up and the Grid Point snap to place it.

Figure 4.19
Click the Refine button in Modify panel, Geometry roll-out.

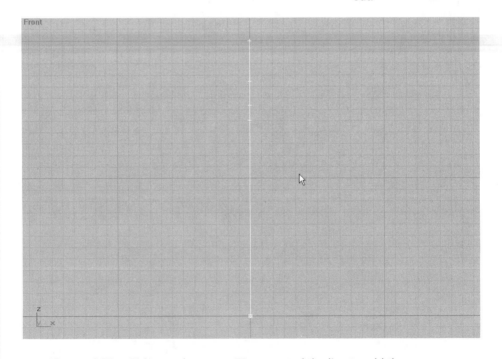

Figure 4.20   Pick near the upper 75 percent of the line to add three new vertices.

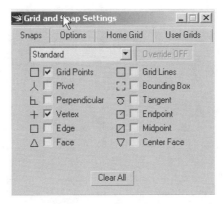

Figure 4.21   Grid Points and Vertex must both be checked in the Snaps
tab of Grid and Snap Settings.

6. In the toolbar, click the Select and Move button and pick the second vertex from
the top. Holding the mouse down, move the vertex to the right to a Grid Point
that is 10 inches to the right of the line and 2 inches from the top of the line,
similar to Figure 4.22.

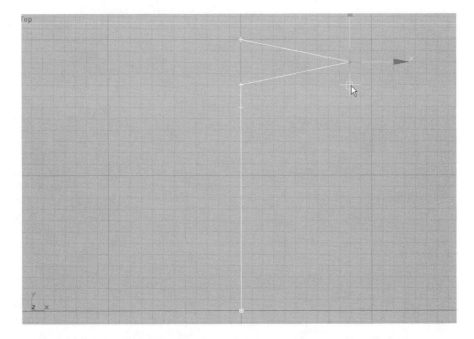

Figure 4.22   Move the second vertex from the top to a point 10 inches
to the right and 2 inches down from the top.

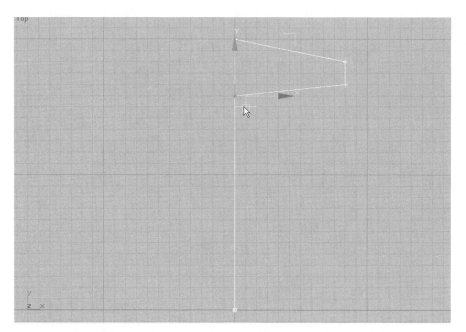

Figure 4.23   Move the next two vertices to the positions shown.

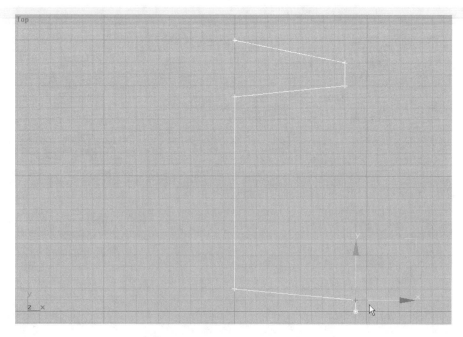

Figure 4.24   Use Refine to add new vertices and move them to form the
base of the stool_profile shape.

7. Select the next vertex down the line and move it to a point 2 inches below the one you just repositioned. Move the third vertex from the top straight up or down to a point 1 inch below the last. The stool_profile shape should look like Figure 4.23.

8. Using the same techniques of refining the line and snapping vertices into place, form the base of the stool_profile shape to resemble that shown in Figure 4.24.

9. The stool_profile shown would be a bear to sit on, so in the next step you will round the top somewhat. Click the Select button and, in the Top viewport, select the top vertex of the line. With the cursor over the vertex, right-click and choose Bézier from the Tools1 Quad menu (see Figure 4.25). This adds tangency handles to the vertex. Because there was no curvature at that vertex the green tangency handles lie on the line itself.

10. Toggle 3D Snap off. While in Select and Move mode, pick and hold on the green tangency handle to the right and down from the vertex. Move it straight up until it is at the level of the top of the line. This introduces outgoing tangency to round the top of the stool_profile (see Figure 4.26).

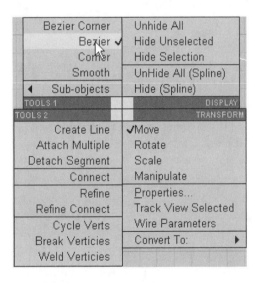

Figure 4.25   Select the top vertex of the line and right-click over it. Choose Bézier from the tangency options in Tools1 Quad menu.

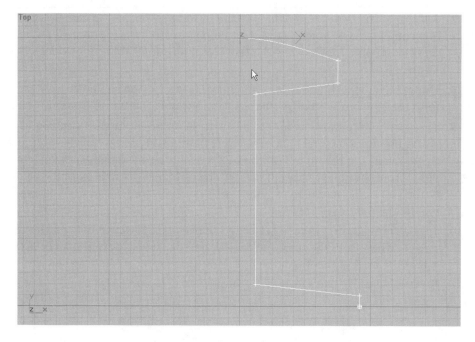

Figure 4.26   Select and move the right most green Bézier handle to adjust the tangency of the top vertex to give the stool a round cushion.

---

caution   Avoid the temptation to make all vertices have curvature, even if the model would look "better." Unnecessary curvature in models increases the density of the mesh exponentially and your models will quickly become unmanageable and inefficient.

Also, don't move the Bézier handle higher than the top vertex of the line. Doing so will result in a cup or dip in the top of the stool when the spline is converted to 3D.

---

11. In the Modify panel, Stack view, click the Segment option (see Figure 4.27). You will move the segment representing the stool support shaft 1.5 inches to the right to create a 3 inch shaft when converted to 3D. Click the Select button if it is not already active and pick the long vertical segment between the top of the base and the bottom of the seat. It will turn red to indicate it is selected.

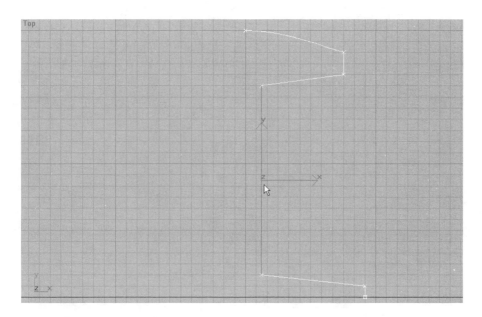

Figure 4.27   Choose the long vertical segment in the shape.

Figure 4.28   You can type accurate data into the Transform Type-in fields
in the status bar in 3ds max 4. A toggle is available for
either Absolute coordinate or Offset coordinate entries.

12. Click the Select and Move button to activate it. In the status bar, click the
Absolute Mode Transform Type-in button to toggle it to Offset Mode Transform
Type-in mode. Enter 1.5" in the X: numeric field (see Figure 4.28) and press Enter.
The selected segment moves 1-1/2 inches to the right and should look like Figure
4.29.

13. In the Modify panel, Stack view, click Line to exit Sub-object mode. Save the file,
it should already be named Ch4_stool_profile.max.

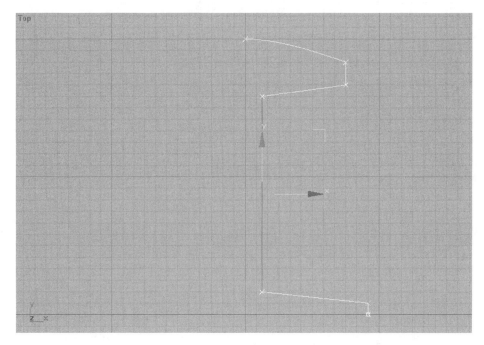

Figure 4.29   Stool_profile with shaft segment offset by 1.5" to the right.

Work with simple 2D shapes and investigate the various options available in Sub-object editing mode for Vertex, Segment, and Spline level editing. Becoming familiar with the tools that are available will help when you get in a production crunch.

caution

You must type the inch mark after the number or max 4 will assume the number is in feet.

2D Modifiers

There are two different types of modifiers in 3ds max 4 that are available only when you have a 2D shape selected in a scene. There are modifiers for editing the 2D shape as a 2D shape. There are also modifiers that convert 2D shapes into 3D mesh objects, several of which you will learn about later. In this section of this chapter, you will learn about some of the modifiers that edit 2D shapes, including:

- Edit Spline
- Fillet/Chamfer
- Trim/Extend

tip

Even though you have your Display Units set to Feet w/Fractional Inches, you can still enter numeric data in other forms, such as decimal. Also, if you type 5mm in a numeric field it will convert it to inches for you.

You have already seen how selecting a 2D shape, right-clicking on the shape, and choosing Convert to: Editable Spline gives you access to sub-object level editing, that is, editing the Vertices, Segments, and Splines that make up the shape. Converting a shape to an Editable Spline bakes in any changes or edits into the shape so that those changes and edits can not be reversed. For example, you create a Rectangle, convert it to Editable Spline, and, in Vertex sub-object mode, you change the curvature of the Bézier tangency for a freeform shape. You now right-click and convert to Editable Spline again. There is no way to get back to the original rectangle to make changes to it.

 tip

If you do not know if a tool is available, you cannot use it. This may sound like a superfluous tip, but it is an absolute hindrance to production and warrants mentioning.

note

The edits and changes can be reversed with the Undo command, but that is a linear reversal and subject to the state of your Undo buffer. For example, if you save the file, close 3ds max 4, and reopen the file, the contents of the Undo buffer is lost.

There are circumstances in which you want to retain edits in the Modifier Stack history so you can have more options to go back to alter those changes. As in the previous example, you create a rectangle, but now apply an Edit Spline modifier. At Vertex sub-object level you make similar changes to Bézier tangency. Now you can drop below the Edit Spline level in the Modifier Stack to access the Base Parameters of the rectangle to change the Length and Width parameters. The Bézier edits from the Edit Spline modifier are still intact. You can, at any time, choose the Edit Spline modifier in the Modifier Stack and remove it or disable it.

caution

As previously mentioned in this chapter and in Chapter 2, if you make topological changes in an Edit Spline modifier, that is, one that adds or deletes vertices, you often cannot go back in history to make changes without unexpected results. 3ds max 4 issues a warning to that effect.

In the previous example, you cannot use Refine in the Edit Spline modifier to add an extra vertex and change the Length and Width without problems. Conversely, you could not drop to the rectangle Base Parameters and change the Corner Radius as the process adds new vertices.

You can apply as many Edit Spline modifiers as you like, each acting as a container for particular edits. This gives you a flexibility and freedom to design and experiment not offered in most software.

In Exercise 4.7 you will apply an Edit Spline modifier to a rectangle and perform some editing functions to see the effects on the rectangle.

Exercise 4.7: Edit Spline Modifier

1. Open 3ds max 4 or go to File, Reset to start a new scene. Save the file as Ch4_edit_spline01.max.

2. Right-click in the Top viewport to activate it and type W to maximize the viewport. In the Create panel, Shapes panel, click the Rectangle button and click and drag a Rectangle of any size in the Top viewport.

3. In the Modify panel, Parameters rollout, type 5 in the Length and 10 in the Width fields. When you press Enter, max 4 will enter the number as whole feet by default.

4. In the Modify panel, click the Modifier List and double-click Edit Spline in the Patch/Spline Editing area (see Figure 4.30).

5. In Stack view, click the plus sign to the left of Edit Spline and choose Vertex. In the Top viewport, select the upper-right vertex of the rectangle. Click the Select and Move button and move the left, green Bézier handle upward to introduce tangency curvature similar to Figure 4.31. In the Stack view, choose Edit Spline to exit Vertex sub-object mode.

Figure 4.30
Double-click Edit Spline in the Modifier List.

> **tip**
>
> Choosing Hold/Yes saves the current scene in a Hold buffer on your hard drive. If something unexpected should happen as a result of dropping back in history you can recover by clicking the Edit pull-down menu and choosing Fetch. This restores the scene to the same state it was when you clicked Hold/Yes.
>
> You may also use the Edit menu Hold option at any time to save the current scene in the buffer for later Fetch actions. The Hold buffer is not cleared by Fetch or when you shut down max 4 or the computer. Clicking Hold again overwrites any information in the buffer.

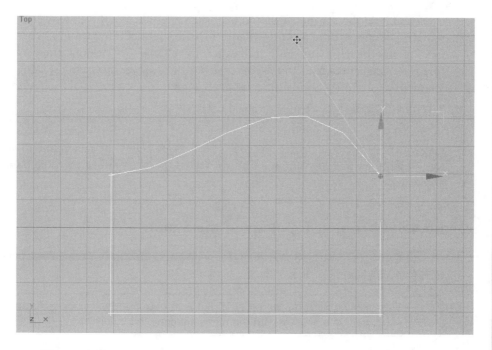

Figure 4.31   In Vertex sub-object mode, move the left Bézier handle
                   upward.

6. In the Stack view, choose Rectangle to drop back in history to the Rectangle Base
   Parameters. A warning dialog appears letting you know that dropping below the
   Edit Spline modifier may cause problems (see Figure 4.32). Click the Hold/Yes
   button.

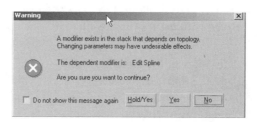

Figure 4.32   Click Hold/Yes in the warning dialog.

7. Click and hold the left mouse button over the Length or Width spinners and move the mouse up and down to change the size, right-clicking while you are still holding the left mouse button to cancel the change. You see that the curvature is retained and adapts to the size changes. In the Stack view, choose Edit Spline to return to the top of the Modifier Stack list.

8. Save the file. It should already be called Ch4_edit_spline01.max.

In Exercise 4.8, you will use Ch4_edit_spline01.max to investigate the possible consequences of changing the topology of the shape below the Edit Spline modifier. Results will vary in many situations but you will learn the value of the Hold buffer in any case.

Exercise 4.8: Changing Topology of the Shape

1. Open the file Ch4_edit_spline01.max if it is not still open from Exercise 4.7. Save it as Ch4_edit_spline02.max.

> **tip**
>
> Remember, you can pick the plus sign button in the File, Save As dialog to save a new file with the name incremented by one.

2. In the Stack view, choose Rectangle to return to the Base Parameters of the rectangle. Click the Hold/Yes button in the warning dialog to store the scene in the Hold buffer. Click and hold the left mouse button on the Corner Radius spinner and move the mouse to change the setting. Right-click to cancel the operation when you see the results. The rectangle is destroyed by changing the topology as Corner Radius adds two vertices at each corner of the rectangle.

3. In the Stack view, choose the Vertex level of the Edit Spline modifier. In the Top viewport, click the Select button, and pick the lower-right vertex to select it. In the Modifier panel, Geometry rollout, type 1 in the Fillet field and press Enter. The vertex is replaced with a 1 foot radius fillet at that corner.

4. Select the lower-left vertex of the rectangle, hold the Ctrl key and add the upper-left vertex to the selection set, type 1 in the Fillet field, and press Enter. Those vertices are also replaced by a 1-foot radius fillet (see Figure 4.33). In the Stack view, choose Edit Spline to return to the top of the Modifier Stack.

> **tip**
>
> You should get into the habit of always returning to the top of the Modifier Stack, otherwise the next modifier you apply may only be acting on the last sub-object selection below that level.

5. Save the file, it should already be called Ch4_edit_spline02.max.

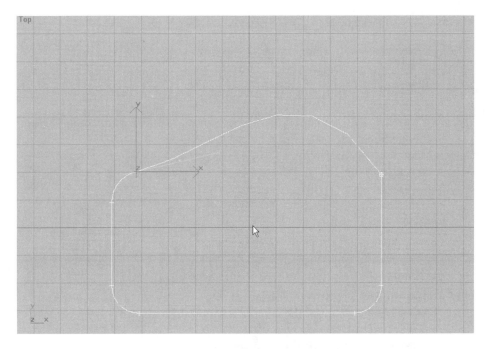

Figure 4.33   Modified rectangle with three filleted corners.

By converting the original Rectangle shape to an Editable Spline, you could have made the edits that you performed in Exercise 4.7 and Exercise 4.8, but you would not have had the capability at any time to have changed the length or width of the original rectangle as that information would have been baked in when converting.

By applying an Edit Spline modifier, you were able to make adjustment to the tangency and were still able to drop to the bottom of the Modifier Stack to change the length and width of the rectangle, but as soon as you tried to make topology changes the rectangle was destroyed.

But you were able to move up the Modifier Stack and change the Fillet radius of any vertex with the Vertex level Fillet command. You changed one, then another's Fillet radius.

As it stands now, however, if you wanted to go back and remove the Fillet from the lower-right corner vertex, for example, you cannot do it. The Fillet edits are in the same Edit Spline modifier and not a reachable part of the Modifier Stack history.

There is yet another option available to you as you will learn in Exercise 4.9.

Exercise 4.9: The Fillet/Chamfer Modifier

1. In a new 3ds max 4 scene, maximize the Top viewport, and create a new Rectangle shape. In the
   Modify panel, set it to Length = 5'0" and Width =
   10'0". Click the Zoom Extents button to zoom in on
   the Rectangle.

2. In the Modifier List, click on the Fillet/Chamfer
   modifier under Patch/Spline Editing (see Figure
   4.34). Click on the upper-left vertex of the rectangle
   in the Top viewport and type 2 in the Fillet Radius
   field in the Edit Vertex rollout (see Figure 4.35). Press
   Enter to fillet the vertex.

3. Choose the upper-right vertex of the rectangle in the
   Top viewport. In the Edit Vertex rollout, type 1 in
   the Radius field and press Enter to set the fillet.

4. Choose the lower-right vertex, type 1 in the
   Chamfer Distance field of the Edit Vertex rollout,
   and press Enter. That corner becomes a 45-degree
   chamfer in 1 foot from the original vertex (see
   Figure 4.36). Click the top Fillet/Chamfer in the
   Stack view to ensure that you are out of Vertex
   sub-object mode.

   You now have a situation where you can apply new
   modifiers to the Modifier Stack and, depending on
   topology changes, you can return to this
   Fillet/Chamfer modifier to remove it. It contains only
   the Fillet/Chamfer information and no other edits as
   an Edit Spline modifier might have. You do not need
   to save this file.

Figure 4.34
In the Modifier List, click
Fillet/Chamfer under
Patch/Spline Editing.

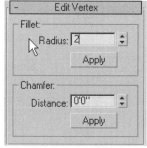

Figure 4.35
Type 2 in the Fillet Radius
field of the Fillet/Chamfer
modifier and press Enter.

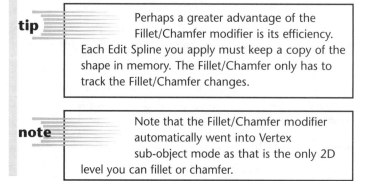

tip
Perhaps a greater advantage of the
Fillet/Chamfer modifier is its efficiency.
Each Edit Spline you apply must keep a copy of the
shape in memory. The Fillet/Chamfer only has to
track the Fillet/Chamfer changes.

note
Note that the Fillet/Chamfer modifier
automatically went into Vertex
sub-object mode as that is the only 2D
level you can fillet or chamfer.

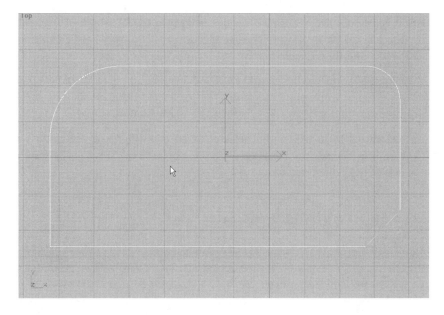

Figure 4.36   A rectangle with two filleted corners, one chamfered corner in a Fillet/Chamfer modifier.

Figure 4.37   Three complex shapes created quickly with Trim/Extend modifier.

Another useful modifier that can only be applied to 2D shapes is the Trim/Extend modifier. It can either be applied to a selection of 2D shapes or to a compound shape, each with slightly different results.

By using the Trim/Extend modifier you can create complex 2D shapes that would be difficult, if not impossible to create with other methods. See Figure 4.37 for three examples of shapes created quickly with the Trim/Extend modifier.

In Exercise 4.10 you will apply the Trim/Extend modifier to a selection of two shapes to learn the process, then in Exercise 4.11, you will use the Trim/Extend options at the sub-object level of a compound shape.

Exercise 4.10: Trim/Extend Modifier

1. Open a new session of 3ds max 4 or use File, Reset to clear your present session.

2. Right-click in the Top viewport to activate it. Type W to maximize the viewport. In the Create panel, Shapes panel, click Circle and click and drag a circle in the Top viewport. In the Parameters rollout, type 1 in the Radius field and press Enter.

3. In the Create panel, Shapes panel, click Star and click and drag a star of any size in the Top viewport.

4. With Star01 still selected, click the Align button on the toolbar and pick on the Circle01 shape in the Top viewport. In the Align dialog, check the X Position and Y Position options to center the star in the circle (see Figure 4.38). Click OK in the Align dialog.

 **tip**

> If the star shape had an odd number of points, the Center to Center alignment would be different. Remember that the options are based on the bounding box of the shape, which is rectangular for a five-pointed star.
>
> In the case of an odd number of points, Pivot to Pivot alignment would give the same results as Center to Center and an even number of points.

5. With Star01 still selected, in the Modify panel, enter Radius 1 = 1'6", Radius 2 = 0'6", and Distortion = 20. Click Zoom Extents and the Top viewport should look similar to Figure 4.39.

6. Click the Select button and click and drag a selection rectangle across both shapes to select them. In the Modify panel, click the Modifier List and choose Trim/Extend in the Patch/Spline Editing area (see Figure 4.40). You have applied a single modifier to two separate shapes.

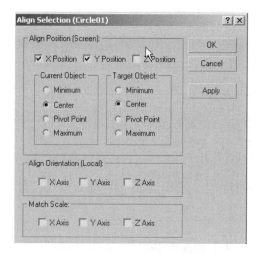

Figure 4.38   Check the X Position and Y Position options to align Star01 Center to Center to Circle01.

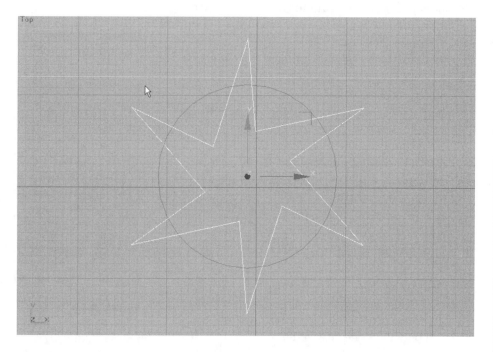

Figure 4.39   Distorted Star01 aligned to center of Circle01.

note   The Distortion setting of the Star shape rotates the inner apex point around the Star center in degrees.

note   By default you are in Crossing mode and only need to enclose or touch the objects to select. You can toggle to Window selection mode by clicking the Crossing Selection button on the status bar. This requires that all objects are completely inside the selection rectangle, circle, or polyline.

7. In the Modify panel, Trim/Extend rollout, click the Click Locations button (see Figure 4.41) and pick on the shapes as shown by the arrows in Figure 4.42. Click the Pick Locations button to disable it. The areas you picked were trimmed from the other shape based on the nearest boundary from your pick point. The resulting shapes should be similar to Figure 4.43.

8. To make the shape useful for converting to a 3D object, there are still two steps. Select the remains of Star01, move the cursor over the shape, right-click, and choose Convert To: Editable Spline in the Transform Quad menu. Right-click again and choose Attach in the Tools 2 Quad menu.

9. Move the cursor over Circle01 until you see the Attach cursor and pick to Attach. The shape is now a compound shape, but still not a fully closed polygon.

10. In the Modify panel, Stack view, click the plus sign to the left of Editable Spline and choose Vertex sub-object. The shape in the Top viewport has several First Vertex indicators, a white square on a vertex. This means this is an open spline. A closed spline will only have one First Vertex.

Figure 4.40
Choose Trim/Extend in the Modifier List.

Figure 4.41
Click the Pick Locations button in Modifier panel, Trim/Extend rollout.

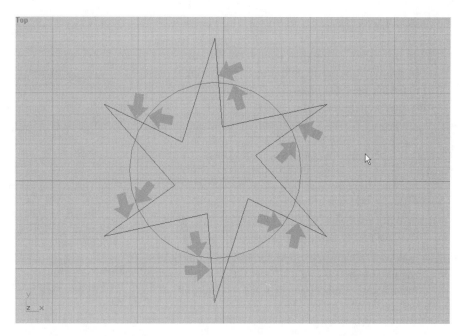

Figure 4.42   Pick segments to trim as shown by the arrows.

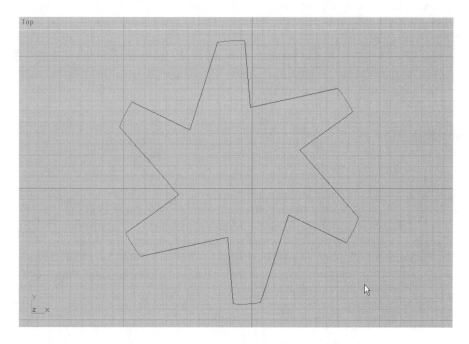

Figure 4.43   Star01 and Circle01 trimmed to create two new shapes.

11. Click the Select button and, in the Top viewport,
drag a selection rectangle around all vertices to select
them. In the Modify panel, Geometry rollout, enter
1" in the Weld numeric field and click the Weld button (see Figure 4.44). However, you should still have
four First Vertex indicators in the shape.

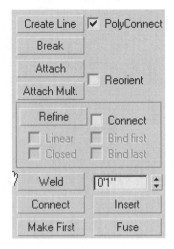

Figure 4.44   Enter 1" in
the Weld field and click
Weld.

note

Welding is an important process in
3ds max 4. It combines two or more
vertices into a single vertex. The Weld
number describes a sphere around each selected
vertex of that size. If two spheres overlap, the vertices are welded to a single sphere at the centroid
of the selection set.

max 4 does its best to weld vertices according to
the parameters you set, but is not always successful.
In such cases, select pairs or small selection sets of
vertices and try again.

12. You should have two sets of vertices at the top and bottom of the shape that did
not weld correctly. (If not, skip this step.) Select each pair individually, and click
the Weld button. Another option would be to select one vertex of a pair and drag
it over the other with Select and Move. When you release the left mouse button,
the Editable Spline dialog appears and asks if you want to weld the vertices. Click
Yes. You now should have a closed polygon shape with one First Vertex that
could be turned into a 3D mesh.

warning

If you set the Weld number too high you might weld vertices you do
not intend to weld and collapse parts of the shape.

tip

A useful tool when working with shapes is found in the Utility panel.
Click the More button, and double-click Shape Check in the Utilities
list dialog (see Figure 4.45). In the Modify panel, Shape Check rollout, click the
Pick Object button. Pick on any shape and it will report if the shape is self-
intersecting. The areas of self-intersection will be highlighted in red in the viewports. Self-intersecting shapes can be created during welding and are relatively
common on shapes imported from other software.

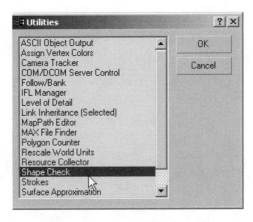

Figure 4.45   The Shape Check utility found in Utilities panel, More.

The more tools you are aware of for creating and using 2D shapes, the more efficient your models can be and the greater your productivity. When you find yourself with a few extra minutes, investigate the various Command panels and options within the panels. When you find an option you want to know more about, use the Online Reference under the Help pull-down menu.

In Exercise 4.11 you will use the Trim and Extend options at the sub-object Spline level of a compound shape. The Trim and Extend options in sub-object level editing function as they did in the Trim/Extend modifier, but are not discreet operations that can be removed or disabled in the Modifier Stack. Trim and Extend options are also found at the sub-object Spline level of Edit Spline modifier. By working with the various methods available you will develop your own style choosing the best method for any given situation.

Exercise 4.11: Sub-Object Spline Level Trim and Extend Options

1. Open a file called Ch4_trim_extend.max from the CD-ROM that accompanies this book. Click No when asked Do You Want to Save Your Changes?, if you are still in 3ds max 4 from the previous exercise. The file is a compound shape containing an arc within a rectangle. It should look like Figure 4.46.

2. Click the Select button and, in the Top viewport, select the shape. In the Modify panel, Stack view, choose Spline to enter sub-object Spline editing mode.

3. In the Geometry rollout, click the Extend button, and pick at each end of the arc as shown by the arrows in Figure 4.47. This extends the arc until it finds a segment that is part of the same compound shape.

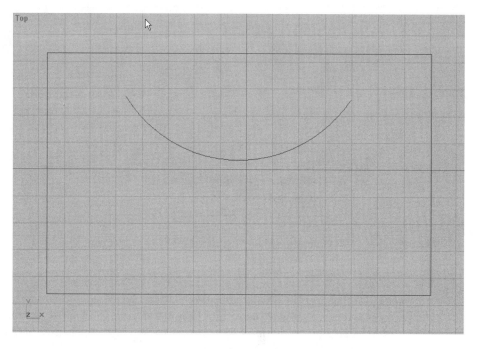

Figure 4.46   A compound shape containing an arc within a rectangle. One shape made of two splines.

4. In the Geometry rollout, click the Trim button and pick the portion of the top horizontal line between the two end point intersections (see Figure 4.48) to remove it.

5. In the Stack view, click Vertex for vertex sub-object mode. You will notice there is only one First Vertex. This is not the case, but an illusion. Coincidentally, the First Vertex of the rectangular spline and the First Vertex of the arc spline are at the same point. This shape still needs to be welded to become a closed polyline.

6. To double-check, right-click the shape and choose Properties in the Transform Quad menu. In the Object Information area of the Properties dialog, notice there are 12 Vertices and 2 Curves in the shape (see Figure 4.49). If you count the vertices in the viewport you will see only 10 vertices. Click OK to close the Properties dialog.

tip

The Extend option with the Infinite Bounds checked on is a good method of closing open splines. As you pick the end of a spline the line will extend until it meets the projected extension of the other end. Provided, of course, that the splines are not parallel or would never meet in space.

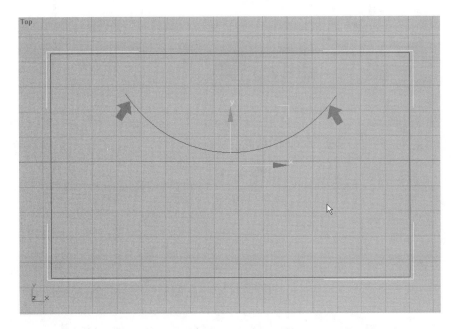

Figure 4.47   Click the Extend button in Geometry rollout and pick at each end of the arc.

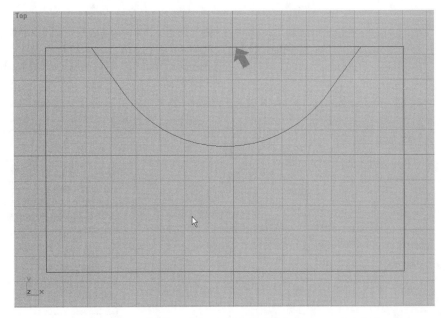

Figure 4.48   Click the Trim button in Geometry rollout and pick the segment between the ends of the arc.

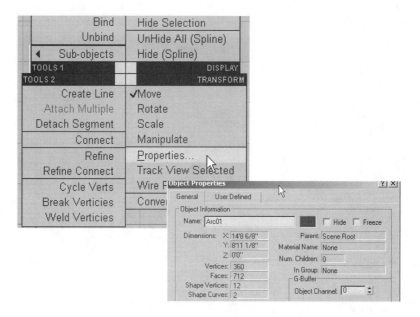

Figure 4.49   Right-click on the shape and choose Properties in the Transform Quad menu. There are 12 Vertices and 2 Curves listed.

7. Click the Select button in the toolbar and, in the Top viewport, click and drag a window around vertices at the two ends of the arc. In the Modify panel, Geometry rollout, enter 1" in the Weld numeric field and click the Weld button.

8. Right-click in the Top viewport and choose Properties again in the Transform Quad menu. The Properties dialog now reports 10 Vertices and 1 Curve. The vertices were welded and the shape is one continuous polygon. You do not need to save this file.

What you see at first glance is not always what you expect. This example would not have created a valid capped 3D mesh object if it was converted to 3D before the welding had been performed. Always be suspicious that all is not what it seems and, armed with the knowledge of max 4, be prepared to use deductive reasoning to correct potential problems.

If you have a scene with 2D shapes and you render a viewport, the 2D shapes do not appear in the rendered image. They have no third dimension, therefore are not mesh objects by default.

There is a option available at Vertex and Segment sub-object level called Break that will create two vertices for each selected vertex. It is the opposite of Weld.

However, it can be desirable to use 2D shapes to define lines and have them show up in a rendered scene. It would be possible to use a simple shape as a loft path and extrude a cross section along it to create a mesh object. But if the shape is a compound shape or something along the idea of a spider web it cannot be used as a loft path.

Renderable Splines

Luckily for us, there is an option in 3ds max 4 to make any 2D shape renderable. In Exercise 4.12, you will create a 2D spider web shape and turn it into a renderable spline. You will refresh what you know about the Outline option at sub-object Spline and to create new segments with Create Line option.

Exercise 4.12: Renderable Splines

1. Open the file from the CD-ROM called Ch4_ren-derable01.max. It contains a 2D shape created from a six-sided NGon primitive. The primitive was converted to an Editable Spline and the Bézier tangents were adjusted at the vertices to produce inward curving sides. This will be the start of your spider web.

2. In the File pull-down menu, choose Save As, and click the plus sign button left of the Save button to save with an incremented name. Select the shape and in the Stack view, choose Spline sub-object level to activate it. Click the spline in the Top viewport to highlight it red.

3. In the Modify panel, Geometry rollout, type –1" in the Outline numeric field and press Enter (see Figure 4.50).

4. Select the new spline, type –1" in the Outline field and press Enter.

5. Repeat step 4.

6. Repeat step 4, again. The resulting compound shape will look like Figure 4.51.

Figure 4.50
Type –1" in the Outline numeric field.

7. In the status bar, click, and then right-click the 3D Snap button. In the Grid and Snap settings dialog, click the Clear All button, then check the Vertex option (see Figure 4.52). Close the dialog.

8. In the Modify panel, Geometry rollout, click the Create Line button and, working out from the center, click each vertex to create a connecting radial line for the vertices at the three o'clock side. Right-click after picking the last vertex to finish the line. It should look like Figure 4.53.

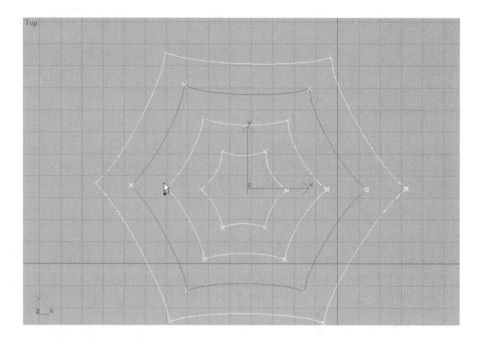

Figure 4.51   Repeat step 4 several times to create the rings of the spider web.

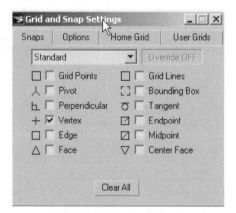

Figure 4.52   Clear all snap options, then only check Vertex.

9. Repeat step 8 for each set of vertices. The spider web should look like Figure 4.54. Click the Create Line button to disable it and, in the Stack view, choose Editable Spline to exit sub-object mode.

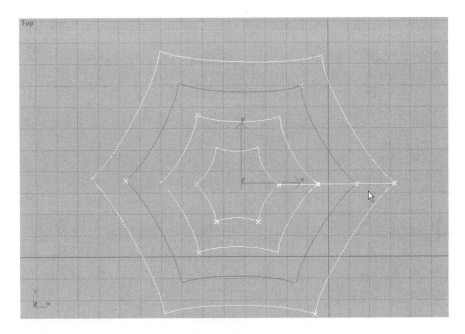

Figure 4.53   Using Create Line in the Geometry rollout, connect each
vertex and right-click to finish the radial line.

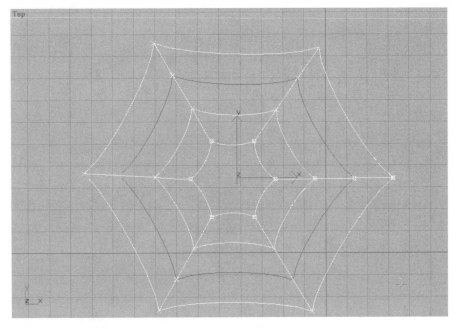

Figure 4.54   Create radial lines for each set of vertices.

10. On the toolbar, click the Quick Render button. The Virtual Frame Buffer will not show any rendered image because all you have is a default 2D shape.

11. In the Modify panel, Rendering rollout, check the Renderable option (see Figure 4.55). The Virtual Frame Buffer will display a rather fat spider web-shaped 3D mesh object like the one in Figure 4.56. Close the Virtual Frame Buffer.

12. In the Rendering rollout, type 0.125" in the Thickness field and press Enter.

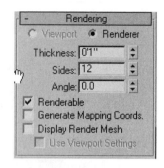

Figure 4.55
Check Renderable in the Modify panel, Rendering rollout.

| caution | Entering a number smaller than 0.125" or 1/8" will have no result, because the Display Units is set to show the nearest 1/8" in your maxstart.max prototype file. |

13. Click the Quick Render button in the toolbar and see that you have a more proportional spider web (see Figure 4.57). Close the Virtual Frame Buffer.

14. Save the file as Ch4_renderable02.max.

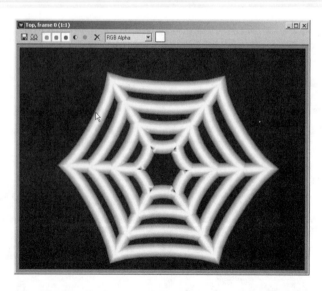

Figure 4.56   Fat rendered spider web in Virtual Frame Buffer.

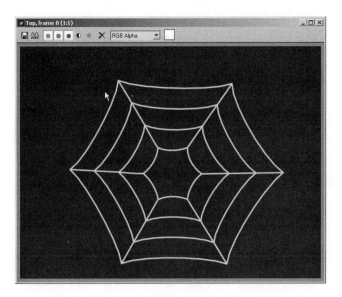

Figure 4.57   The rendered spider web with more pleasing proportions in Virtual Frame Buffer.

Chapter Summary

- **Setting up a scene**   In this chapter, you have learned to set up a prototype file with the Units and Grid Spacing setting you would like to use as a default and to save that file to maxstart.max. This helps hold consistency throughout a company or project and saves time at the beginning. This file may be edited at any time to change it.

- **2D shapes**   You have learned the fundamentals of working with 2D shapes both at the object and sub-object level. It is extremely efficient and flexible to get much of the base work done in 2D.

- **2D modifiers**   You have applied modifiers specific to 2D shapes such as, Fillet/Chamfer and Trim/Extend.

- **Renderable splines**   Complex 3D grids or webs can often be created easily by using the Renderable Spline feature of 2D Shapes.

3D Fundamentals: Creating the World Around Us

In This Chapter

Congratulations, you have made it through the chapter on creating 2D shapes. While it is an incredibly important aspect of working with 3ds max 4, it is not exactly the most satisfying in terms of seeing results of your labors. In this chapter you will begin to convert some of the shapes you have created and some shapes you will import into 3D mesh objects. This is the 3D world to which you will eventually be applying materials, lights, cameras, and animation to create a world around you, the viewer.

Read through the exercises and explanations in this chapter and then go step-by-step through the exercises. Keep in mind that the purpose of the exercises is to illustrate work methods and concepts. Pay more attention to the process than the end results. As you learn more about 3ds max 4, you will be able to tweak and adjust to get just the right look and feel to your scene. But first you must be able to quickly and cost effectively get to a point where you can afford to spend the time on the all-important artistic aspects.

Throughout this chapter, you will learn production techniques that may be applied in your day-to-day work that will be efficient and allow flexible editing. These techniques will allow you to be responsive to changes by the client, and in many cases, to monitor and adjust the density of the mesh objects for a balance between efficient rendering and sufficient model detail on the fly.

Again, it is beyond the scope of this book to cover all the techniques and methods of modeling in 3D, but if you learn the core tools presented in this chapter, you will have the essential fundamental skills to build perhaps 90 percent of the objects you will need including:

- Extrude modifier
- Bevel modifier
- Bevel Profile modifier
- Lathe modifier
- Lofting methods

The diner that you will create will be a mix of methods to show you various approaches to modeling. There is no right or wrong method for any given task, but the more methods you are familiar with, the easier it will be for you to choose one that works for your scenario.

Often new users want to know about NURBS modeling and Patch modeling right from the start. NURBS and Patches are not the fundamental modeling tools that most of you will need to get the vast majority of your work done. Take the time to learn these fundamental modeling techniques, and you will have a good base to build more advanced 3ds max 4 modeling on.

Key Terms

Sub-object   Some types of objects let you change to a sub-object level to edit their component parts. For example, editable meshes have Vertex, Edge, Face, Polygon, and Element sub-object levels. NURBS models can have Surface, Curve, Point, Surface CV, Curve CV, and Import sub-object levels. You change the active sub-object level using the Modifier Stack rollout on the Modify panel. The right-click menu provides an alternative way to change the sub-object level.

Vertex   A vertex is a nondimensional point in space. Vertices are found in both 2D and 3D objects.

Edge   The edge of a 3D face or patch is the boundary of a triangular face that connects two vertices.

Face   A face is a flat triangular plane that is the building block of mesh surfaces.

Polygon   A polygon is a collection of triangular faces surrounded by visible edges.

Element   An element is a sub-object level collection of faces that is treated as a single entity.

Modifier   A modifier changes an object's geometrical structure, deforming it in some way. When you apply a Taper modifier to the end of a cylinder, for example, the vertices near the end move closer together. Modifiers make changes in the geometry that stay in effect until you adjust or delete the modifier.

Modifier Stack   The Modifier Stack is a hierarchical list of modifiers that represents the history of changes to an object.

Some of the lessons you learned in Chapter 4 on 2D fundamentals will be revisited here to illustrate efficient editing methods. In addition, there are parallels in working with 2D shapes that are found when working with 3D mesh objects including:

- **Convert to Editable Mesh**   This is very similar to the method of converting a shape to Editable Spline. It gives you access to sub-object editing of the fundamental parts that make up a 3D mesh: vertex, edge, face, polygon, and element. Once you have converted a 3D Primitive, for example a Box, you no longer can adjust the base parameters of the box.

- **Applying modifiers at sub-object level**   You can apply modifiers to just the selected sub-objects much the way you did with 2D modifiers. For example, a Bend modifier could be applied to the top half of a cylinder instead of to the whole object.

- **Some modifiers only operate on 3D mesh**   In the same way that Fillet/Chamfer modifier will only function correctly on 2D shapes, MeshSmooth, Mesh Select, and UVW Map only do their job when applied to 3D mesh.

tip

Feel free to experiment with a variety of modifiers on either 2D or 3D objects. For example, most users think of the Bend modifier as being intended for 3D objects. However, you can get some interesting results by applying a Bend modifier to a 2D shape that has enough vertices to bend and then converting it to 3D. See Figure 5.1 for an ellipse with added vertices that has a Bend modifier applied at the 2D level and then a Bevel to convert to 3D. The object would be difficult to model with other techniques.

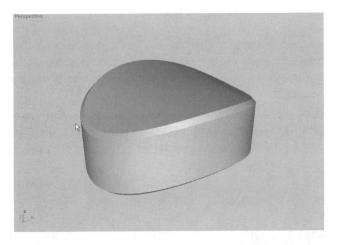

Figure 5.1   The ellipse has added vertices, a Bend modifier, and a Bevel modifier.

In the next sections you will use several modifiers that can be applied to 2D Shapes to turn the 2D into 3D Mesh objects. The following modifiers can only be applied to 2D Shapes. If you have a 3D Mesh selected, the modifiers do not even appear in the Modifier List. You will apply:

- Extrude modifier
- Bevel modifier
- Bevel Profile modifier
- Lathe modifier

The Extrude Modifier

The Extrude modifier is a simple but powerful modifier that can only be applied to 2D shapes. It extrudes the 2D shape in only the positive or negative z-axis of the shape as it was created.

You will start with Exercise 5.1 by creating a new master scene for your diner. You will create a rectangle of the overall floor dimensions as a guide. You will start modeling by creating a simple wall with a single large window opening. You have already created the necessary 2D shapes for the wall, the window sash, and the window trim in Exercise 4.2 and Exercise 4.3 from the previous chapter. You will then apply a modifier to convert the compound shape to a 3D wall with a window opening.

note   If you have anything other than a 2D shape selected, it will either be grayed out or will not show in the Modifier List.

Exercise 5.1: The Extrude Modifier

1. Open 3ds max 4 or use File, Reset to clear the current session. You should already have architectural units of Feet w/Fractional Inches and a default grid spacing of 1 foot. This information was saved in the maxstart.max file in Exercise 4.1 of the previous chapter.

2. Right-click in the Top viewport to activate it and press W to maximize the display. Click, then right-click on the 3D Snap button, click the Clear All button, and then check the Grid Points checkbox (see Figure 5.2). Close the dialog.

3. In the Create panel, Shapes panel, click the Rectangle button, and in the Top viewport, pick in the upper left of the viewport and drag down and right to create a rectangle with length = 18 feet, 0 inches and width = 38 feet, 0 inches. Edit the name to be floor_outline. Click the Zoom Extents button to fill the display with the rectangle. You will use this as a guide to construct the walls of the diner.

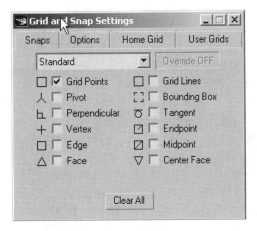

Figure 5.2   Set 3D Snap to Grid Points only.

4. From the File pull-down menu, choose Save As and name this file MASTER_DINER01.MAX. During the exercises in this book, you will save incremental copies of this file in much the same way that many production offices work. With a history of files, it will be easier to go back to previous revisions and to recover from possible data loss.

5. You will now use the File, Merge option to merge 2D shapes from an earlier exercise. In the File pull-down menu choose Merge (see Figure 5.3). In the Merge File dialog, find and double-click Ch5_frontwall_shape02.max on your hard drive or on the CD-ROM.

> **tip**
>
> While you are dragging the cursor to define the lower-right corner of the rectangle, you probably will not have enough viewport to complete the rectangle. While still holding the left mouse button, press I and the display will center on the current cursor position.

6. In the Merge-Ch5_frontwall_shape02.max dialog, choose frontwall in the list, and click OK (see Figure 5.4). This merges just that selected shape and not the window_sash and window_trim shapes.

> **note**
>
> In the Top viewport you will only see a white line with an axis indicator appear when you merge the shape. The shape was originally created in the Front viewport and retains that orientation and because it is 2D you are only seeing the edge from above.

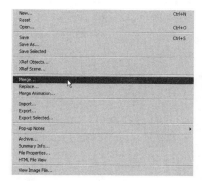

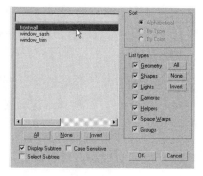

Figure 5.3
Choose the Merge option in
the File pull-down menu.

Figure 5.4
Choose frontwall to merge only
that shape into your current
scene.

7. Type W to minimize the viewports and you will see
the frontwall shape better. With the frontwall shape
selected, in the Modifier panel, Modifier List, choose
Extrude. The 2D shape will be converted to a 3D
object with no thickness. Rename this object
FRONTWALL with all caps to indicate a 3D object
(see Chapter 2, "Object Naming Standards").

8. In the Modify panel, Parameters rollout, type 6" and
press Enter in the Amount field to create a six-inch
thick wall (see Figure 5.5). Because the frontwall
shape was a compound shape the 3D wall becomes
a solid wall with a window opening.

tip

Do not use the Extrude
modifier to create flat surfaces with no thickness.
This object is actually two
sets of coplanar faces with
the Face Normals in oppo-
site directions. It is more
dense than necessary and
could cause problems with
materials later.

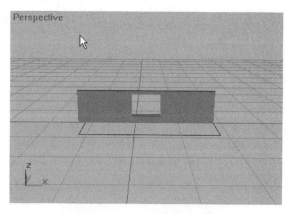

Figure 5.5   You create a six-inch thick wall with window opening.

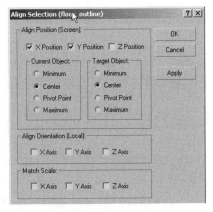

Figure 5.6   Align FRONTWALL Center to Center to floor_outline in the X- and Y-axes of the Top viewport while in View Reference Coordinate System.

9. You will now use the Align command to place the wall on the floor_outline shape. Right-click in the Top viewport and type W to maximize it. Make sure FRONTWALL is selected and click the Align button in the toolbar. In the Top viewport, click on the floor_outline shape. In the Align Selection dialog, check X Position and Y Position. Center is the default for the Current and Target objects columns (see Figure 5.6). *DO NOT* close the Align Selection dialog.

> **note**
>
> You do not want to align center to center in the Z Position as the FRONT-WALL would drop down through the grid plane.

10. This is not the final position for FRONTWALL, but this alignment has gotten you to a known position, and there are no combinations that would put the wall where it belongs. In the Align Selection dialog, click the Apply button. This sets the position of the wall, clears the alignment axes, but leaves the Align Selection dialog open for more alignment.

> **tip**
>
> For the last step in a series of alignments, you do not need to click the Apply button. Clicking OK applies the settings and closes the dialog.

11. Check the Y Position checkbox, and in the Current Object and Target Object columns, check the Minimum options (see Figure 5.7). This aligns the farthest bounding-box point in the negative y-axis of the FRONTWALL with the farthest bounding box point in the negative y-axis of the floor_outline. Click the OK button to close the dialog and finish the alignment.

12. In the File pull-down menu, choose Save As. In the Save As dialog, click the plus sign button left of the Save button to save and increment the name of a new file to MASTER_DINER02.MAX.

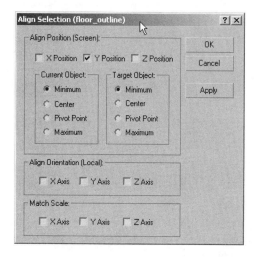

Figure 5.7   The outer edge of the wall aligned with the outer edge of the shape by checking the Y Position checkbox, and in the Current Object and Target Object columns, checking the Minimum options.

The Bevel Modifier

In Exercise 5.2 you will create a window sash and window trim for the interior of the wall. You will merge the other 2D shapes from the same file you used in Exercise 5.1. While you could apply an Extrude modifier to each of the shapes to create efficient mesh objects, you will instead use a modifier called Bevel. It is similar to Extrude in that it creates a 3D object from a 2D shape in the positive or negative z-axis of the shape, but it has options to outline the shape as well as extrude it.

This allows you to create beveled edges at the front and back of the object. It is intended for creating beveled text to use in logo animations, but it is very useful for many objects. Bevel modifier does increase the mesh density by adding new faces, but in many cases, the extra faces can add significant visual interest to the objects by catching the light in the scene (see Figure 5.8). You must ultimately weigh the cost of extra geometry versus acceptable visual results in every scene, but with practice the choice will become easier and easier.

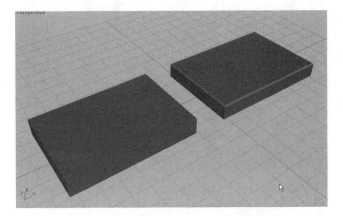

Figure 5.8   The box on left has the Extrude modifier applied, while the
box on right has the Bevel modifier applied. The box with
Bevel applied has edges that catch the light and define the
shape of the box in 3D space. The box with Extrude applied
has no definition and appears flat in the scene.

Exercise 5.2: The Bevel Modifier

1. Open the file called MASTER_DINER02.MAX if you are not still in it from the last
   exercise. From the File pull-down menu, choose Save As, and save a new file
   called MASTER_DINER03.MAX.

2. From the File pull-down menu, choose Merge, and find
   Ch5_frontwall_shape02.max. In the Merge dialog, highlight window_sash and
   window_trim in the list. Click the OK button to merge the shapes and close the
   dialog. Press W to minimize the viewports, right-click in Perspective viewport,
   and press W to maximize it.

3. Use the ArcRotate and Zoom navigation tools to position the Perspective viewport
   similarly to that shown in Figure 5.9. Click the Select button, press H, and in the
   Select Objects dialog, double-click window_trim.

4. In the Modify panel, Modifier List, choose Bevel in the Mesh Editing area (see
   Figure 5.10). The 2D shape converts to a 3D mesh with no thickness just as with
   the Extrude modifier in the previous exercise. Name the object WINDOW_TRIM
   to indicate it is now a 3D mesh.

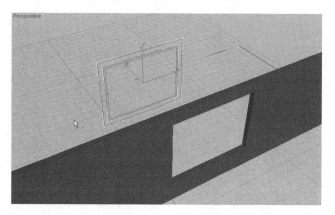

Figure 5.9   Use the Zoom and ArcRotate tools in the Perspective viewport to attain a similar view.

caution   Do not choose Bevel Profile modifier by mistake. If you do, click the Remove Modifier From Stack button in the Modifier panel to remove it.

note   If you look in the Modifier List again, you will see that Bevel is not an option. This is because you have already applied a modifier to convert the shape to 3D and Bevel is only available for 2D shape.

5. There are three levels to the Bevel modifier that need to be adjusted to create the 3D trim. In the Bevel Values rollout, check Level 2 and Level 3 checkboxes and type the following numbers in the fields as shown in Figure 5.11:

Level 1
    Height = 0.5"
    Outline = 0.5"
Level 2
    Height = 0.75"
    Outline = 0
Level 3
    Height = 0.5"
    Outline = –0.5"

Figure 5.10

Choose the Bevel modifier in Modifier list, Mesh Editing area.

The window now has bevel edges front and back. See Figure 5.12 for a close up view of the top corner of the window trim.

6. Click the Select button, press H, and double-click window_sash in the Select Objects list. In the Modifier panel, Modifier List, choose Bevel. The values you had entered in the Bevel modifier for the trim are remembered until you change them or exit this scene. Rename the object WINDOW_SASH. In the Modify panel, click on the object color swatch right of the object name and choose a different color for the sash. Select the WINDOW_TRIM and change its display color.

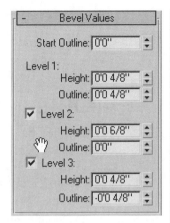

note 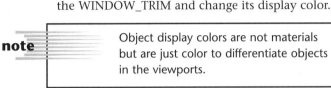 Object display colors are not materials but are just color to differentiate objects in the viewports.

Figure 5.11
Check the Level 2 and Level 3 checkboxes and fill in the numeric fields.

7. Click the Select button, press H, choose WIN-DOW_TRIM and WINDOW_SASH in the list, and click the Select button. Click the Align button, and in the Perspective viewport, pick the FRONTWALL object. In the Align dialog, check the X Position, Y Position, and Z Position checkboxes (World Coordinate System). In both Current and Target columns, check the Pivot Point options. This aligns the trim and sash with the opening and flush to the inside of the inside wall.

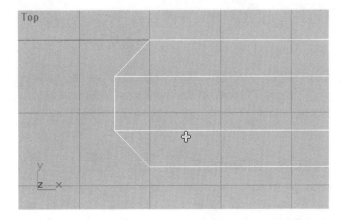

Figure 5.12   This is a Top view close-up of a corner of the wireframe trim showing beveled edges front and back.

> **tip** This alignment is partially luck. If you remember the merged 2D shapes were all derived from the same original rectangles. Therefore, they all share common pivot points and can be aligned as such. If the objects were created separately, you would have to use 3D Snap option to move them into place accurately.

8. Click the Select button, press H, choose WINDOW_TRIM, and click the Select button. Click Align and in the Perspective viewport, pick FRONTWALL. In the Align Selection dialog, check the Y Position option and set Current Object to Minimum and Target Object to Maximum. This aligns the trim flush to and projecting from the inside wall surface.

9. Click the Zoom Extents All Selected button and the scene should look similar to Figure 5.13. Save the file, which should already be named MASTER_DINER03.MAX.

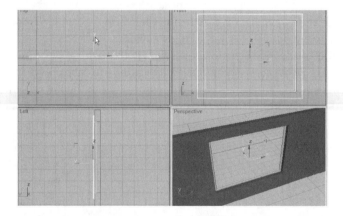

Figure 5.13   WINDOW_TRIM is aligned flush to and projecting from the inside wall surface. WINDOW_SASH is flush to and projecting inward from the inside wall surface.

The Bevel Profile Modifier

There is another modifier that functions similarly to Extrude and Bevel modifiers. It extrudes a 2D shape in the positive or negative z-axis direction to create a 3D mesh. Bevel Profile requires two objects: a base (which can be an open or closed spline) and a profile (which must be an open spline). The Bevel Profile modifier is applied to the base shape.

The Bevel Profile modifier goes one step farther and extrudes based on another open 2D shape. You could have created the front wall or the window trim and sash with the Bevel Profile modifier, but it was overkill for the objects you needed to create. What Bevel Profile offers that you do not get with Extrude or Bevel is the ability to edit the 2D profile at any time to change the 3D mesh.

In Exercise 5.3 you will use Bevel Profile to create the stools for the diner counter from the 2D shape you saved in Exercise 4.6.

Exercise 5.3: The Bevel Profile Modifier

1. Open the file you saved in Exercise 4.6 called Ch5_stool_profile.max or from the CD-ROM. It is a half shape of a diner stool created in the Top viewport. It should look like Figure 5.14. Save the file with the name Ch5_STOOL01.max.

2. In the Create panel, Shapes panel, click the Circle button, and in the Top viewport, pick and drag any circle. In the Modify panel, Parameters roll-out, type 10.5" in the Radius field. Rename Circle01 to stool_base for now.

3. With stool_base selected, in the Modify panel, Modifier List, choose Bevel Profile in the Mesh Editing area. Click the Select button, press W to minimize the viewport, and click the Zoom Extents All button to zoom all viewports. You will notice in the shaded Perspective viewport that the circle is now a solid disk with no thickness (see Figure 5.15).

tip

The viewport in which the shape was created is of no consequence to the final 3D mesh. The profile shape will move to the base shape with the first vertex attached to the base shape and the profile in the z-axis.

The position of the base shape should be created in a viewport that will give the 3D mesh the correct orientation in space.

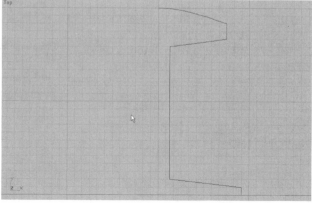

Figure 5.14   This is a 2D shape of half a counter stool in Top viewport.

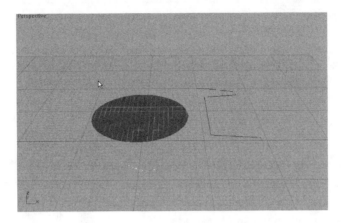

Figure 5.15   The circle with Bevel Profile applied becomes a disk with no thickness before picking any profile.

4. In the Modify panel, Parameters rollout, click the Pick Profile button (see Figure 5.16), and in any viewport, pick on the stool_profile shape. Rename this object STOOL01. You now have a 3D stool mesh as seen in Figure 5.17.

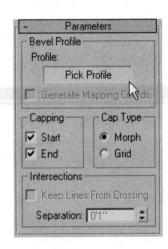

note

> The direction of the extrusion depends on the position of First Vertex on stool_profile. Had the First Vertex been on the other end of the shape, the result would have been different (see Figure 5.18).
>
> Changing the First Vertex on the shape automatically updates the 3D mesh object, as any change to the profile or the base shapes is automatically reflected in the 3D mesh.

Figure 5.16
Click the Pick Profile button in Parameters rollout and then pick stool_profile in any viewport.

5. Save the file, which should already be called Ch5_STOOL.MAX. You will use this stool in your diner scene in later exercises.

Figure 5.17   The Bevel Profile option extrudes stool_base in the positive
z-axis with the profile described by stool_profile.

The Lathe Modifier

One more modifier that can only be applied to 2D shapes that you will look at in this
chapter is the Lathe modifier. It does not extrude a shape in a shape's z-axis, rather it
revolves the shape around itself to generate the 3D mesh. Both Lathe and Bevel Profile
modifiers could have been used to create the same stool you just created in Exercise
5.3. But each method has slightly different editing capabilities. Become familiar with
both modifiers and you will be able to choose the one that is best for your particular
application. Choosing the appropriate method is more an art form than hard rule.
The beauty of 3ds max 4 is that you can usually change your mind and switch from
one method to the other without re-creating any new shapes.

In Exercise 5.4 you will use the Lathe modifier to create a 3D mesh of a ceiling fan
body.

Exercise 5.4: The Lathe Modifier

1. Open a file from the CD-ROM called Ch5_fan_body_profile.max. It contains a 2D
   shape created in the Front viewport. Because the Lathe modifier revolves the
   shape around its own local y-axis, you will have better results if the shape is
   created in the viewport that gives the correct orientation to the 3D mesh. Save
   the file with the name FAN_BODY.MAX.

2. Click the Select button, and in the Perspective viewport, pick the fan_body_profile 2D shape. In the
Modify panel, Modifier List, choose Lathe in the
Patch/Spline Editing area. The shape is revolved
around an axis that passes through the geometric
center of the shape and runs parallel to the shape's
local y-axis (see Figure 5.18). Rename the object FAN_BODY.

3. In the Modify panel, Parameters rollout, click the Max button in the Align area.
This aligns the axis with the maximum x-axis point of the shape resulting in
what appears to be two objects (see Figure 5.19).

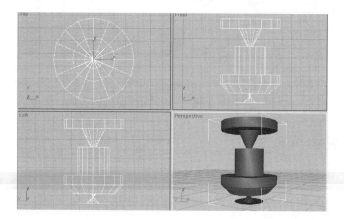

Figure 5.18   In the Lathe modifier the shape is revolved around the local
y-axis at its centroid.

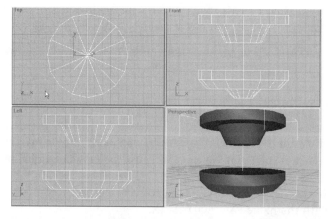

Figure 5.19   Clicking the Max button in Parameters rollout, revolves
the shape on the maximum point on the geometry in the
positive x-axis.

4. In the Modify panel, Stack view, pick the plus sign left of Lathe to expand it (see Figure 5.20). Click on Axis to highlight it yellow and you will see the Lathe axis appear as a yellow line in the viewports.

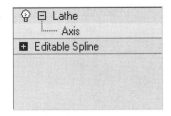

5. Click the Absolute Mode Transform Type-in button left of the coordinate fields in the status bar to toggle to Offset Mode Transform Type-in. Type 0.5" in the X coordinate field to move the axis one-half inch in the positive x-axis. The FAN_BODY mesh now appears to have a one-inch connector between the parts as seen in Figure 5.21.

Figure 5.20
Expanding Lathe in the Stack view and choosing Axis allows you to edit the Lathe Axis.

6. In the Stack view, choose Lathe to exit sub-object Axis mode. Save the file, which should already be named FAN_BODY.MAX.

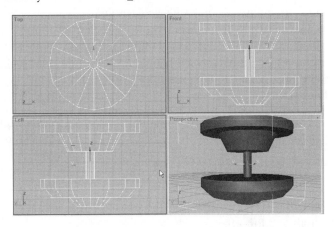

Figure 5.21   Move the Lathe axis_0.5" to the right to create a solid appearing mesh.

Lofting Cross-Section Shapes Along Complex Path Shapes

The most powerful method of converting 2D shapes into 3D mesh objects is probably the loft capabilities in 3ds max 4. In concept it is an extremely simple process requiring two objects, both 2D shape. You will need:

- **Path**   The loft path is a 2D shape made of one spline only. It can be open or closed but must be a continuous polyline. Although it is a 2D shape, it can occupy 3D space. For example, a Helix primitive shape can be a loft path.

- **Shape**   In lofting, shape refers to an open or closed 2D shape with one or more splines that acts to define the cross section of the lofted 3D mesh. The only real restriction is that all loft shapes must contain the same number of splines. For example, you cannot loft a Circle primitive and a Donut primitive on the same loft path.

Much of the power of lofting in 3ds max 4 lies in the ability to have more than one cross-section shape along a single loft path creating a transition in the form of the 3D mesh. The 2D shapes, either the cross-section shape or loft path, can be edited at any time at sub-object level to affect the result of the 3D mesh when you use the Instance clone option during lofting. Refer back to Chapter 2 for more information on the basic concept of cloning.

Material assignments can be based on the 2D information, and, of course, most of the editing can be animated by turning the Animate button on, setting the Frame slider to a frame other that zero, and making the edit change.

This section of Chapter 5 will walk you through several exercises illustrating the process of lofting. You will start out by lofting a relatively simple wall, and then you will edit that example to learn some important fundamentals of lofting. You will create several other loft objects, each time learning new options in the loft process. Some of the important fundamental topics covered will include:

- Get Shape versus Get Path loft methods
- Shape orientation
- Path and shape steps density control
- Shape instance control
- Path editing and more density control
- Materials and loft objects
- Multiple shapes on a single path

Lofting Two Walls of the Diner

You have already created the front wall of your diner by extruding a compound shape. Because this scene is of the interior of a diner and because the camera will never turn more than, say, 60 degrees left or right you only need two more walls at the end and left side of the diner.

In Exercise 5.5 you will use 2D information extracted from an existing 2D object to create the path for the

tip

You are taking a page from the film director's book here: if you can't see it, don't model it. The scene focuses on the interior of the diner looking from one end to the other. Neither the exterior walls nor the end wall behind the camera will be seen so it makes no sense to have the overhead of the mesh objects slowing down the rest of production.

Movie sets often use facades of buildings rather than the whole buildings or rooms built in the middle of studio space.

walls and you will merge a 2D wall profile shape from a file on the CD-ROM.

In lofting it is important to understand the relationship of the orientation of the shapes, both cross-section shapes and path shapes, to be able to take full advantage of the loft process.

As each shape is created it has a pivot point based on the local coordinates of the shape. The local coordinates of any shape always have the positive z-axis pointing away from the grid plane the shape was created on. A shape created in the Front viewport will have different local coordinates than a shape created in the Top viewport.

tip

During lofting the pivot point of the shape starts on the First Vertex, and the original local z-axis of the shape is extruded along the path.

Also, the original local y-axis of the shape aligns with the local z-axis of the path, and the local x-axis of the shape aligns to the local x-axis of the path.

tip

Lofting always uses the original local axis to determine how the shape is oriented on the path.

Adjusting the pivot point orientation in the Hierarchy panel, Adjust Pivot rollout will do nothing to loft orientation.

The only way to affect the original local axis of an object is to attach it to an object with a different local-axis system and then detach it to turn it back to an independent 2D shape again.

Exercise 5.5: Lofting Walls

1. Open the file called MASTER_DINER03.MAX that you saved in Exercise 5.2 or from the CD-ROM. Click the Zoom Extents All button to fill the viewports with all geometry. Save the file as MASTER_DINER04.MAX.

2. You will extract two 2D segments from the floor_outline rectangular shape in the scene. The new shape will be used as the loft path for the end and back wall of the diner. Right-click in the Top viewport to activate it. Click the Select button, press H, and double-click floor_outline in the list.

3. In the Modify panel you will notice that the shape is still a Rectangle primitive. To access sub-object level editing you will convert it to an Editable Spline. In the Top viewport, right-click, choose Convert To in the quad menu Transform quad, and then choose Convert to Editable Spline (see Figure 5.22).

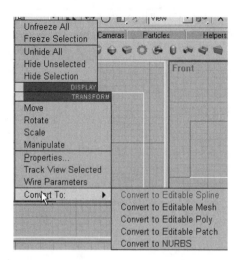

Figure 5.22   Choose Convert to Editable Spline to gain access to sub-object level editing.

4. In the Modify panel, Stack view, click the plus sign left of Editable Spline, and choose Segment in the list. In the Top viewport pick the right vertical segment, hold the Ctrl key and pick the top horizontal segment to highlight them both in red (see Figure 5.23). In the Geometry rollout, check the Copy option below the Detach button, and then click the Detach button. Enter wall_path in the Detach as dialog (see Figure 5.24) and click OK. In the Modify panel, Stack view, choose Editable Spline to exit sub-object Segment mode.

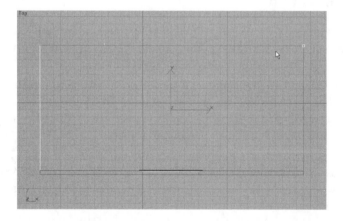

Figure 5.23   In sub-object Segment mode, pick the right vertical segment, and holding down the Ctrl key, pick the top horizontal key. Holding down Ctrl, add to the selection set.

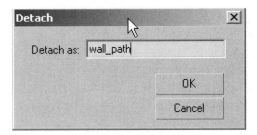

Figure 5.24   Name the newly detached shape wall_path.

5. You will now merge the 2D wall profile for lofting on the wall path. In the File pull-down menu, choose Merge. Find the file called Ch5_wall_loft_shape.max, and in the Merge dialog, double-click wall_profile (see Figure 5.25) to merge it into the current scene.

6. Press W to minimize the viewport, right-click in the Front viewport, and click the Zoom Extents Selected viewport. This fills only the Front viewport with the wall_profile 2D shape (see Figure 5.26). The profile is a single line depicting a base board at the bottom, a chair rail in the middle, and some molding at the top.

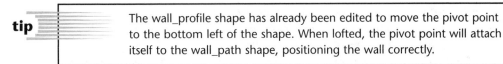

tip   The wall_profile shape has already been edited to move the pivot point to the bottom left of the shape. When lofted, the pivot point will attach itself to the wall_path shape, positioning the wall correctly.

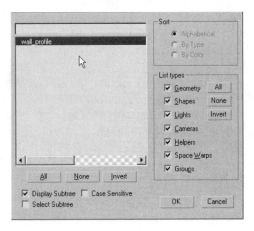

Figure 5.25   Double-click on wall_profile in the Merge dialog to merge it into the scene.

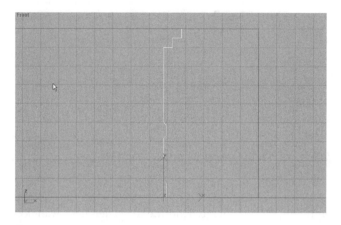

Figure 5.26   In the Front viewport, click the Zoom Extents Selected viewport to view the wall_profile shape.

7. Right-click in the Perspective viewport to activate it
    and press W to maximize the viewport. Click the
    Select button, press H, and double-click wall_path in
    the list. In the Create panel, click Standard
    Primitives and choose Compound Objects in the list
    (see Figure 5.27). In the Object Type rollout, click
    the Loft button.

8. In the Creation Method rollout, click the Get Shape
    button, press H, and double-click wall_profile in the
    Pick Shape dialog. The shape is lofted along the path
    to create two new 3D walls (see Figure 5.28).

Figure 5.27
In the Create panel,
Standard Primitives list,
choose Compound Objects.

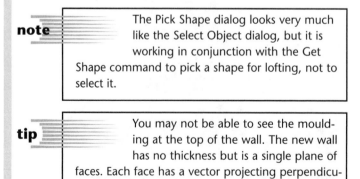

note   The Pick Shape dialog looks very much
like the Select Object dialog, but it is
working in conjunction with the Get
Shape command to pick a shape for lofting, not to
select it.

tip   You may not be able to see the mould-
ing at the top of the wall. The new wall
has no thickness but is a single plane of
faces. Each face has a vector projecting perpendicular from its center called a Face Normal. Faces that
have the Face Normal pointing toward the viewer
are visible. When Face Normals point away from
the viewer, they are invisible.

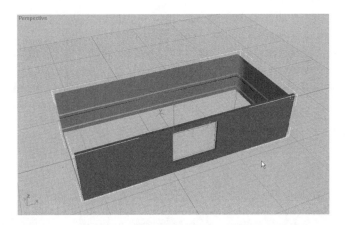

Figure 5.28   You selected a loft path and used Compound Objects, Loft, Get Shape to loft a profile along the path to create a 3D wall.

9. Save the file, which should already be named MASTER_DINER04.MAX. You will make some adjustments to the wall in Exercise 5.6.

You have selected a simple L-shaped line as a path and lofted a simple wall profile line to create a fairly complex wall system. All work is done in 2D so far, and the resulting 3D mesh is quite efficient. However, you are just beginning to see the power of lofting.

tip

You can flip the shape's orientation on the path by using Get Shape while holding the Ctrl key. The local negative z-axis of the shape now points down the path.

You have already learned the fundamentals of editing 2D splines at sub-object levels, Vertex, Segment, and Spline. You also learned in Chapter 2 about a 3ds max 4 concept called cloning. Cloned objects can be linked to the parent they were derived from.

When you lofted wall_profile along wall_path, you may have noticed an Instance option checked just below the Get Shape button. The means that the original 2D stayed where it was and a linked Instance clone was used to actually create the wall. Instance within a Loft command means that if you change the original shape, the shape on the loft path will update as well. This is an incredibly powerful feature to enable you to change your models on-the-fly, even to animate the changes.

In Exercise 5.6, you will modify some of the parameters of the loft command to make the model even more efficient than it is already. You will adjust two parameters called

Shape Steps and Path Steps. Path and Shape Steps are intermediate points between each vertex of a 2D shape that define curvature as described by the vertex tangency. The path Steps option affects the path and the Shape Steps option affects the shape. Each step also creates a new segment in the mesh object, thus increasing the number of faces in the 3D mesh.

tip

Creating lofted walls that are one continuous shape with no thickness can be a big advantage if you decide to render scenes with a Radiosity render such as Lightscape or Mental Ray.

Exercise 5.6: Editing a Lofted Wall in Modify Panel

1. Open MASTER_DINER04.MAX that you saved in Exercise 5.5 or from the CD-ROM. Make sure Loft01 is selected. In the Modify panel, rename Loft01 to WALLS. Save the file with the name MASTER_DINER05.MAX.

2. In the Perspective viewport, move the cursor over WALLS, right-click, and choose Properties in the Transform quad menu (see Figure 5.29). Notice in the Object Properties dialog that the WALLS object contains 871 vertices and 1584 faces (see Figure 5.30).

3. In the Perspective viewport, right-click on the Perspective label and choose Edged Faces in the menu (see Figure 5.31). This shows the wireframe mesh as well as the object surfaces. You can see the segments in WALLS defined by the shape and path steps (see Figure 5.32).

4. In the Modify panel, Skin Parameters rollout you will see Shape Steps and Path Steps numeric fields, both set to 5 steps by default. Right-click on the spinners to the right of the field to set them to 0 (see Figure 5.33).

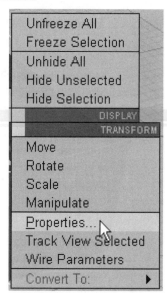

Figure 5.29
Right-click on WALLS and choose Properties in the Transform quad menu.

5. In the Perspective viewport, right-click on WALLS and go to the Properties dialog. The object now has only 36 vertices and 44 faces, a very substantial savings that can be seen in a much cleaner mesh in the viewport. Right-click on Perspective label and choose Edged Faces to turn it off in the viewport.

6. In the Modify panel, Surface Parameters rollout, clear the checkboxes for Smooth Length and Smooth Width in the Smoothing area. This cleans up the illusion of the inside-back corner of WALLS being rounded slightly. The walls are clean and efficient.

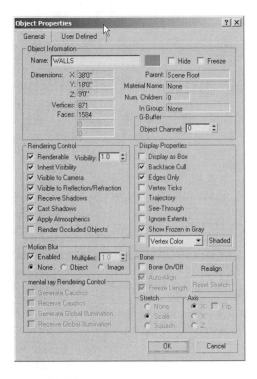

Figure 5.31
Right-click on the Perspective label in Perspective viewport and choose Edged Faces in the menu.

Figure 5.30
The Object Properties dialog shows that WALLS 3D mesh contains 871 vertices and 1584 faces.

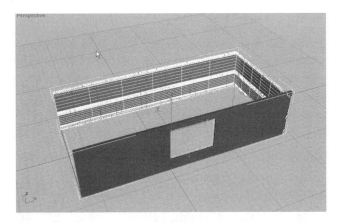

Figure 5.32   WALLS 3D mesh with Edged Faces shows the result of five steps between each vertex on the shape and path.

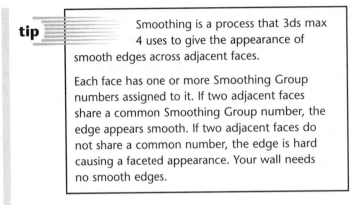

tip | Smoothing is a process that 3ds max 4 uses to give the appearance of smooth edges across adjacent faces.

Each face has one or more Smoothing Group numbers assigned to it. If two adjacent faces share a common Smoothing Group number, the edge appears smooth. If two adjacent faces do not share a common number, the edge is hard causing a faceted appearance. Your wall needs no smooth edges.

7. Save the file. It should already be named MASTER_DINER05.MAX.

Now that you have created a fairly complex wall system by lofting two simple 2D shapes, you will make some changes to the 2D wall shape to see how the powerful Instance Clone connectivity makes editing an easy task.

While you are performing the edits to change the wall, try using your imagination to project this process to some aspect of your modeling needs. As with the other exercises in this book, the simplicity of

Figure 5.33

Right-click on the Shape Step and Path Step spinners to set them to 0.

the exercise is to illustrate the technique without requiring you to concentrate so much on what is being created. Do not finish this exercise with the attitude that you now know how to create a wall—that is not the point. Project the loft methods to other tasks. For example, you could use the same process to create:

- **Exterior curtain wall systems**   Loft a cross section of one floor of an exterior wall along a path representing the foundation line. Clone this as an instance to make many floors.
- **Highway systems**   Loft a cross section of sidewalks, curbs, and roadbeds along a road center line.
- **Waterslide chutes**   A complex slide system could be done quickly.
- **A trombone**   The snaking curves of the tubing can easily be lofted.
- **A snake or arms of a squid**   A circle lofted along a curved path is the basis of both these objects.

The list could go on, but you get the idea, and later exercises will delve more deeply into lofting.

In Exercise 5.7 you will edit the 2D shape called wall_profile to change the height of the chair rail. This again is just a simple example to acquaint you with the fundamental process. The reason this works is because the Instance option was checked when you performed the Get Shape function of lofting. This retains a connection between the original and the Instance clone used on the loft path.

Exercise 5.7: Editing an Instance Shape on a Loft Path

1. Open the file called MASTER_DINER05.MAX that you saved in the last exercise or from the CD-ROM. Save it as MASTER_DINER06.MAX. Press W to minimize the viewport.

2. In the Front viewport, pick the wall_profile 2D shape or press H and select it from the list. In the Modify panel, Stack view, choose Vertex to activate sub-object Vertex editing mode. Click the Select button, and in the Front viewport, drag a window around the four vertices that make up the chair rail in the middle of the wall (see Figure 5.34).

3. In the toolbar, click the Select and Move button, and in the status bar, toggle Absolute Transform Type-in to Offset Transform Type-in. In the status bar, type –6" in the Y field (see Figure 5.35) and press Enter. You will notice in all viewports that the 3D chair rail has moved in accordance with the movement of the vertices that define it. Any valid modifications that you make to wall_profile will be reflected in the 3D mesh, and you have free reign to design almost any wall you want.

4. In the Modify panel, Stack view, choose Line to exit sub-object Vertex mode. This exercise is, again, a very simple example of a two powerful 3ds max 4 concepts at work: first, the concept of sub-object editing and second, the concept of Instance cloning.

5. Save the file. It should already be named MASTER_DINER06.MAX.

note

The four vertices are still selected from a previous exercise; however, select them again just to make sure you have the correct vertices.

tip

You do not need to be concerned about accidentally selecting any vertices of the other objects in the scene. You have access to the sub-object level of the currently selected object only.

tip

Get into the habit of exiting sub-object mode when you are finished with sub-object edits. You cannot select any other objects in the scene while you are in sub-object mode.

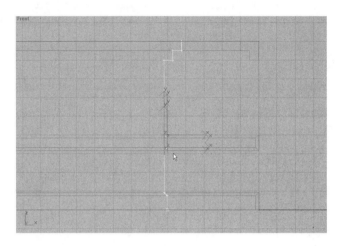

Figure 5.34   In sub-object Vertex mode, select the four vertices that form the chair rail.

Figure 5.35   Toggle to Offset Transform Type-in, type –6" in the Y field, and press Enter.

You have modified the 2D shape of the wall cross section to change the 3D wall itself. In Exercise 5.8 you will import a counter with overhead trim that was lofted in the same manner as the walls in Exercise 5.7. Here you will edit the loft path instead of the loft shape. The point of this exercise will be to introduce new options to keeping the density of mesh objects to a minimum for the requirements of the scene. It cannot be stressed enough that this should be a primary concern while modeling. If you learn some of the methods while you are new to 3ds max 4, you will develop good work habits that will become automatic as you learn more of the program.

Exercise 5.8: Editing a Loft Path and Controlling Mesh Density

1. Open MASTER_DINER06.MAX from the last exercise or from the CD-ROM. Save the file as MASTER_DINER07.MAX. You will merge a lofted 3D counter and the 2D shapes that it was created from.

2. In the File pull-down menu, choose Merge, locate and double-click on a file called Ch5_counter.max on the CD-ROM (see Figure 5.36).

3. In the Merge dialog, click the All button (see Figure 5.37) and then click OK to merge the two 2D shapes and the 3D counter into the scene. The Shape and Path Step fields have already been set to 0 and Smooth Length and Smooth Width fields have been cleared to form an efficient, clean counter.

4. The counter now takes a 90-degree turn toward the wall. You will change the counter to be rounded on the corner by modifying the loft path and still be as efficient as possible. Right-click in the Top viewport to activate it. Click the Select button, press H, and double-click counter_path in the list to select it.

5. In the Modify panel, Stack view, expand Line (pick the plus sign), and choose Vertex. In the Top viewport pick the vertex on the path at the corner of the counter.

tip

The counter is a single object lofted from a compound shape. Previous compound shapes in this chapter have taken advantage of nested shapes to create 3D objects with holes in them. Nested shapes are not necessary, however. The only situation to avoid is overlapping splines in a compound shape.

tip

The vertex is hidden by the counter 3D mesh, but if you drag a selection Window around the corner area, you will select the vertex. You do not need to worry about other vertices because they are only at the ends of the path.

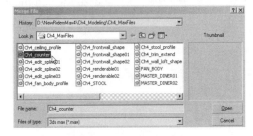

Figure 5.36
In File, Merge, double-click on Ch5_counter.max in the CD-ROM.

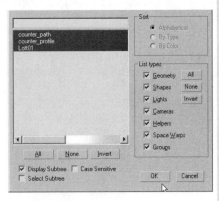

Figure 5.37
In the Merge dialog, click the All button to select everything in the list, and then click OK to merge.

6. In the Modify panel, Geometry rollout, type 3 in the Fillet field (see Figure 5.38) and press Enter to fillet the path corner with a 3-foot radius. The counter does not show a fillet, however, but has a 45-degree chamfer (see Figure 5.39).

7. You actually have filleted the path, but the 3D mesh does not reflect the curvature because Path Steps is set to 0 in the loft parameters. Path and shape steps are intermediate steps between vertices that define curvature. In the Modify panel, Stack view, choose Line to exit sub-object mode. In the Top viewport, select COUNTER.

8. In the Modify panel, Skin Parameters rollout, increase Path Steps to 5. The corner of the counter is now rounded because there are enough intermediate steps between the two vertices to create segments in the mesh (see Figure 5.40). However, this has also added segments between the other vertices thus increasing the Vertex/Face count from 152/288 to 722/1428. This is unnecessarily high. Set the Path Steps back to 0.

9. You will edit the rounded segment in the loft path and add new vertices with the Divide option. This adds the extra vertices where needed to define the

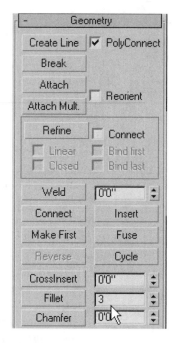

Figure 5.38
In Modify panel, Geometry rollout, type 3 in the Fillet field, and press Enter to finalize the command.

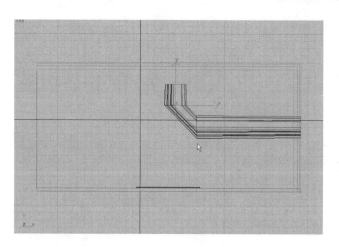

Figure 5.39   The top viewport shows apparent chamfer created with the Fillet option.

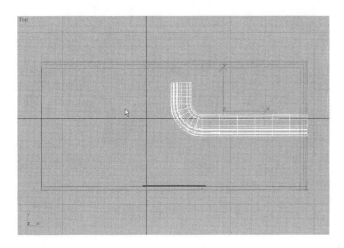

Figure 5.40   Increasing the Path Steps adds vertices between each vertex on the path. This does round the corner but adds unnecessary detail in the straight sections of the loft.

curvature without affecting any other segments. In the Top viewport, select the counter_path 2D shape. In Modify panel, Stack view, choose Segment. In the Top viewport, pick on the curved segment at the corner of the counter.

> **note**   It may be difficult to see the rounded segment, but if you pick several times where you suspect it is, you will see the axis tripod move when it is selected.

> **tip**   If you really cannot select the segment, go to Display panel, Hide rollout, and click the Hide Unselected to hide everything except the path. When you have selected the correct segment, you can click Unhide All to make your objects visible.

10. In the Modify panel, Geometry rollout, type 3 in the field to the right of the Divide button, and then click the Divide button (see Figure 5.41). Divide adds new vertices on the select segment. This increases the

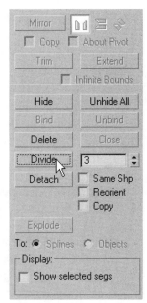

Figure 5.41
In the Modify panel, Geometry rollout, type 3 in the Divide field, and then click the Divide button to add vertices to the curved segment of counter_path.

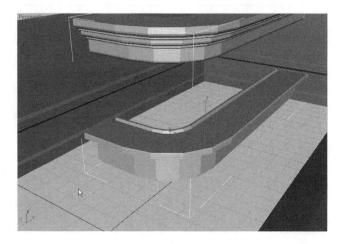

Figure 5.42   Smoothing is turned off in lofting surface parameters causing a faceted appearance at the edges of adjacent faces.

curvature of the counter locally rather than globally and the increase in the Vertex/Face count is only to 266/512.

11. Right-click in the Perspective viewport and then type W to maximize it. Use the Zoom and ArcRotate options in the Perspective viewport for a view similar to Figure 5.42. You will notice faceting instead of a smooth curve in the counter. This is because Smooth Width and Smooth Length were cleared. You will add a Smooth modifier to remove the faceted look.

12. Click the Select button, and in the Perspective viewport, select COUNTER. In the Modify panel, Modifier List, choose Smooth in the Mesh Editing area (see Figure 5.43). In the Parameters rollout, check Auto Smooth. The surfaces have lost most of their faceted look as seen in Figure 5.44.

Patch/Spline Editing
Edit Patch
DeletePatch
Mesh Editing
DeleteMesh
Edit Mesh
Face Extrude
Normal
Smooth
Tessellate
STL Check
Cap Holes
VertexPaint
Optimize
MultiRes

Figure 5.43
In Modify panel, Modifier List, choose Smooth.

tip   Auto Smooth smooths edges based on the angle that adjacent faces form. By default it is 30 degrees. Smoothing does not occur between edges and background so you still see some segmentation. You have to decide when the balance between appearance and efficiency is reached.

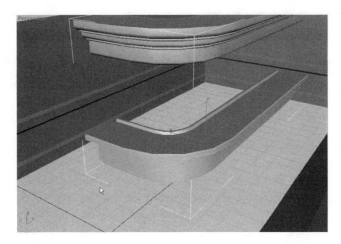

Figure 5.44   Auto Smooth option in the Smooth modifier smoothes the edges of adjacent faces.

13. Press W, to minimize the viewport. Save the file. It should already be called MASTER_DINER07.MAX.

    In Exercise 5.9 you will learn a little something about materials, plus you will learn about another of the advantages of lofted 3D mesh objects.

    It is possible to assign a Multi/Sub-object material (one material made of several other materials) to a loft object. You can then edit the loft shape and assign the various materials by either Segment or Spline sub-object editing. This makes it very easy to change materials and material assignments at any time while still dealing with just a single mesh in the scene.

Exercise 5.9: Assigning Material at Sub-Object Shape or Spline Level of a Lofted Mesh

1. Open MASTER_DINER07.MAX from the last exercise or from the CD-ROM. Save it as MASTER_DINER08.MAX. The important part of this exercise is the assignment of materials, not the material itself. Materials will be covered later. Assigning the Multi/Sub-object material is a three-step process. Tell the loft object to Use Shape IDs for material assignments, set the proper IDs at Segment or Spline level, and apply the material to the mesh.

2. In the Perspective viewport, pick WALLS to select it. In Modify panel, Surface Parameters rollout, check the Use Shape IDs option in Materials area (see Figure 5.45).

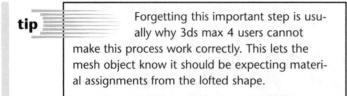

tip   Forgetting this important step is usually why 3ds max 4 users cannot make this process work correctly. This lets the mesh object know it should be expecting material assignments from the lofted shape.

3. Press W to minimize the viewport, and in the Front viewport, pick wall_profile to select it. In the Modify panel, Stack view, choose Segment. In the Front viewport, pick low and right of the bottom of wall_profile and drag the mouse to just above the chair rail (see Figure 5.46). Because the selection rectangle is in Crossing mode, all segments that are in or touching the selection rectangle are selected. While holding down the Alt key, pick on the vertical segment between the baseboard and chair rail segments and the segment above the chair rail to subtract them from the selection set. You are left with only the baseboard and chair rail segments selected.

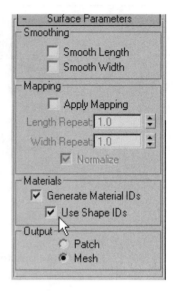

Figure 5.45
In the Modify panel, Surface Parameters rollout, check the Use Shape IDs checkbox in Materials area.

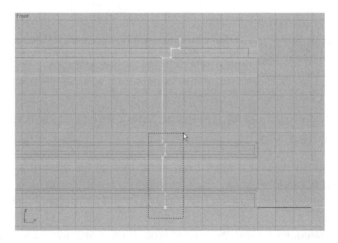

Figure 5.46   Drag a Crossing selection rectangle from below the spline to just above the chair rail segments.

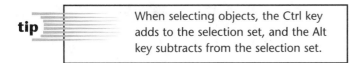

tip

When selecting objects, the Ctrl key adds to the selection set, and the Alt key subtracts from the selection set.

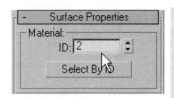

4. In the Modify panel, Surface Properties rollout, type 2 in the ID field (see Figure 5.47). This tells the mesh that is generated from those two segments to use the second material of a Multi/Sub-object material.

5. In the Front viewport, pick the segment between baseboard and chair rail segments, hold down the Ctrl key, and pick the long segment above the chair rail segments. In the Surface Parameters rollout, type 3 in the ID field. Mesh generated from these segments will get the third material in a Multi/Sub-object material. In Modify panel, Stack view, choose Line to exit sub-object mode.

Figure 5.47

Type 2 in the Modify panel, Surface Parameters rollout, ID field. Mesh generated from those segments will use the second material in a Multi/Sub-object material.

6. In the toolbar, click the Material Editor button to open it (see Figure 5.48). Click on the Type: Standard button and double-click Multi/Sub-Object in the Material/Map Browser list (see Figure 5.49). Click OK to accept the Keep old material as sub-material option in the Replace Material dialog (see Figure 5.50).

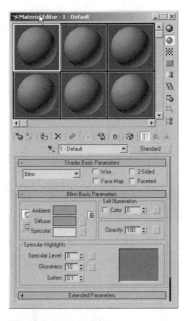

Figure 5.48

Open the Material Editor.

Figure 5.49

Click on the Standard button and double-click Multi/Sub-Object in the Material/Map Browser.

7. From the Material Editor, drag and drop the first Sample Sphere onto WALLS in the Perspective viewport to assign the new material to the walls. The lofted WALLS will become gray in the viewport.

8. In the Material Editor, Multi/Sub-Object Basic Parameters rollout, click on the gray color swatch to the right of the material name. In the Color Selector set the color to a bright red (see Figure 5.51). The cove molding in the Perspective will also turn red. Change the second color swatch to bright blue and the third to bright green. You should have green walls and blue baseboard and chair rail in the Perspective viewport. Close the Material Editor.

9. Save the file. It should already be named MASTER_DINER08.MAX. You have created, edited, and changed materials on a 3D object by changing attributes of the 2D shapes that made up the object. This is a very efficient, flexible work method for many of your modeling needs.

Figure 5.50
Click the OK button to accept the Keep old material as sub-material? option.

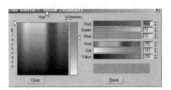

Figure 5.51
Change the Color Selector bright red for the first material.

Loft Multiple Shapes on a Single Path

You have seen some of the power in creating simple cross-section 2D shapes, lofting them on a simple 2D path, and editing the original 2D shapes to change the resulting 3D mesh. You will take this work method a bit farther to learn about these concepts:

- Path levels
- Multiple shapes on a path
- Loft deformations

While there is a lot you can do with what you have already learned about lofting in 3ds max 4, learning how to implement these topics will give you a quantum leap in productivity. Again, the object will be a simple one so you can concentrate on the methods used and not the end result.

You will create the ubiquitous ketchup bottle found in any self-respecting diner. The base of a typical glass ketchup bottle is round and about two-thirds of the way up it transitions into a hex-shaped neck and tapers into a small, round cap. There is no way to accomplish such a transition with Extrude, Bevel Profile, or Lathe modifiers.

You will start the loft with a circle at the beginning of the path, and then you will get a new hex shape on the path at approximately two-thirds of the way up the path.

Finally, you will get the circle on the path approximately nine-tenths of the way up the path and again at halfway up the path. This creates a cylinderlike object that starts round, changes to hex, and then back to round. However, it has straight sides and does not taper in to become smaller at the top.

tip

At the diner, go ahead and stick your knife into the bottle to get the ketchup flowing through that hex neck, for it's too much work banging on the bottom, and too dangerous.

The tapering will be handled by Loft Deformations options, found in the Modify panel. One of the deformations is called scale, and it allows you to define a side profile of the bottle to change the scaling of the shapes along the path.

In Exercise 5.10 you will loft a circle, a hex, and then the circle again to modify the cross sections along a straight path. You will also learn how to move the cross-section shapes once you have them on the path.

Exercise 5.10: Lofting Multiple Shapes on a Single Path

1. Open a file called Ch5_ketch_bottle_shape.max from the CD-ROM. It contains three 2D shapes: a line for the path, a circle, and a hex for the cross-section shapes (see Figure 5.52). Save the file as Ch5_KETCHUP_BOTTLE01.MAX.

2. In the Perspective viewport, select the straight line called k_bottle_path. Type W to maximize the viewport. In the Create Panel, Geometry panel, click on Standard Primitives, and choose Compound Objects in the list. In Compound Objects, Object Type rollout, click the Loft button (see Figure 5.53).

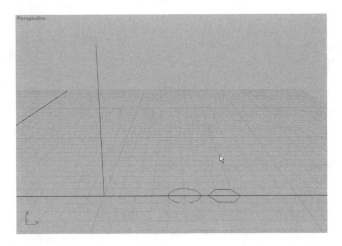

Figure 5.52   A straight line path, and circle and hex cross-section shapes are shown.

3. In the Creation Method rollout, click the Get Shape button (see Figure 5.54), and in the Perspective view pick the circle called bottle_body_round 2D shape. The resulting loft object should be just a straight cylinder. The circle cross section defines the object over the entire path.

> **tip**
>
> You have a Get Path button as well as Get Shape. Whichever option you use causes the selected object to stay stationary and the picked object to move to it. Get Shape causes the shape to move, Get Path causes the path to move.
>
> Another option would be to select the circle and do a Get Shape to pick the line. This would create an open-ended cylinder (line lofted around the circle) at the position of the circle.

4. Right-click on the Perspective label in the viewport and choose Wireframe. Notice the yellow tick at the bottom of the path. That is the active path level. You will also see a green circle that is the instance circle on the path. In the Modify panel, Path Parameters rollout, type 65 in the Path field and press Enter. If you look carefully in the Perspective viewport you will see that the yellow tick has moved 65 percent of the way up the path.

5. In the Creation Parameters rollout, click the Get Shape button and pick the hex called bottle_body_hex in the Perspective viewport. Right-click on the Perspective label and choose Smooth + Highlights for a shaded viewport. It should look similar to Figure 5.55. The loft object is round at the bottom and quickly transitions to a hex shape. Too quickly, actually.

6. At 50 percent of the way along the path, you will use Get Shape to get the circle again. This will hold the circle cross section to 50 percent and then transition to hex within the next 15 percent. In the Path Parameters rollout, type 50 and press Enter. Click the Get Shape button, and in the Perspective viewport, pick the circle shape. The transition is much quicker (see Figure 5.56).

Figure 5.53
In Create panel, Geometry panel, Compound Objects, Object Type rollout, click the Loft button.

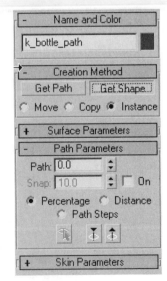

Figure 5.54
Pick Get Shape in the Creation Method rollout.

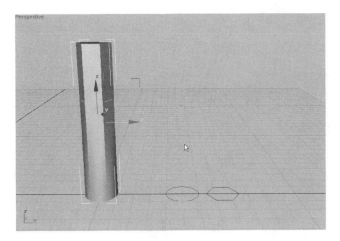

Figure 5.55   A loft object is created with a circle shape at the base and a hex shape at 65 percent.

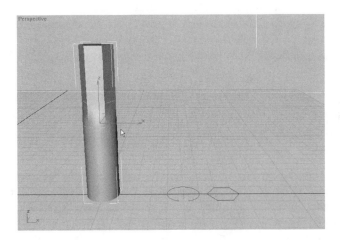

Figure 5.56   The circle is shown at 0 percent and then at 50 percent. The hex is 65 percent along the path.

7. In the Path Parameters rollout, type 95 in the Path field and press Enter. In the Perspective viewport, pick the circle. The loft object now transitions back to a round cross section (see Figure 5.57).

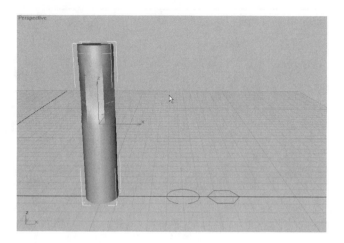

Figure 5.57   New circular shape is shown at 95 percent along the path.

tip

You can have as many shapes as you like on a path. Each shape must have the same number of splines if it is a compound shape. Technically speaking, each shape can have any number of vertices.

However, you will have much more control of the transitions and get a more manageable mesh if all shapes have the same number of vertices.

The circle you are using in this exercise is not a parametric 3ds max 4 Circle primitive. Rather, it is a NGon primitive with six sides and with the circular option checked.

In 3ds max 4 there is much less math to calculate when it can build the mesh from vertex to vertex. With unequal vertices in each shape, 3ds max 4 must interpolate segments during the transition, which can cause irregularities in the mesh.

8. Click the Select button to exit Get Shape mode. In the Modify panel, rename Loft01 to KETCHUP_BOTTLE. Save the file. It should already be called Ch5_KETCHUP_BOTTLE01.MAX.

You have the approximate transitions that will make this object a convincing ketchup bottle so now you will add the tapering. It would be possible to use a Taper modifier on the 3D mesh, but there is an option in the Loft command to give you exceptional control of the side profile of the lofted object. It is called Scale Deformations.

In Exercise 5.11 you will use Scale Deformation to taper the sides of the ketchup bottle, to round the bottom, and to create the appearance of a cap.

Exercise 5.11: Loft Object Scale Deformation

1. Open Ch5_KETCHUP_BOTTLE01.MAX that you saved in the last exercise or from the CD-ROM. Save the file as Ch5_KETCHUP_BOTTLE02.MAX. Right-click on the Perspective label in the viewport and choose Edged Faces in the menu. This shows the shaded object plus the wireframe mesh in the viewport.

2. Make sure KETCHUP_BOTTLE is the selected object in the Perspective viewport. In the Modify panel, Deformations rollout, Click the Scale button (see Figure 5.58). This opens the Scale Deformation(X) window.

3. The Scale Deformation(X) window shows a red line with a black square at each end running along the 100 percent line (see Figure 5.59). The red line is the scaling of the shapes on the path and the black squares are at each path vertex. The vertical lines represent the position of each shape on the path. To get the scaling you need, you must add more control points to the scaling line. In the Scale Deformation(X) window, click the Insert Corner Point button and pick seven times on the red line near the positions shown in Figure 5.60. Click the Move Control Point button to toggle it on and to toggle the Insert Corner Point button off.

> **caution**
>
> Each time you add a new control point, it is the same as adding a new vertex to the path. There are new segments created between each control point. This can increase the density of a mesh very rapidly.

> **tip**
>
> The (X) in the window name indicates you are viewing the x-axis scaling line. However, because the yellow Make Symmetrical button is toggled on, this line scales both the x- and y-axes at the same time for a symmetrical object. The z-axis is along the path and has no Scale Deformation.

Figure 5.58
In Modify panel, Deformations rollout, click the Scale button to open Scale Deformation(X) window.

4. In the Scale Deformation(X) window, pick the black control point furthest left on the red line. It will turn white. There are two numeric fields at the bottom of the

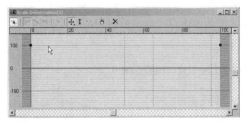

Figure 5.59
Scale Deformation(X) window shows a red line with a black square at each end.

Figure 5.60
Click the Insert Corner Point button and pick seven times to add new corner points as shown.

Scale Deformation(X) window. The left field is the percent along the path, and the right field is the percentage of scaling at that point. Type 75, press Enter in the right field, and you will see the bottom of the bottle has become smaller.

5. Select the third control point from the left. In the left field type 50. This aligns the control point with the shape at 50 percent on the path for a more efficient mesh.

6. Select the fourth control point from the left. Enter 65 in the left field and 50 in the right field. This lines the control point with the shape and scales the loft to 50 percent (see Figure 5.61).

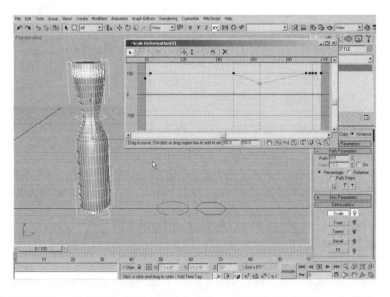

Figure 5.61   This shows 50 percent scaling at 65 percent along the loft path for the fourth control point.

7. For the fifth control point, type 90 in the left and 50 in the right field. For the sixth point, type 90.01 in the left and 40 in the right field. For the seventh point, type 91.99 in the left and 40 in the right field. For the eighth point, type 92 in the left and 50 in the right field. For the last point, type 50 in the right field. The bottle is now taking shape. Right-click on the Perspective label and choose Edged Faces to turn Edged Faces visibility off in the viewport. (see Figure 5.62).

tip

Two points that have the same percent along the path number (left numeric field in the Scale Deformation(X) window) can cause unexpected results. Always separate the percent along the scale by at least 0.01.

8. The changes in scaling are a bit harsh, especially at the bottom and on the neck. You created corner points on the scale line that have no curvature. You will now convert some of the points to Bézier control points. In the Scale Deformation(X) window, pick and drag a selection window around the second, third, and fourth control points from the left. Move the cursor over any one of the white selected control points, right-click, and choose Bézier-Smooth in the menu (see Figure 5.63). This converts those control points to Bézier-Smooth and smooths the scaling.

9. Click the second control point from the left and type 6.25 in the left field and 100 in the right field to smooth that transition more. Pick on the control point furthest to the right, right-click on it, and then choose Bézier-Corner. Pull the black Bézier handle up and to the right and move the point itself downward to round the top of the cap slightly. The Scale Deformation line and the bottle should look similar to Figure 5.64. Close the Scale Deformation(X) window.

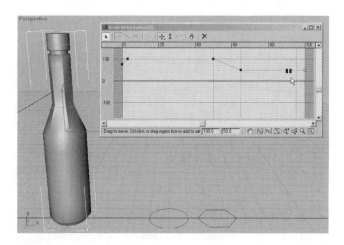

Figure 5.62   The form of the bottle is more clearly seen with Edged Faces turned off.

10. If you right-click in the Perspective viewport and choose Properties in the quad menu, you will see that the bottle has 3950 faces. This is very dense unless you must view the bottle closely. Right-click on the Perspective label and choose Edged Faces to see the mesh in the viewport. In the Modify panel, Skin Parameters rollout, type 2 in both the Shape Steps and Path Steps fields. The bottle now only has

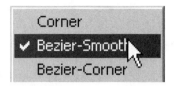

Figure 5.63
Choose Bézier-Smooth in the menu.

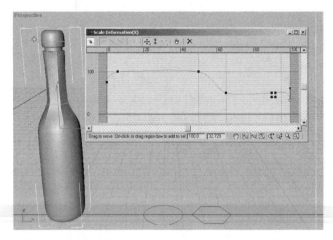

Figure 5.64 Bottle and Scale Deformation window with Bézier handles adjusted.

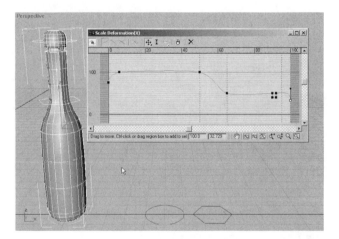

Figure 5.65 Face density drops from 3950 to 1004 when Shape Steps and Path Steps are both set to 2. Appearance of bottle is still acceptable.

1004 faces and still looks practically the same (see Figure 5.65). If you had many bottles seen from a distance, you could reduce this further.

11. Save the file. It should already be called Ch5_KETCHUP_BOTTLE02.MAX.

You have again created a fairly complex 3D model with only three simple 2D shapes. You have used Shape and Path Steps to reduce the density of the bottle to 20 percent of the original without compromising on the visual quality much. The bottle can also be edited at any time by changing shapes on the path or by adjusting the Scale Deformation curve. This could be a flower vase in a matter of minutes.

Feel free to play with the adjustments and to modify the bottle to your liking, you are the artist in control here. All exercises are presented as guidelines and learning tools, not as gospel.

Modeling with Primitives

In this section of the chapter you will build objects by creating 3ds max 4 primitives and modifying them into more detailed 3D objects. The exercises will point out some new modifiers and sub-object levels within the modifiers applied to primitive 3D objects and turned into a variety of fixtures that could be used in the diner. The objects will include:

- Wire shelves using Lattice modifier
- A modern table with the Taper modifier
- An overstuffed chair with the new PolyMesh object

Some options of cloning objects in a scene will also be introduced in this chapter to illustrate some of the tools available, including:

- Shift Transform cloning
- Array cloning
- Spacing Tool cloning

You will focus on creating efficient mesh objects and applying modifiers in a way that will leave you with flexible, easy editing capabilities. This will help make you more productive in modeling and leave more time for the important lighting and materials that make the scene convincing to the viewer.

In Exercise 5.12 you will create some wire shelving for the cooking area of the diner. You have several styles of wire shelving that you might need in the diner, and you may even need some enclosed wire baskets. Instead of creating each object from scratch, you will set up the model so it can be copied and edited into almost any box-shaped wire object you can think of. You will start with a Box Standard primitive, increase the density, and use the Lattice modifier to convert it to a visible wire mesh.

Exercise 5.12: Easy to Modify Wire Mesh

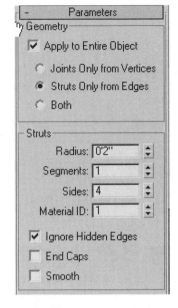

Figure 5.66
In the Modify panel,
Parameters rollout, check
Struts Only from Edges
option in the Geometry area.

1. Open a new 3ds max 4 session or, from the File pull-down menu, choose Reset, save any files that are important to you, and click Yes to reset. Save this empty file as Ch5_SHELF.MAX.

2. In the Create panel, Geometry panel, Standard Primitives panel, click the Box button. In the Perspective viewport, pick and drag any size box. In the Modify panel, Parameters rollout, type the following dimensions: Length = 1'0", Width = 6'0", Height = 0'6". Name the object SHELF01.

3. In the Modify panel, Modifier List, choose Lattice in the Parametric Modifiers area. Lattice uses visible edges of a mesh object to create struts and vertices of the mesh to create junctions. You only need the struts. In the Modify panel, Parameters rollout, check Struts Only from Edges option in the Geometry area (see Figure 5.66). The junctions disappear and you are left with struts where the outer visible edges of the box are. However, the wire is too large, and the spacing is too far to use for shelving (see Figure 6.67).

4. In the Modify panel, Stack view, choose Box. This drops you to the bottom of the history for access to the Box parameters. In the Parameters rollout, type Length Segs = 3, Width Segs = 6, Height Segs = 2. You can see the lattice changing, but you cannot see the original box. In the Stack view, click the lightbulb icon left of Lattice to disable it. In the Perspective viewport, right-click on the Perspective label and choose Edged Faces option to see the wireframe and shaded box in the viewport. The visible edges of the Box primitive get the struts (see Figure 5.68).

5. In the Stack view, choose Lattice, and click the lightbulb icon to enable Lattice. In the Parameters rollout, type 0.25" in Struts Radius field. Type 6 in the Sides field for hex struts. Turn Edged Faces off in the viewport. The wire shelf now has more segments and smaller hex wire.

6. To function as wall-mounted shelving, you only need four sides of wire. You will use a Mesh Select modifier to select the top and back of the box and then a Delete Mesh modifier to delete them. In the Stack view choose Box to drop to that level. Click to disable the Lattice modifier so you can see the Box primitive. In the Modify panel, Modifier List, choose Mesh Select in the Selection Modifiers area. Expand Mesh Select and choose Polygon sub-object level (see Figure 5.69).

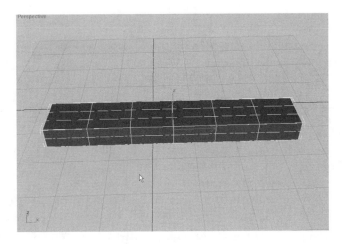

Figure 5.67   This Box primitive with Lattice modifier is set to Struts Only from Edges.

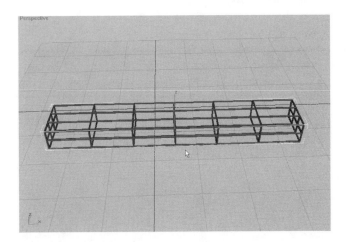

Figure 5.68   This Box primitive has the segments' fields increased and Edged Faces option enabled.

7. In the Customize pull-down menu, choose Preferences. In the Preference Settings dialog, Scene Selection area, check the new Auto Window/Crossing by Direction. It is set to Right->Left=>Crossing mode (see Figure 5.70). Now when you select in a viewport, dragging right to left is Crossing mode, left to right is Window mode. This will help you select sets of faces for modification.

Figure 5.69
Choose Box in the Stack view, apply a Mesh Select modifier, expand the Stack view, and then choose Polygon sub-object level.

> **tip** This is the type of setting that you would save in the MAXSTART.MAX prototype file that you created at the beginning of the chapter so it would always be on when you reset or open a new file.

8. Right-click in the Top viewport to activate it. Make sure the Select button is toggled on and pick and drag, from right to left, a Window selection around only the back faces. You can recognize the selection window as Window by the fact it is solid lines, not dashed (see Figure 5.70).

9. Right-click in the Front viewport, hold the Ctrl key to add to the selection set and pick and drag from right to left around the top faces of the box.

10. In the Modifier panel, Modifier List, choose DeleteMesh in the Mesh Editing area (see Figure 5.72). The back and top faces will be deleted.

> **note** You may no longer see the ends of the box, not because they were deleted but because the Face Normals point away from you.

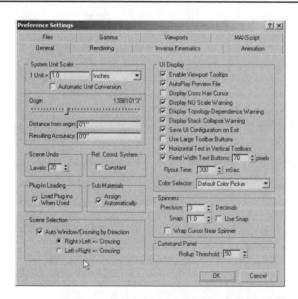

Figure 5.70   In Customize, Preferences, Preference Settings dialog, Scene Selection area, check Auto Window/Crossing by Direction.

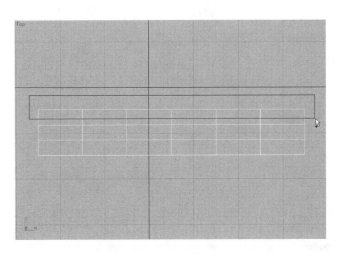

Figure 5.71   Pick and drag from right to left for a Window selection around the back faces of the box.

11. In the Modify panel, Stack view, choose Lattice to return to the top of the stack and enable Lattice by picking the lightbulb icon. You now have wires on four sides of the box, creating open shelving (see Figure 5.73).

tip   The advantage of working this way is that you can move up and down the Modifier Stack to change the size and density of the original box or to change the selections for the DeleteMesh and the Lattice attributes. One box could become many types of wire objects with simple edits. The Mesh Select and DeleteMesh may be removed or disabled at any time.

tip   Lattice uses the visible edges of a 3D mesh object. You can edit at sub-object edge to modify the visibility and direction of edges, as well as to create new edges for Lattice to use.

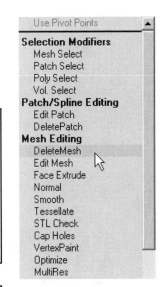

Figure 5.72
Choose DeleteMesh modifier. It deletes only the faces selected in the Mesh Select modifier below it.

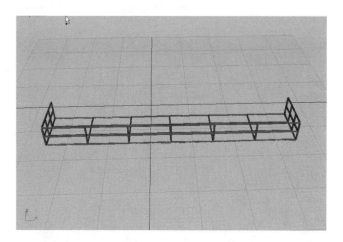

Figure 5.73   Faces deleted with Mesh Select and DeleteMesh do not get Lattice wires applied.

12. Save the file. It should already be called. Ch5_SHELF.MAX. This exercise is a simple example of using the Lattice modifier and, more importantly, of inserting modifiers lower in the stack to affect the edges Lattice uses. It highlights the flexibility of utilizing modifiers.

In Exercise 5.13 you will look into some of the sub-object editing capabilities of modifiers. The object you will create will be a simple molded plastic table that you might have encountered in the '60s or '70s. You will apply a Taper modifier to a Cylinder primitive and change parameters of the taper to create the table.

Exercise 5.13: Modifier Sub-Object Level Editing

1. Start a new 3ds max 4 session or reset the current scene. Save any information that may be important to you. Save the new empty scene as Ch5_TABLE.MAX. In the Customize pull-down menu, choose Units Setup. In the Units Setup dialog, check US Standard, and choose Feet w/Fractional Inches in the list. In the Create panel, Geometry panel, Object Type rollout, click the Cylinder button, and in the Perspective viewport, create a Cylinder primitive of any size.

2. In the Modify panel, Parameters rollout, type the following: Radius = 0'6", Height = 2'0", Height Segments = 8. Click the Zoom Extents button to fill all viewports with the cylinder. Name the object TABLE01.

3. In the Modify panel, Modifier List, choose Taper from the Parametric Modifiers area (see Figure 5.74).

4. In the Modifier panel, Parameters rollout, adjust the Amount spinner by picking, holding the mouse and moving the mouse. Right-click to cancel the adjustment. The cylinder tapered from a point at its base, actually, from its pivot point which happens to be at the base. You want the taper to start higher up the cylinder. You can accomplish this by adjusting the Taper center point.

5. In the Modify panel, Stack view, Modifier List, expand the Taper modifier and choose Center subobject (see Figure 5.75). You will see a yellow center marker at the base of the cylinder in any of the wireframe viewport.

6. Right-click in the Front viewport, click the Select and Move button in the toolbar. Pick on the y-axis of the Transform Gizmo and move the center almost onehalf the way up the cylinder (see Figure 5.76). Choose Taper in the Stack view.

7. In the Modify panel, Parameters rollout, type 2 in the Amount field and press Enter. This tapers the cylinder with a 2:1 ratio from the new center position. Above the center, it tapers outward; below the center, it tapers inward from the center (see Figure 5.77). This table would tip over for sure.

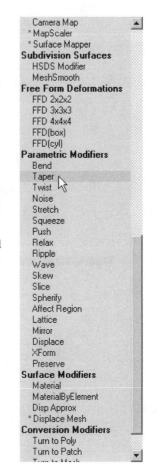

Figure 5.74
Choose Taper from the Modifier List, Parametric Modifiers area.

Figure 5.75
Expand the Taper modifier in the Stack view and choose Center sub-object.

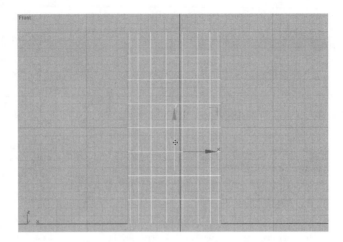

Figure 5.76   Click the Select and Move button and move the Center up approximately halfway to the top of the cylinder. Use the y-axis Transform Gizmo to restrict movement to y-axis only.

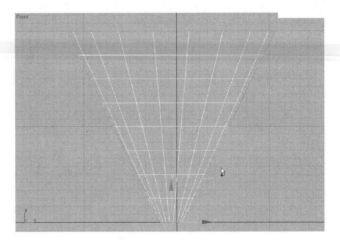

Figure 5.77   The cylinder has a 2:1 taper from the center.

8. In the Modify panel, Parameters rollout, check the Symmetry option in Taper Axis area. The taper is outward both above and below the center. Type 2 in the Curve field in Taper area of Parameters rollout. The tapers are now rounded instead of straight (see Figure 5.78).

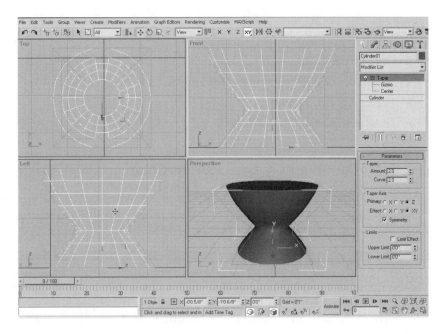

Figure 5.78   The tapered cylinder has Curve field set to 2 and Symmetry option checked on.

9. Save the file. It is already called Ch5_TABLE.MAX. You have changed a modifier at sub-object level to adjust the point in the 3D mesh that the modification springs from. Many modifiers allow sub-object editing, make sure you experiment with the various settings on simple objects and use the Online Reference in the Help pull-down file to learn more about the modifiers. This table is as ugly now as it was in the '60s.

The next exercise will introduce you to a new 3D object type in 3ds max 4 called Editable Poly. This is different than an Editable Mesh in that the surface is constructed from four-sided polygons rather than triangles in the mesh. The difference may seem like a minor detail at first glance, but for game developers or companies that need to extract polygon data from a surface, it is a very big improvement. Editable Poly may not be critical information to you, the new user of 3ds max 4, at this point. However, most of what you do in this exercise is applicable to Editable Mesh, as well. Whether you choose Editable Poly or Editable Mesh in your production depends on your needs, but it is important to know that both exist.

In Exercise 5.14 you will start with a segmented box and convert it to an Editable Poly. At the Polygon level you will extrude and bevel faces to create a rough overstuffed chair. You will then use built-in subdivision capabilities to smooth the edges, resulting in a flowing, rounded chair. Although this process is being used to create an overstuffed chair, the same methods could be applied to create, for example:

- Organic tree trunks with branches
- Aerodynamic automobiles and other vehicles
- Humanoid and animal characters
- Smooth rock outcroppings

Exercise 5.14: Editable Poly Overstuffed Chair

1. Open a file from the CD-ROM called Ch5_OVERSTUFF01.MAX. It is a Box primitive with segments added in all axes. Click the Select button in the toolbar and pick the box to select it. Edged Faces is checked in the Display menu so you can see edges and shaded surfaces. You will convert this to an Editable Poly. Save the file as Ch5_OVERSTUFF02.MAX.

2. In the Perspective viewport, right-click, choose Convert To in the Transform quad menu, and choose Editable Poly in the flyout menu. The object is no longer a parametric box, but you have access to sub-object level editing for an Editable Poly. In the Modify panel, Stack view, expand Editable Poly, and choose Polygon (see Figure 5.79).

3. In the Perspective viewport, make sure the Select button is active and pick any polygon on the top of the box. You should see the edges of the selected polygon turn red. It can be difficult to see exactly which faces are selected, however. Right-click on the Perspective label and choose Configure at the bottom of the menu. In the Viewport Configuration dialog, check Shade Selected Faces in the

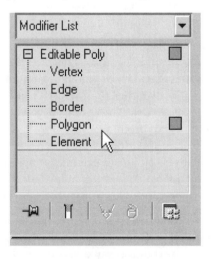

Figure 5.79   In Stack view, expand Editable Poly, and choose Polygon.

Rendering Options area (see Figure 5.80). Close the dialog. Now the entire selected polygon is a shaded red and easier to see. In the Modify panel, Selection rollout, check the Ignore Backfacing option. This allows you to select only faces with Face Normals pointing in your general direction (see Figure 5.81).

4. In the Perspective viewport, pick one polygon at the top corner of the box, hold the Ctrl key, and pick the polygon's other three sides as seen in Figure 5.82.

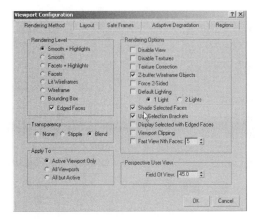

Figure 5.81
In Modify panel, Selection rollout, check Ignore Backfacing to avoid selecting faces with Face Normals pointing away from the viewer.

Figure 5.80
In the Viewport Configuration dialog, check Shade Selected Faces in the Rendering Options area to make it easier to see the selected polygons in the viewport.

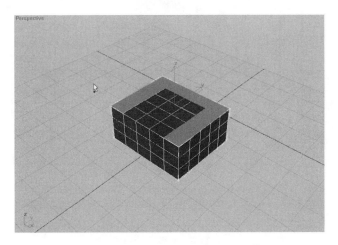

Figure 5.82   Pick one corner polygon, and then holding the Ctrl key, pick the polygon's other three sides.

5. In the Modify panel, Edit Geometry rollout, type 1 in the Extrusion field (see Figure 5.83). Press Enter and the selected polygons will move out one foot, creating new faces along the sides.

6. In the Perspective viewport, pick the polygons along the middle of the front of the box, type 2" in the Extrusion field and press Enter (see Figure 5.84).

7. ArcRotate the Perspective viewport so you can see the polygons that make up the seat and seatback and select them (see Figure 5.85). In the Modify panel, Edit Geometry rollout, check the By Polygon option under Extrusion Type.

8. In the Edit Geometry rollout, type 1" in the Extrusion field and –0.5" in the Outline field. This extrudes each polygon individually and bevels in on its own center point (see Figure 5.86). In the Stack view, choose Editable Poly to exit sub-object mode.

9. In the Modify panel, Surface Properties rollout, check Use NURMS Subdivision and type 1 in the Iterations field (see Figure 5.87). The chair is rounded based on edge configuration resulting in a smooth object.

Figure 5.83
Type 1 in the Extrusion field and press the Enter key to extrude the selected faces.

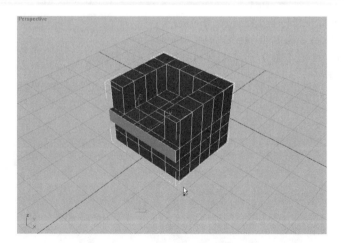

Figure 5.84   Select the front-middle row of polygons and type 2" in the Extrusion field. Press Enter to finalize the process.

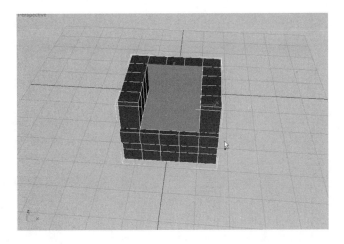

Figure 5.85   Select the polygons that make the seat and seatback surfaces.

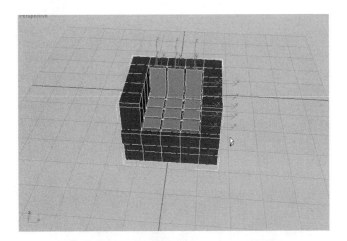

Figure 5.86   With By polygon checked, extrude 1" and outline –0.5".

<table>
<tr><td>tip</td><td>In most cases, the simpler the object is before applying NURMS Subdivision, the better the results will be. Mesh objects can have a MeshSmooth modifier applied for similar results.</td></tr>
</table>

10. In the toolbar, click the Quick Render button to see how the rendered object appears. It should be similar to Figure 5.88. Close the Virtual Frame Buffer.

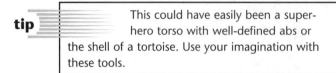

> **tip**   This could have easily been a super-hero torso with well-defined abs or the shell of a tortoise. Use your imagination with these tools.

11. You will optimize the chair farther with a new 3ds max 4 modifier called MultiRes. In the Modify panel, Modifier List, choose MultiRes from the Mesh Editing area (see Figure 5.89). You can read in the MultiRes rollout that the chair has 1680 faces.

12. In the MultiRes rollout, click the Generate button to generate a MultiRes solution. In the Percent field in Vertex Resolution area, type 50 and press Enter. The face count drops to 838 (see Figure 5.90).

13. Quick Render the image in the Perspective viewport, and you will see little or no difference in the rendered images. This face economy is critical in any of your scenes. Any extra faces that do not add to the end result should be trimmed from the scene.

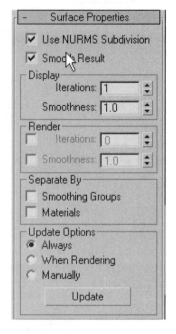

Figure 5.87
In Surface Properties rollout, check Use NURMS Subdivision, and type 1 in Iterations.

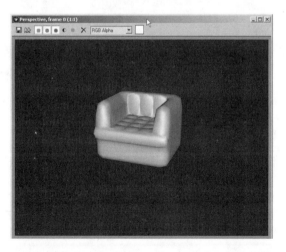

Figure 5.88   Quick Render the overstuffed chair. It is a smooth, relatively efficient 3D object.

Figure 5.89
Choose MultiRes in the
Modifier List.

Figure 5.90
Type 50 in the Percent field
in Vertex Resolution area of
the MultiRes rollout. The face
count drops by nearly half.

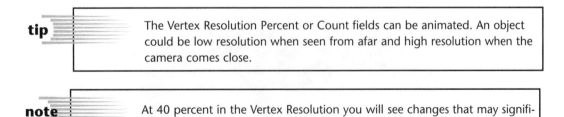

tip The Vertex Resolution Percent or Count fields can be animated. An object could be low resolution when seen from afar and high resolution when the camera comes close.

note At 40 percent in the Vertex Resolution you will see changes that may significantly alter the visual quality.

14. Save the file. It should already be called Ch5_OVERSTUFF02.MAX.

Perfection is one of the biggest enemies to getting a convincing scene in computer rendering. Of course, there are objects that might be perfect, but only if it tells the viewer something about the scene. Most objects in real-life are dented or sagging in various degrees. Some of these effects can be accomplished with materials, but in Exercise 5.15 you will apply modifiers to rough up the chair so it has that lived-in look. You will also learn some new functionality in the Modifier Stack, Stack view that can make editing easier.

The overstuffed chair needs a little more organic look to reduce some of the angular appearance. You will use an FFD (Free Form Deformation) modifier to round the back a little, and then you will use a Noise modifier to rough the whole chair.

Exercise 5.15: Organic Modeling

1. Open the file called Ch5_OVERSTUFF02.MAX from your hard drive or from the CD-ROM. It is the chair from Exercise 5.14 to which you have applied MultiRes modifier to reduce the face count. Save the file as Ch5_OVERSTUFF03.MAX.

2. Make sure the chair is selected, and in Modify panel, Modifier List, choose FFD 4×4×4 in the Free Form Deformations area. The modifier applies a matrix of control points over the object (see Figure 5.91). Those control points can be transformed to affect the vertices on either side of a given control point. This might be analogous to modeling with clay, for when to pull a bit of clay, the effect is over an area depending on the elasticity of the clay. In the FFD modifiers, the more control points you have, the smaller the influence of any point.

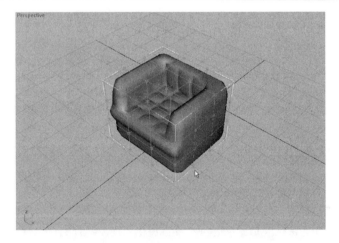

Figure 5.91   FFD 4x4x4 modifier is applied to chair. A 4x4x4 matrix of control points fills the bounding box of the chair. Edged faces is disabled for clarity.

note In FFD modifiers the numbers are the matrix size. In FFD(Box) and FFD(Cylinder) modifiers you can set the number of control points and the matrix is shaped according to which you choose.

3. In the Modify panel, Stack view, expand FFD 4×4×4, and choose Control Points (see Figure 5.92). Click the Select button, and in the Perspective viewport, select the four control points that make a square at the center-top back of the matrix (see Figure 5.93). The control points will turn yellow when selected.

4. Click the Select and Move button, and in the Perspective viewport, pick the z-axis Transform Gizmo axis arrow and move the four control points upward to round the back of the chair (see Figure 5.94). In the Modify panel, Stack view, choose FFD 4×4×4 to exit sub-object mode.

Figure 5.92
In Modify panel, Stack view, expand FFD 4x4x4, and choose Control Points.

tip There are times that the Transform Gizmo tripod is either too large or too small to be useful. You can increase or decrease the Transform Gizmo with the plus or minus key on the keyboard while the Transform Gizmo is visible in the viewport.

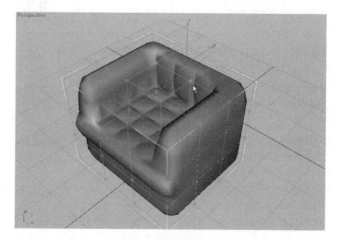

Figure 5.93   Select four control points at the center-top back of the FFD matrix.

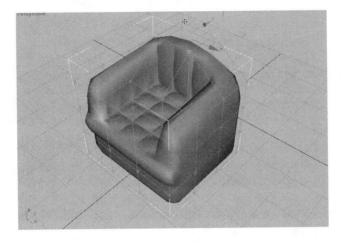

Figure 5.94   In the Perspective viewport, move the four control points upward on the z-axis to round the back of the chair.

caution

> When working in a non-orthographic viewport, make sure you use the Transform Gizmo to constrain the transform to the correct axis. It is very easy to edit in a non-orthographic viewport and have the edit look correct. However, when it is viewed in another viewport, the edit is radically different.

Free Form Deformations
FFD 2x2x2
FFD 3x3x3
FFD 4x4x4
FFD(box)
FFD(cyl)
Parametric Modifiers
Bend
Taper
Twist
Noise
Stretch
Squeeze
Push
Relax
Ripple
Wave
Skew
Slice
Spherify
Affect Region
Lattice
Mirror
Displace
XForm
Preserve

5. You will now add some overall roughness to the chair using the Noise modifier. The Noise modifier randomly moves vertices based on a Strength and Scale that you define. In the Modify panel, Modifier List, choose Noise in the Parametric Modifiers area (see Figure 5.95).

6. In the Modify panel, Parameters rollout, type 2" in the X, Y, and Z Strength fields. This means that a random number will be generated and any vertex will be moved randomly between –1" and +1". However, not much happens to the chair because the scale is too high. Type 10 in the Scale field and the chair will distort noticeably (see Figure 5.96).

Figure 5.95

In the Modify panel, Modifier List, choose Noise modifier in the Parametric Modifiers area.

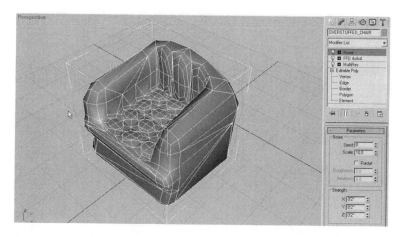

Figure 5.96   With Strength set to 2" in all axes and Scale set to 10, the chair distorts noticeably.

7. This effect is not the look you want, however. You do not want to ruin the chair, just rough it up. Both FFD and Noise work by moving vertices in space. The chair has a MultiRes modifier below the FFD and Noise in the Modifier Stack that removed vertices and faces for efficiency. In 3ds max 4, this is not a problem in this case. You can drag and drop modifiers in Stack view to reposition them. You need to have the MultiRes modifier on top of FFD and Noise for a better result.

8. In the Modify panel, Stack view, highlight MultiRes in the stack, right-click, and choose Cut in the menu. This cuts the modifier to a buffer with the current settings intact. Highlight the Noise modifier in the stack, right-click, and choose Paste to paste the MultiRes modifier above the Noise modifier. The FFD and Noise modifiers now have more vertices to operate on, giving a more predictable result. In the Modify panel, MultiRes rollout, click the Generate button to update the optimization of the mesh (see Figure 5.97).

9. Save the file. It should already be called Ch5_OVERSTUFF03.MAX. You have learned that modifiers in the Stack view can be repositioned up or down the stack by dragging and dropping in 3ds max 4. This adds to the flexibility and versatile nature of working with 3ds max 4.

tip

You can also right-click in the Stack view to access other stack editing tools (see Figure 5.98).

caution

Repositioning modifiers in the Stack that affect sub-object level changes is still dependent on the validity of the modification.

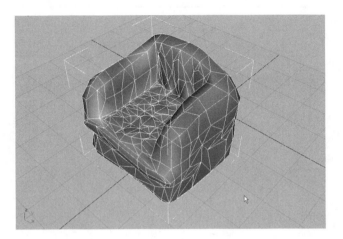

Figure 5.97   In Modify panel, Stack view, drag and drop MultiRes modifier from below FFD 4x4x4 to the top of the Stack. Click the Generate button to regenerate the optimized mesh.

You could have gotten similar results in several other ways: You could have added Mesh Select and Face Extrude modifiers before applying a MeshSmooth modifier, and then FFD, Noise, and MultiRes.

You could also have converted the box to Editable Mesh and used the right-click Extrude options, added a MeshSmooth modifier, raised the back with SoftSelection, and applied the other modifiers.

You will have to develop a feel for which method works in any given situation for you and the editing capabilities you anticipate you will need. Familiarize yourself with as many options as you can and the task will be easier.

Cloning Objects in a Scene

A chapter on 3D modeling fundamentals would not be complete without a section on cloning, the process of creating copies of objects in 3ds max 4.

Figure 5.98
Right-clicking in the Stack view offers a menu of Stack view editing options.

The options in cloning allow you to make copies of object, either 2D or 3D, that may or may not connect to the original object. This offers the opportunity for *edit one/edit many* scenarios that can speed production and make animating the changes in multiple objects much easier. There are three types of clones available in 3ds max 4:

- **Copy**   A Copy clone has no connection to the original and stands alone as an exact replica of the original. You might use a copy if you model a generic base character and then modify the copies to create different characters.

- **Instance**   An Instance clone is a copy with a two-way connection to the original object. If you modify the original, all instances change, and if you modify any instance, all instances and the original will change. Instances would be handy for the fish in a school. Selecting any one and modifying it would change all.

- **Reference**   Reference clones have a one-way connection to the original. If you modify the original, the clone changes, but if you modify the Reference, the original is *not* affected. This would be good for many objects that are similar to the original, but each with its own modifications. Global changes could be made by adjusting the original, but each could have it own identity.

You will clone objects with three different methods in this section:

- Shift Transform cloning
- Array cloning
- Spacing Tool cloning

In Exercise 5.16 you will use the most commonly applied cloning method, holding the Shift key while transforming an object in space. The three transforms being Move, Rotate, and Scale in 3ds max 4.

tip

Cloning can become very complex. For example, you could create a window, make a Reference clone of it and then make a Reference clone of the clone. If you repeated that process to create many objects, you could now select the tenth clone in the series, modify it, and all the clones downstream would change. However, none of the clones upstream are affected.

tip

Another major advantage of Instance and Reference clones is that they take up a fraction of the computer resources of the original.

caution

Cloning with the Shift key and Move or Rotate is safe way to clone. However, using Scale to clone at the object level can be a dangerous task. Any object scaling is evaluated after transforms and the objects can behave unpredictably. Always apply an Xform modifier and scale the Xform Gizmo. This evaluates the scale at the proper point in the history.

Exercise 5.16: Shift Transform Cloning with Instance

1. Open the file called MASTER_DINER08.MAX that you saved in Exercise 5.9 or from the CD-ROM. This is the interior view of the diner. Save the file as MASTER_DINER09.MAX.

2. In the File pull-down menu, choose Merge and find the file called Ch5_SHELF.MAX. In the Merge dialog, choose SHELF01 in the list (see Figure 5.99) and click OK. The wire shelf is merged near the center of the floor. Click the Align button in the toolbar, and in the Perspective viewport, pick WALLS. In the Align Selection dialog, check Y Position, and check Maximum in both Current Object and Target Object columns (see Figure 5.100). This aligns the back of the shelf with the outside of the back wall.

3. In the Align Selection dialog, click the Apply button to set the position of the shelf and reset the Align dialog. Check Z position and Center in both columns to align the shelf half way up the wall. Click OK in the dialog to close it.

4. Click the Align button again, and in the Perspective viewport, click COUNTER. In the Align Selection dialog, check X Position and check Minimum in both columns. Click OK. This aligns the left edge of the shelf with the left edge of the counter while the shelf remains on the wall (see Figure 5.101).

5. In the Perspective viewport, make sure the Select and Move button is toggled on, hold the Shift key, and pick and drag the SHELF01 by the z-axis Transform Gizmo to move it approximately one foot higher up the wall.

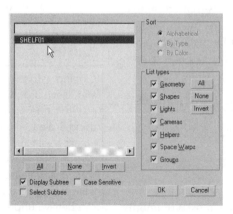

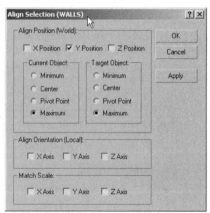

Figure 5.99
In the File, Merge dialog, choose SHELF01, and click OK to merge the wire shelf into the scene.

Figure 5.100
In the Align Selection dialog, check Y Position and Maximum in both Current Object and Target Object columns.

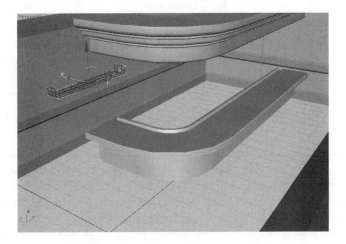

Figure 5.101   Align SHELF01 to WALLS and then align again to
COUNTER.

6. Release the mouse button and the Clone Options dialog appears. In the Clone
Options dialog, check the Instance option (see Figure 5.102), and click OK to
accept the new name of SHELF02. You have created an Instance clone. Modify
either one and the other will also change.

As you transform an object in space, you can read the coordinate offsets in the
status bar. When you release the mouse button, the coordinates report the
absolute position of the cursor again.

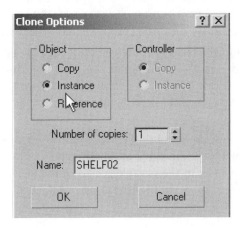

Figure 5.102   In the Clone Options dialog, check Instance, and then click
OK to accept the incremented name.

---

tip ▤ If you type a number other than 1 in the Number of Copies field in the Clone Options dialog, you will get that number of instance copies (in this case) that are offset the distance and direction of the first offset. This is a quick method of creating arrays with any of the transforms.

---

7. Save the File. It should already be called MASTER_DINER09.MAX. This is a common method of creating clones in 3ds max 4.

---

tip ▤ If you need a clone an exact distance from the original you can use 3D Snap to a Grid that is adjusted appropriately. Or you can use Edit pull-down, Clone to make a single clone in place, and then use the Transform Type-in in the status bar to transform it an exact offset amount.

In Exercise 5.17 you will merge the overstuffed chair and make a radial array of four chairs. The radial array requires that you change the position of the pivot point, for otherwise the chair will array on its own center. You will simply move the pivot point.

Exercise 5.17: Array Cloning with Reference

1. Open the file called MASTER_DINER09.MAX that you saved in Exercise 5.16 or from the CD-ROM. Save the file as MASTER_DINER10.MAX.

2. In the File pull-down menu, choose Merge. Find the file called Ch5_OVERSTUFF03.MAX that you saved in Exercise 4.27 or from the CD-ROM. In the Merge dialog, choose OVERSTUFFED_CHAIR in the list and click OK. In the Top viewport, move the chair approximately as shown in Figure 5.103.

3. The pivot point of the chair is at the center of the base because the object started as a Box primitive. To do a radial array, the pivot point must be offset to the center of the array. This will be a point approximately two feet in front of the chair. In the Hierarchy panel, click Affect Pivot Only in the Adjust Pivot rollout (see Figure 5.104).

4. In the status bar, toggle the Absolute Mode Transform Type-in button to Offset Mode Transform Type-in. In the Y axis field, type –3, and press Enter. The pivot point moves three feet in the negative y-axis of the viewport. The chair remains in place (see Figure 5.105). In the Hierarchy panel, click Affect Pivot Only to toggle it off.

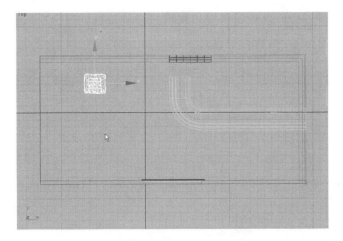

Figure 5.103   In the Top viewport, move the chair to the back left of the diner. You will not see the chair in the Perspective viewport.

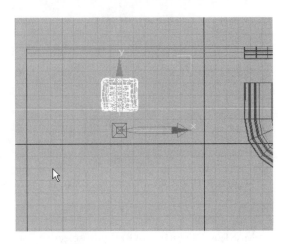

Figure 5.104
In the Hierarchy panel, click Affect Pivot Only in the Adjust Pivot rollout.

Figure 5.105
In Affect Pivot Only mode the pivot point is transformed, but the chair remains in place.

5. In the toolbar, click the Array button. In the Array dialog, type 90 in the Incremental, Z axis, Rotate field. In the Type of Object area, check Reference, and in the Array Dimensions area type 4 in the Count field for a 1D array. Press Enter and you will see the Total in Array field shows 4 (see Figure 5.106). You should have a cluster of four chairs around a common pivot point (see Figure 5.107).

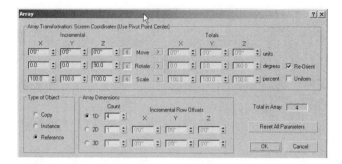

Figure 5.106   Type 90 in the Incremental, Z axis, Rotate field. Check Reference in Type of Object area, and type 4 in the Count field in the Array Dimensions area. Click OK.

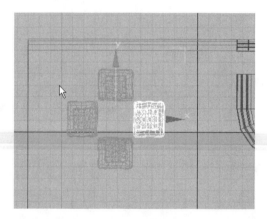

Figure 5.107   A radial array of four chairs appears around a common pivot point.

6. Save the file. It should already be called MASTER_DINER10.MAX. If you select the original chair and modify it, all chairs will reflect the same changes. If you select any of the three Reference clones and modify it, none of the others will change.

In Exercise 5.18 you will use a tool called the Spacing Tool. The Spacing Tool offers a variety of options, but you will use the Path option to set a series of stools at the counter. To use the Path option, you must first have a path, which you will extract from the 2D shape that is the loft path for the counter. It already has the correct curvature.

tip

The 3ds max 4 Array tool is very powerful. To use it correctly, you must be aware of the current active viewport and current Reference Coordinate system being used.

Exercise 5.18: Spacing Tool Cloning

1. Open MASTER_DINER10.MAX from the last exercise or from the CD-ROM. Click the Select button in the toolbar, press H, and double-click counter_path in the list. This is the 2D loft path of the COUNTER. Save the file as MASTER_DINER11.MAX.

2. You will clone it in place and make a Copy clone. In the Edit pull-down menu, choose Clone. In the Clone Options dialog, check Copy, and name the clone stool_center (see Figure 5.108). Click OK. You will notice that stool_center is the currently selected object.

3. In the Modify panel, Stack view, expand Line and choose Spline sub-object level. In the Modify panel, Geometry rollout, type 2 in the Outline field and press Enter. The result is a closed polyline with two curved sides. You only need the outer most segment, however.

4. In the Modify panel, Stack view, choose Segment sub-object. In the toolbar click the Select button if it is not already activated. Pick either of the new segments at the end of the new polyline, and holding the Ctrl key, select all segments except those at the front (see Figure 5.109). Press the Delete key to delete the selected segments.

5. In the Modify panel, Stack view, choose Line to exit sub-object mode. In the File pull-down, choose Merge and find Ch5_STOOL.MAX to open it. In the Merge dialog, choose STOOL01 and stool_profile, and click OK. Select the STOOL01 and move it away from the counter.

6. In the toolbar, click and hold the Array button to call the flyout buttons. Click the Spacing Tool button. In the Spacing Tool dialog, click the Pick Path button, and in the Top viewport, pick the stool_center 2D shape. You will see three new

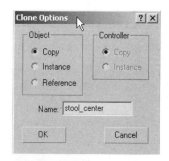

Figure 5.108

Check Copy in the Object area of the Clone Options dialog and name the clone stool_center.

tip

At the bottom of the Modify panel, Selection rollout, you will see that you have 8 Segments Selected (see Figure 5.110). If you have a different number, try selecting the segments again.

tip

By merging both the 3D and 2D information into your scene, you will be able to edit the stools by modifying the 2D profile.

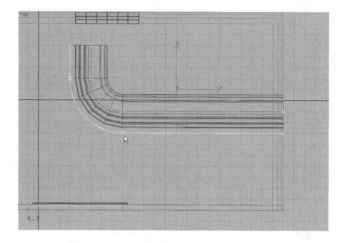

Figure 5.109   Select all segments except those along the front of the counter and delete them.

stools on the path. In the Spacing Tool dialog, click on Divide Evenly, Objects at Ends and choose Centered, Specify Spacing in the list. In the Spacing field, type 3, and press Enter. Check Instance in Type of Object area and click the Apply button, and then close the dialog. This places nine stools at 3-foot centers along the line.

7. Press the Delete key to delete the original STOOL01. You only need the Instance clones. Select and delete the last stool on the right, which is the one against the wall (see Figure 5.111). The eight stools are placed evenly along the counter and all stools may be edited at any time by modifying the 2D shape called stool_profile.

8. Save the file. It is already called MASTER_DINER11.MAX. Cloning is a powerful feature that, when used thoughtfully, can increase productivity in 3ds max 4.

Figure 5.110
You should see a line that states "8 Segments Selected" in the Selection rollout before you delete the segments.

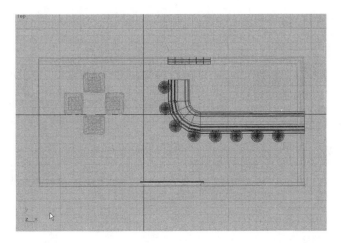

Figure 5.111   Spacing Tool option places Instance clones along a path on 3-foot centers.

Other Modeling Methods

Mesh and Polygon modeling are the most common methods of building models in 3ds max 4. Whether you are using the program for architecture, either specifically as an architect or as part of everyday 3D worlds for backgrounds, designing characters for computer games or television, designing engineering prototypes and concepts, or for just plain artistic reasons, mesh modeling is a flexible and efficient use of time and resources.

However, there are situations where Mesh and Polygon modeling can become difficult to manage when creating flowing, smooth surfaces. The sheer number of points that need to be manipulated to keep the surface smooth becomes counterproductive.

In this section you will learn about some alternatives to Mesh and Polygon modeling including:

> **tip**
>
> If backgrounds are an important part of what you do with 3ds max 4, a great reference to have on hand is *Architectural Graphics Standard* published by John Wiley & Sons. It is updated often and contains dimensioned drawings for many everyday and occasional items from windows to sports fields, from boats to bakeries.

- **Patch modeling**   Patches are surfaces defined by a series of weighted control vertices. Patches offer an efficient method of creating and modifying organic, curved surfaces.

- **NURBS modeling**   NURBS (Non Uniform Relational Bézier Spline) modeling is similar to Patch modeling in many ways, but the main difference is the underlying math that defines the surface (see Figure 5.112).

- **XRef**   While not a modeling method in itself, XRef is worth mentioning in this chapter. XRef (external reference) is a process of merging scenes or objects into another scene with a one-way reference connection between the files. Modify the original and all references change.

A complete coverage of Patch and NURBS modeling is beyond the scope of this book on fundamentals of 3ds max 4. However, many of the concepts and lessons you have learned about 2D shapes and 3D meshes are the same or have parallel techniques in Patch and NURBS modeling.

Patch Modeling

3D mesh models are defined by triangular flat faces. Each face has three vertices that have no relationship to each other. Move a vertex in space, and the faces defined by that vertex form a spike (see Figure 5.113).

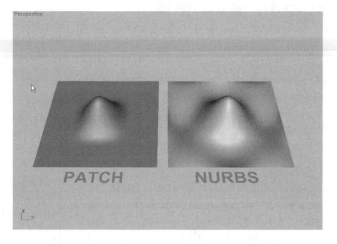

Figure 5.112   In the Patch surface on left, control vertices are weighted to the next control vertex only with no effect beyond adjacent control vertices. In the NURBS surface on right, control points are weighted beyond adjacent vertices to counteract the adjustment.

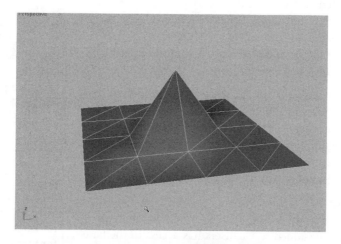

Figure 5.113   In this mesh surface with a single vertex moved in space, the triangular faces form a spike with no relationship between vertices. All edges are visible for clarity.

Patch modeling in 3ds max 4 is a technique of building and modifying surfaces defined by vertices and edges in which the vertices have a relationship that affects the curvature of the surface between them. There are three methods of creating Patch surfaces:

- **Native Patch surfaces**   Flat Patch surfaces that can be modified to change the curvature by manipulating Vertex, Edge, or Patch sub-object levels or by applying modifiers.

- **Surface tools**   A process of creating a 2D wire cage and skinning it with a Patch surface.

- **Convert to Editable Patch**   Any mesh or NURBS surface can be converted to an Editable Patch for patch editing functionality.

The appropriate method to use will depend on your needs and skill level, but with a little practice, you can create smooth, flowing objects quickly in either method.

Native Patch Surface

Starting a model with native Patch grids has two options:

- **Quad Patch**   The default Quad Patch is a flat plane made of 36 quad facets, each made of two triangular faces. The density can be adjusted for more control.

- **Tri Patch**   A Tri Patch is similar but made of 72 triangular faces.

The Patch surfaces can be subdivided for more control vertices in areas where needed, and new patch surfaces can be "grown" from edges or whole patches. A good example of this work method might be a human face (see Figure 5.114).

The first native Quad Patch was manipulated to create the nose, and then a Quad Patch was grown from each side edge to form cheeks and from the bottom edge to form an upper lip. After modifying each new surface into shape, it was in turn grown to form the next adjacent area until the head was finished.

The patches can be converted to Editable Patch for access to sub-object edit levels, or an Edit Patch modifier can be added so the users has access to the base Patch parameters in the Modifier Stack. In 3ds max 4, Patch edges can be Shift Transform cloned to form new surfaces and the edges can be welded together to close seams. You can also animate Patch vertices in 3ds max 4.

Other uses for Quad Patches might be hilly landscape, wavy water surfaces, draping fabric, or modern kitchen appliances.

tip

Most users find Quad Patches easier to manipulate. They also have fewer visible edges in the viewport, making it easier to see what you are working on.

note

The same restrictions apply for Patch modifier stacks as for Mesh stacks. If topological changes have been made to the sub-object level, you may not be able to drop below that point in the stack with predictable results.

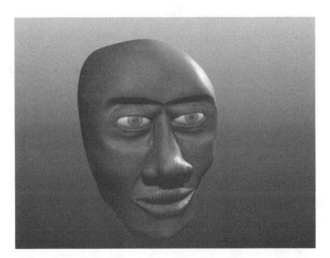

Figure 5.114   The head began as a Quad Patch manipulated to become a nose, and then edges were grown to form cheeks and the upper lip. From there the chin and forehead were created, and so on.

Patch surfaces can have Material IDs and Smoothing Groups options applied to the surface to change the characteristics of each surface also.

Surface Tools Patch Surface

With Surface Tools Patch modeling, you create a wire cage from 2D shapes and then apply a Surface modifier to skin the cage with the Patch surface. This method can certainly be used to create a human head, but it also works well for flowing automobile surfaces or body parts. It is often easier to rough out the form in 2D shapes and then fine-tune the surfaces as a patch.

Figure 5.115 shows a 2D wire cage that is the basic form of an automobile fender. After applying a Surface modifier and an Edit Patch modifier and making a few simple adjustments to the Bézier vertices, the result is a smooth, efficient surface that could pass as a fender (see Figure 5.116).

The surface resulting from this method has most of the editing qualities of the native Quad Patch. Surface Tools method has the advantage of quickly roughing out the object in 2D before getting into the less efficient Patch editing. Moving up and down the Modifier Stack from 2D to 3D editing can offer a flexibility not found in Quad Patch creation methods.

NURBS Modeling

Modeling in NURBS is not a fundamental topic in 3ds max 4. To be treated properly, NURBS needs a small book of its own.

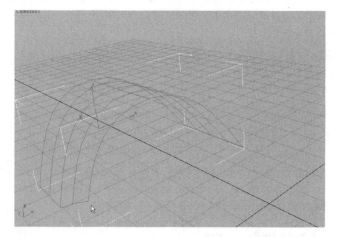

Figure 5.115   A 2D wire cage is used to form the underlying structure of a fender. All the 2D shape editing tools are available.

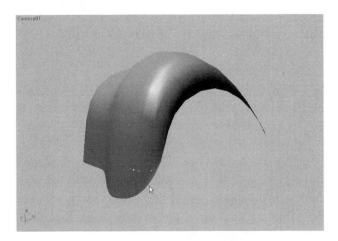

Figure 5.116   The 2D wire cage with Surface modifier applied to create a
skin and Edit Patch modifier to adjust the Bézier vertices for
a more curved, flowing surface.

In a nutshell, NURBS is very similar to Patch modeling. It can be started as native
NURBS quad surfaces and edited and manipulated with similar processes to those
described in the previous section on Patch surfaces. Or the process can start with a
2D wire cage of NURBS Point Curves or CV (Control Vertex) Curves to which a
NURBS skin surface is applied and manipulated into the final 3D object.

NURBS surfaces can be blended into each other with smoother results than Patch surfaces, and it is possible to cut holes and extract data from the curved surfaces much
easier than with patches.

The surfaces that are created with NURBS can sometimes be exported from 3ds
max 4 using the IGES translator in a form that other engineering software can use in
construction documents and still retain the NURBS relationships.

The major disadvantage with NURBS in general modeling is the overhead and
demand on computer resources. Even the smallest objects can quickly overwhelm the
largest systems and make the process frustrating and nonproductive.

NURBS is a powerful tool that allows you to create objects that would be difficult with
other methods, but only use them when necessary and approach the project with
careful planning to utilize the tools efficiently.

XRef: External Reference Files

While XRef is not a method of modeling, it is important in terms of modeling efficiency in the overall project. XRef allows you to merge scenes or objects from other

3ds max 4 files while retaining a reference link with the original files. This is a good situation for collaborative projects where many people are working on different aspects of the project. For example, the animation team needs to be setting up the preliminary motion of objects, but you are not finished with the model. The animation team can XRef your object and start animating it in the scene. As you make changes to the model and save the file, the animation team can update the object they have merged in at any time. The update can be automatic whenever the file containing the merged object is opened. This allows concurrent work to be done, keeping the project on schedule.

Whole scenes may be XRefed from a file but may not be edited in the new file. Individual objects may be XRefed, and while the base work can only be changed in the original file, new modifiers may be added in the new file to edit those objects.

In Exercise 5.19, you will XRef objects from two files. One will be a ceiling object, and the other a ceiling fan. You will learn a few of the capabilities of XRefing that can make your work more productive.

Exercise 5.19: XRef Objects

1. Open the file called MASTER_DINER11.MAX that you saved from Exercise 5.18, or from the CD-ROM. Save the file as MASTER_DINER12.MAX.

2. In the File pull-down menu, choose XRef Objects (see Figure 5.117). The XRef Object dialog contains two fields. The top field is for files from which you have merged XRef Objects, the lower field is for the objects themselves.

Figure 5.117   From the File pull-down menu, choose XRef Objects.

3. In the XRef Objects dialog, click the Add button and open the file called Ch5_DINER_CEILING.MAX on the CD-ROM (see Figure 5.118). It only contains one object called CEILING, so choose CEILING in the XRef Merge dialog. In the XRef Merge dialog, double-click on CEILING to merge that object into your scene (see Figure 5.119).

note

The ceiling is not completely visible in the Perspective viewport because of Face Normals. An interior view will show the ceiling in its entirety.

4. In the XRef Objects dialog, click the Add button again and double-click on a file on the CD-ROM called Ch5_DINER_FAN.MAX to open it. In the XRef Merge dialog, double-click on [FAN01] in the list. The XRef Objects dialog now lists two files in the top field and the objects that were merged from the selected file in the bottom field.

note

When names in lists have brackets, this indicates a 3ds max 4 group, not necessarily a single object.

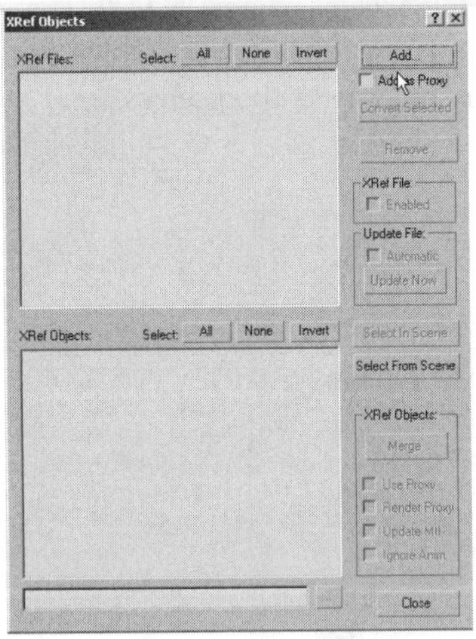

5. In the top field, select Ch5_DINER_FAN, and in the bottom field, click the All button to select everything in the XRef Objects list. Check the Use Proxy option in the XRef Objects area and notice that the fan objects in the viewport have been replaced by tick marks (see Figure 5.120). This can speed viewport performance but still allow you to render the full objects in the scene. Close the dialog.

Figure 5.118
Click the Add button and find the file called Ch5_DINER_CEILING.MAX.

Figure 5.119
Double-click on the CEILING object in the XRef Merge dialog to merge it into your scene.

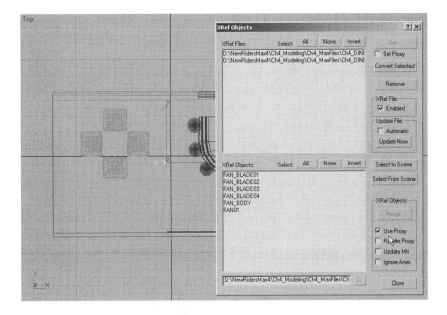

Figure 5.120   When XRef Objects, Use Proxy is checked, the mesh objects in the display become tick marks. When the scene is rendered, the original mesh objects are rendered, however.

tip   To break the reference link between the original and the XRef Object, but still have the objects in the scene, use the Merge button found in the XRef Object dialog.

6. Save the file, it is already called MASTER_DINER12.MAX.

Chapter Summary

- **More 2D Modifiers**   You have learned about other 2D shape-specific modifiers that let you turn the 2D into 3D mesh objects. These included Extrude, Bevel, Bevel Profile, and Lathe.

- **Lofting**   Extruding complex 2D shapes along complex 2D paths is one of the most powerful tools you have learned in this chapter. You have seen that the 2D shapes can be edited at any time to affect the 3D mesh and that materials can be assigned based on the 2D information.

- **3D Primitives**   You created 3D primitive objects such as boxes and cylinders, and by applying modifiers, you have changed the primitives so they were new objects.

- **3D Modifiers**   By applying modifiers to 3D mesh objects you have created a complex history of edits that can often be transversed to make changes at any point in the history without affecting others before or after.

- **Patch modeling**   You learned about the more organic methods of manipulating patch surfaces to create flowing objects, both with native Quad Patches and Surface Tools methods.

- **NURBS**   A discussion of NURBS surfaces has set the foundation for you to explore the modeling technique to see if it can be productive in your situation.

- **XRef scenes and objects**   Collaborative projects can be streamlined by using XRef functions to allow scenes and objects to be merged into a master scene while retaining an editing link from the original to the XRef.

Materials: Applying Surface Colors and Patterns

In This Chapter

Materials, together with lighting in 3ds max 4, should usually take precedence over modeling when budgeting your time on a project. It is possible to create a beautiful detailed model and make it look very mediocre with materials and lights. On the other hand it is possible to create a simple model and make it stunning with good materials and lights.

In Chapter 6 you will be learning the fundamentals of creating materials that you will apply over and over in various combinations to create top-notch materials for your scenes. Think of the fundamentals presented in this chapter as the building blocks from which you will be able to construct complex structures of color, shading, and texture.

3ds max 4 uses a modeless dialog, meaning it can remain open as you work on other things. An example would be Material Editor in which you build your materials layer by layer.

In this chapter you will also learn about mapping, the process of correctly fitting patterns within the materials on a surface. This is important to show the scale of a map for a convincing representation to the viewer.

A very important concept of materials in 3ds max 4 is the ability to simulate geometry. Refer to the section on maps in Chapter 2, "3ds max 4 Concepts: The Fundamentals" for more information on the concepts of materials and maps. Always remember that you should model with the minimum number of faces and vertices required to get sufficient detail to convince the viewer of your intentions. Often, rather than build geometry, you can simulate the geometry with materials, thus increasing efficiency.

Some of the topics that will be covered in Chapter 6 include:

- Fundamental material types
- Navigating the Material Editor
- Material basic parameters: color, patterns, shininess, and transparency
- Fundamental maps and mapping coordinates
- Concepts and use of shaders
- Organizing with Material Libraries

Learn the fundamentals well, and in simple scenes, experiment with the basic concepts and the interaction with of your materials with different lighting combinations. Then move on to more complexity and layering a step at a time. Essentially you will be repeating the same steps over and over in different combinations to get the effects you desire. Build on experience rather than trying to do everything at once, and you will be more productive.

Key Terms

Materials   A material is data that you assign to the surface or faces of an object so that it appears a certain way when rendered. Materials affect the color of objects, their shininess, their opacity, etc.

Maps   The images you assign to materials as patterns are called maps. 3ds max provides several different map types. They include standard bitmaps (such as .bmp, .jpg, or .tga files), procedural maps (such as Checker or Marble), and image-processing systems such as compositors and masking systems.

Diffuse color   The diffuse color is the color that the object reflects when illuminated by "good lighting," that is, by direct daylight or artificial light that makes the object easy to see.

Ambient color   Ambient color is the color of the object in the shaded portion or where the object is in the shadow of another object.

Specular color   Specular color is the color scattered off the surface of a material.

Specular level   Specular level is the brightness of the specular highlights, scattered light from a surface.

Glossiness   Glossiness adjusts the size of the specular highlights scattered from the surface.

Shader   A shader is an component of a material that adjusts the shape and edge transition of specular highlights.

Opacity   Opacity is the ability of a material to block the passage of light. It is the opposite of transparency.

Self-Illumination   Self-Illumination creates the illusion of incandescence by replacing any shadows on the surface with the diffuse color. At 100 percent, the shadows are completely replaced by the diffuse color, creating the illusion of self-illumination.

Material Libraries   Material Libraries are files on the hard drive used to store material and map definitions. They can be accessed from any 3ds max 4 file.

Bump maps   Bump maps are maps that use the brightness values of pixels to cause the rendered illusion of raised or depressed areas on objects without generating new geometry.

Opacity maps   Opacity maps use the brightness of pixels to create the illusion of opacity or transparency on surfaces.

Tiling   Tiling is an adjustment of maps to vary the repeating patterns.

Smoothing   Smoothing is a render effect that causes adjacent faces to appear faceted or smoothed at their shared edge. The Smoothing Group Numbers option can be assigned to faces. If two faces share a common number, the edge is smoothed.

Face Normals   Face Normals are vectors that defines the direction a face surface points. If the Face Normal points toward the viewer, the faces are visible in the display and rendered image. Face Normals may be flipped or overridden with 2-Sided materials.

Use the sample materials and maps that ship with 3ds max 4 as templates and guides to create your own materials. There is nothing more disconcerting than to go into a presentation with exactly the same materials in your scene as your competition.

It is not within the scope of Chapter 6 to make you an expert in creating materials but to familiarize you with some of the fundamental tools available. The final results are a very subjective, and sometimes elusive, goal where your artistic side must come into play. Once you are comfortable with the fundamentals, move on to the more advanced topics in other 3ds max 4 books.

Material Editor, Materials, and Maps

The terms Material Editor, materials, maps, and mapping can cause some confusion to the new user of 3ds max 4. Repeating the short definition of each from the Key Terms section at the beginning will be helpful in clarifying the role of each.

- **Material Editor**   This is the workspace of 3ds max 4 that you use to create and save your materials. It might be thought of as the equivalent of the painter's palette.
- **Materials**   A material is a combination of all the attributes that make up the surface appearance. Materials can be simple or complex and can interact closely with lighting in a scene.
- **Maps**   Maps are the various patterns that the viewer sees in a material. These can be used singly or in combinations with other maps.
- **Mapping**   Mapping is the process of applying and adjusting a coordinate system to change the size and repetition of any map.

As you explore the process of creating materials for a scene, you will soon discover that it is not a linear event. You do not start at the top and work to the bottom of the Material Editor; instead, you jump around adding layers, making adjustments, and test rendering. Then you come back to the Material Editor and repeat the process in a different sequence until you have the result (or near to it) that you want.

There are many styles of materials just as there are many different map types available. Probably the most commonly used material type for new users to 3ds max 4 is the Standard material because the default Sample Windows are set up as Standard materials. This chapter will introduce you to several others to give you a feel of some differences. Experiment with materials types but go slowly. The complexity can quickly become overwhelming and can confuse even veteran users.

tip

Knowing when to stop tweaking a material is a great boon to production. Often you are your own worst critic, and the client may not perceive more infinite adjustments on a material.

There are several material types other than the Standard default available in 3ds max 4:

- **Blend** Blends any two material types together with mixing or masking options.

- **Composite** Composites two or more materials, taking advantage of Alpha channel in the materials.

- **Double-sided** Made of two materials; one is applied to the side of faces with the Face Normal, and the other is applied to the back side of faces.

- **Matte/Shadow** Objects with Matte/Shadow material always show the background image through the object for masking and shadow-catching capabilities.

- **Morpher** Material that changes based on Morph modifier changes on mesh objects.

- **Multi/Sub-object** A material made of any number of other materials, each assigned to faces according to the Material ID numbers.

- **Raytrace** A material that blends material components with Raytrace reflections and refractions.

- **Shellac** Two materials blended based on face angle to the viewer.

- **Top/Bottom** Two materials assigned to faces based Face Normal direction in the World or Local Z-axis.

The Material Editor

As mentioned earlier in the chapter, the Material Editor is a modeless dialog that may be open while you are working on other aspects of your 3ds max 4 scene (see Figure 6.1).

You will learn the important elements from the Sample Windows, the Shader Basic Parameters rollout, and the Blinn Basic Parameters rollout. You will also learn about navigating throughout the Material Editor, an important aspect of being productive.

Face Normals

Before embarking on a discussion of materials in 3ds max 4, a review of the concept of Face Normals is appropriate.

It is simple. Each face in 3ds max 4 has an imaginary vector pointing perpendicular from the surface. If that Face Normal vector points toward the viewer, the face is visible. If the Face Normal points away from the viewer, the face is invisible.

This is done for efficiency, to avoid calculating reflections inside a sphere, for example. However, it is often useful to see both sides of a surface. For example, a pane

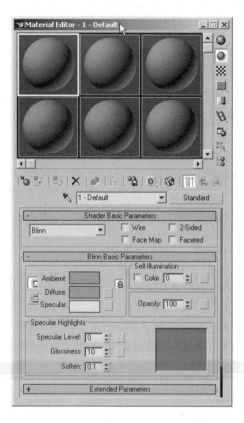

Figure 6.1   This is the default Material Editor modeless dialog in
3ds max 4.

of glass or the page of a book can be made up of a single collection of faces without thickness. Because of Face Normals, you can only see one side of the pane or page. In order to see both sides without giving the object thickness, which would more than double the face/vertex count, you can use a Double-sided material type or check the 2-Sided option in Shader Basic Parameters of a material to make the material visible regardless of the direction of the Face Normal.

Remember it is important to model as efficiently as possible. This is one tool that helps you maintain that goal.

The Sample Windows

At first glance at the Material Editor, the most notable feature is the six Sample Windows with gray spheres. Probably one of the most frequently asked support questions is "How do I use more than six materials in my scene?" The number of visible sample spheres has nothing to do with the number of materials in any scene. There is no limit, other than perhaps computer resources, on the number of possible materials in a given scene.

Think of the Sample Windows area of your scene as a box of crayons. You have a box with six crayons. If you right-click in a Sample Window and choose 6 × 4 Sample Windows in the pop-up menu, you are presented with 24 Sample Windows, the maximum setting (see Figure 6.2).

Selecting the maximum setting is like having a box of 24 crayons. Assume you have a bag of thousands of crayons at your side to color with. However, you can only have any 24 of the crayons in the box at any one time. Materials not shown in the Sample Windows can be assigned to objects in a scene or saved in Material Libraries (the bag in this scenario), which you will learn about later in the chapter.

note

If you switched to 24 Sample Windows, right-click on a Sample Window and choose 3 × 2 Sample Windows in the menu.

tip

You can also navigate among the 24 Sample Windows by positioning your cursor on the edge of any window to reveal the hand cursor and picking and dragging or by using the sliders below and right of the Sample Windows.

The currently selected Sample Window has a heavy white border to indicate it is active.

You will learn the function of some of the buttons below and right of the Sample Windows as we progress through this chapter. Centered below the bottom row of buttons is a name field for the current material. It is very important to name materials with logical names so everyone knows what the material is.

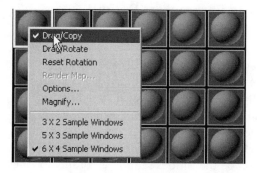

Figure 6.2   Right-click on a Sample Window to switch to a 6 × 4 array, the maximum possible.

Double-clicking on a Sample Window or right-clicking on a Sample Window and choosing Magnify, will "tear off" a copy that can be resized for better visibility.

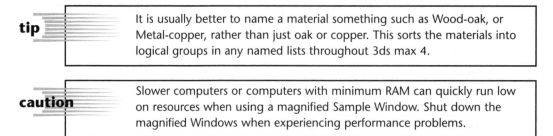

tip It is usually better to name a material something such as Wood-oak, or Metal-copper, rather than just oak or copper. This sorts the materials into logical groups in any named lists throughout 3ds max 4.

caution Slower computers or computers with minimum RAM can quickly run low on resources when using a magnified Sample Window. Shut down the magnified Windows when experiencing performance problems.

Shader Basic Parameters Rollout

In the Shader Basic Parameters rollout, you can choose a shader for the material from the pull-down list, the default being Blinn for the Standard material type (see Figure 6.3). You will learn more about the shaders later in the chapter.

Two of the checkboxes in Shader Basic Parameters rollout that can be important to the new user include:

- **Wire** When the Wire option is checked, the mesh object is shown with all visible edges in the mesh treated as if they were made of wire and the faces become transparent. This is a good material attribute to simulate simple wire objects without creating each physical wire in the scene (see Figure 6.4).

- **2-Sided** The 2-Sided checkbox allows transparent and wire materials to appear on faces regardless of the direction of the Face Normals. In the sample sphere shown in Figure 6.5, it allows the viewer to see the inside of the back of the sphere. Compare Figure 6.5 with Figure 6.4.

Material Basic Parameters Rollout

The Material Basic Parameters rollout is of prime importance in creating materials as you will soon learn. In the default Standard material type the rollout is named Blinn Basic Parameters because of the Blinn shader currently in use. Each type of material has its own features in the Material Basic Parameters rollout, but there is a lot of cross-functionality and common features throughout the material types. This chapter section will describe the various settings according to the group they belong to in the rollout.

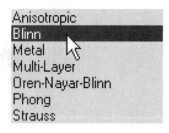

Figure 6.3

Click Blinn in the Shader Basic Parameters rollout for a list of available shader types.

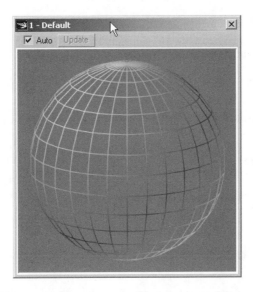

Figure 6.4   Checking the Wire option shows the object with all visible edges in the mesh treated as if they were made of wire and the faces become transparent.

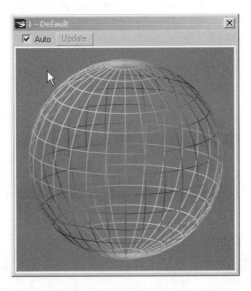

Figure 6.5   Transparent and wire materials appear on faces regardless of the direction of the Face Normals when the 2-Sided checkbox is selected.

Color Swatches

The first area in the upper left of the rollout contains three color swatches. These set various color components of a material:

- **Ambient**   The color of a material where no direct light hits the object.
- **Diffuse**   The color of a material in direct light.
- **Specular**   The color of scatter highlights from the shininess of the surface.

By clicking on the color swatch you can call up the Color Selector for that component (see Figure 6.6). This allows you to choose a color by these selections:

- Hue
- Blackness
- Whiteness
- Red, Green, or Blue sliders
- Hue, Saturation, or Value sliders

The method you use to set the desired color is your preference. All aspects of the Color Selector are interconnected, and as you adjust one setting, the others adjust accordingly.

> **tip**   It is possible to change the default Color Selector in the Preferences menu, General tab, if you have a Color Selector that was created in accordance with the 3ds max 4 Software Developers Kit.

The small gray box to the right of the Diffuse and Specular color swatches is a short-cut button to apply maps to the components.

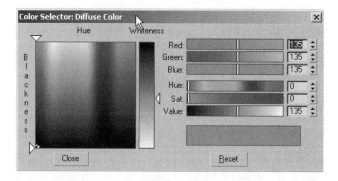

Figure 6.6   This shows the Default Color Selector in 3ds max 4.

note   To the right of the Ambient and Diffuse color swatches you will see a padlock toggle. This locks any map applied to the Diffuse color swatch to the Ambient, so your material looks the same in direct light as in shade. You can unlock this for special effects.

tip   The lock button to the left of the Ambient and Diffuse color swatches locks the two colors to be the same. This author suggests you unlock Ambient and Diffuse colors and adjust the Ambient color to be a much darker version of the Diffuse color. This makes the shaded areas and shadows in a scene darker, increasing the overall contrast and adding to the apparent 3D depth in the scene.

Self-Illumination Area

Increasing the number in the Self-Illumination field makes the materials appear to glow from within (see Figure 6.7).

In effect, increasing the Self-Illumination amount boosts the color values in the Ambient portion of the material where no direct light hits the object. This cancels out shading and shadows giving the appearance of a glow. The material does not actually cast light.

An example would be the monitor and status lights on a computer. You would not want the monitor and lights to disappear in shadows. When you apply a material with 100 percent Self-Illumination, it is not affected by the shadow.

By default, the pixel color of the material is boosted to cause the effect, but you can toggle a color swatch to cause the glow to be a different color than the material.

Opacity Area

The Opacity area has a single numeric spinner and a map shortcut button. Decreasing the Opacity setting increases the transparency of a material (see Figure 6.8).

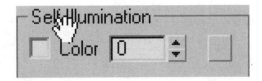

Figure 6.7 The Self-Illumination area of Blinn Basic Parameters rollout.

Figure 6.8   The Opacity area of Blinn Basic Parameters rollout.

Specular Highlights Area

Specular Highlights options, which will be covered in more depth in the exercises of this chapter, are controlled partially from this dialog area (see Figure 6.9).

The three settings available in this area of the dialog are

- **Specular Level**   This is the brightness of the specular highlights, the glint from scattered light, of a material.

- **Glossiness**   This adjusts the size of the specular highlight of a material. Smaller specular highlights make a material appear more shiny and hard; large specular highlights make it appear flat and porous.

- **Soften**   This controls the softness of the transition between specular and diffuse area at the edge of the specular highlight.

The gray window at the right of the Specular Highlights area shows a graphical representation of the specular highlight. The height of the graph indicates Specular Level or brightness, and the width of the graph represents size of the specular highlight.

Maps Rollout

The next most important rollout for the new 3ds max 4 user is the Maps rollout (see Figure 6.10). You have buttons marked None in this area where you can assign different types of maps that describe the pattern of a material component, in the Diffuse Color or Bump map slots, for example.

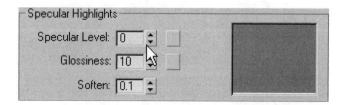

Figure 6.9   Specular Highlights area of Blinn Basic Parameters rollout is shown.

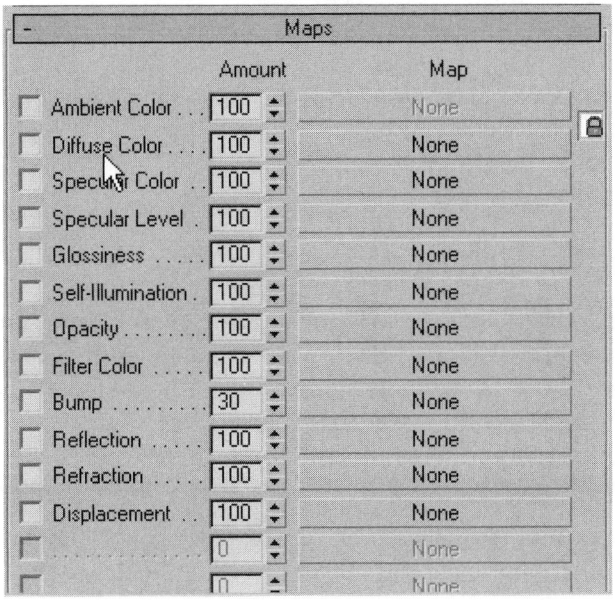

Figure 6.10   In the Maps rollout, you can assign maps or patterns to different aspects of the material.

The Maps rollout contains four columns of information starting with a checkbox to indicate if a map is active, followed by the component name. Next is an Amount column indicating an amount of a given map.

In the Diffuse Color slot, the Amount field can range from 0 to 100. At 100 the map in the slot to the right has full effect on the color of the object, and at 50 the map contributes 50 percent to the color. The color you set in the Diffuse color swatch in Blinn Basic Parameters rollout contributes 50 percent.

In the Bump Amount field, however, the value ranges from –999 to 999 and is the relative amount of the affect of the maps used to give the illusion of a bumpy surface at render time.

tip   In 3ds max 4 and with a DirectX version 8 or higher graphics card and drivers, you can see the bump effect in the viewports.

> **note** As in the Blinn Basic Parameters rollout, the padlock toggle to the right of and between Ambient Color and Diffuse Color map slots locks the two to apply the same map to both components. The slots may be unlocked and contain separate maps for special effects.

The Standard Material Type

By default, each Sample Window contains a dull gray material on the sample sphere. You will perform a series of exercises to create some simple materials that will be applied to objects in the diner scene from Chapter 4, "2D Modeling: Create Your World." You will learn the basics of material creation, and you will learn to navigate the Material Editor. The basic materials you create in this section on Standard materials will be:

- **Flat paint** You will set the Diffuse and Ambient colors and adjust the shininess of a paint to apply to the front wall of the diner.

- **Window glass** This will be a 2-Sided, semitransparent material representing glass.

- **Tile floor** In this exercise, you will apply a map to the Diffuse and Ambient slots of a material to generate a tile floor color pattern.

- **Chrome stool** This material will be a generic chrome material applied to the counter stools in the diner.

You will apply the materials you make in this chapter section to objects in the diner scene, and then return to the materials to edit them for a more convincing appearance. Pay close attention to the process of creating these simple materials and navigating through the Material Editor. Learning in manageable steps and building on previous knowledge can cut the confusion and steep learning curve of trying to create complex materials for the new user.

Exercise 6.1: Creating a Flat Paint Material with Homogeneous Color

1. Open the file called MASTER_DINER12.MAX that you saved at the end of Chapter 4 or from the CD-ROM. Save it as MASTER_DINER13.MAX. The file already has a Multi/Sub-object material that you created to learn about assigning materials to objects by changing the Material ID of the segment on the 2D shape they were generated from. You will come back to this material later in this chapter for editing.

> **note**
>
> The MASTER_DINER12.max file includes some objects, DINER_CEILING and DINER_FAN, which are external reference objects (XRef) from other files.
>
> If the ceiling and ceiling fan do not show up when you open MASTER_DINER12.max, you will get an error message about Missing XRefs. Use the Browse button in the Missing XRefs dialog to locate the file(s) listed in the dialog window.

2. Pick and drag on the title bar of the Material Editor to position it in the display to allow full view or the Perspective viewport. In the Material Editor, click on the second Sample Window in the top row to activate it, and drag it onto the FRONT-WALL object in the Perspective viewport. You will see the ToolTip with the object name FRONTWALL appear when the cursor is over the correct object. This assigns the material to the wall object. The corners of the Sample Window will have triangles indicating a hot material in the scene, and the wall will turn gray in the shaded viewport (see Figure 6.11).

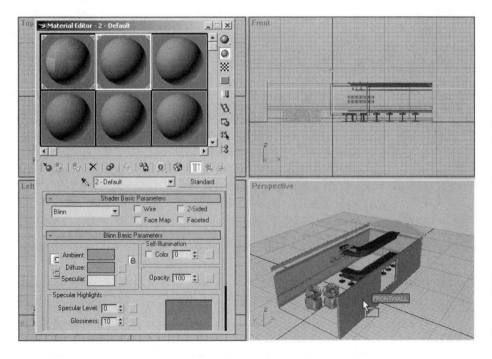

Figure 6.11   Drag and drop the second Sample Window onto FRONT-WALL. The wall turns gray and the triangles in the Sample Window indicate a hot material, that is, one that will change in the viewport after it is changed in the Material Editor.

3. In the Material Editor, Blinn Basic Parameters roll-out, click the Diffuse color swatch to call Color Selector. To create a beige hue, enter the following values in the numeric fields for each primary color: Red = 225, Green = 220, and Blue = 200. Examine the sample sphere to see the relationship between the lightest color (diffuse) and the darkest color (ambient) on the sphere.

4. In the Blinn Basic Parameters rollout, click the color lock toggle left of Ambient and Diffuse to unlock the Ambient from the Diffuse colors. Click on the Ambient color swatch and enter 100 in the Value numeric field. This retains the basic hue of the color but is a much darker value. Compare the relationship between the lightest and darkest area of the sample sphere again, and you will notice an increase in contrast.

5. In the Material name field overwrite 2-Default with PAINT_BEIGE. In the Blinn Basic Parameters rollout, click on the Specular color swatch, and in the Color Selector, enter 255 in the Value field for a pure white color.

6. In the Blinn Basic Parameters rollout, Specular Highlights area, enter 20 in the Specular Level field. This increases the level, or brightness, of the white color giving a low gloss specular highlight in the lit areas of the sample sphere. Notice the graph in the Specular Highlights area is a low bulge indicating a dull broad highlight. Click the Close button in the Color Selector.

7. Save the file. It is already named MASTER_DINER13.MAX.

tip

If you change the Diffuse color at a later time, you can drag and drop the Diffuse Color swatch onto the Ambient Color swatch and make a copy. Then, double-click on the Ambient Color swatch to bring up the Color Selector and drag the Value slider to a darker setting.

tip

Most materials in the real world have specular highlights that are pure white. The exceptions are materials such as gold and anodized aluminum that have specular highlights derived from the base color of the metal. You will learn much more on specular highlights later in this chapter.

You have created your first material and assigned it to an object in the scene by dragging and dropping the SampleWindow on the object. You will repeat this and similar processes over and over in 3ds max 4, adding new layers of information each time, perhaps, but these are the essential steps of material creation. Congratulations.

In Exercise 6.2 you will create a glass material in a new Sample Window that will be assigned to the glazing of the window in the front wall of the diner. Glass is, of course, somewhat transparent and is significantly shinier than low gloss paint.

You will create a window-pane object from the existing 2D window data and assign the new material to it. From the view in the Perspective viewport and the orientation of Face Normals on the window-pane object, you will not be able to drag and drop the material onto the object in the scene, but will instead learn a new method of assigning materials.

Exercise 6.2: Creating a Transparent Glass Material and a Window Pane Object

1. Open the file called MASTER_DINER13.MAX that you saved from the last exercise or from the CD-ROM. Save the file as MASTER_DINER14.MAX. You must first create a window-pane object to receive the glass material. You will use existing 2D data to extract the information needed for the window pane. Minimize the Material Editor in the 3ds max 4 scene.

2. Click the Select button and type H. Double-click WINDOW_SASH in the list to select it (see Figure 6.12). In the Modify panel, choose Spline in the Stack View to enter Spline sub-object mode (see Figure 6.13).

3. Right-click in the Front viewport to activate it and pick the inner rectangle of the WINDOW_SASH compound shape to select it. It will turn red when selected. In the Modify panel, Geometry rollout, check the Copy option below the Detach button, and then click the Detach button (see Figure 6.14). Enter WINDOW_PANE in the Detach dialog (see Figure 6.15) and click OK.

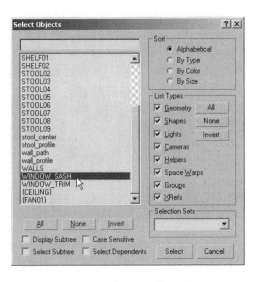

Figure 6.12   Double-click WINDOW_SASH in the Select Objects dialog.

Figure 6.13   Choose Spline sub-object level in the Stack View.

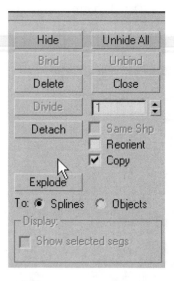

Figure 6.14   Check the Copy option before clicking the Detach button.

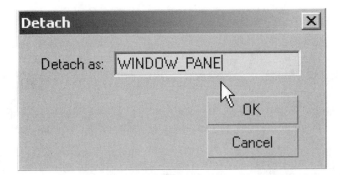

Figure 6.15   Enter WINDOW_PANE in the Detach dialog and click OK.

4. Use Select by Name to select the WINDOW_ PANE object, and in the Front viewport, right-click, and in the Convert To option, choose Convert to Editable Mesh in the quad menus (see Figure 6.16). This converts the 2D shape to a 3D flat plane mesh. The mesh becomes visible in the window opening of the diner front wall. If you were to look from the inside you would not see the mesh because the Face Normals point outward. In the Top viewport, with WINDOW_PANE selected, click the Select and Rotate button and rotate the WINDOW_PANE 180 degrees in the z-axis. This points the Face Normals into the room.

tip

You are naming the detached shape with all caps which denotes 3D objects in our naming scheme. However, you will convert the 2D shape to a flat mesh object in the next step. This saves having to rename the object.

5. Maximize the Material Editor and pick the right Sample Window in the top row. In the Window Name field enter WINDOW_GLASS. In the Material Editor, click the Assign Material to Selection button just above the eyedropper button next to the material name. This assigns the WINDOW_GLASS material to the selected object or objects in the scene, in this case, to the WINDOW_PANE. This is a method of assigning a material to multiple objects at once or to objects that would be difficult to hit with drag-and-drop methods. The window pane will turn gray in the shaded Perspective viewport.

6. In the Material Editor, Shader Basic Parameters rollout, check the 2-Sided option. This allows the material to be seen on the object regardless of the direction of the Face Normals. In the Blinn Basic Parameters rollout, click the Diffuse color swatch, and in the Color Selector, enter Red = 205, Green = 215, and Blue = 220, a light blue color. Click on the Specular color swatch and change the color to pure white in the Color Selector.

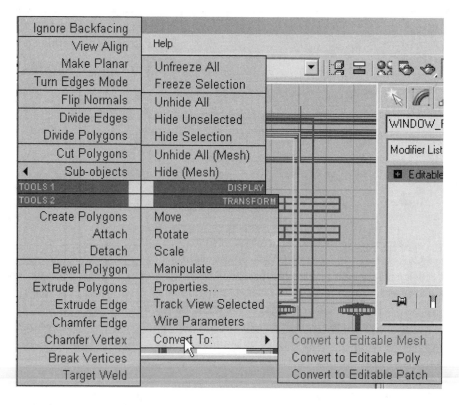

Figure 6.16   Choose Convert to Editable Mesh in the Convert To quad
menu option.

7. In the Material Editor, Specular Highlights area,
   enter 30 in the Specular Level field. Enter 60 in the
   Opacity field to make the material 40 percent transparent.

8. In the Material Editor, click on the Background button. It is the third button down on the right side of
   the Sample Windows. This toggles a checker background in the active Sample Window to make the
   transparency more apparent on the sample sphere
   (see Figure 6.17). The transparency should be apparent on the WINDOW_PANE in the shaded
   Perspective viewport.

tip

Bluish color is perceived as
a cold color that can be
used to make glass and
metal materials more con-
vincing. Because the glass
is transparent and is not
obviously different in light
or shade, there is little reason to unlock and adjust
the Diffuse and Ambient
color swatches. Close the
Color Selector.

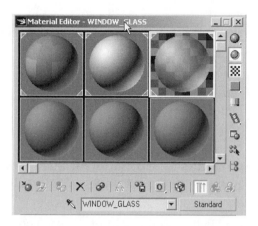

Figure 6.17   Toggle on the Background in the Sample Window to better
see the effect of lowered Opacity settings.

9. Save the file. It should already be called MASTER_DINER14.MAX. You have
   created your first transparent material. It needs more work, but you will make
   those changes in a later exercise. This might be a good time to take a break.

Using Maps in the Material Editor

As mentioned previously in this chapter, materials are the surface-attribute definitions
applied to objects in the scene to simulate materials found in the real world.

Maps, on the other hand, are patterns that are used
in the various components of a material, for example,
as color, bump, or opacity patterns.

Maps can be accessed from the Material Editor in
several ways including:

- Clicking the small gray box to the right of component's fields or swatches in the Material
  Editor rollouts and choosing a map in the
  Material/Map Browser. Once a map is assigned
  to a component, a capital M, for active maps, or
  lowercase m for inactive maps will appear in the
  gray box (see Figure 6.18). Maps may be activated or disabled with the checkbox in the Maps
  rollout.

caution

When using Keyboard
Shortcuts you should be
aware that they are con-
text sensitive. For example,
when you are in a view-
port the P key switches to
Perspective viewport.
However, if you are cur-
rently in the Material
Editor, pressing P brings
up the Create Material
Preview dialog.

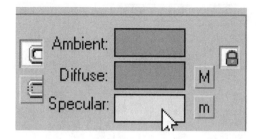

Figure 6.18   Map shortcut buttons with an active map in the Diffuse slot and a disabled map in the Specular slot are shown.

- Click the None button to the right of the component in the Maps rollout of Material Editor. This also brings up the Material/Map Browser for you to choose a map type from (see Figure 6.19).

- Click the Get Material button, the first button on the left below the Sample Windows in the Materials Editor, to open the Material/Map Browser and drag and drop the map onto the None button or the map shortcut button in the Material Editor. Maps in the Material/Map Browser have a green or red parallelogram left of the map name. A blue sphere in the Browser (see Figure 6.20) indicates materials.

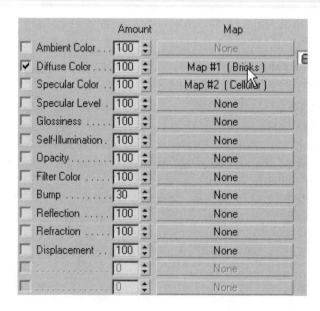

Figure 6.19   Assign maps to components by clicking the None button in the Maps rollout.

Figure 6.20   Drag and drop maps from the Material/Map Browser to the map shortcut button or to the None button in Material Editor.

- In the Utilities panel, click on Asset Browser to load it and drag and drop from the Asset Browser thumbnails to the map shortcut buttons or the None buttons (see Figure 6.21). From the Asset Browser you can browse from your network or, in cases where ActiveX iDrop ® has been implemented, directly from manufacturers' Web sites. For example, www.formica.com is a site where you can access special maps of flooring materials (see Figure 6.22).

caution   Dragging and dropping a map with any of the preceding methods directly onto the Sample Window does not create a material that can be assigned to objects in the scene. Maps entered directly into the Sample Windows can only be used as viewport or render backgrounds or as projected images in lights. Thinking otherwise is a common error for new max users to encounter.

Map Types

Maps that can be used in 3ds max 4 come in several forms and are applied to objects in different ways. The following bullet list looks at some of the map types and explains the basics of each. The Material/Map Browser has a filter at the lower left of the Browser to show only one type of map in the list at a time (see Figure 6.23).

Figure 6.21

In Utilities panel, choose Asset Browser to access maps on your network.

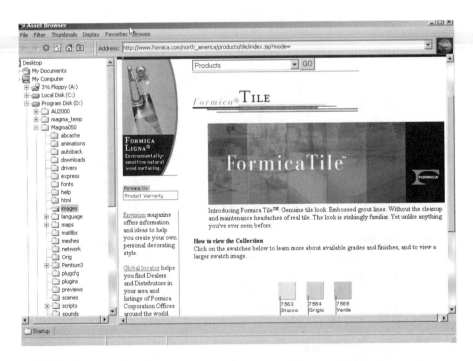

Figure 6.22   You can also access selected manufacturers' Web sites to drag and drop images or mesh objects into your 3ds max 4 scenes.

tip   It is important for you to experiment with different maps and map types to develop a feel for which maps might be appropriate for a given situation.

Also, do not rely on the map name for an indicator of where to use the map in a material. For example, many people use the Brick map to generate bricks, but you can also use it to create suspended ceiling tiles or tire-tread patterns (see Figure 6.24).

The following is an overview of map types in 3ds max 4:

- **2D maps**   Are applied to surfaces as if painted or projected onto the surface. Bitmap images are a good example of 2D maps.

- **3D maps**   Emanate from the center of objects and are procedurally generated throughout the volume of the object. Cutting away the mesh reveals the material correctly.

- **Compositor maps**   For compositing and masking other maps or colors as you would in a photo-imaging software. A mask map could be used to hide or reveal other maps or apply decals to surfaces.

Figure 6.23
In this filter-toggle area of Material/Map Browser, you can choose to show maps of certain types only.

Figure 6.24   A Brick map is used for a tire-tread pattern in the Bump slot of a tire material.

- **Color Modifier maps**   Alter the color of pixels in other maps or materials. You can use this map for correcting colors in bitmaps, for example.

- **Other maps**   Map filter category which includes reflection and refraction maps.

Using Maps to Control Color in Materials

In Exercise 6.3 you will create a floor plane in the diner scene and then create a material that will represent terracotta tile. This exercise will be an example of using a map as color information in a material.

When any map is applied to the Diffuse Color slot of a material, the default setting controls the material color 100 percent. This is set in the Amount field of the Maps rollout. Also the default is that the both Diffuse and Ambient areas have the map applied. This is controlled by the lock button to the right of the slots in the Maps rollout.

tip   Interesting special effects might be created by unlocking the Diffuse map from the Ambient map and applying different maps in each. Area in light would have one pattern while areas in shade would have another.

Again, the exercises are simple so you can learn the process. Once you are comfortable with the fundamental process, you can build on your knowledge to create more complex materials.

Exercise 6.3: Using a Map in the Diffuse Color Slot as a Color Pattern

1. Open the file called MASTER_DINER14.MAX that you saved from Exercise 6.2 or from the CD-ROM. You will first create a Plane primitive object in the Top viewport to represent a floor surface in the diner. Save the file as MASTER_DINER15.MAX.

2. Right-click in the Top viewport to activate it. In the Create panel, Geometry panel, click the Plane button, and in the Top viewport, click and drag a Plane that is a little larger than the diner walls (see Figure 6.25). Name the object FLOOR.

3. Right-click on the Top viewport label and choose Smooth + Highlights from the menu to shade the Top viewport to see the floor surface.

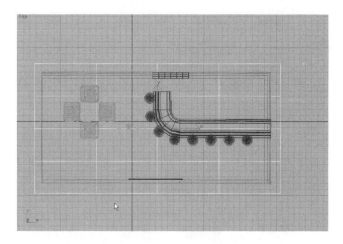

Figure 6.25   Click and drag a Plane primitive larger than the diner walls in the Top viewport. Name it FLOOR.

4. Open the Material Editor and click in the left Sample Window in the bottom row to activate it. Enter TILE_TERRACOTTA in the name field of the material and drag and drop the Sample Window onto the FLOOR object in the Top viewport. FLOOR should turn gray in the display.

5. You will now assign a map to control the color of the material rather than use the current Diffuse Color Swatch Setting shortcut button to the right of the Diffuse color swatch. Double-click on Bricks in the Material/Map Browser list (see Figure 6.26).

note

When you shade the Top viewport, you cannot see the ceiling of the diner. This is because the Face Normals are pointing away from you, making the faces invisible in both the display and renderings from this viewpoint.

6. The brick pattern shows up on the sample sphere in the Sample Window but does not show in the display. Click on the Show Map in Viewport button, the fourth from the right below the Sample Windows. This makes the map visible on the object in any shaded viewport (see Figure 6.27). The brick pattern is very large on the floor, but you will adjust that in the next exercise. For now you will work on color and shape of the bricks.

7. In the Material Editor, expand the Advanced Controls rollout. This shows the colors of the brick as well as the Horiz. Count and Vert. Count fields that show the number of bricks in one repetition of the pattern. In the Standard Controls rollout, click on Preset Type option, Running Bond, and choose Stack Bond from the list. This pattern is more appropriate for floor tiles.

Figure 6.26   Double-click on Bricks in the Material/Map Browser list of
maps to load it into the Diffuse Color map slot.

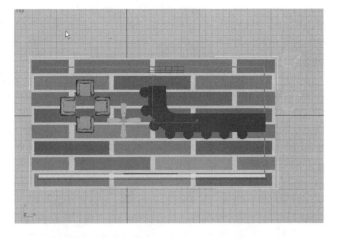

Figure 6.27   Toggle the Show Map in Viewport button to see the map on
the objects in shaded viewports.

8. In the Advanced Controls rollout, Bricks Setup area, enter 3 in the Vert. Count field. This makes a brick pattern that is three bricks by three bricks for a total of nine bricks in one repetition. Three bricks by three bricks should be a square pattern, but that is not what you see in the shaded Top viewport. Again, this will be adjusted in the next exercise with mapping coordinates.

9. The bricks in the pattern vary somewhat in color and saturation. In the Advanced Controls rollout, Bricks Setup area, enter 0 in both the Color Variance and Fade Variance fields to make all bricks the same color as determined by the Bricks Setup Texture color swatch (see Figure 6.29). The bricks appear rectangular instead of square because the pattern is stretched to fit the rectangular floor object.

tip

Instead of viewing the brick pattern on a sample sphere in the Sample Window, you can click and hold on the Sample Type button at the top right of the Sample Windows and choose a flyout button that shows the pattern on a sample cube or cylinder (see Figure 6.28). By right-clicking a Sample Window and choosing Options, you can even have your own mesh object appear in the Sample Windows.

tip

Instead of entering 0 in the variance fields, you could also right-click on the spinner arrows to set the value to 0, in this case, or the lowest setting when 0 is not appropriate.

10. Save the file. It should already be named MASTER_DINER15.MAX. You have assigned a map to the Diffuse Color slot of a material. This overrides the color in the Diffuse color swatch, and because the two are locked together, it also

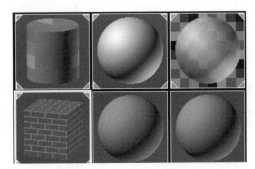

Figure 6.28   Sample Windows can have a sample sphere, cube, cylinder, or custom object.

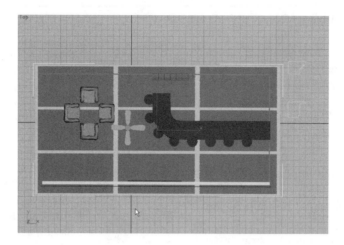

Figure 6.29   A three by three brick pattern is stretched over the floor
with no fade or color variation in the bricks.

overrides the color in the Ambient color swatch. You have adjusted one repetition of the pattern to contain three bricks by three bricks and removed any variations that affect color. Keep in mind that you are adjusting a map that controls the color of the material only.

Using Maps to Simulate Geometry in Materials

In this section of the chapter you will learn how to simulate geometry using map patterns without generating new faces or vertices in the mesh object. This is a very important concept to understand and use to increase your productivity, both in modeling and rendering time.

You will simulate the tiles being higher than the mortar grout lines in the floor. Rather than building each tile and grout line separately as objects, you will take advantage of properties of materials to give the illusion of extra geometry when rendered.

In this particular case you will apply a map in the Bump slot of the material. The luminance value or brightness of each pixel in the map is translated into bumps or no bumps when rendered. White or high-luminance pixels appear to bump while black or low-luminance pixels have no effect. Gray pixels show the effect somewhere inbetween.

> **tip**
> The pixels in colored maps also have luminance values, but it is often difficult to judge the effect. For example, a bright yellow pixel looks very different from a bright green pixel to the eye, but the luminance values may be similar thus making it inappropriate for a Bump map.
>
> Converting or viewing maps as grayscale images makes it much easier to judge what the effect will be at render time.

The luminance values of maps affect other components of a material such as opacity, glossiness, self-illumination, and specular level.

> **tip**
> There is a map slot called Displacement in most material types. This uses the luminance values of map pixels to actually generate new faces and vertices in a mesh object.
>
> Be careful with Displacement mapping as it can compound the complexity of your scene exponentially, bringing any computer system to its knees.

In Exercise 6.4 you will clone the Bricks map in the Diffuse Color slot to the Bump slot. This will create an illusion of bumps on the surface of the sample sphere, but not exactly as you would want for floor tiles. You will then learn to adjust the colors to maximize the bump illusion for a more convincing material.

Exercise 6.4: Simulating Geometry with Bump Maps in Materials

1. Open the file MASTER_DINER15.MAX that you saved in Exercise 6.3 or from the CD-ROM. Save it as MASTER_DINER16.MAX. You will clone the Diffuse Color map into the Bump map slot and adjust it for effectiveness.

2. In the Material Editor, Maps rollout, click and hold on the map slot to the right of Diffuse Color; it should say something like Map #0 [Bricks]. Then drag and drop it onto the None button to the right of Bump. Make sure the Copy option is checked in Copy (Instance) Map dialog (see Figure 6.30) and click OK. Enter 100 in the Bump Amount field and clear the checkbox to the left of Diffuse Color to disable that map.

> **tip**
> In this case you do not want to use the Instance option because if you change one, the other will also change. You want to have different colors in the Bump map.
>
> Instance maps can often increase productivity by allowing you to change one map and have all Instance clones of that map adjusted automatically. This is just like Instance mesh or shape objects in modeling.

Figure 6.30   Drag and drop the Diffuse Color map button onto the Bump None button, choose Copy in the Copy (Instance) Map dialog, and click OK.

3. You can clearly see the illusion of grout lines in the Sample Window caused by the Bump map. You have not generated any new geometry. To maximize the effect you will change the colors in the Bricks map. To make it easier to navigate in the current material, pick the Material/Map Navigator button

> **note**
>
> The Map# associated with the buttons may vary for each user.

below and right of the Sample Windows. The Material/Map Navigator shows a hierarchical representation of the current material with the current level high-lighted in yellow (see Figure 6.31). Click on Bump: Map#2 [Bricks] to drop to that level in the Editor.

4. In the Advanced Controls rollout, click on the Bricks Setup: Texture color swatch and set the color to pure white, Red, Green, and Blue values are all set to 255. Click on the Mortar Setup: Texture color swatch and set it to pure black, Red, Green, and Blue values all set to 0. Remember white pixels bump to the fullest extent set in the Amount field, black pixels have no bump effect.

5. With the Top viewport active, click the Quick Render button, and you will see the bump pattern on the floor. In the Material/Map Navigator, click the top TILE_TERRACOTTA (Standard) level, and in the Material Editor Maps rollout, check Diffuse Color to enable it.

6. Click the Render Last button and you will see the effect of Diffuse Color and Bump mapping on the floor (see Figure 6.32). Because you are looking straight down on the bumps and because of the default lighting, the illusion will not be extremely strong, but you will see it.

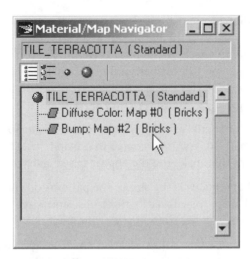

Figure 6.31   Use the Material/Map Navigator to move through the hierarchy of a material.

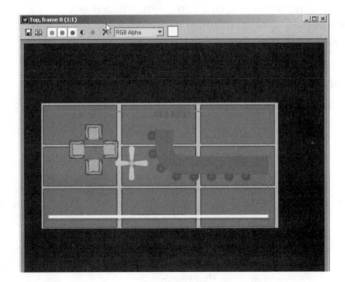

Figure 6.32   The Top viewport is rendered to show combination Diffuse Color and Bump maps on the floor.

7. Close all dialogs and windows and save the file. It should already be named MASTER_DINER16.MAX. You have used a map as color information in a

material and adjusted the pattern repeats. With the drag-and-drop technique, you then cloned the map into the Bump slot as a copy and changed the map colors for maximum bump effect. White pixels give the illusion of bumps while black pixels do nothing. You will further modify this material in a later exercise.

Adjusting the Size of Map Patterns

So far in the floor material exercise, you have created a map that determines the color pattern of the material. You then copied that map to use it to create a pattern for the illusion of bumps that make the tile appear raised above the grout.

The problem that remains is the size of the patterns on the floor. You set one repetition of the brick maps to be three by three tiles, and when applied to the floor object, the nine bricks were stretched to fit the entire floor.

The key to the process of adjusting map coverage is called mapping coordinates. There will be more discussion later in the chapter of various methods of determining mapping coordinates, but a common method will be introduced in the next exercise.

In Exercise 6.5 you will adjust the size of one repetition of the map you have created to fit a predetermined area that corresponds to real-world floor tiles. You will take a simple two-step approach to adjusting the size of your map so it can be used for many of your everyday materials.

- Analyze the map pattern to determine size of the area one repetition of the pattern would cover.
- Adjust the mapping coordinates to fit area determined above.

In your floor-tile case, you have already set the pattern to three bricks by three bricks. Now make the determination of how big each brick is. For this example you will use 12-inch × 12-inch tiles. You now have the coverage area for one repetition of the pattern, 3 bricks × 12 inches by 3 bricks × 12 inches, or 3 feet by 3 feet.

tip

> The Bricks map you used is a special procedural map that allows you to adjust the number of bricks horizontally and vertically. If, however, you are using a bitmap image that is a photograph of a brick pattern, you would multiply the horizontal and vertical size of each brick by the number of bricks across the image and courses up the image and use that number.
>
> It would have been possible to set the Bricks procedural map to, perhaps, 12 by 12 tiles and assumed a 4-inch tile size. You would then enter 4 feet by 4 feet as the Gizmo Length and Width.

For this exercise you will add a modifier called UVW Map and adjust its size accordingly. By default, maps use tiling to repeat the pattern over an entire object, which is just what you want in this example.

Exercise 6.5: Applying Map Coordinates to an Object to Adjust Pattern Repeats

1. Open the file called MASTER_DINER16.MAX that you saved in Exercise 6.4 or from the CD-ROM. Save it as MASTER_DINER17.MAX. You should be in the maximized Top viewport that is shaded, and in the Material Editor, Show Map in Viewport has been toggled on so you can see the Diffuse Color Bricks map on the floor.

2. Click the Select button, type H, and double-click FLOOR in the list of objects. In the Modify panel, click on Modifier List, and click UVW Map in the UV Coordinate Modifiers section (see Figure 6.33).

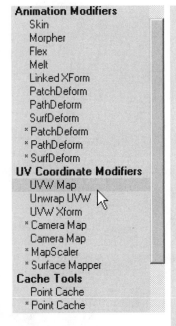

Figure 6.33
In Modify panel, Modifier List, UV Coordinate Modifiers areas, choose UVW Map modifier.

> **note** UVW is not an acronym for anything. Objects use XYZ to rotate coordinate axis in space; materials simply use the next three letters in the alphabet to try to avoid confusion.

3. If you look closely at the FLOOR object in the Top viewport you will see a new orange line surrounding the floor. This is the Gizmo for the UVW Map modifier. It represents one repetition of the material map pattern, and because it automatically fits the object it was assigned to, nothing has visibly changed. In the Modify panel, Parameters rollout, enter Length = 3 and Width = 3. (see Figure 6.34). The Gizmo is now 3 feet by 3 feet, and the bricks in the pattern are the size you determined in the two-step process explained above.

4. Type W to minimize the viewports, and right-click in the Left viewport to activate it. In the Create panel, Lights panel, Object Type rollout, click the Omni button (see Figure 6.35). In the Left viewport, pick just below the ceiling fan to place the Omni light (see Figure 6.36). This gives appropriate light so you can see the floor pattern in a rendered image.

Figure 6.34
Enter 3 in both Length and Width fields of Parameters rollout. The UVW Map Gizmo is now 3 feet by 3 feet.

Figure 6.35
In Create panel, Lights panel, Object Type rollout, click the Omni button.

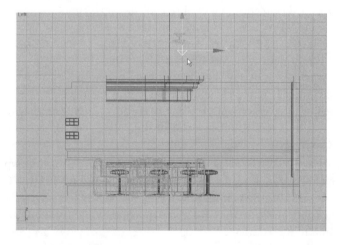

Figure 6.36   In the Left viewport, pick just below the ceiling fan to place the Omni light.

5. Right-click in the Perspective viewport to activate it. Use Arc Rotate, Pan, and Zoom to get a view looking down the diner from approximately eye level. Click the Quick Render button in the toolbar and the Virtual Frame Buffer should look similar to Figure 6.37. The color and bump pattern should give the appearance of raised tile higher than the grout.

tip

In the Perspective viewport, the map being shown in the viewport may appear distorted. To correct this, right-click on the Perspective viewport label, and choose Texture Correction in the menu (see Figure 6.38). The tile may still not be clear, depending on your graphics card and monitor, but the distortion will be gone. The map will render fine in any case.

6. Save the file, which should already be called MASTER_DINER17.MAX. You have used a UVW Map modifier to adjust the size of one repetition of the map you created. The resized pattern repeats itself over the entire object by a process called tiling.

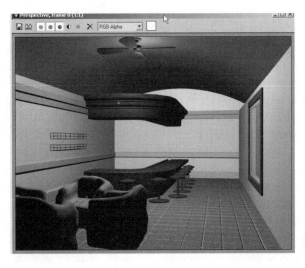

Figure 6.37
Navigate the Perspective viewport for a view down the diner and click Quick Render to see the floor material.

Figure 6.38
Right-click on the Perspective viewport label and choose Texture Correction to remove distortion of maps in the viewport.

Adding Reflections

You have created a tile color pattern and a tile bump pattern in a material, applied it to a mesh surface, and rendered it to see the result of color and simulated geometry in the scene. A real tile floor similar to the one in your scene would undoubtedly have at least some reflections, unless it were old, dirty, and scuffed. Your diner is a bit classier, so you will add some reflection to add more depth to your scene.

tip

Plain color materials, those with no pattern, and reflection maps do not require you to assign specific mapping coordinates to an object.

There are several methods of creating reflections in 3ds max 4. The following is a list and description of the methods available:

- **Bitmap**   With bitmap reflections, you apply bitmap images in the Reflection slot of the material. 3ds max 4 assigns mapping coordinates to simulate the distortion of curved reflective surface, so no mapping coordinates are needed. Bitmap reflections are efficient, but not usually accurate. You would use them to simulate vague reflections from small objects, for example a smudged-gray image as reflections on silverware on a table. Bitmap reflections only work on curved surfaces.

- **Reflect/Refract maps**   These are special maps that take six snapshots (front, back, top, bottom, left, and right) from the center of the object with the material assigned and maps the images back on to the surface with spherical distortion. The process is less efficient than Bitmap reflections, but more accurate as the actual scene is reflected in the surface. Reflect/Refract is used to simulate refraction in transparent objects when applied in the Refraction slot. Reflect/Refract map type only works on curved surfaces.

- **Flat Mirror maps**   Flat Mirror reflections work similarly to Reflect/Refract reflections, but they must be applied to contiguous flat sets of faces. Flat Mirror uses six snapshots mapped to only flat surfaces. Flat Mirror reflections are fairly efficient and somewhat accurate.

- **Raytrace maps**   These are the most accurate and slowest calculating reflection type in 3ds max 4. Raytrace reflections work on either curved or flat surfaces, making it well-suited for complex objects. Raytrace map may also be applied to the Refraction slot of a material to calculate refractions. Raytrace material type will be discussed later in this chapter.

Try to use the most efficient reflection type for any given situation by starting with the fastest method appropriate and working up to higher quality. For example, Raytrace map reflections on all the silverware in a restaurant would be totally unnecessary and not cost-effective.

In Exercise 6.6 you will create a material for the counter stools in the diner. The material will represent a chrome finish, but because of the distance from the viewer to the stools and the fact that the stools are not important items in the scene, you will use a Bitmap reflection type. This will give the illusion of chrome without much overhead on computer resources.

Exercise 6.6: Efficient Chrome Material

1. Open the MASTER_DINER17.MAX file you saved in Exercise 6.5 or from the CD-ROM. Save this file as MASTER_DINER18.MAX. Open the Material Editor and click in the next unused

> **You can type the keyboard shortcut M to call the Material Editor.**

   Sample Window to activate it. Enter CHROME_STOOL in the material name field. In this material you will be adding only a map to the Reflection slot so you must adjust the Diffuse and Ambient color swatches for the color you want as an underlying material color.

2. In the Material Editor, Blinn Basic Parameters rollout, click on the lock button to the left of Diffuse and Ambient color swatches to unlock them. Click on the Diffuse color swatch, and in the Color Selector, enter Blue = 160, leave Red and Green at the default 150. This gives the base color a slight blue tint that adds a cold feel to metallic and glass surfaces. Drag and drop the Diffuse color swatch onto the Ambient color swatch, release the mouse button, and click Copy in the Copy or Swap Colors dialog (see Figure 6.39). In the Color Selector, enter 80 in the Value field to darken the Ambient color for better contrast.

3. In the Blinn Basic Parameters rollout, click the Specular color swatch and change it to pure white by moving the Value slider to the far right or by moving the Whiteness slider to the bottom. In the Specular Highlights area make Specular Level = 60 and Glossiness = 35 for a moderately bright, smallish Specular highlight (see Figure 6.40).

4. In the Material Editor, Maps rollout, click on the None button to the right of Reflection, and double-click Noise map in the Material/Map Browser list. In the Noise Parameters rollout, enter 4 in the Size field to make the randomly generated grayscale pattern smaller.

5. Click the Select button in the toolbar, type H, and highlight STOOL02 through STOOL09 in the Select Objects dialog list (see Figure 6.41). Click the Select button in the dialog. In the Material Editor, click the Assign Material to Selection button below left of the Sample Windows. This assigns CHROME_STOOL material to all the selected stools.

Figure 6.39

Drag and drop the Diffuse color swatch onto the Ambient color swatch and click Copy in the Copy or Swap Colors dialog.

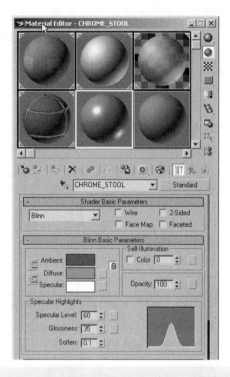

Figure 6.40   Set the Diffuse, Ambient, and Specular color swatches and adjust Specular Level and Glossiness values.

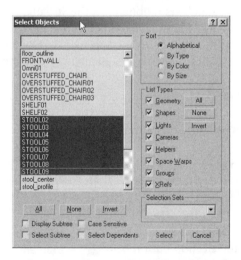

Figure 6.41   Select all the STOOL objects in the Select Objects dialog list and click the Assign to Selection button in the Material Editor.

6. Make sure the Perspective viewport is active and click the Quick Render button. The Virtual Frame Buffer should look similar to Figure 6.42. The Noise bitmap in the Reflection slot is a soft mix of grayscale pattern that passes for acceptable chrome when seen from a distance. In the Material Editor, click on the Material/Map Navigator button at the bottom right of the Sample Windows and choose CHROME_STOOL [Standard} to go to the top of the material (see Figure 6.43). In the Maps rollout, enter 90 in the Amount field to the right of Reflection. This tones down the reflection slightly and allows some of the base color to show through.

> **caution**
>
> Materials with 100 percent reflection can appear self-illuminated in a scene as the reflections override any shading or shadows. Usually lower the reflection amount except on mirror surfaces.

7. Save the file, which should already be named MASTER_DINER18.MAX. You have created a material with a Noise Bitmap in the Reflection slot to simulate a generic chrome material. It is an efficient method of giving the illusion of shiny reflective surfaces. Do not worry about the fact that you have made the cushions chrome as well as the stands. You will correct that in a later exercise.

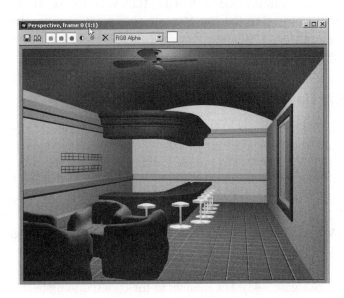

Figure 6.42   CHROME_STOOL material assigned to STOOLS is shown in the Perspective viewport and after the scene is rendered.

Figure 6.43   In the Material/Map Navigator, choose CHROME_STOOL to go to the top level of the material in the Material Editor.

In Exercise 6.7 you will modify the TILE_TERRACOTTA material in your scene to add some reflections using the Flat Mirror map type. Remember that Flat Mirror only works on coplanar, contiguous faces. The floor object is a Plane primitive that passes the requirements.

Exercise 6.7: Flat Mirror Reflection Maps

1. Open MASTER_DINER18.MAX that you saved in Exercise 6.6 or from the CD-ROM. Save the file as MASTER_DINER19.MAX. Open the Material Editor and click on TILE_TERRACOTTA Sample Window to make it the current active material. The triangular corners in the Sample Window indicate it is a hot material in the scene. When you change the material, it will automatically update on the objects you assigned it to.

2. In the Material Editor, Maps rollout, click on the None button right of Reflection, and in the Material/Map Browser, double-click on Flat Mirror (see Figure 6.44).

3. In the Flat Mirror Parameters rollout, Render area, check the Apply to Faces with ID box (see Figure 6.45). The number in the corresponding field is 1. This means that all the coplanar, contiguous faces that have a Material ID of 1 will reflect the scene. Material ID of 1 is assigned by default to all the faces of a Plane primitive.

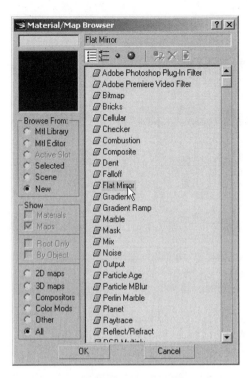

Figure 6.44   Click the None button for Reflection and double-click on Flat
Mirror map in the Material/Map Browser.

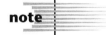

note

In this particular case, it is not absolutely necessary to use the Material ID
checkbox. This just guarantees that the faces with the default settings of
Material ID #1 will get the Flat Mirror reflections.

In the case of a Box primitive object, in which each side of the Box (2 faces) has
Material ID's 1 through 6, it would be important to use the checkbox with the
appropriate ID number for the side that will get the Flat Mirror reflection.

4. With the Perspective viewport active, click the Quick Render button and you will
   see strong reflections on the floor surface (see Figure 6.46). Use the Material/Map
   Navigator to return to the top level of the TILE_TERRACOTTA material and enter
   15 in the Reflection Amount field. Click on the Render Last button in the toolbar.
   The reflections are much more subdued and appropriate for the scene.

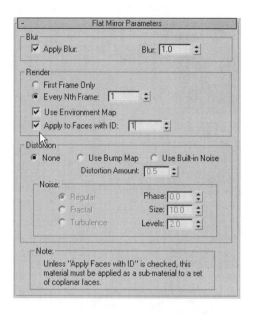

Figure 6.45   In the Flat Mirror Parameters rollout, Render area, check Apply to Faces with ID of 1 checkbox.

Figure 6.46   Flat Mirror Reflection set to the default 100 percent is applied to the floor in the diner scene.

5. In the Material Editor, click on the WINDOW_GLASS Sample Window. Click on the Get Material button below the Sample Windows. In the Material/Map Browser, check Scene in the Browse From area. In the list, drag and drop Reflection Map #4 [Flat Mirror} from the list onto the Reflection button in the Maps rollout (see Figure 6.47). Check Copy in the Instance (Copy) Map dialog and click OK (see Figure 6.48). Enter 30 in the Reflection Amount field. This copies the Flat Mirror map from the floor in the scene to the WINDOW_GLASS material with its settings intact.

6. Save the file. It should already be called MASTER_DINER19.MAX.

You have created a Flat Mirror map reflection in a material and then copied it from the material in the scene to a new material in the Material Editor. This allows you to use maps in a variety of places without starting from scratch. If you clone the map with the Copy option, there is no connection between the old and new maps. If you choose the Instance option, either one of the maps automatically changes when you change one.

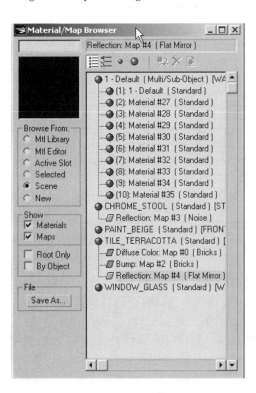

Figure 6.47   Drag and drop the Flat Mirror map from a material in the scene to a new material in the Material Editor to copy the map with all settings intact.

Figure 6.48   Choose the Copy option in the Instance (Copy) Map dialog
to make changes to each map independently.

note   If you render the Perspective viewport, you may not see much reflection
on the WINDOW_PANE object. Viewing angle and lighting in a scene can
greatly influence the final rendered material.

tip   When working with reflecting materials, it is often helpful to hide all objects
except the object with the reflecting material, then create a primitive object
such as Box or Cylinder close to the object to test the reflective qualities. When you see
the reflection is correct, you can delete the new primitive object and unhide the rest of
the scene.

Raytrace Material Type

Up to this point in the chapter you have been working with the Standard material
type. Many of the materials you will create for your 3ds max 4 scenes will probably
be Standard materials. Standard does not mean simple or boring. On the contrary,
you can create some very beautiful and complex materials with the Standard type.

It is beyond the scope of this book to delve into all the material types available in 3ds
max 4. But in this section you will learn the fundamentals of using a Raytrace material. You could obtain similar reflection results with a Standard material and a

Raytrace map in the Reflection slot. However, the Raytrace material type has attributes that other material types do not have and are worth a basic introduction.

In Exercise 6.8 you will learn to create a Raytrace material to apply to the COUNTER object in the diner scene. You will create the material as a polished stainless steel and assign it to the whole counter. Later in the chapter you will return to the material and adjust it for use on selected parts of the counter mesh.

Exercise 6.8: The Raytrace Material Type

1. Open the file called MASTER_DINER19.MAX from Exercise 6.7 or from the CD-ROM. Save it as MASTER_DINER20.MAX. Click on the lower-right Sample Window to activate it. Click on the Standard button to the right of the material name field. Make sure that New is checked in the Browse From area and double-click in Raytrace in the material list (see Figure 6.49).

Figure 6.49   In the Material Editor, click the Standard button, and double-click Raytrace in the Material/Map Browser to change the material type.

2. The Raytrace Basic Parameters rollout is considerably different from the Standard material Blinn
Basic Parameters rollout (see Figure 6.50). Instead of
adding a Raytrace map to the Reflection map slot as
you did in Standard material, you adjust the brightness of the Reflect color slot to activate reflections
here. Black is no reflection, and white is 100 percent reflection. In the Raytrace Basic Parameters
rollout, click the Reflect color swatch, and in the
Color Selector, enter 150 in the Value field to make
it a middle gray.

> **tip**
>
> If you change the color in
> the Reflect color swatch to
> something other than a
> gray color, the hue is
> mixed into the reflection
> as a tint. This allows for
> subtle variations with
> Raytrace map reflections
> that are not possible with
> other material types.

3. In the Material Editor, enter COUNTER_RAYTRACE
in the material name field. Drag and drop the
COUNTER_RAYTRACE Sample Window onto the COUNTER object in any viewport. Make sure the Perspective viewport is active and click the Quick Render button in the toolbar. You will briefly see a dialog appear in the Virtual Frame Buffer
showing the status and progress of the raytrace calculations (see Figure 6.51).
When the scene is rendered accurately, reflections are apparent on both the
curved and flat surfaces of the counter as if it were made of a polished steel sheet.

4. Close all the dialogs and save the file. It should already be called
MASTER_DINER20.MAX.

You have created a new Raytrace material type and adjusted the reflections to be
moderately strong to simulate polished steel.

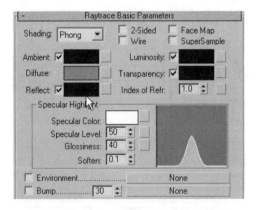

Figure 6.50   Reflection amount is based on the brightness of the
Reflection color swatch in Raytrace material.

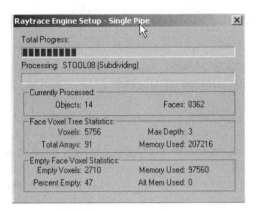

Figure 6.51   Raytrace Engine Setup dialog appears briefly as the raytrace reflections are calculated.

tip   Raytrace material does not have all the options for shader types that the other materials have. For cases where you need to control the specular highlights, you may want to use another material type with Raytrace map in the Reflection slot.

Multi/Sub-Object Material Type

One of the most powerful and flexible material types is the Multi/Sub-object material, a single material made of two or more sub-materials. The material itself is applied to a mesh object and the sub-materials are assigned to faces on the object based on the Material ID number of the face. There is no practical limit to the number of materials in a Multi/Sub-object material. The order of the sub-material corresponds to the Material ID number of the face.

In Exercise 6.9 you will learn to change an existing Standard material into a Multi/Sub-object material while retaining the original material to be assigned to all faces with Material ID #1. The example will require editing one of the STOOL objects to select the cushion faces and assigning Material ID #2 to those faces. The faces with Material ID #2 will then receive the second material in the Multi/Sub-object material list. All the stools will change accordingly because you used the Instance option when you cloned them.

Exercise 6.9: Creating and Assigning a Multi/Sub-Object Material Type

1. Open MASTER_DINER20.MAX that you saved in Exercise 6.8 or from the CD-ROM. Save the file as MASTER_DINER21.MAX. Open the Material Editor and click the CHROME_STOOL Sample Window if it is not already active. In the Material Editor, click on the Standard material type button below right of the Sample Windows. Double-click on Multi/Sub-object material type in the Material/Map Browser list. In the Replace Material dialog, make sure Keep old material as sub-material? option is checked (see Figure 6.52) and click OK. The CHROME_STOOL material is now the first material in the Multi/Sub-object material list. It will be assigned to all faces with Material ID #1 which, on the current object, is all faces.

2. In the Multi/Sub-Object Basic Parameter rollout, click the Set Number button and change the Number of Materials to 3. In the Material Editor, click on the Material/Map Navigator button, and in the Material/Map Navigator dialog, choose [2]: Material #37 [Standard] in the list to go to that material (see Figure 6.53). The number in the name could be different in your scene. Name this material VINYL_RED. It is a Standard material type.

3. In the Blinn Basic Parameters rollout, click on the Diffuse color swatch, and in the Color Selector, change it to a bright red: Red = 200, Green = 65, Blue = 45. Click the lock toggle to unlock the Ambient color swatch, click on the Ambient color swatch, and enter 80 in the Value field of the Color Selector. This makes it much darker. Click on the Specular color swatch and make it pure white.

4. In the Blinn Basic Parameters rollout, Specular Highlights area, make Specular Level = 60 and Glossiness = 40 for a fairly bright, small specular highlight. Close all dialog windows.

5. Click the Select button in the toolbar, and in the Front viewport, pick any one of the STOOL objects. Click on the Zoom Extents Selected button to zoom on the selected stool in the Front viewport (see Figure 6.54).

Figure 6.52   With the Keep old material as sub-material? option checked, click OK in the Replace Material dialog.

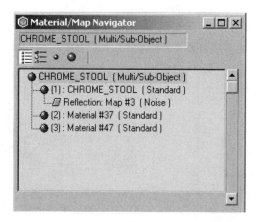

Figure 6.53   In the Material/Map Navigator dialog, choose [2]: Material #37 [Standard] in the list to go to that material.

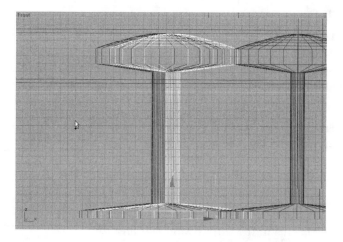

Figure 6.54   With any stool selected in the Front viewport, click Zoom Extents Selected to fill the viewport with the selected stool.

6. In the Modify panel, click Modifier List, and click Mesh Select in the Selection Modifiers area of the Modifier List (see Figure 6.55). The Mesh Select modifier allows you to select at sub-object level only. You can then apply other modifiers to the selection made in Mesh Select. In the Stack view, expand Mesh Select and choose Polygon (see Figure 6.56).

Figure 6.56
In Stack view, expand Mesh
Select, and choose Polygon.

Figure 6.55
Choose Mesh Select modifier
in the Selection Modifiers
area of the Modifier List.

7. In the Front viewport, type W to maximize the
   viewport, click the Select button, and drag a
   Crossing selection window around the cushion
   faces of the stool. The selected faces will highlight
   red.

8. In the Modify panel, click on Modifier List again,
   and click Material in the Surface Modifiers area (see
   Figure 6.57). In the Parameters rollout enter 2 in the Material ID field (see Figure
   6.58). This changes the Material ID number of the selected faces to 2 to receive
   the second material of the Multi/Sub-object material, red vinyl.

9. In the Modify panel, click on the Modifier List, and click Mesh Select again. This
   is an important step. It applies an empty Mesh Select to give you control of the
   whole stool object, not just the last selection set. Render the Perspective viewport
   and the stools will have flat gray bases with red vinyl cushions. What has hap-
   pened is that a Bevel Profile modifier creates a mesh object with Material ID #1

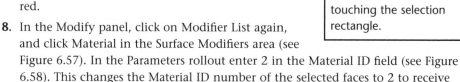

note

Crossing selection mode
selects all faces inside or
touching the selection
rectangle.

on the top cap, Material ID #2 on the bottom cap, and Material ID #3 on the body. You have selected specific faces of the body and changed the Material ID number from 3 to 1.

10. In the Material Editor, Multi/Sub-Object Basic Parameters rollout, drag and drop the CHROME_STOOL [Standard] button from slot 1 to slot 3. Choose Swap in the Instance (Copy) Material dialog (see Figure 6.59) and click OK. Render the scene and the bases of the stools should be chrome.

11. Save the file. It should already be named MASTER_DINER21.MAX.

You have learned to change a material into a Multi/Sub-object material while retaining the original as a sub-material. You then modified a second material in the Multi/Sub-object material. Next you edited an object in the scene by selecting faces and adding a Material modifier to change the ID number of the selected faces. Finally, you added another Mesh Select modifier to get control of the whole mesh. Rendering shows two materials on one object. Either the Material IDs on objects or the order of the materials in the list can be changed to affect material assignments on objects.

tip

Another option would be to change the ID number in the ID column of the Multi/Sub-Object Basic Parameters rollout in the Material Editor. When you enter 3 in the ID column for the first material you will get an error message warning of Duplicate Material ID's. Enter 1 in the ID column for the third material and the error message will clear.

This exercise shows the flexibility of Multi/Sub-Object materials and that you have options to change the Material ID numbers on the faces, reorder the numbers in the ID column, or reorder the materials themselves.

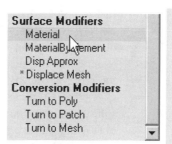

Figure 6.57
Choose Material modifier in the Surface Modifiers area of the Modifier List.

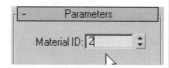

Figure 6.58
Enter 2 in the Material ID field of the Parameters rollout. This assigns Material ID #2 to only the selected faces.

Figure 6.59
Choose Swap in the Instance (Copy) Material dialog and click OK.

In Exercise 6.10 you will learn a method of assigning Multi/Sub-object materials to objects created from 2D shapes by Lofting, Extrude modifier and Lathe modifier. Each of these modeling techniques starts with a 2D shape that can have Material IDs assigned to the sub-object Segment or Spline. Then in the Modifier panel for the mesh object there is a checkbox called Use Shape IDs under the Generate Material IDs checkbox. The faces of the mesh object that are created from any given segment or spline will have that corresponding material from the Multi/Sub-object material list. Lofted objects have the extra bonus of generating mapping coordinates that follow the loft path.

Exercise 6.10: Multi/Sub-Object Materials Assigned by Segment or Spline Level

1. Open the file called MASTER_DINER21.MAX from Exercise 6.9 or from the CD-ROM. Save it as MASTER_DINER22.MAX. You will change the material on the counter top by editing the 2D cross-sectional shape and changing the Material ID at Segment sub-object level. You will then make the material a Multi/Sub-object material and add a brown wood-colored material to be assigned to the part of the mesh defined by the 2D segments.

2. Right-click in the Top viewport to activate it and press W to maximize it. Click the Select button, press H, and double-click counter_profile in the Select Objects list (see Figure 6.60). Use the Region Zoom viewport navigation button to zoom in to the lower part of the compound shape (see Figure 6.61).

Figure 6.60   Click the Select button and double-click counter_profile in the list to select it.

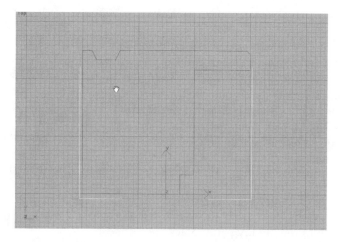

Figure 6.61   In the Top viewport, Region Zoom in on the lower counter spline of the compound shape.

3. In the Modify panel, Stack view, choose Segment, and in the Top viewport, pick the seven segments that make up the top and front of the counter top. They will highlight red (see Figure 6.62). In the Modify panel, Surface Properties, change the Material ID to 2 (see Figure 6.63). Any mesh generated in the loft object from these segments will get the second material in a Multi/Sub-object material list. By default all segments have Material ID #1 assigned. In the Stack view, choose Editable Spline to exit sub-object editing.

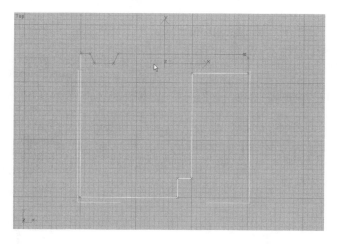

Figure 6.62   In sub-object Segment mode, select the seven segments at the top and front of the counter top spline.

note Some of the Modify panels have many rollouts, and it can take a fair amount of scrolling to find the rollout you want. Position the cursor in the Modify panel to get the hand cursor, right-click, and choose the rollout you want from the pop-up menu (see Figure 6.64). In 3ds max 4 you can also drag and drop rollouts to rearrange them in the Modifier Stack for faster access.

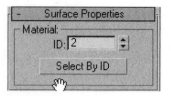

Figure 6.63
In the Surface Properties of the Modify panel, change the Material ID to 2.

4. Press W to minimize the Top viewport. In the Perspective viewport, select the COUNTER object in the scene. In the Modify panel, Stack view, choose Loft to drop to that level. In the Surface Parameters rollout, Materials area, check the Use Shape IDs (see Figure 6.65). This lets 3ds max 4 know to use the Segment Material ID that you assigned to the 2D shape. In Stack view, choose Smooth to return to the top of the Modifier Stack.

caution Forgetting to check the Use Shape IDs option for the mesh object is the most common reason this process appears to fail for users.

5. Open the Material Editor and choose COUNTER_RAYTRACE Sample Window. It is the Raytrace chrome material used on the entire counter. You will change it to a Multi/Sub-object material and keep this material as a sub-material. In the Material Editor, click the Raytrace material type button on the right of the material name. Double-click Multi/Sub-Object in the Material/Map Browser list (see Figure 6.66). Check Keep old material? as sub-material in the Replace Material dialog (see Figure 6.67). Click OK.

Figure 6.64
With the hand cursor in the Modify panel, right-click to choose a new rollout from the pop-up menu. The figure shows the Surface Properties rollout highlighted as an example. Clicking on Surface Properties would take you directly to the rollout.

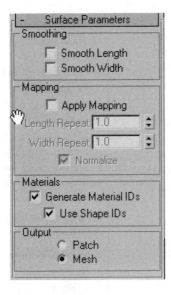

Figure 6.65
In the Modify panel, Surface Parameters rollout, check Use Shape IDs.

Figure 6.66
Click the Raytrace material type button and double-click Multi/Sub-Object in the list.

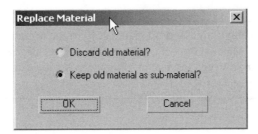

Figure 6.67   Choose Keep old material as sub-material? in the Replace Material dialog and click OK.

6. In the Material Editor, Multi/Sub-Object Basic Parameters rollout, click on the material name button in the list of sub-materials. In the material name field enter WOOD_BROWN. In the Blinn Basic Parameters rollout, unlock the Ambient and Diffuse color swatches. Click on the Diffuse color swatch, and in the Color

Selector, adjust it for a medium-brown color to simulate wood. Drag and drop the Diffuse color swatch
onto the Ambient, choose Copy in the Copy or
Swap dialog, and darken the Value in the Color
Selector. Click in the Specular color swatch, and in
the Color Selector, set it to pure white.

7. In the Blinn Basic Parameters rollout, set Specular
   Level = 60 and Glossiness = 45 for a polished look.
   Right-click in the Perspective viewport to activate it
   and click the Quick Render button in the toolbar.
   The top of the counter and the base should have
   the polished steel while the countertop itself
   appears to be wood.

8. Close all dialogs and save the file. It should already
   be called MASTER_DINER22.MAX.

You have used the Material IDs generated by the
Segment Material ID assignments made on the original 2D cross section. Use this method of material
assignment for flexible and rapid changes on simple or complex objects.

note

No specific color numbers
are given to allow you to
think about what is appropriate for you. Start developing your artistic talents
as soon as you can in the
process. Avoid using pre-
made materials and maps
"out of the can" or adjust
them to put your signature
on the rendering you
create.

Tutorials should guide you
in thinking, not teach you
to make this or that. You
are the artist.

Take the time to experiment with the material on the walls that is in the first Sample
Window. You created this as a dummy material to see the effects of Segment Material
IDs in Chapter 4.

tip

You can also drag and drop materials from the Material/Map Browser
onto the Material slots of the Multi/Sub-object material. This is handy
for retrieving materials stored in Material Libraries that you will learn about in the
next section.

Material Libraries

As mentioned earlier in the chapter, you can only have a maximum of 24 Sample
Windows at any time, but there is no limit to the number of materials in a scene. You
have created six materials, not counting the sub-materials, and assigned them to
objects in the scene.

When you save the scene, the materials that have been assigned to objects are saved
in the file as well as in the Material Editor. However, if you open a new 3ds max 4 session or do a File/Reset, you are presented with the default Material Editor with gray

materials in all Sample Windows. You have no access to the materials you created in the diner scene.

In 3ds max 4 you can create Material Libraries, files with a .mat file type that are stored on your hard drive. These can be opened from any max file for access to the materials defined in them.

It is usually appropriate to create a Material Library for each project, and perhaps, libraries for metals, woods, plastics, and so on. Use whatever works for you and your coworkers for organizational purposes.

The process is simple. To use materials stored in a Material Library, you use the Get Material button in the Material Editor and choose Browse From: Mtl Library. This shows a list of materials and maps in the currently active library (see Figure 6.68). Materials are designated with a blue sphere while maps have a green or red parallelogram. You can drag and drop a material from the Browser to the Material Editor.

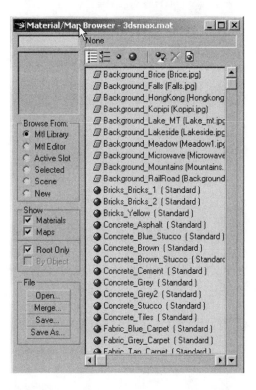

Figure 6.68   In the Material/Map Browser, you see a typical Material Library.

To create you own Material Library you first clear the existing library by picking the Clear Material button at the top right of the Material/Map Browser (see Figure 6.69). You are presented with a dialog asking Are you sure you want to delete all materials in the library? (see Figure 6.70). Answer Yes.

tip

This only clears the materials in the list; it does not delete the materials from the library on the hard drive.

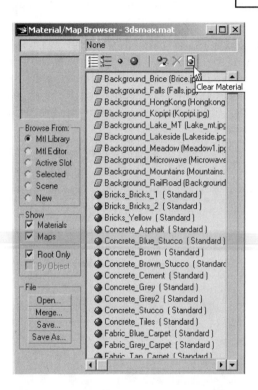

Figure 6.69   Click the Clear Material button in Material/Map Browser to start a new library.

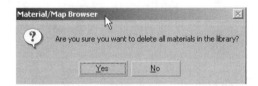

Figure 6.70   Answer Yes to Are you sure you want to delete all materials in the library? This does not delete any files or material definitions on the hard drive.

Now you can drag and drop the Sample Windows from the Material Editor into the Browser list to put the materials into the unnamed library. Use the Material/Map Browser File: Save As button to save the current Material Library to the hard drive with a new name. Name the file and click the Save button in the Save Material Library dialog (see Figure 6.71). Conversely, you can use the File: Open button to open new Material Libraries at any time.

After you have saved a Material Library with a name of your choice, you can put new materials into it without resaving. It will be saved automatically after you exit the file.

warning

On computers with Microsoft Access, the .mat file type may be registered in File Associations for Access. This can cause the 3ds max 4 .mat library files not to show in the Material/Map Browser. Change the file type association to 3ds max 4 to correct the situation.

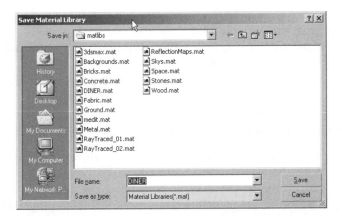

Figure 6.71   Name the new Material Library file (.mat) and click Save to create a new Material Library on your hard drive.

Shader Fundamentals

The following discussion is to encourage you to develop an eye for details in scenes that we take for granted and often leave out of our computer renderings. Read the chapter section and look around in the real world for examples.

As mentioned earlier in the chapter, specular highlights are the very first clue to the viewer as to what a material may be, and it is the least understood and unappreciated aspect of materials. A quick look around a typical office will reveal many different materials. You will quickly identify metal, plastic, cardboard, paper, rubber, and cloth. But what is it that causes you to recognize the differences? It is generally the specular highlight, the (usually) white spot of bounced light from the surface. The specular highlight's size, shape, and sharpness are based on the hardness and porosity of the surface. The specular highlights are the effect of the light scattering as it hits the surface and is affected at the molecular level of the material and by the surface conditions.

Materials with molecules that are tightly packed are hard and not very porous, a billiard ball, for example. Many materials appear shiny but, if you look closely, the type of shininess is very different for each material. Plastic, for example, can be very hard, but its specular highlights are rounder and have a softer edge than chrome in the same light.

Additionally, metals can have a grain similar to that of wood and, depending on the manufacturing process (cast, rolled, or forged, for example), often have elongated specular highlights. Compounding the elongation of the specular highlights are the surface scratches and coatings that may even cause metals to have two specular highlights at differing angles as can be seen on stainless steel. How sharp or soft a specular highlight is at its edge is also an important factor in providing a clue as to the type of material. At the other edge of the spectrum are the soft materials such as rubber and fabric, which typically have a duller specular highlight with a very soft edge.

3ds max 4 has shaders that help define the specular highlights of materials in conjunction with the Specular Level and Glossiness values. You can use the Online Reference to see the descriptions of each shader and the general usage. Then look through some of the sample materials included with each program and compare the settings for various materials.

Most importantly, however, spend some time studying specular highlights in the real world to determine what it is you are trying to replicate in the Material Editor. It is the myriad of small, bright specular highlights that give the scene a crispness and snap that are often missing in computer renderings, leaving the scene flat with no depth.

You have already seen how you can adjust the brightness and size of specular highlights in a material with the Specular Level and Glossiness settings.

The other available specular controls are the various shaders. These are used to adjust the shape of specular highlights and edge transition from specular to diffuse. Figure 6.72. shows the Shaders pull-down in the Material Editor.

The following is a fundamental description of the shaders available in most material types:

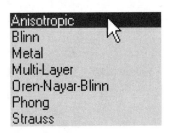

Figure 6.72
These types are available from Shader pull-down in Material Editor.

- **Anisotropic** Anisotropy is the elongation of the specular highlight that can be caused by surface scratches or molecular alignment in metals and extruded materials.

- **Blinn** This gives round specular highlights and is good for plastic and paint. Phong shader is very similar to Blinn, with Blinn being the newer method.

- **Strauss** Strauss and Metal shaders are similar. The color of the specular component is derived directly from the Diffuse color. This is appropriate for metals like gold, bronze, or anodized aluminum.

- **Multi-Layer** This has two separate anisotropic specular components and would be similar to the specular highlights of stainless steel. One set of highlights is from the metal, and another is from the surface scratches giving a cross-pattern effect.

- **Oren-Nayer-Blinn** This is a soft, round specular highlight good for representing porous materials like rubber, cloth, and human skin.

Use this list as a guide only. Experiment with the various settings to try to interpret what you see in the real world using your own artistic sensibilities.

Mapping Coordinates

You have already applied a UVW Map modifier to your floor in the diner scene to adjust the pattern of the floor tiles for size and position. A fundamental overview of some mapping options will help you investigate the subject further as you work with 3ds max 4.

UVW Map Modifier

Think of the UVW Map modifier as sort of a projector. In the floor example you used in this chapter, the mapping type was Planer where the maps are projected in a plane and mapped on a surface. There are other options for the style of mapping (see Figure 6.73). Usually the best option to start with is the most closely fits the shape of the object. Use the Online Reference for more detail on each mapping type.

The Tile setting for the three axes allow you to repeat the map pattern independently of adjusting the size of the Map Gizmo. You can flip images used as maps with the checkboxes.

There are also handy alignment tools for the Map Gizmo to help position the pattern on objects.

UVW Unwrap Modifier

The UVW Unwrap modifier allows you access to the vertex position on the mesh as it relates to maps. You can move coordinate vertices to adjust the position of the map on the surface. Figure 6.74 shows an over-stuffed chair from the diner scene with a bitmap and the vertex coordinate points of the optimized mesh as seen from the top.

You can select the vertices and transform them to better fit the map for your purposes. This can be very helpful in fine-tuning the placement of maps on surfaces.

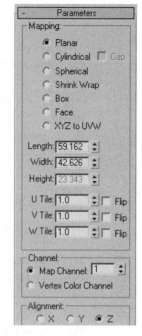

Figure 6.73
The UVW Map modifier, Parameters rollout.

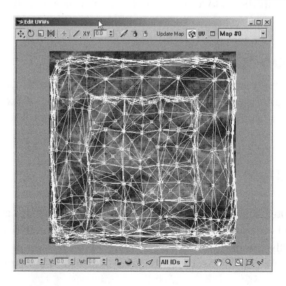

Figure 6.74   UVW Unwrap modifier is applied to an overstuffed chair as seen from the top.

Loft Mapping Coordinates

One of the advantages of lofting objects over other forms of modeling is that the loft process generates mapping coordinates along the loft path. When you modify the object to change its shape, the mapping coordinates are adjusted to the new shape. Good examples of this type of mapping would be the skin on a snake or the dotted passing line on a road. See Figure 6.75 for a simple lofted object with a checkered pattern applied with Loft Coordinates. The Length Repeat and Width Repeat are adjusted in the Surface Parameters rollout of the loft mesh object.

Again, it is beyond the scope of this book to delve into the nuances of mapping, but be aware that you have several options and experiment with simple examples to get a feel for how each works.

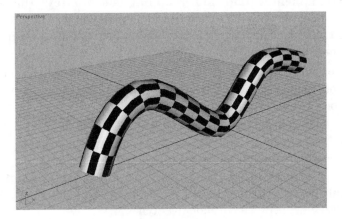

Figure 6.75   In this Loft object with checkered pattern, mapping coordinates are derived from the loft path and adjusted in the Surface Parameters rollout of the object.

Chapter Summary

- **Fundamental material types**   You learned about the difference between materials and maps and about the material types available in 3ds max 4.

- **Navigating the Material Editor**   In this section you learned about the different areas of the Material Editor and how to navigate around from materials to maps and back. Navigating quickly throughout the Material Editor is a boon to productivity.

- **Material basic parameters**   This section afforded an overview of some of the commonly used parameters of a Standard material type. By understanding the basic information and layering it over and over, you can create complex materials that make your rendered images stand out against the competition.

- **Fundamental maps and mapping coordinates**   This section aided you in understanding the fundamentals of maps and mapping coordinates that are so important in sizing and positioning the material patterns for a more convincing rendered images.

- **Concepts and use of shaders**   Developing a sense of how shaders affect your perception of materials is probably the most important aspect of creating convincing materials. The specular highlights give the viewers the cue they are looking at steel, wood, cloth, or any other material you want to represent in the scene.

- **Organizing with Material Libraries**   You learned how to create and store your materials in Material Libraries that can be accessed from other files or by other users. It is critical to use logical libraries to avoid duplication of effort and disparities between collaborative scenes.

Lighting: Get a Grip on max 4 Lights

In This Chapter

Lighting a scene in 3ds max 4 is one of the most challenging aspects of creating convincing rendered images. In this chapter you will learn the fundamentals of the mechanics of setting and adjusting lights. Take the time to become comfortable with the tools available. Start with a minimum number of lights in a scene, and work your way up to more complexity and artistic expression.

> **note**   Reread the sections in Chapter 1 and Chapter 2 of this book on the general concepts of lighting in an artistic sense and the concepts of lighting issues specific to 3ds max 4 before proceeding.

Adding a lot of lights to a scene early in the cycle is usually a shortcut to disaster. Keep in mind as you add lights that they are not only allowing you to see the scene but they also will be having a profound effect on the materials in the scene. Try to develop a workflow where you apply your materials and lights in conjunction with each other for a more predictable results.

Shadow casting lights are an important part of most scenes. It is the shadows that give objects the appearance of having weight and that anchor those objects to the ground. The mathematics and computer resources involved in calculating shadows can quickly bring even the most powerful computer to its knees.

You will also learn about 3ds max 4 cameras in this chapter. While cameras and lights are certainly different types of objects created for entirely different reasons, they do share some similarity in placement and controls.

Some of the fundamental topics that will be covered in this chapter include:

- Deciphering 3ds max 4 light types
- Basic light parameters
- Adjusting light intensity
- Light exclude/include features
- Principles of shadow casting lights
- Light attenuation
- Using Projector maps in lights
- Applying Environment effects
- Placing and adjusting cameras

Key Terms

Angle of incidence   The more a surface inclines away from a light source, the less light it receives and the darker it appears. The angle of the surface normal relative to the light source is known as the angle of incidence.

Omni light   An Omni light provides a point source of illumination that shoots out in all directions and casts light to infinity.

Spotlight   A spotlight casts a focused beam of light in a cone like a flashlight, a follow spot in a theater, or a headlight.

Direct light   Directional lights cast parallel light rays within a cylinder, as the sun does (for all practical purposes) at the surface of the earth.

Ambient light   Ambient light is the general light that illuminates the entire scene. It has a uniform intensity and is uniformly diffuse. It has no discernible source and no discernible direction

Radiosity   Radiosity is the light bounced from surfaces in the scene onto other surfaces. 3ds max 4 does not calculate radiosity; you must use a program like Lightscape.

Attenuation   In the real world, light diminishes over distance. Objects far from the light source appear darker; objects near the source appear brighter. This effect is known as attenuation.

Shadow maps   A Shadow map is a bitmap that the renderer generates during a pre-rendering pass of the scene. Shadow maps don't show the color cast by transparent or translucent objects. Shadow maps can have soft-edged shadows.

Raytrace shadows   Raytraced shadows are generated by tracing the path of rays sampled from a light source. Raytraced shadows are more accurate than shadow-mapped shadows. They always produce a hard edge.

tip

There are three settings in Shadow maps that can have profound effect on the quality of the shadows. The settings are found in the Shadow Map Params rollout in the Modify panel. In 3ds max 4, Shadow maps are actual bitmap images that are generated at render time and composited into the final image. The adjustments include:

Bias   Bias moves the shadow toward or away from the light source. Smaller numbers move the shadows toward the light, and larger numbers move it away. The Absolute Map Bias checkbox in the Shadow Map Params rollout should be checked for large scenes such as exterior architectural or civil landscapes.

Size   Map size is the resolution of the Shadow map that is superimposed onto the image at render time. The default is 512×512. A good rule of thumb is to start with a resolution that is equal to the largest size of the rendered image. For example, a 1024×768 rendering would start with a 1024 Shadow map size. Larger maps require more computer resources.

Sample range   Sample range adjusts the softness of edge of the shadow. Small numbers give a saw tooth appearance, and large numbers result in soft edges.

The three settings work in concert with each other, so adjusting one may require adjusting the others. For example. A higher map size makes the shadows crisper and will override the sample range settings. Large scenes with large and small objects will require different settings than small scenes with large objects or small scenes with small objects.

This is not a science, but an art. You must experiment with each combination of lights and scenes to find appropriate settings.

In the diner scene, a small scene with moderate sized objects, the default settings will be fine, and you will not likely need any adjustments for acceptable shadows.

Raytraced shadows only have a bias adjustment to move the shadows toward or away from the light source.

Light Types in 3ds max 4

There are four light types available in 3ds max 4. Three of the light types, Omni, Spot, and Direct are physical objects that you can treat similarly to any other object type in 3ds max 4. The fourth light type, Ambient, is not a physical object but an overall level of illumination that can be raised or lowered in the scene.

Each type of light has particular qualities that offer flexibility in placement and control. The following list is a thumbnail sketch of the general properties of the different light types:

■ **Ambient** General level of illumination from no apparent source.

■ **Omni** Single point source light radiating in all directions to infinity by default.

■ **Spot** Light radiating from the source within a cone to infinity by default.

> **tip**
>
> You will generally have better lighting results if you keep the Ambient light color set to pure black, which is off. This increases contrast between lit and unlit area. Only adjust it for special effects.

■ **Direct** Light radiating from the source within a cylinder to infinity by default.

Light can be created by accessing the Create panel, Lights panel, (see Figure 7.1) or from the Lights & Camera tab panel (see Figure 7.2).

You will notice in the both the Create panel and the Lights & Camera tab panel there are more than four types of lights. The Ambient light does not show up in the either panel because it is not a physical object that can be created and placed in a scene.

The Spot and Direct lights each have a Target or Free version as options in the panels. The light, either Spot or Direct, has the same attributes and controls in Target or Free variations, and the differences are more in how the light is used in the scene.

■ **Target Spot or Direct** These are created by picking anywhere in a scene to set the light source object and dragging and releasing the mouse to set the target. The light always points at its target. Target lights (and Cameras) are primarily used as fixed or limited motion range lights. Both the light and its target can be animated independently but in general use they would be stationary.

■ **Free Spot or Direct** These are created with a single pick anywhere in the scene to place the light source. The direction of the light is in the negative z-axis of the active viewport. Free lights (and Cameras) are best for animating along a path. For example, the headlights of a moving car. The headlight always points straight ahead in relation to the car and does not track a single point in space.

Figure 7.1

Access Create panel, Lights panel to create lights.

Figure 7.2   You can also create lights from the Lights & Camera tab panel.

These suggestions are not hard-and-fast rules, for either of the light types can be used interchangeably but are the intended general application. Feel free to experiment.

Ambient Light

Ambient light does not have an equivalent light in the real world. Perhaps the closest analogy might be the light you would find if you crawled under your car on a foggy day. It is light enough for you to see, but there is no apparent light source.

> **note**
>
> By default there is one Omni light in the scene in 3ds max 4. The default light goes out as soon as you add a light of your own and returns if you delete all your own lights.

Think back to Chapter 6, "Materials: Applying Surface Colors and Patterns" where you learned about Ambient color in the Material Editor. Ambient color is the color of a material where there is no direct light striking the surface. The intensity of the Ambient light in the scene affects the Ambient colors much more than the Diffuse or Specular colors. Increasing or decreasing the light in these shaded or shadowed portions of the scene can greatly affect the overall contrast in the scene. Low Ambient light gives high contrast while high Ambient levels give low contrast.

In Exercise 7.1 you will adjust the Ambient light in two places: one will be in the current scene, and the other will be in the System Preferences. By setting the Ambient light level in the System Preferences you ensure that the light will be set to that level for all new 3ds max 4 scenes. Adjusting the Ambient light in the current scene affects only that scene.

The general consensus among most 3ds max 4 users is to set the Ambient light to black so it has no effect on your scene. This allows better control of contrast. Raise the Ambient light levels for special cases including:

- **Night scenes**   Push the Ambient light level up with a bias toward blue color. This adds a cool atmosphere that accentuates the warmth of any reddish or yellow lights in the scene.

- **Bright sun or snow scenes**   Again with a slight level of blue color added to the Ambient light, the shadows take on the bluish tint you see in photographs making the scene more convincing to the viewer.

- **Foggy or hazy atmospheres**   This reduces the contrast of colors much the same way real fog does. Gray or very light blue can be effective.

> **tip**
>
> What our eyes see and what our brains perceive can be very different. While a the film in a camera often shows very blue shadows in bright sunlight, our brains tend to counteract that effect and we perceive just the color we expect. You have to develop a critical eye to discern the difference between perception and reality and translate that into a convincing image for the viewer.

Exercise 7.1: Adjusting Ambient Light

1. Open the file called MASTER_DINER22.MAX that you saved in Chapter 6 or from the CD-ROM. Save the file as MASTER_DINER23.MAX. The scene has a single Omni light as the illumination source set high in the middle of the room, and, therefore, that scene has many areas shaded from direct light.

2. The default Ambient light setting in 3ds max 4 is pure black or a color Value setting of 0. In the Rendering pull-down menu, choose Environment (see Figure 7.3). In the Environment dialog, Common Parameters rollout, click on the Ambient color swatch in the Global Lighting area (see Figure 7.4).

Figure 7.3
In the Rendering pull-down menu, choose Environment.

Figure 7.4   Click on the Ambient color swatch in Common Parameters rollout. The default setting is a Value of 0, or pure black.

3. Right-click in the Perspective viewport to make sure it is the active viewport. In the toolbar, click the Quick Render button to render the scene. Close the Virtual Frame Buffer, and in the Rendering pull-down menu, choose RAM Player. In the RAM player, click the teapot button for Channel A to open the last rendered image in Channel A (see Figure 7.5). Click OK in the RAM Player Configuration dialog to load the image you just rendered. Minimize the RAM Player.

4. In the Rendering pull-down, choose Environment. In the Environment dialog, click on the Ambient color swatch, and in the Color Selector, slide the Value slider to the far right or enter 255 in the Value field. This makes the Ambient color pure white or full brightness. Close the Environment dialog.

> **note**
>
> Do not adjust the Background color instead of the Ambient color.
>
> The Background color is only the backdrop against which the scene is rendered. It is black by default. It adds no colored light to the scene.

> **tip**
>
> You could also drag and drop the Global Tinting, Tint color swatch onto the Ambient swatch and copy it.

Click the Render Last button in the toolbar, and then close the Virtual Frame Buffer. Maximize the RAM Player and click the teapot button for Channel B. Click OK in the RAM Player Configuration dialog to load the last rendered image into Channel B. A comparison of the two images shows a radical difference in rendered images (see Figure 7.6). With the full intensity Ambient light, the scene in Channel B is washed out with no contrast. The image in Channel A has a much

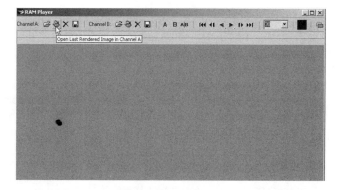

Figure 7.5   Click the teapot button in Channel A of the RAM Player to load the last rendered image into that channel.

Figure 7.6   Load the high Ambient setting image into Channel B of the RAM Player to compare the two.

more 3D feel caused by the differences between the lightest and darkest areas. You can click and drag on the small white triangle at the top or bottom of the images in RAM Player to show more of less of the images in each channel. Close the RAM Player.

5. While it would be unlikely to set the Ambient light to the full amount, even small increases in the setting can wash out a scene, leaving it flat. Adding slight amounts of color to the Ambient color swatch can shift the material you see in the rendered image to be very different from what you create in the Material Editor. In the Rendering pull-down, Environment dialog, set the Ambient color swatch back to pure black and close the Environment dialog.

6. Save the file which should already be named MASTER_DINER23.MAX. You have learned to adjust the Ambient color setting to lower the contrast of a scene.

note

At this point, your file is no different than the file you started with at the beginning of the exercise. You have saved it with a new name for consistency in the exercises.

It is important to be aware of the Ambient light color setting and its effect on scenes. At some point you may encounter a tutorial or situation in which you increase the setting and forget to set it back to black.

tip

If you are consistently having trouble getting good scene lighting and good materials, always check the Ambient light level as a possible cause.

Omni Lights

Omni lights are point lights that cast light equally in all directions. By default, shadow casting for all lights is disabled in 3ds max 4, therefore the light shines through objects in the scene to infinity.

 caution

Placing three or more default Omni lights in a scene will quickly confuse even experienced users. Because the lights shine in all directions to infinity you lose control of where light originates on any particular surface.

In Exercise 7.2 you will learn to place and adjust Omni lights for a starting point in illuminating your scene. The point of the exercise is to introduce you to the fundamentals of light parameters, not to light your diner scene artistically. A very important aspect of all lighting is that of angle of incidence. This exercise will illustrate the effect and show you how to use it to your advantage. You will also learn how to adjust the intensity of the light at its source.

Exercise 7.2: Placing and Adjusting Omni Lights

tip

Each viewport can be saved in its own buffer, but only one version of each viewport can be saved at any time.

1. Open the file called MASTER_DINER23.MAX that you saved in Exercise 7.1 or from the CD-ROM. Save the file as MASTER_DINER24.MAX. You already have one Omni light in the scene that you will delete to return to a default lighting scheme. With the Perspective viewport active, in the Views pull-down menu, choose Save Active Perspective View (see Figure 7.7). This stores the viewport in a disk buffer area. You will later restore this view after zooming out in the viewport.

2. Click on the Zoom Extents All button to zoom all viewports to show all objects in the scene. Click the Select button, type H, and double-click Omni01 in the Select Objects list to select it (see Figure 7.8). Press the Delete key to delete the light from the scene.

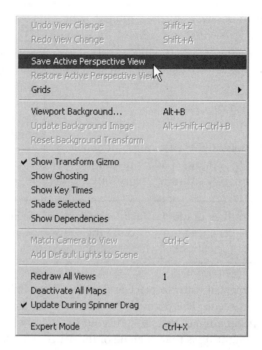

Figure 7.7   With the Perspective viewport active, choose Save Active
Perspective View in the Views pull-down menu.

Figure 7.8   Click the Select button, type H, and double-click Omni01.
Press the Delete key to delete it and return to default lighting.

3. In the Views pull-down menu, choose Restore Active Perspective View to get the view back to the state before you did a Zoom Extents All.

4. In the Create panel, Lights panel, click the Omni button (see Figure 7.9). In the Top viewport, pick in the middle of the ceiling fan. This places an Omni light on the World Grid plane directly below the ceiling fan. The floor appears to turn black in the shaded viewports. With the Perspective viewport active, click the Quick Render button. The end wall is evenly lit and the ceiling and front and back walls show some diminishing of the light toward the end wall. (see Figure 7.10). Load the last rendered image into Channel A of the RAM Player.

Figure 7.9
In the Create panel, Lights panel, click the Omni button, and then click in the middle of the ceiling fan in the Top viewport.

Figure 7.10   The floor object appears black in the viewports and in a rendered perspective image.

> **tip**
>
> By default, the distance of a light from a surface has no effect on the brightness of the light hitting that surface. What does have a profound effect on the brightness of the light is the angle of incidence of the light to the surface. Because the Omni light is on the same plane as the floor, the angle of incidence is 0, and there is no light hitting the surface. The light is a distance from the narrow end wall with an angle of incidence ranging from 90 degrees at the bottom-middle of the wall to somewhat less at the top, giving fairly even light. The front and back walls are longer and the light is closer so the diminishing of the angle of incidence is more pronounced.

5. In the Left viewport, click the Select and Move button, or right-click in the viewport and choose Move in the Quad menu. Move the Omni01 light about halfway up the wall (see Figure 7.11). Render the Perspective viewport, close the Virtual Frame Buffer, and load the last rendered image into Channel B of the RAM Player for comparison with Channel A (see Figure 7.12). There is a noticeable change in light values on surfaces based solely on the angle of incidence.

6. In the Modify panel, General Parameters rollout, are color spinners like those found in the Color Selector. Changing the V (Value) spinner adjusts the intensity of the light from 0 to 255, or black to white color (see Figure 7.13).

> **tip**
>
> Omni, Spot, and Direct lights are all affected the same in regards to angle of incidence of the light to the receiving surface.

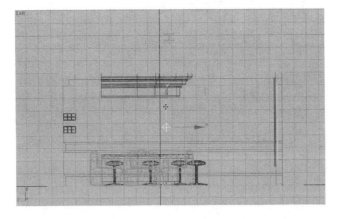

Figure 7.11   In the Left viewport, move the Omni01 light about halfway up the wall.

Figure 7.12   Note the comparison of the angle of incidence affect with an Omni light. The left side shows the light at the plane of the floor, and the right side shows the light about halfway between the floor and ceiling.

> **tip**   You can use the spinner values in General Parameters rollout or the Color Selector to change the color of any light as well as its intensity. It is advisable to wait until you have all your materials correctly in the scene before adding color to lights. Slight amounts of color in the lights can make it difficult to get accurate materials until you have considerable experience with 3ds max 4.

7. In the Modify panel, General Parameters rollout, you will see a Multiplier spinner and numeric field. Enter 2 in the Multiplier field and render the Perspective viewport. The light appears twice as bright and the scene is burned out. Enter 0.5 in the Multiplier field and click the Render Last button. This is very similar to the result you would get if you entered 128 in the Value field. Set the Multiplier back to default 1.0. Multiplier values of between 0 and 1.0 have the same effect as 0 to 255 in the Value field on light intensity. However, if you had a brightly lit scene such as a supermarket interior or a bright sunny day and you needed a light intensity above the 255, you could set higher Multiplier values to boost beyond the 255 setting.

tip If you enter negative numbers in the Multiplier field you can actually draw light out of a scene. This is an excellent method of controlling the viewer's gaze toward the important parts of the scene and away from others. Lights with negative Multiplier values should generally use attenuation (covered later in this chapter) and not have shadow casting on. Negative light values can also be used in combination with the Exclude/Include feature of lights for a powerful control tool.

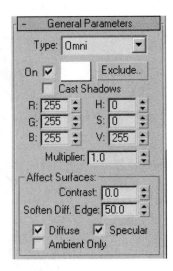

8. Save the file. It should already be named MASTER_DINER24.MAX. You have learned the fundamentals of light intensity. Angle of incidence is a prime consideration when placing lights in a scene. To get an even spread of light on the ceiling of the diner you would have to place the light far below the floor. You can also adjust intensity with the Value setting of the Color Selector or with the Multiplier to boost or diminish the current Value setting.

Figure 7.13
Adjust the Value spinner in the Modify panel, General Parameters rollout, or click on the Omni color swatch and adjust Value in the Color Selector to change the intensity of the light.

Spotlights

Spotlights in 3ds max 4 are lights that emanate from the source within a cone and shine to infinity within that cone. There are actually two cones that define the light:

- **Hotspot cone** Within the inner cone, shown as light blue in the display, the light has the full intensity defined by the Color Value and Multiplier.

- **Falloff cone** Outside the outer, dark blue cone the light has no effect, neither illumination nor shadow casting. Within the space between the Hotspot and Falloff cone the light diminishes in a linear fashion. This has the effect of softening or hardening the edge of the light where it strikes a surface.

tip It is virtually impossible to light a 3ds max 4 scene by placing lights in the positions that you would place lights in the real world. You have to "paint" the scene with light using an approach similar to more traditional artists.

Up until now you have learned that, by default, all 3ds max 4 lights shine to infinity within their defined illumination patterns, a cone for Spot, a cylinder for Direct, or omnidirectional for Omni. This is almost never a good situation to work with because you quickly lose control of where light is coming from, especially in the case of Omni lights. For Spot and Direct lights, the areas where two lights overlap on a surface becomes twice as bright, looking unconvincing.

In physics, light attenuates or diminishes based on something called the Inverse Square Law. The light on a surface is diminished according to the inverse of the square of the distance from the source ($1 \div$ distance $\times$ distance). For example, if you hold a light meter at a light and it reads 100 lumens, and then you move the meter 2 feet from the light, it will read 25 lumens ($1 \div 2 \times 2$, or $1 \div 4$), and at 4 feet from the light it will read 6.25 lumens ($1 \div 4 \times 4$, or $1 \div 16$). This is a very rapid falloff.

Lights in 3ds max 4 work differently, the default being no attenuation. However, you do have several options for simulating attenuation:

- **Far Attenuation**   This method allows you to adjust two ranges from the light source, the Start and End ranges. The light has full intensity from the source to the Start range, and then attenuates linearly to the End range. Beyond the End range you have no illumination or shadows. This is not physically accurate but very controllable.

- **Near Attenuation**   This is similar to Far Attenuation with a Start and End range; however, the light has no intensity from the light source to the Start range, and then it ramps up to full intensity at the End range. This is useful for special effects.

- **Inverse Decay**   The light has full intensity from the source to a Start range, and then attenuates based on the inverse of the distance ($1 \div$ distance) from the Start range.

- **Inverse Square Decay**   Similar to Inverse Decay, but the light attenuates based on Inverse Square of the distance from the Start range ($1 \div$ distance $\times$ distance). This is not true Inverse Square Attenuation because has a user defined starting point.

Attenuation is one of the most important factors you have available to give you the control you need to light 3ds max 4 scenes. The Far Attenuation method is easy to use and flexible and can create a convincing effect in most situations.

In Exercise 7.3 you will place a Target Spot light under the counter valance, shining on the counter. It represents the style from a recessed bowl reflector. You will then make several Instance clones of the light and adjust the Attenuation for a more convincing result.

Exercise 7.3: Placing and Adjusting Spotlights

1. Open MASTER_DINER24.MAX that you saved in Exercise 7.2 or from the CD-ROM. Save it as MASTER_DINER25.MAX. You will place a Target Spot light in the Left viewport with the source just under the counter valance and the target on the floor. Right-click in the Left viewport to activate it and type W to maximize it. In the Create panel, Lights panel, click on the Target Spot button, and in the Left viewport, click at the bottom middle of the valance and drag the mouse. Release the mouse at the floor plane to set the Target position (see Figure 7.14). Type W to minimize the viewports.

2. Right-click in the Top viewport and type W to maximize it. Right-click on the Top label and choose Wireframe in the menu. The light and target have been created in the plane that passes through 0,0,0 Absolute World Coordinate. If you move the light now, the light source will move but the target will stay in place because it is not selected. Pick the blue line that connects the light source and the light target (see Figure 7.15). The light and target are both selected. Click on the Transform Gizmo X axis constraint and move the light and target under the valance (see Figure 7.16). Type W to minimize the viewports. Right-click in Perspective viewport to activate it.

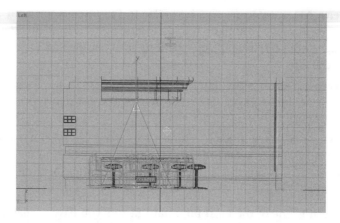

Figure 7.14   In the Create panel, Lights panel, click on the Target Spot button, and in the Left viewport, click below the bottom middle of the valance and drag to the floor plane.

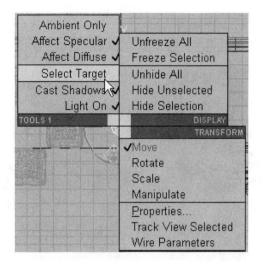

Figure 7.15   By picking on the blue line that connects the light source and the light target in the viewport you can select both the light and the target so you can move them both at the same time.

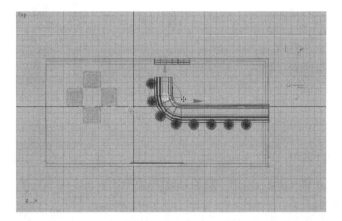

Figure 7.16   Use the Transform Gizmo X axis constraint to move the light and target under the valance.

3. Click the Quick Render button to render the Perspective viewport. There is a bright hard-edged circle of light on the counter and spilling onto the floor (see Figure 7.17). You may change the angle of view in the viewport and render again

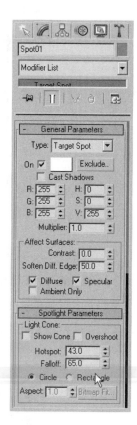

Figure 7.17   Adjust the Perspective view if necessary and click the Quick Render button. The lighted area of the Target Spot cone has a harsh edge.

to better see the result. The Hotspot and Falloff setting are at the default 43 and 45 degrees respectively. This makes a very harsh edge to the lighted area. Close the Virtual Frame Buffer.

4. Click the Select button, and in the Perspective viewport, select the Spot01 object. In the Modify panel, Spotlight Parameters rollout, enter 65 in the Falloff field (see Figure 7.18). Click the Render Last button and you will see the lighted area is larger with a softer edge transition. In the Modify panel, General Parameters rollout, check the Cast Shadows option. Click Render Last again and you will see shadows cast from the counter and stools that add apparent weight to those objects (see Figure 7.19). Close the Virtual Frame Buffer.

5. In the Top viewport, select Spot01 and Spot01.Target. Right-click and choose Move from the Transform Quad Menu. Hold the Shift key, move the light, choose Instance in the Clone Options dialog, and click OK. Repeat this for a total of four Target Spots along the counter. Select any one of the spotlights and in the Modify

Figure 7.18
Enter 65 in the Falloff field of Spotlight Parameters rollout to soften the edge of the lighted area. The light intensity is the same within the area defined by the Hotspot but is a more gradual transition to the cutoff at the edge of the Falloff cone.

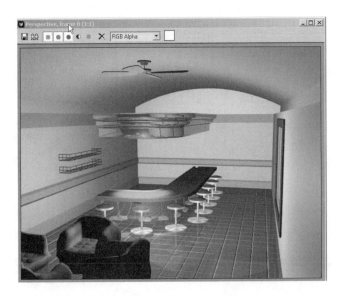

Figure 7.19   Check the Cast Shadows option in General Parameters
rollout to cast shadows from the counter and stools.

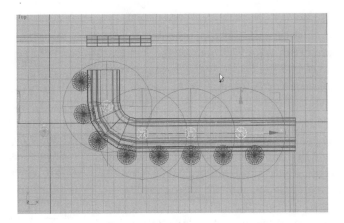

Figure 7.20   Check the Show Cone option in the Spotlight Parameters
rollout. With this checked, the Hotspot and Falloff Cones
show in the viewports whether or not the light is selected.
All your spots show because they are Instance clones.
Modify one, and they all change.

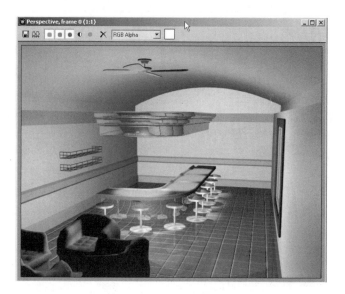

Figure 7.21 You have twice the light intensity where the Hotspot cones overlap, and the light is just as intense on the floor as on the counter due to lack of any attenuation.

panel, Spotlight Parameters rollout, check the Show Cone option (see Figure 7.20). Click the Render Last button to render the Perspective viewport. You will see bright areas corresponding to the overlapping Hotspot cones in the Top viewport (see Figure 7.21).

6. You will now make attenuation adjustments to a spotlight. Make the Left viewport active and maximize it to full display. Select any one of the spotlights in the scene. In the Modify panel, Attenuation Parameters rollout, check the Use checkbox in the Far Attenuation area (see Figure 7.22). You should see two lens shapes appear within the light cone, a tan Start lens near the top of the counter, and a darker brown End lens below the floor. You may have to zoom or pan in the viewport to see them both. The light has full intensity from the source to the tan Start range, and then diminishes linearly to the brown End range. Beyond the End range there is no light.

tip

The Quick Render command will only render the active viewport in 3ds max 4. After you have rendered any viewport, you can use Render Last to render that same viewport regardless of which viewport is currently active.

note
The Show checkbox is similar to the Show Cone in the Spotlight Parameters rollout. You do not need to show the Attenuation Ranges in this scene, however. You already know that the spotlights are Instance clones, and when you modify one, they all change.

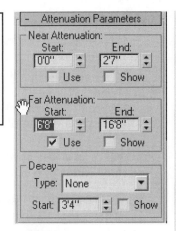

7. In the Far Attenuation Start field, enter 4. That causes the spotlight to have full intensity to approximately the top of the counter. In the Far Attenuation End field, enter 6. The light has no effect beyond the midpoint of the stools. This eliminates the overlapping bright areas and softens the effect of the light. You can still increase the intensity of the spotlights by increasing the Multiplier value, say to 1.5, without causing distracting effects. (see Figure 7.23).

8. Close any open windows and dialogs and minimize the display to show all four default viewports. Save the file, it should already be called MASTER_DINER25.MAX. You have learned about placing Target Spot lights and adjusting the intensity and color. You also learned about controlling the distance a light shines from its source by adjusting the Far Attenuation.

Figure 7.22
Check the Use checkbox in Modify panel, Attenuation Parameters rollout, Far Attenuation area, to activate attenuation.

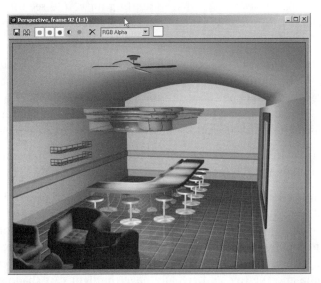

Figure 7.23   You can increase the Multiplier value to 1.5, for example, to brighten the light.

Direct Lights

Direct lights in 3ds max 4 share many of the same properties of spotlights. Like spots, Direct lights can either be Target Direct or Free Direct, there are Hotspot and Falloff adjustments, and the different forms of attenuation are available. Where Direct lights differ from spotlights is the shape of the beam emanating from the source. While spotlights shine within an area defined by two cones, the Direct lights shine within two cylinders.

The biggest advantage of using light in a cylindrical shape is the fact that the shadows cast from Direct lights are parallel to each other. In a scenario where you have a small section of city with a spotlight as the sun, the shadows on one side of town will go in one direction, while the shadows on the other side of town go in another direction. Both are defined by the angle of the light cone. A Direct light used as the sun in the scene will be more convincing because the parallel shadows look correct.

Direct lights can also be used to concentrate the light beam more sharply on objects without affecting nearby objects, as theatrical lighting. Direct lights with Volume Light effect added can be used as laser beams or other special effects lighting.

In your diner scene, the overall lighting is coming from an Omni light centered in the room. That is not a lighting scheme that is particularly convincing for a diner. The Omni light gives enough overall lighting for you to see the scene only when it is rendered. Usually, a diner would have several fixtures in the ceiling that give the bulk of the light in the room.

In Exercise 7.4 you will add ceiling fluorescent light fixtures from another file using the File, Merge command. These are six simple mesh fixtures that have been previously constructed and positioned in the scene with no lights. It would be possible to place a 3ds max 4 spotlight for each of the six fixtures in the ceiling and play with the adjustments until the cones and attenuation ranges are convincing.

However, in this exercise you will learn about two important lighting features: Projector maps and the Include/Exclude capabilities of lights.

The Projector Map option allows you to project any map from the light source as if the light were a slide or movie projector. Lights can then be used as actual projectors or for creating special "gobo" effects as it is known in the film world. For example, if you want the illusion of light from a window with a tree outside shining over your shoulder into a room, it would be expensive, in computer resources, to build the window frame and the tree and actually have the light cast shadows. It can be much more cost-effective to use an image of a window, branches, and leaves and project them through the light to create the illusion of complex geometry.

One Direct light will be placed above the ceiling shining straight to the floor. Direct lights cast light within a cylinder, generating parallel light and shadows. One option of Direct lights and spotlights is to have a rectangular shaped cone or cylinder to allow you to direct the light beam more precisely. You will set the Direct light in the exercise to fit the floor aspect ratio and size.

However, with shadow casting turned on and the light placed above the ceiling, light fixtures, and ceiling fan you will get shadows cast from some of the objects causing a unconvincing results. You will use a feature, available on all lights, called Include/Exclude. With Include/Exclude you can tell lights to ignore certain objects in the scene. The objects can be excluded or included for the illumination, the shadow casting, or both illumination and shadow casting.

note

The Include option is just to make it easier to manage lights. By default, all objects are included by all lights. For example, rather than try to exclude 300 out of 320 objects in your scene it is easier to select just the 20 and include them. Also, when you add new objects to the scene, they will not be affected by that particular light, and you do not have to remember to exclude them.

There is a Light Include/ Exclude button in the Lights & Cameras tab menu, that brings up a Light Incl/Exl dialog. (see Figure 7.24).

Figure 7.24   In the Lights & Cameras tab, there is a Light Include/Exclude button to bring up the Light Incl/Exl dialog to help manage light Include/Exclude assignments in the scene.

Exercise 7.4: Direct Lights with Projector Maps

1. Open the file called MASTER_DINER25.MAX. Save it as MASTER_DINER26.MAX. There are no light fixtures in the ceiling, so to make the scene more convincing you will merge several fluorescent light fixtures created previously. From the File pull-down menu, choose Merge. In the Merge File dialog, find a file on the CD-ROM called FLUORESCENT.MAX and double-click it. In the Merge-FLUORES-CENT.MAX dialog (see Figure 7.25), choose the six FLUORESCENT fixtures and BALLAST in the list and click OK. You will see the fixtures appear on the ceiling.

2. Right-click in the Top viewport to activate it, type W to maximize it, and click the Zoom Extents button to fill the viewport with all objects. In the Create panel, Lights panel, click the Free Direct button. In the Top viewport, click near the center of the room to place a Free Direct light on the floor level, pointing downward. In the toolbar, click the Align button, and double-click floor_outline in the Pick Object dialog. In the Align Selection dialog, check X Position, Y Position, and Center in both columns (see Figure 7.26), for this aligns the Free Direct light to the center of the room exactly. Click OK in the Align dialog.

3. Click the Align button again, type H, and double-click {CEILING} in the Pick Objects list. Check Z Position, Maximum,, and Maximum in the Align Selection dialog (see Figure 7.27). Click OK to close the dialogs. The top of the Free Direct light is aligned with the top of the ceiling. You can see the light

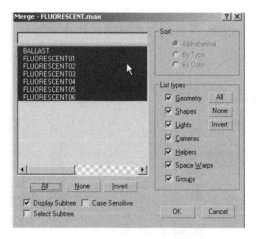

Figure 7.25   From File, Merge pull-down menu, choose Merge, and merge the fixtures and ballast into the scene. They appear in the correct location in the scene because they were constructed in that position beforehand.

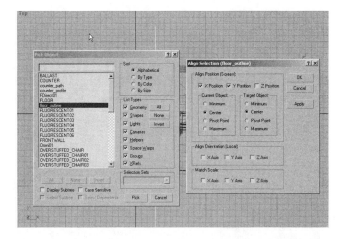

Figure 7.26   Click the Align button in the toolbar, double-click floor_outline
in the Pick Object lists, and in the Align dialog, check X
Position, Y Position, Center, and Center.

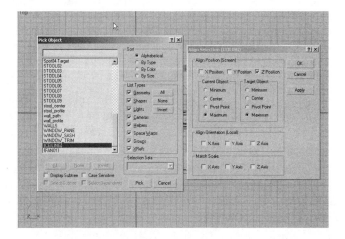

Figure 7.27   Click the Align button in the toolbar, double-click {CEILING}
in the Pick Object lists, and in the Align dialog, check Z
Position, Maximum, and Maximum to align the light with
the top of the ceiling.

position in the Front viewport. Type W to minimize the viewports, right-click in
the Perspective viewport, and click Quick Render. There is a new circle of light in
the corner of the counter (see Figure 7.28).

Figure 7.28   Render the Perspective viewport to see the new round pool
of light from the Free Direct at the ceiling.

The install from the CD-ROM will give access to the paths. I try to use as many standard maps as will be on the shipping paths.

4. Right-click in the Top viewport to activate it. With the FDirect01 light selected, in the Modify panel, General Parameters rollout, check the Cast Shadows checkbox. In the Directional Parameter rollout, check the Rectangle option, the shape of the Hotspot and Falloff ranges become rectangular as seen from the Top viewport.

5. You will now adjust the aspect ratio of the rectangle to match that of the room. You will use a feature called Expression Evaluator to calculate the ratio. The dimensions of the room are 38 feet by 18 feet. In the Directional Parameters rollout the Aspect field is set to 1.0 or square. Select the numeric value in the Aspect field to highlight it blue (see Figure 7.29). Hold down the Ctrl key and press N to call the Numeric Expression Evaluator. Enter 38/18 and the result of 2.1111 will appear in the window below (see Figure 7.30). Click Paste to enter the result in the Aspect field. The aspect ratio of the light now matches the room dimensions. In the Directional Parameters rollout, enter 19 (which is half the full length of the 38 foot room) in the Hotspot field and press Enter. The parallel rectangular light now fills the room.

Figure 7.30
With the Aspect field highlighted in blue, press Ctrl+N to call the Numeric Expression Evaluator. Enter the formula 38/18 and the result will appear in the window below. Click the Paste button to enter the result in the highlighted field.

Figure 7.29
In the Modify panel, Directional Parameters rollout, highlight the Aspect field in blue by clicking and dragging the cursor over the text.

6. Click the Render Last button in the toolbar to render the Perspective viewport again. The light is much too bright and there are shadows of the light fixtures and ceiling fan on the floor. You will fix both problems. In the Left viewport, select Omni01. In the Modify panel, General Parameters rollout, enter 125 in the Value field to lower the intensity of the Omni. Render the Perspective viewport and notice the walls and ceiling are much darker.

note   The walls, except for the top edge of the chair rail are not affected by the Free Direct because the angle of incidence is zero degrees.

The stools do not appear to cast shadows because the reflection maps are overriding the ambient area of the shadows.

7. Select the FDirect01 light in the Top viewport. In the Modify panel, General Parameters rollout, click the Exclude button. In the Exclude/Include dialog, choose CEILING, {FAN01}, and all six FLUORESCENT fixtures in the left panel. Click the double-arrow button pointing to the right to send the selected names into the right panel to exclude them from both shadow casting and illumination (see Figure 7.31). Render the Perspective viewport and notice the shadows on the floor from the fixtures and fan are gone. Also the fixtures and fan blade are no longer brightly lit from the Free Direct light above it.

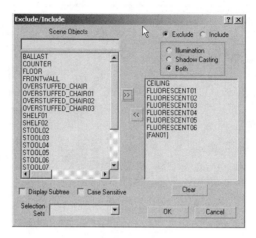

Figure 7.31   In the Exclude/Include dialog, the fan and fixtures are
moved to the Exclude panel.

8. You will now load a map into the Material Editor to make it available for use in
the Projector Map slot of the Free Direct light. Open the Material Editor and
click the next available Sample Window to make it current. Click the Get
Material button below left of the Sample Windows. This opens the Material/Map
Browser that lists all available material and map types. This is not a material you

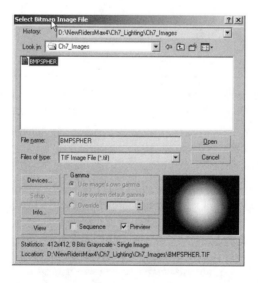

Figure 7.32   In the Material/Map Browser, double-click Bitmap. Find and
open BMPSPHER.TIF on the CD-ROM.

are creating but a map that can be used as a projector image or display and render background image. Double-click on Bitmap in the Material/Map Browser. In the Select Bitmap Image File dialog, find and choose BMPSPHER.TIF on the CD-ROM (see Figure 7.32). Click the Open button to load the file into the Sample Window. Name the map in the Sample Window PROJECTOR MAP.

> **note**
>
> This is not a gray material on a Sample Sphere. This is an image of a gray gradient circle blurred at the edges. You cannot assign this map to objects in the scene.

Move the Material Editor to one side and select FDirect01 in the scene. In the Modify panel, Directional Parameters rollout, you will see a None button in the Projector Map area (see Figure 7.33). Drag and drop the BMPSPHER.TIF map from the Sample Window to the None button. In the Instance (Copy) Map dialog, check Instance, and click the OK button (see Figure 7.34).

9. Quick Render the Perspective viewport, and you will see that there is an oval area of light being projected through FDirect01. You will now adjust the map to simulate multiple lights. In the Material Editor, Coordinates rollout, enter 3.0 in the U:Tiling field, 2.0 in the V:Tiling field, and 0.25 in the V:Offset field. This repeats

Figure 7.33
You will drag and drop the BMPSPHER.TIF map from the Material Editor Sample Window to the Directional Parameters rollout, Projector Map, None button.

Figure 7.34
Check the Instance option in the Instance (Copy) Map dialog and click OK. This allows you to adjust the map in the Material Editor and have it update in the FDirect01 light.

the pattern 3 by 2 times and offsets the map by 25 percent to center the six white dots (see Figure 7.35). You now have the illusion that there are six lights from overhead fixtures without the hassles of adjusting the overlapping areas of separate beams (see Figure 7.36).

note

This pattern is not exactly matched to the light fixtures, but most viewers would not be the wiser. For a more accurate representation, create 2D shapes on the floor where the light would fall. Convert the shapes to Editable Mesh flat planes and assign a pure white, fully self-illuminated material. Hide all objects except the new planes and render the white planes against a black background from the Top viewport. Open the rendered image in a paint program and apply an appropriate blur to soften the edges. Use this new image as the Projector map.

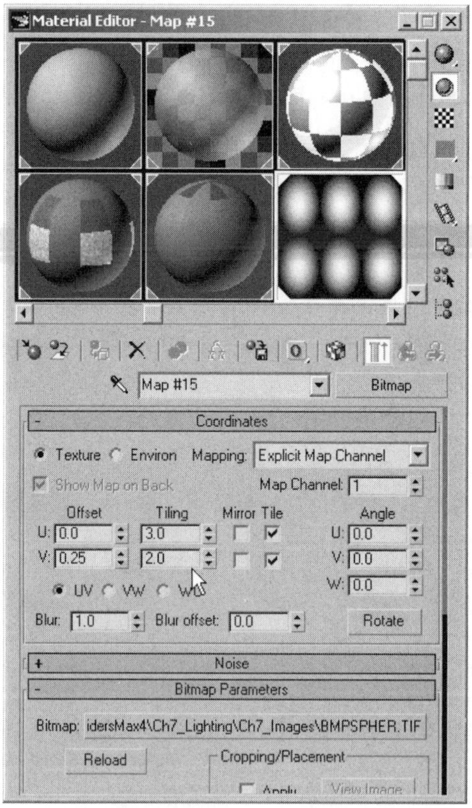

Figure 7.35   In the Material Editor, Coordinates rollout, set the U:Tiling to 3.0, the V:Tiling to 2.0 and the V:Offset to 0.25 to create a pattern of 3 by 2 white dots for the projected image.

Figure 7.36   Quick Render the Perspective viewport to see the illusion of multiple light sources produced by one light and a Projector map.

tip   Simulating multiple lights with a single light and Projector map combo can be very effective in large outdoor scenes at night to simulate the light from street lights, parking lots lighting, or walkway lights.

10. Close all dialogs and save the file. It should already be called MASTER_DINER26.MAX.

You have learned to use a Projector map in a direct light to simulate multiple lights in a scene. You have also learned about the Exclude/Include feature of lights to include or exclude objects from the lights influence.

Adding lights to a scene is an art form that you will need to practice and develop your own style. Use a minimum number of lights to start and add and adjust lights to get the right feel to the scene. Again, you are painting the scene with lights, not lighting the scene as you would with real lights. All lights in 3ds max 4 should have attenuation enabled for full control and you should take advantage of the Exclude/Include features.

In Exercise 7.5 you will add an effect to the scene that is not a light control, but a material effect to make the light fixtures in the scene more convincing. The viewer is often more comfortable knowing where the light is emanating from. You will add a Environment Effect glow to the fluorescent bulbs in the ceiling fixtures.

Exercise 7.5: Adding a Glow Effect for More Convincing Fluorescent Bulbs

1. Open the file called MASTER_DINER26.MAX that you saved in Exercise 7.4 or from the CD-ROM. Save it as MASTER_DINER27.MAX. Open the Material Editor and find a Sample Window with FLUOR_FIXTURE Multi/Sub-Object material in it. If there is no such material in the Material Editor, select the next available Sample Window, and click the eyedropper button to the left of the material name field. In any viewport, pick the one of the fluorescent light fixtures on the ceiling. This gets the material from the object into the Sample Window. The Multi/Sub-Object material is made of two materials: ENAMEL_WHITE and FLUOR_BULB (see Figure 7.37).

2. Click the Material/Map Navigator button and choose FLUOR_BULB in the list. This is a Standard material with green self-illumination to make it appear to glow from within by overriding any ambient light areas. You will now add an external glow effect. Click and hold the mouse button on the Material Effects Channel button below the middle of the Sample Windows. This shows a flyout of buttons from 0 to 15. Highlight the 1 button and release the mouse button to set the Effects Channel to 1 (see Figure 7.38). Close the Material Editor.

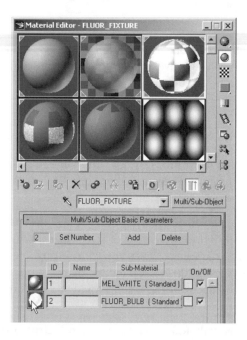

Figure 7.37   Select the FLUOR_FIXTURE Sample Window in the Material Editor or use the Eyedropper button to get the material from the light fixture in the scene.

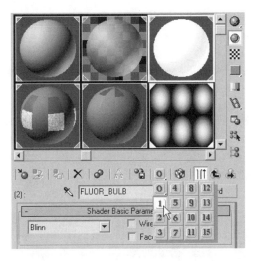

Figure 7.38   In the Material Editor, click and hold the Material Effects Channel button and choose the 1 button in the flyout.

note   The numbers do not have any significance. Zero is no effects and the other numbers are just options used to cue material effects. Each material can cue up to 15 effects, which the programmers thought would be enough to cover all cases.

3. In the Rendering pull-down menu, choose Effects (see Figure 7.39). In the Rendering Effects dialog, click the Add button. In the Add Effect dialog, double-click Lens Effect (see Figure 7.40). In the left column of the Lens Effect Parameters rollout, choose glow and click the right-arrow button to send it to the right column. Right-click in the Perspective viewport to make sure it is active. In the Effects rollout, check the Interactive checkbox. The Perspective viewport will appear to render. However, it is a Effects Preview window, not the Virtual Frame Buffer window you get after you render.

4. Make sure Glow is highlighted in the right column of the Lens Effects Parameters rollout. In the

Figure 7.39
In the Rendering pull-down menu, choose Effects.

Rendering Effects dialog, Glow Element rollout, enter 0.1 in the Size field and 90 in the Intensity field (see Figure 7.41). Nothing will happen yet because you have not told 3ds max 4 where to apply the Glow effect.

5. In the Glow Element dialog, click on the Options tab. In the Image Sources area, check the Effects ID checkbox (see Figure 7.42.) It is set to 1 to match the Material Effects Channel 1 you set in the FLUOR_BULB material. Any objects with that material assigned in the scene will get the Glow effect applied at render time. When you check the option, the scene will appear to render again, and in a second pass, the Glow effect will be applied to the fluorescent bulbs causing a glowing halo (see Figure 7.43).

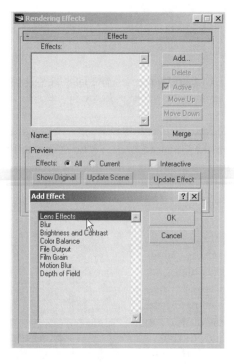

Figure 7.40
In the Rendering Effects dialog, click the Add button, and double-click Lens Effects in the list.

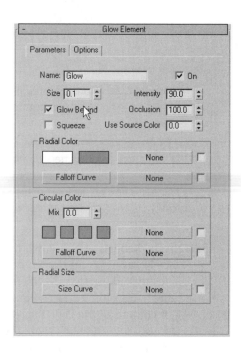

Figure 7.41
In the Glow Element rollout, enter 0.1 in the Size field and 90 in the Intensity field.

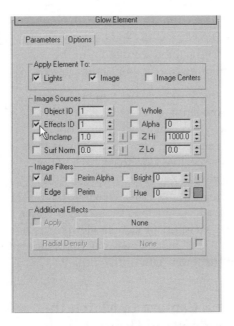

Figure 7.42   In the Rendering Effects dialog, Glow Element rollout, check the Effects ID option in the Image Sources area. It is set to 1 by default and will cue a glow on any material in the scene with Material Effects Channel 1.

Figure 7.43   Perspective viewport Effects Preview with Glow effects applied to the material on the fluorescent bulbs in the scene.

6. Close all dialogs and save the file. It should already be called MASTER_DINER27.MAX. You have added a small glow effect to the fluorescent bulbs in the diner to make them more convincing to the viewer.

Up to this point in the diner exercises you have been working with and rendering a Perspective viewport. You have used the Views pull-down menu option called Save Active Perspective View to allow you to use Restore Active Perspective View to get back to the same view in cases where a Zoom Extents All or other viewport navigation change the viewpoint. In Exercise 7.6 you will add a camera to the scene, and then switch the Perspective viewport to a Camera01 viewport. A camera viewport is not affected by Zoom Extents or Zoom Extents All, but has its own navigation tools that replace the zoom/pan buttons located at the lower right of the display.

tip

Large glow size settings can be slow to preview or may be so large as to be undetectable in the preview window. Start with a smaller size setting than the default 30 usually makes it easier to see the effect.

Exercise 7.6: Placing a Camera to Match the Existing Perspective View and Using Manipulators

1. Open the file called MASTER_DINER27.MAX that you saved in Exercise 7.5 or from the CD-ROM. Save the file as MASTER_DINER28.MAX. Right-click in the Top viewport to activate it. In the Create panel, Cameras panel, click on the Target button (see Figure 7.44).

2. In the Top viewport, pick and drag to create a camera and a target object. It does not matter where the camera or the target are located for this exercise.

tip

A Target Camera is similar to a Target Spot or Direct light. It is intended for situations where the camera is likely to be pointing to a specific spot or area in the scene with minimal movement of the target. Free Cameras are for cameras that move along a given path.

Figure 7.44
In the Create panel, Cameras panel, click the Target button in the Object Type rollout.

3. Right-click in the Perspective viewport to activate it, and with Camera01 still selected, click on the Views pull-down menu, and choose Match Camera to View in the menu (see Figure 7.45). This moves the camera into position and adjusts the field of view for an exact match. Press C and the viewport label will switch from Perspective to Camera01 but you will not see a change in the view.

4. In the Modify panel, Parameters rollout, click on the 28mm button in the Stock Lenses area (see Figure 7.46) for a wider angle view.

5. Use the Dolly Camera and Orbit Camera buttons at the lower right of the display to adjust the view so the camera is inside the room and you have a view of the whole diner. (see Figure 7.47.).

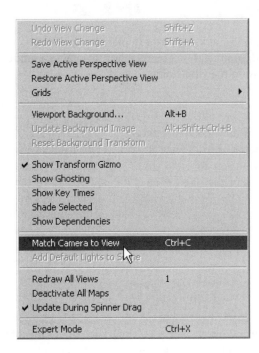

Figure 7.45
With a camera selected and a Perspective viewport active, use Match Camera to View in the Views pull-down menu. Press C to switch from a Perspective to a matching Camera01 view.

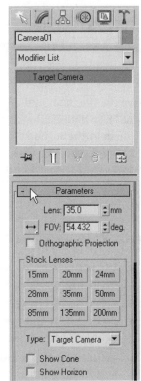

Figure 7.46
In the Modify panel, Parameters rollout, click the 28mm button for a wider angle view.

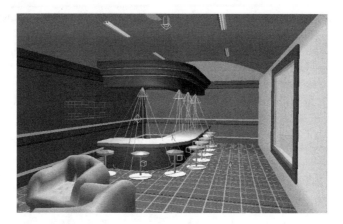

Figure 7.47   Using the Dolly Camera and Orbit Camera buttons that have replaced Zoom and ArcRotate, adjust the camera inside the room viewing the whole diner.

6. Save the file, it should already be called MASTER_DINER28.MAX. You have created a Target Camera in the scene and matched its view with an existing Perspective view. You then adjusted the camera with the new buttons in the navigation buttons.

tip

The Stock Lens presets are based on lenses for a 35mm film camera. The 50mm lens is considered the equivalent of a normal field of view for most people.

Chapter Summary

- **Deciphering 3ds max 4 light types**   You have learned some of the differences and similarities between Omni, Spot, Direct, and Ambient light and their uses.

- **Basic Light Parameters**   You have used the basic parameters of the various light types to get general lighting in the scene.

- **Adjusting light intensity**   You adjusted the intensity of light on surfaces by adjusting the angle of incidence of the light to the surface, by adjusting the Value, and by changing the Multiplier settings.

- **Principles of shadow casting lights**   You have learned some of the principles of Shadow map and Raytrace shadows and some of the important adjustments for good shadows such as Bias, Map Size, and Sample Ranges.

- **Light attenuation**   The importance of light attenuation cannot be stressed enough. You learned to adjust the attenuation of Omni lights and spotlights.

- **Light Exclude/Include features**   3ds max 4 lights have controls that movie lighting professionals can only dream of in the Include/Exclude features.

- **Using Projector maps in lights**   You learned to use Projector maps to simulate multiple lights with only one light.

- **Applying Environment effects**   You learned to use Environment effects cued to a material to cause light bulbs to glow in the scene. This makes the object more convincing as a light source.

- **Placing and adjusting cameras**   You learned to place a camera in the scene and match it to a perspective view you had set previously.

Animation: A Moving Experience

In This Chapter

Understanding the underlying control systems that handle animation is a very important first step to being able to set up basic animation. You can then tweak these for that extra edge that makes the difference between a great animation and a mediocre animation.

Many new users are frustrated with unexpected motion in animated objects because they have not taken the time to look at what makes animation happen in the first place. For example, you may move an object and have it stop at a wall. However, the object does not stop at the wall but goes into the wall and backs out to the final resting place. Or you may rotate an object 180 degrees, but the object counter-rotates slightly before rotating in the direction you specified.

3ds max 4 uses a technique called keyframe animation, which is an adaptation of the process used in the traditional 2D cell animation that you may have grown up seeing every Saturday morning. In a traditional animation shop, there are master animators who draw the important poses of characters to determine the mood and pacing of the animation. Those drawings are then given to junior animators who draw all the in-between images that make it an animation when played back at 24 frames per second, the speed of traditional animation. In 3ds max 4, you are the master animator. You determine the starting pose at frame 0, and then set the major keyframes throughout the animation at specific times. 3ds max 4 acts as the junior animator and fills all the in-between frames to create the animation when played back at 30 frames per second, the traditional speed of animations in countries using the NTSC TV/video standard.

Figure 8.1   In this sample Track View, each component with a green
arrow to the left of it can be animated.

While the position and rotation of objects in the scene will be the focus of the animation in this chapter, it is by no means the only animation that can be performed in 3ds max 4. Practically every change you make in 3ds max 4 will become an animated change if you have the Animate button toggled on and are at a frame other than frame 0 when you make the change. Figure 8.1 shows a sample Track View in which every parameter that has a green triangle next to it has a controller associated that can be animated. Each material, each modifier, and each sub-object level adjustment, with few exceptions, can be animated.

Some of the topics to be covered in this chapter include:

- **Keyframing**   You will learn the concept of keyframe animation. Keyframing is analogous to setting up a daily schedule calendar. An object must be at a certain place at a given time. You mark the calendar with a key to schedule the event.

- **Basic animation calculations**   Part of this chapter will introduce you to basic calculations to get an object traveling at a known speed within your scene. If you do not start with a constant speed, adjusting the animation to be convincing to the viewer is difficult.

- **Configuring time**   You will learn how to configure time in 3ds max 4 to set the length of a new animation or to change the speed of an existing animation.

- **Track Bar and Track View**   You will also use the Track Bar and Track View to see graphical representations of your animation. You can select and adjust keys to aid in fine-tuning the animation.

- **Tangency controls**   Keys often have tangency information associated with them that allows you to add or remove follow-through and anticipation at the keys. You will learn to adjust the tangency.

- **Animation controllers and constraints**
  All objects have controllers or constraints when created to define how an object moves. You will explore several alternate controllers and constraints.

- **Ease Curves**   You will learn about basic Ease Curves. Ease Curves are superimposed on base animation to allow for graphical control of velocity.

note

Ease Curves are not often introduced to new 3ds max 4 users. This author believes that a basic knowledge of Ease Curves is essential to controlling animation.

Key Terms

Keyframe   Keyframes record the beginning and end of each transformation of an object or element in the scene. The values at these keyframes are called keys.

Animation controller   Controllers are plug-ins that handle all the animation tasks in 3ds max 4. All objects have controllers of one form or another by default.

Animation constraint   Constraints are a new form of animation controller in 3ds max 4 that allow multiple weighted objects or parameters to modify animation.

Track Bar   The Track Bar provides a timeline below the viewports showing the frame numbers (or appropriate display units). It provides a quick alternative to Track View for moving, copying, and deleting keys and for changing key properties.

Track View   With Track View you can view and edit all the keys that you create. You can also assign animation controllers to interpolate or control all the keys and parameters for the objects in your scene. Some of the functions in Track View, such as moving and deleting keys, are also available on the Track Bar near the time slider. Thirteen Track View layouts can be named and stored in the Track View buffer.

Tangency   The tangent of a Function Curve affects the interpolated values between keys of an animation. Most animation controllers use fixed tangents to define the Function Curve at a key location. By default, 3ds max 4 assigns smooth tangents to the keys in a Position Function Curve. This is the reason that an animated object moves in smooth curves through the keyframes. 3ds max 4 assigns smooth tangents because they usually provide the most natural motion.

Hierarchical link   The Select and Link and Unlink buttons on the left side of the toolbar are used to make and break links between objects in your scene. The links are in the form of Parent/Child relationships. The Parent controls the Child.

Dummy object   A Dummy helper object is a wireframe cube with a pivot point at its geometric center. It has a name but no parameters, you can't modify it, and it doesn't render. Its only real feature is its pivot, which is used as a center for transforms. The wireframe acts as a reference for transform effects.

Keyframe Animation

Again, the concept of keyframe animation in 3ds max 4 is that you start with a pose at frame 0, you toggle the Animate button on, and then advance the Frame slider to any frame other than 0. Making a change to your scene results in an animation of that change that starts from frame 0 at the frame where you set the key.

Keyframing is essentially a simple process. However, there are factors that are inherent in the process and factors predetermined by the software that make it confusing for the new user and, sometimes, for the experienced user, too. For example, the changes you make at a given frame are interpolated from the previous key or from the key that is created automatically at frame 0 to record the base pose. This means that if you toggle on the Animate button, go to frame 50, and move an object, the object starts moving at frame 0 and moves until the final position you indicated at frame 50. The distance in frames between these two keys determines the speed of the object. Speed = Distance × Time.

Often you want the object to stay at rest until, perhaps, frame 40, and then cover the same distance in 10 frames, a much faster speed. Two methods to accomplish this include:

- You can copy the starting position key at frame 0 to frame 40, advance the Frame slider to frame 50, and set the final position.

- You can set the Frame slider at frame 40 and right-click on the Frame slider to set a key with the Source Time = 40 and the Destination Time = 40. This records the object's position in a key at frame 40. After you proceed to frame 50 and set the new key, the position change will be interpolated from frame 40 to frame 50.

You will use each method in the exercises of this chapter.

The Fundamentals: Finding Your Way Around

In this section of the chapter, you will learn how to calculate the base speed of an object and to set the timing correctly in 3ds max 4. You will be setting up an animation that will include a vehicle moving across a parking lot at a given speed and stopping after it reaches the other side. You will learn about animation controllers, how to find them, and where to change them in either the Motion panel or in the Track View.

Keys are generally adjusted in either the Track View or in the Track Bar just below the Frame slider at the bottom of the viewports (see Figure 8.2).

Figure 8.2   The Track Bar appears as a ruler and is found just below the Frame Slider, at the bottom of the viewports. The default setting for the Track Bar is 100 frames.

Calculating Total Number of Frames and Timing

You job as animator at this point is to animate a vehicle moving across a parking lot and stopping after it reaches the other curb. The client would like a reasonably convincing feel to the speed and timing. For this you need several pieces of information:

- The overall time of the scene
- The time allotted to the actual vehicle movement
- The distance the vehicle moves

> **tip**
>
> For basic camera moves and characters walking, a good base speed to start from is 30 inches, or 1 stride, per second. This works out to 1 inch of forward motion per frame of animation. This corresponds to a leisurely walking speed.

The total length of the scene is not necessarily the same as the animation time of the vehicle because it will sit still for a period of time before and after the move.

In this exercise you will be using the NTSC standard frame playback rate of 30 frames per second. The client requires a total length of 3 seconds or 90 frames. You will set the total length of the scene in the Time Configuration dialog. The vehicle will sit still for 0.5 seconds, or 15 frames, before and after the move. This leaves 60 frames for the animation of the vehicle to take place or 2 full seconds. You will calculate the distance the vehicle moves by measuring in the scene in Exercise 8.1.

Time Configuration Controls

You can configure time for your animation in the Time Configuration dialog (see Figure 8.3). Here you can choose a standard frame rate from NTSC, PAL, or film, or set a custom rate. You can also display time in several convenient formats.

The Playback area controls how the animation is played back in the display viewports only. It has nothing to do with the playback speed of any final rendered images. In the Animation area you can set the Start Time and End Time of your animation or the total Length or total Frame Count. The Re-scale Time button calls a panel similar to the Animation area options.

In Exercise 8.1 you will configure the time of the animation as directed in the previous section of this chapter. The scene is a hilly landscape with a roller coaster. In front of the roller coaster are a parking area, a jeep-type vehicle, and a roller coaster car for use in a later exercise in this chapter.

> **caution**
>
> Changing settings in the Re-scale Time dialog stretches or compresses any existing animation. Changing settings in the Animation area will either add empty frames to, or chop frames from, existing animations.

Figure 8.3   The Time Configuration dialog.

---

tip

As with any exercises in this book that have elements already set up, it is a good idea to explore the modeling methods, materials, and lighting to see techniques that are not specifically covered in the exercises. Keep an open mind as you explore and try to think of ways to reuse techniques for other purposes. For example, many of same methods used on the landscape model and materials could be used to make a rough ocean scene with very few changes.

Exercise 8.1: Configuring Time

1. Open the file called Ch8_ANIMATON01.MAX from the CD-ROM. It is the hilly landscape with a roller coaster and vehicles. Save the file as Ch8_ANIMATION02.MAX. As a reminder, you can click the Save As option in File pull-down menu, and then use the plus sign button to increment the name of the newly saved file (see Figure 8.4).

2. Your first task is to measure the distance the vehicle will move to cross the parking lot in a straight line. You can use a Helper object called Tape to measure distances in scenes. Right-click in the Top viewport to activate it and type W to maximize the viewport. In the Create panel, Helpers panel, click the Tape button (see Figure 8.5).

note

The letters visible in the Front viewport at ground level are the cardinal compass points indicated in the Sunlight System Compass applied to the scene.

Figure 8.4   In the File pull-down menu, choose Save As, and click the plus sign button to increment the newly saved file name.

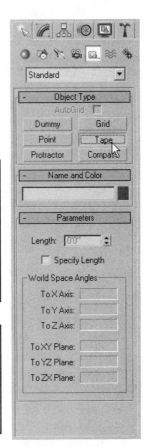

3. In the Top viewport, pick near the front of the front wheels and drag the mouse to the curb at the left of the parking lot. A green Tape object appears in the viewport and the total length of the tape is indicated in the Parameters rollout. It reads approximately 60 feet, rounded to the accuracy you require for this exercise (see Figure 8.6). Click the Select button in the toolbar to exit Tape mode.

tip   The Tape is a Helper object that will never render in a scene. Selecting the tape end (triangle) and going to the Modify panel will reveal the statistics of the tape and moving the tape end or the target end will change the statistics accordingly. You can have as many Tape objects in the scene as you need. Using the Snap settings to place the Tape and target can increase accuracy.

caution   Using Snap settings can also give bogus readings. If you snap to a vertex in the Top viewport and there are several vertices in the z-axis, you may have snapped to a vertex far below or above the point you intended, resulting in unexpected length measurements.

4. Click the Time Configuration button that is left of the Region Zoom button at the lower right of the display. In the Time Configuration dialog, enter

Figure 8.5

In the Create panel, Helpers panel, click the Tape button.

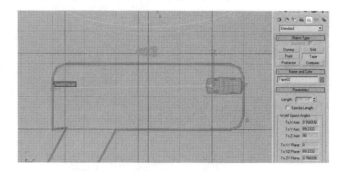

Figure 8.6   In the Top viewport, click left of the front wheels and drag the mouse to the curb at the left. The Length field in the Parameters rollout should read approximately 60 feet.

90 in the Frame Count field of the Animation area. This sets a total of 90 frames or 3 seconds of animation. The Frame slider will read frames 0 through 89. Click the OK button to close the Time Configuration dialog.

5. Type W to minimize the viewports and save the file. It should already be named Ch8_ANIMATION02.MAX. You have configured the frame count in 3ds max 4 for a total animation time of 3 seconds at 30 frames per second.

> **tip**   Except for particularly dramatic scenes, you should try to keep your rendered scenes short. This makes it easier to correct and avoid animation problems. Take a cue from current movies and television. If you count the seconds that any scene is on screen it is generally between 2 and 10 seconds or the equivalent of 60 to 300 frames of animation. Scenes are then edited together to make the entire story. Viewers are comfortable with this pace, and with the new video styles, an even faster pace is becoming popular. It is not unusual to see scenes of only 10 frames in films and on television today.

Motion Panel Controllers and Constraint Assignment

In this section you will perform a simple exercise to familiarize yourself with where animation controllers and constraints can be assigned and modified. Understanding the concept of controllers and constraints and being able to access them quickly is a boon to productivity. While this chapter will only cover the fundamentals, you should take it upon yourself to experiment with simple animations to get the feel for when it is appropriate to use any given controller or constraint.

Position, Rotation, and Scale controllers or constraints can be assigned in two places, either in the Motion panel or in Track View. For object or scene parameters such as object color or scene ambient light level, you have to use the Track View for access to those controllers or constraints.

In Exercise 8.2 you will select the vehicle in the parking lot and check to see what controller is assigned in both the Motion Panel and the Track View. You will learn what the available controllers and constraints are for position changes of the object.

Exercise 8.2: Using Motion Panel to Assign Controllers and Constraints

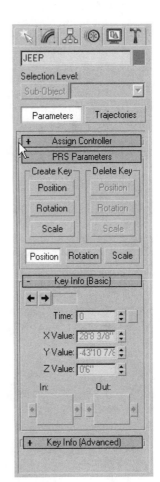

1. Open the file called Ch8_ANIMATION02.MAX that you saved in Exercise 8.1 or from the CD-ROM. You will select the vehicle in the parking lot and check the currently assigned controller in the Motion panel.

2. In the Top viewport, select the vehicle named JEEP, either by picking it in the viewport, or by typing H and double-clicking it in the Select Objects list.

3. Click the Motion panel button to open the Motion panel (see Figure 8.7). In the Motion panel, you can assign controllers or constraints for transforming objects only. You can also adjust trajectories, create new keys or delete existing keys in this panel, change basic or advanced key information in the appropriate rollouts. Click on the Assign Controller rollout to expand it (see Figure 8.8).

4. In the Assign Controller list, choose Position:Bézier Postion to highlight it in yellow. This activates the Assign Controller button at the upper left of the rollout. The appropriate object must be selected in the scene for you to be able highlight the Transform in the list.

5. Click the Assign Controller button in the Assign Controller rollout. This calls a list of possible controllers that can be assigned to the Position option of the object (see Figure 8.9). The "greater than" right arrow next to Bézier Position indicates that it is the current controller assigned to the Position Transform. Click the OK button to close

Figure 8.7

In the Motion panel for selected JEEP object in the scene, you can assign Transform controllers or constraints.

the Assign Position Controller dialog. You will not assign a new controller at this time.

> **warning**
>
> You will see at the bottom of the dialog that Bézier Position is the default Position controller assigned by 3ds max 4 to all new objects. Bézier Position controller allows you to select and move the object with the Select and Move button. Many new users will assign a Path Constraint and check the Make Default button in the dialog.
>
> Any new objects will have a Path Constraint controller assigned by default with no path indicated. This means the object will be created at 0,0,0 World Coordinate position and you will not be able to move it.
>
> If this happens to you, assign a Bézier Position controller to the object and pick the Make Default button to correct the problem.

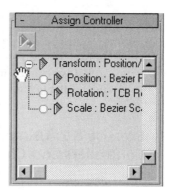

Figure 8.8
Assign Controller rollout in the Motion panel. The green triangles to the left of the Transform name show a controller is assigned. The name of the controller or constraint is indicated to the right of the Transform name, that is, Bézier Position or TCB Rotation.

6. Click on Rotation:TCB Rotation to highlight it and click the Assign Transform Controller button. The Assign Rotation Controller list is different from the Assign Position Controller list (see Figure 8.10).

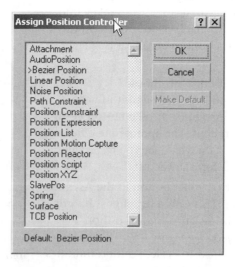

Figure 8.9   Assign Position Controller dialog with list of possible Position controllers and constraints.

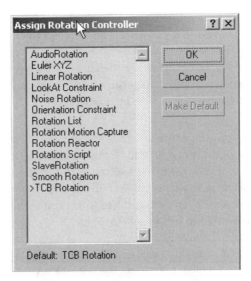

Figure 8.10   In Assign Rotation Controller dialog, the controllers can only be assigned to the rotation component of an object.

Some of the controllers behave similarly, but you cannot assign a Position controller to a Rotation and vice versa. Exit this file without saving any changes, just in case you might have made changes by mistake. You have learned to access the Motion panel and to locate Transform controller assignments.

Track View Controllers and Constraints Assignment

The next place in 3ds max 4 you will learn to assign controllers and constraints is in the Track View. While the Motion panel allowed you access to the Transform controllers and constraints, the Track View allows that and more. All possible controllers and constraints may be assigned from the Track View and you can see a graphical display of the keys used by the controllers as well as compare two or more controllers in the same Track View. Where the Motion panel is a quick and easy access to transformations, the Track View is a complete panel with much more control and flexibility. In Exercise 8.3. you will open the Track View and explore some of its capabilities.

Exercise 8.3: Using Track View to Assign Controllers and Constraints

1. Open the file called Ch8_ANIMATION02.MAX. You used this file in Exercise 8.2, but did not make any changes to the file and, therefore, did not save it with a new name. Select the object called JEEP if it is not already selected.

2. In the Graph Editors pull-down menu, Track View sub-menu, choose Untitled 1 from the menu (see Figure 8.11). This is an existing Track View created when the scene was initially set up but was never given a name. Resize the Track View by picking and dragging one edge to see the entire Track View (see Figure 8.12). It is a hierarchical representation of the entire scene. Sounds are indicated by a green cone, scene controls by a blue cylinder, materials by a blue sphere, and objects by a yellow cube.

3. Click the plus sign in the white square to the left of Objects to expand all objects in the scene. Pan up to reveal JEEP in the list. It has a yellow background behind the yellow cube to indicate it is the selected object in the scene. Click the plus sign in the white circle to the left of JEEP to expand its options. Click the plus sign in the white circle to the left of Transform to see the same information that was available to you in the Motion panel (see Figure 8.13).

tip

You can also right-click on the white squares or circles for a menu to expand, collapse, or select levels in Track View.

Right-clicking on an object in the scene and choosing Track View Selected is a shortcut to the object parameters in the Track View for that particular object only.

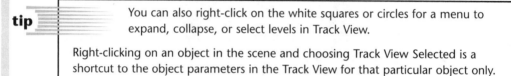

Figure 8.11   In the Graph Editors pull-down menu, Track View sub-menu, choose Untitled 1 to open an existing Track View.

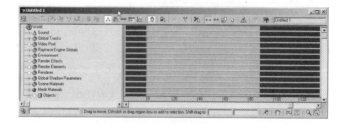

Figure 8.12   Resize the Track View by picking and dragging on one edge to view the entire dialog.

4. Click on the Position field in the Track View list and you will see the Assign Controller button become available in the toolbar for Track View. It is the same green arrow with a black arrow button you saw in the Motion panel, Assign Controllers rollout. Picking this button calls the Assign Controller dialog as it did before. Close the Assign Controller dialog without changes if you have opened it.

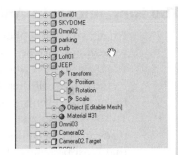

Figure 8.13
By picking the plus signs in the white circles or squares you can expand the various components of the Track View to reveal more options.

5. Rename this Track View by highlighting Untitled 1 in the upper-right name field and call it JEEP. In the upper-left corner of the Track View click on the Filters button. At the right side of the Filters dialog, check Selected Objects in the Show Only area (see Figure 8.14). Click OK to close the Filters dialog. Now when you access it from the pull-down menu, it will be expanded as it is now, showing only the selected and visible objects. Close the Track View.

6. Save the file with the new name Ch8_ANIAMTION03.MAX. You have learned where to assign controllers and constraints in the Track View and to configure the Track View for a cleaner view of the objects you are currently working on.

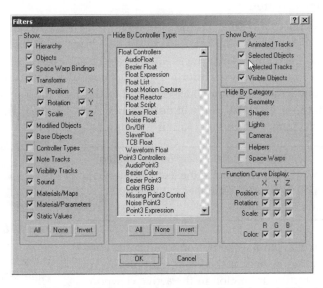

Figure 8.14   Open the Filters dialog and check the Selected Objects option in the Show Only area. This simplifies the information shown in the Track View.

The Fundamentals: Animating Objects

Finally you will actually animate the vehicle moving across the parking lot. You will set keyframes for position and rotation of the jeep in the scene. The position changes will make it move across the parking lot, and the rotation exercise will make it appear to slide. You will then need to make adjustments to remove unwanted motion and to cause the events to happen as described in the storyboard as the client requested. This seems like a simple task, but because of assumptions the programmers have made in the default settings for 3ds max 4, there will be some unexpected motion that must be removed.

Exercise 8.4: Animating a Position Change for the Jeep

1. Open the file called Ch8_ANIMATION03.MAX that you saved in Exercise 8.3 or from the CD-ROM. Save it as Ch8_ANIMATION04.MAX. You will animate the vehicle moving from one side of the parking lot to the other.

2. The JEEP should be selected and the Top viewport should be active. Click on the large Animate button at the bottom of the display to toggle it on. It will turn red along with the Frames slider track and the border around the active viewport. This is a warning that anything you do now could become an animation. You want the JEEP to reach the far side of the parking lot at frame 75, so drag the Frame slider so it reads 75/89 or type 75 in the frame number field to the right of the Animate button.

3. Click the Select and Move button, and then right-click it to call the Move Transform Type-in dialog. Enter –60 in the Offset:Screen x-axis field (see Figure 8.15) and press enter. The vehicle will move 60 feet to the other side of the parking lot. Close the Move Transform Type-In dialog. Click the Animate button to turn it off. Scrub the Frame slider back and forth to see the animation you have created. In the Track Bar you will notice a new key at frame 0 and one at frame 75, the keyframes for this animation (see Figure 8.16).

note If moving the vehicle 60 feet should happen to move the jeep outside the parking lot, adjust the number to move it less, perhaps 50 feet or so.

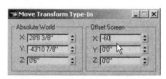

Figure 8.15

Click and then right-click on the Select and Move button. Enter –60 in the Offset: Screen x-axis field and press Enter.

4. Click the Play Animation button located just above the active frame field at the lower right of the display to play the animation in the active viewport. Click the Stop Animation button to stop it. These buttons resemble standard video player control

Figure 8.16   With the Animate button on, you set the active frame to frame 75 and moved the vehicle 60 feet to the left. This created a key at frame 75 to record the new position and one at frame 0 to record the start position.

buttons. There are also buttons to advance one frame forward or backward or buttons to jump to the beginning or end frames.

5. Right-click in the Camera02 viewport and click the Play Animation button. You can now see how the animation looks from the Camera02 perspective.

6. In the Rendering pull-down menu, choose Make Preview (see Figure 8.17). In the Make Preview dialog, be sure that the Active Time Segment is checked at the top of the Make Preview, and click the Create button (see Figure 8.18). In the Video Compression dialog, click OK to use the CinePak video compressor (see Figure 8.19). This renders a preview called _scene.avi and saves it to disk in the /Scenes sub-directory. After the preview is rendered, the Windows Media Player is loaded and you can play the animation back to view the results. Close the Media Player. You can replay the preview animation at any time by double-clicking on the filename in Windows Explorer.

note

This is an example of the master animator and junior animator analogy mentioned earlier. You are setting the master frames, the start position, and the end position of an animation sequence. The junior animator, 3ds max 4, has filled in all the in-betweens to make the motion smooth.

note

A codec, from **co**mpression/**dec**ompression, is software or hardware implementation of algorithms that make images small enough to playback at usable speeds.

AVI and MOV animation file codecs are known as differential or delta compressors. The first frame gets rendered completely, and then the next frame renders only the pixels that have changed, and so on until the scene is rendered. If the compressor has a keyframe option, it renders a new full frame at the indicated spacing. Different compressors or codecs have different qualities and different compression ratios. You need to experiment to determine the codec that fits your requirements for any project.

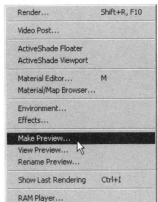

Figure 8.17

In the Rendering pull-down menu, choose Make Preview.

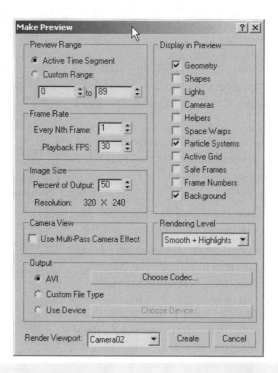

Figure 8.18   In the Make Preview dialog, click Create to accept the default settings.

7. Save the file. It should already be called Ch8_ANIMATION04.MAX.

You have learned to create a position change animation by turning on the Animate button, advancing to a frame other than 0, and making a change in the position of an object to create two keys: one at 0, the other at the current frame. You also learned to render a preview AVI file of the animation.

In Exercise 8.5 you will animate a rotation change for the jeep in the scene to make it appear to slide into position at the other end of the parking lot. The process is similar to the position change you just animated. You determine when the rotation change will be finalized, advance the Frame slider to that frame with the Animate button on, and make the change.

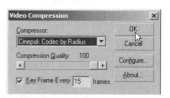

Figure 8.19

In the Video Compression dialog, click OK to use the CinePak by Radius video compressor codec. This renders a quick-and-dirty preview with no shadows, materials, or lighting effects. It is for checking animations, not for final playback.

Exercise 8.5: Animating a Rotation Change for the Jeep

1. Open the file called Ch8_ANIMATION04.MAX from Exercise 8.4 or from the CD-ROM. Save it as Ch8_ANIMATION05.MAX. Drag the Frame slider to frame 0 if it is not already there, or enter 0 in the current frame number field, or click the Go to Start video control button. All have the same effect of setting the current frame to frame 0.

2. Click the Animate button to toggle it on. It will turn red. Advance the Frame slider to frame 75 to make it the current frame.

3. In the toolbar, click the Select and Rotate button, and then right-click the button to call the Rotate Transform Type-In dialog. Enter 90 in the Offset:World z-axis field and press Enter. Click the Animate button to toggle it off and close the Transform Type-in dialog. Scrub the Frame slider back and forth, and you will notice you have a combination move and rotate. However, both the movement and the rotation start at frame 0 and finish at frame 75. The client would like the movement to take place over 60 frames, not 75 frames and the sliding should only occur after the vehicle nears the end. Both actions should end at frame 75 but should begin at different frames. You will correct that in the next exercises.

4. Click the Select button in the toolbar, pick the key that has been created at frame 75 in the Track Bar. It will turn white when selected, and the Track Bar will turn light gray. Position the cursor over the selected key and right-click. A pop-up menu appears showing two keys at that frame, JEEP:Positon and JEEP:Rotation (see Figure 8.20). Click JEEP:Positon to call a dialog that allows changes such as position, time, and key tangency to the specific key (see Figure 8.21). Close the key dialog, you will use it later.

tip

If you have a computer with limited resources or older graphics card, you may not be able to scrub smoothly in a shaded viewport.

To speed the viewport scrubbing, you can toggle the Degradation Override button in the Status bar. The button is all white when it is off and shaded when on.

This causes the viewport to degrade to either Wireframe view or even to Bounding Box mode view to allow smooth scrubbing or playback on any graphics card.

You can also right-click on the viewport label and switch to Wireframe or Other:Bounding Box to force that viewport to a mode that will scrub or playback smoothly.

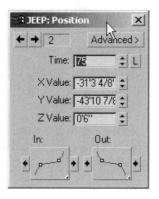

Figure 8.20
Select and then right-click
on the key at frame 75 to
access the pop-up menu.

Figure 8.21
In the key pop-up menu,
choose JEEP:Positon to access
adjustments to the Position
key for the vehicle at frame
75. Close the dialog.

5. Save the file, it should already be called Ch8_ANIMATION05.MAX.

    You have learned to set a Rotation key for an object. You set the Rotation key at the same frame as the Position key and have learned to access adjustments to either key by selecting it in the Track Bar, right-clicking on the key, and choosing the appropriate option in the menu. Much of your day-to-day animation can be handled at this level.

    In Exercise 8.6 you will adjust the animation to the timing requirements of the client. The vehicle should sit for 15 frames before moving. The slide should not start at frame 0 either; it should start at frame 60 for a quick slide into the end position as if the driver had yanked on the parking brake and turned the wheel. You will accomplish these changes by cloning the keys at frame 0 from the start position to frame 15 and the start rotation to frame 60. Cloning keys is done by moving the key with the Shift key held down. This exercise will also illustrate a common issue in basic animation, the anticipation and follow-through programmed into the Bézier Position and TCB Rotation controllers, that can confuse and frustrate new users.

Exercise 8.6: Adjusting the Start Times of Position and Rotation Animation

1. Open the file called Ch8_ANIMATION05.MAX that you saved in Exercise 8.5 or from the CD-ROM. Save it as Ch8_ANIMATION06.MAX. You will clone keys for position and rotation from frame 0 to the respective starting frames for the correct timing.

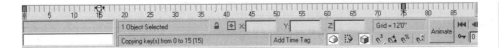

Figure 8.22   Click and then right-click the key at frame 0. Holding down the Shift key, drag the key to frame 15 to clone both the Position and Rotation keys.

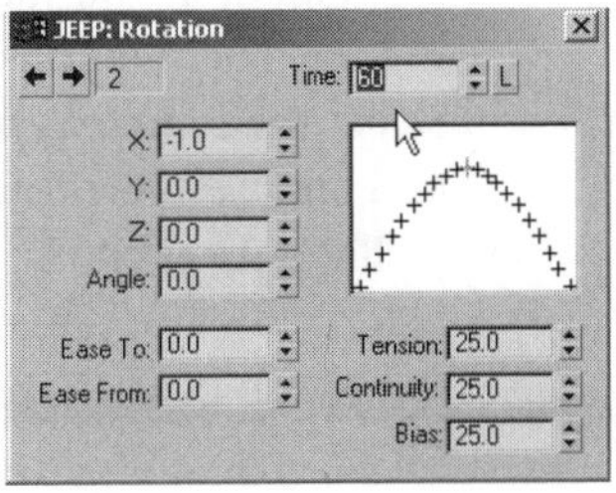

2. With the JEEP object selected, click on the visible key in the Track Bar at the bottom of the display at frame 0 to highlight it white. Hold down the Shift key and drag the animation key to frame 15 on the Track Bar. You can read the frame you are copying from and the frame you are moving to in the Status window below Track Bar (see Figure 8.22). Both the Position key and the Rotation key from frame 0 have been cloned to frame 15.

3. Move the cursor over the new key at frame 15 (it should be selected) and right-click on it. Choose JEEP:Rotation at the top of the menu to access information for that key. In the JEEP:Rotation dialog, enter 60 in the Time field (see Figure 8.23) and press Enter. This moves the Rotation key only from frame 15 to frame 60. Close the JEEP:Rotation dialog.

Figure 8.23
In the JEEP:Rotation dialog, enter 60 in the Time field. This moves the Rotation key from frame 15 to frame 60.

4. Scrub the Frame slider slowly and you will notice two unexpected motions, especially noticeable in the Top viewport. First the vehicle backs up slightly before going forward and it counter-rotates a few degrees at the start. This is caused by preprogrammed tangency information in the Bézier:Position and TCB:Rotation controllers used as default. As mentioned earlier, this is the manner in which characters would move, the wind up and the pitch with follow through, so to speak.

5. To adjust this new motion, you need to change the tangency information of several of the keys from Bézier tangency to Linear tangency for the motion, and you will change the Continuity for the rotation. Click on the Track Bar key at frame 0 and choose JEEP:Positon in the list. In the dialog, click on the In tangency button at the lower left and hold the mouse button to open the flyouts. Choose the Linear flyout button, the second from the top (see Figure 8.24). Click on each of the four black horizontal arrows left and right of the In and Out tangency boxes to copy the Linear tangency to both sides of this key and to the In of the next key. Close the JEEP:Position dialog.

caution   Do not pick the large black arrows at the upper left of the dialog. Those are only for moving from key to key and do not copy the settings.

6. Scrub the Frame slider slowly and watch the vehicle in the Top viewport. There is no more backward movement at the start of the move across the parking lot. There is still some counter-rotation, however. Select the new rotation key at frame 0, right-click and choose JEEP:Rotation in the menu. This is a TCB:Rotation controller. Enter 0.0 in the Continuity field below the tangency graph. This turns the graph to a sharp peak (see Figure 8.25). In the upper left of the dialog, click the right black arrow to advance to Rotation key to frame 60. Enter 0.0 in the Continuity field for this key. Close the dialog and scrub the Frame slider. All anticipation and follow-through for the movement and rotation should be gone, and the vehicle should start cleanly and slide smartly to a stop.

7. Save the file. It should already be called Ch8_ANIMATION06.MAX.

You have learned to access and adjust tangency information for Bézier:Position and TCB:Rotation keys to remove unwanted anticipation and follow-through at certain keys. Play the animation back in the Camera02 viewport or create a new preview animation to overwrite the one you previously created.

The Fundamentals: Path Animation

Animating scenes by creating keys at appropriate frames is certainly a powerful method of moving objects through a scene. However, when the object's path is full of turns in and around other objects, the task of setting the keys and adjusting the tangencies can become daunting, to say the least. The greater the number of keys in the position track, for example, the more difficult it is to remember what each key does.

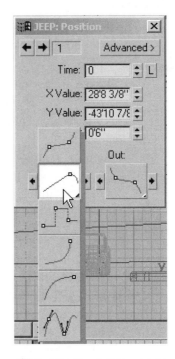

Figure 8.24

In the JEEP:Positon dialog, click and hold the large In tangency button and choose Linear tangency, the second option from the top.

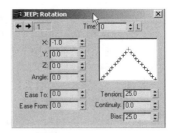

Figure 8.25

For the Rotation keys at frame 0 and at frame 60, set the Continuity to 0.0. This removes tangency from the key, making a clean rotation.

tip There is a field at the bottom middle of the display for adding a Time Tag to a frame to give clues as to what a particular key contributes to the animation.

In the Track View there is also Add Notes Track button that will add a track below the active track. When you add new keys to the Notes Track, you can give a more detailed description of the function of keys in the track above.

note With any Transform animation it is actually the pivot point of the object that is influencing the transformation. For example, the pivot point gets animated during Move; Rotate is around the pivot point; and Scale is about the pivot point in all three axes.

The pivot point is indicated by the gray and red Axis Tripod on selected objects.

There is a method of animating objects through space that can be easier to use in more complex moves. It is a constraint called Path Constraint. Basically you can describe the path an object takes through space by assigning one or more 2D shapes as motion constraints. The motion of the object can be weighted toward one or the other path or paths. This allows for a very flexible method of animating moving objects with incredible control and without the confusion of many keys.

caution The relative positions of the First Vertex of each shape used as a Path Constraint has a profound effect on the end result of the animation.

Assigning Path Constraints

In this section of the chapter you will learn about Path Constraint in its basic form to animate a roller coaster car along the track. However, the exercises will go a little beyond what is normally considered basic animation to introduce you to Ease Curves. Ease Curves are controls superimposed over existing animation that give you a graphical representation of the velocity of objects. You will adjust the Ease Curve to slow and speed the progress of the car on the track.

You will also be introduced to the fundamentals of Hierarchical linking in 3ds max 4. Linking gives you the ability to set up a Parent/Child relationship between objects. Essentially, where the Parent goes, the Child goes with it, but the Child can have its own motion. A human arm is an example of where Hierarchical linking can be used. The hand is linked to the forearm and the forearm is linked to the upper arm. As you move the upper arm its Child the forearm and its Child, the hand, move. Moving the forearm causes only the hand to follow, but the hand can be waving at the same time. This example has a Parent, Child, Grandchild relationship, but the link ancestry can go as deep as necessary.

In the roller coaster example, you will animate something in 3ds max 4 called a Dummy object using a Path Constraint. You will then make adjustments to the velocity of the Dummy object with Ease Curves. Once the animation is satisfactory, you will position the roller coaster car's pivot point in the same position as the Dummy object's pivot point and link the car as a Child of the Dummy. Now you can animate the bouncing or rotation of the car independent of its travel along the path. This simplifies controlling the animation by separating the actions.

In Exercise 8.7 you will create a Dummy object in the roller coaster scene. You will then apply a Path Constraint to it in the Motion panel, Assign Controller rollout, and choose a 2D shape running along the top of the roller coaster structure. This will cause the Dummy object's pivot point to travel along the path.

Exercise 8.7: Creating a Dummy Object and Assigning a Path Constraint

1. Open the file called Ch8_ANIMATION06.MAX that you saved in Exercise 8.6 or from the CD-ROM. Save the file as Ch8_ANIMATION07.MAX. Right-click in the Camera02 viewport to activate it and press C. In the Select Camera dialog, double-click Camera01 to show its view in the viewport (see Figure 8.26). In the Top viewport, select the roller coaster structure called TRACK and click the Zoom Extents All Selected button, found in the flyout below the Zoom Extents All button, to fill the All Orthographic viewports with the selected structure (see Figure 8.27).

Figure 8.26

In Camera02 viewport, press C, and double-click Camera01 in the Select Camera dialog.

2. In the Create panel, Helpers panel, click the Dummy button (see Figure 8.28), and anyplace in the Top viewport, click and drag a small Dummy about the size of the width of the track. The Dummy object will never render and has no adjustable dimensions. It is just a Helper object that can be used effectively in setting up hierarchical links.

3. With Dummy01 selected, open the Motion panel and go to the Assign Controller rollout. Choose Position:Bézier Position in the list to highlight it yellow. Click the Assign Controller button, and in the Assign Position Controller dialog, double-click Path Constraint (see Figure 8.29).

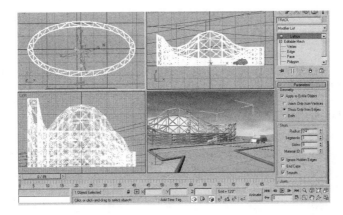

Figure 8.27   Select TRACK in the Top viewport and click the Zoom
Extents All Selected button, found in the flyout below Zoom
Extents All to fill the All Orthographic viewport with the
selected object.

Figure 8.28
In the Create panel, Helpers
panel, click the Dummy
button.

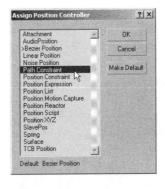

Figure 8.29
In the Assign Controller roll-
out, select Postion:Bézier
Position, and click the Assign
Controller button. In the
Assign Position Controller
dialog, double-click Path
Constraint.

4. In the Motion panel, Path Parameters rollout, click the Add Path button (see
Figure 8.30), type H, and double-click track_path in the Pick Object dialog

(see Figure 8.31). The Dummy01 will jump to the First Vertex on the 2D shape. You will also see two new keys created on the Track Bar, one at frame 0 and one at frame 89. Click the Play Animation button and you will see Dummy01 move along the path in the active viewport. Stop the playback.

The two keys that have been created have values that relate to percentage of the object along the chosen path. The key at frame 0 has a value of 0 percent and the key at frame 89 has a value of 100 percent.

5. Save the file. It should already be named Ch8_ANIMATION07.

You have learned to create a Dummy object and assign a Path Constraint controller to it. You then chose a 2D shape as the path for the pivot point of the Dummy to constrain itself to over the entire length of the animation as set by the number of frames.

note

You can no longer move the Dummy in the scene with the Select and Move Transform button. It is under the control of the Path Constraint, and you have not told it what path to use.

Figure 8.30
In the Motion panel, Path Parameters rollout, click the Add Path button.

Figure 8.31
In the Pick Object dialog, double-click track_path to assign it as the path for the Dummy01 to follow.

Applying Ease Curves for Velocity Control

The speed of the Dummy object along the path is somewhat difficult to calculate. You know the time but not the distance. You will measure the distance shortly, but there is another factor that is not so obvious. The path is a line with Bézier curves. The curvature of the Bézier tangencies affects the speed of the object. The tighter the curve, the slower the object travels.

In Exercise 8.8 you will calculate the current speed of the Dummy on the path and correct the speed variations in the Path Constraint panel by checking the Constant Velocity option. You will then use the Track View for the Dummy to make some basic global changes to the velocity by moving keys. By setting the base animation to a constant velocity you are starting with a known speed, making it easier to make adjustment later.

note

The effect of Bézier curves is more visible when a curved path is used as a Loft path. The segments created by lofting are more tightly packed at the curves and more widely spaced on the straights. The frames are distributed similarly along the animation path.

Exercise 8.8: Setting Constant Velocity

1. Open the file called Ch8_ANIMATION07.MAX that you saved in Exercise 8.7 or from the CD-ROM. Save it with the name Ch8_ANIMATION08.MAX. The first step will be to determine the length of the path to calculate speed of Dummy01 as it travels around the track. In the Top viewport, make sure the Select button is toggled on, type H, and double-click track_path in the Select Objects dialog. In the Utilities panel, click the Measure button (see Figure 8.32). The length of the path is listed in the Shapes area of the Measure rollout as being about 248 feet, rounded to our needs. The speed of the dummy, if it were constant, would be 248 feet ÷ 3 seconds or 82.66 feet per second or around 56 miles per hour. Wow, what a ride!

2. You will now set Dummy01 moving at a constant velocity around the track. In the Top viewport, select Dummy01. In the Motion panel, Path Parameters rollout, check the Constant Velocity option in the Path Options area (see Figure 8.33). The object now travels at a constant velocity.

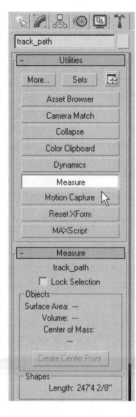

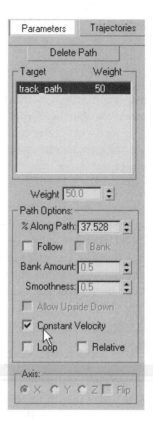

Figure 8.32
In the Utilities panel, click the Measure button to see the length of the path.

Figure 8.33
In the Motion panel, Path Parameters rollout, Path Options area, check the Constant Velocity checkbox to keep the object from slowing down on the curves of the path.

tip

A good way to test to see that this actually works is to apply a Path Constraint to a small box and select an ellipse as the path. Then clone the objects in place as copies and check the Constant Velocity option of one. You will clearly see the difference in velocity of the two boxes when you play the animation.

3. With Dummy01 selected and the Top viewport active, right-click on Dummy01, and choose Track View Selected from the Transform Quad menu (see Figure 8.34). In the Track View, right-click on Dummy01 in the list and choose Expand Tracks. You will see three Range Bars and the two keys in the Percent track. The Track View is where you will assign the Ease Curves.

4. In the Track View, click and drag the key at the far right (frame 89) of the Percent track to about the middle of the track (see Figure 8.35). Play the animation and you will see that the Dummy moves about twice as fast, 100 percent around the track in about half the time. Then it sits still until the animation loops again. You can adjust velocity just by moving the keys in Track View or, if you notice, on the Track Bar.

5. You could also enter 50 in the percent field, and the Dummy would have traveled 50 percent of the way around the track in 40-something frames. In the Track View, right-click on the selected key at frame 40-something and type 89 in the Time field of the Percent dialog (see Figure 8.36). Press enter and the key will go to frame 89.

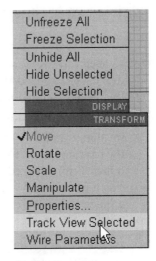

Figure 8.34
Right-click on Dummy01 and choose Track View Selected in the Transform Quad menu to open a Track View for the dummy.

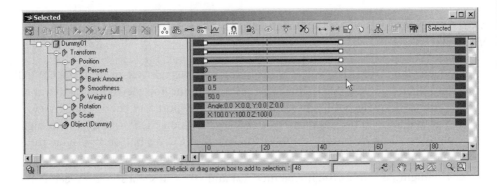

Figure 8.35   Drag the far right key about half way to the left and Dummy01 travels 100 percent of the track in about half the time.

6. Save the file. It should already be named Ch8_ANI-MATION08.MAX. You have set the velocity of the Dummy to a constant speed. You have also learned to open a Track View for the selected object and to move keys to adjust the overall speed or percentage the object travels along the path.

You now have an object traveling at a constant velocity along a path. Next, you will add an Ease Curve to the base animation for a new level of control. As mentioned before, in order to add an Ease Curve to an existing animation you must be in Track View and in a mode called Function Curve with the appropriate track highlighted.

In Exercise 8.9 you will open the Track View for Dummy01 again and go into Function Curve mode to see a graphical representation of the motion of the dummy's pivot point. You will then add the Ease Curve, view it in Track View, and adjust the slope to vary the velocity of the Dummy.

Figure 8.36

Right-click on the selected key, enter 89 in the Time field, and press enter to return the animation to its prior state.

> **note**
>
> Although you are adding an Ease Curve to the percentage track of a moving object, Ease Curves are not restricted to motion animation. The intensity of a light or the color of an object could also have an Ease Curve applied to fine-tune those aspects.

Exercise 8.9: Applying and Adjusting Ease Curves to Change Velocity

1. Open Ch8_ANIMATION08.MAX from the previous exercise or from the CD-ROM. Save it as Ch8_ANIMATION09.MAX. Make sure the Top viewport is active and Dummy01 is selected. Right-click in the Top viewport and choose Track View Selected to open the Dummy01 Track View. Click on the Position label to highlight it yellow. In Track View, click the Function Curves button to display the motion of Dummy01 pivot point as three colored curves (see Figure 8.37).

2. Highlight Percent in the hierarchical list and you will see a straight green curve going up to the right. A straight curve reflects a constant change in the percent along the path. Click on the Apply Ease Curve button toward the right side of the Track View. Be careful to click only once. The Ease Curve appears below and indented from Percent. Highlight Ease Curve in the list. It is also a straight curve to reflect the underlying animation, but it has an extra control point in the middle of the curve.

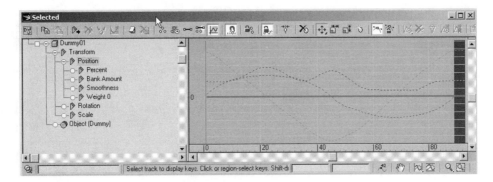

Figure 8.37   In the Track View, with position for Dummy01 highlighted,
click the Function Curves button to display the three curves.

note   Remember the formula XYZ = RGB to see which axis is represented by
which curve. The curves are dotted because they are being determined by
the Path Constraint and the path, not by you directly.

tip   The only reason the Ease Curve appears immediately in the hierarchy is
because you had chosen Expand Tracks in Exercise 8.8. Normally you
would only see a plus sign appear in the white circle to the left of Percent to indicate
the Ease Curve was added lower in the hierarchy.

If you missed the Expand Tracks in Exercise 8.8, you will have to click the plus sign
to expand Percent to show the Ease Curve.

3. Pick the control point in the middle of the Ease Curve to highlight it white. Enter
   25 in the right field at the bottom of Track View and press Enter. The control point
   drops to 25 percent of the way along the path at frame. The curve now starts flat at
   the lower left and gradually gets steeper to the right (see Figure 8.38). Right-click in
   the Camera01 viewport and click the Play Animation button. The Dummy01 starts
   slowly, builds up speed toward the end, and then repeats the loop.

4. In the left field at the bottom middle of Track View, enter 35 and press Enter. The
   Dummy is now 25 percent along the track at frame 35. In the Track View, click
   the Add Keys button and pick on the green curve somewhere to the right of the
   point at frame 35. Click immediately on the Move Keys button to avoid adding
   more new keys. Enter 45 in the left Frame field and 25 in the right Percent field.
   The Ease Curve now rises, dips slightly, and rises again (see Figure 8.39). Play the
   animation in the Camera01 viewport and see that the Dummy starts quickly,
   slows near the top of the first hill, backs slightly on the back side of the hill, and
   then speeds off around the track.

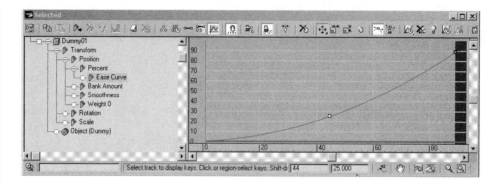

Figure 8.38   Enter 25 in the right field at the bottom of Track View. This
puts the dummy at 25 percent along the path at frame 44.

5. Add new keys and adjust them similarly to those in Figure 8.40. The Dummy
    starts at a steady moderate speed and climbs the hill, pauses, and speeds down. It
    then slowly climbs the second hill, pauses, and shoots down the back side. It is
    then slowed by a brake on the flat and eases into a start position. Play with the
    curve to make your own speeding Dummy. It takes a bit to get a feel for how the
    curve affects the animation but after you learn to do this, you have very good
    control.

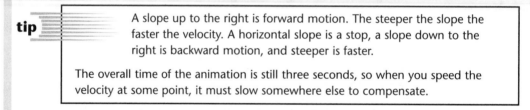

tip

A slope up to the right is forward motion. The steeper the slope the
faster the velocity. A horizontal slope is a stop, a slope down to the
right is backward motion, and steeper is faster.

The overall time of the animation is still three seconds, so when you speed the
velocity at some point, it must slow somewhere else to compensate.

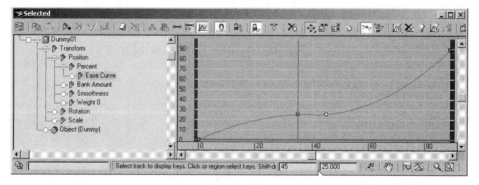

Figure 8.39   Add a new key and set it to frame 45 and 25 percent along
the path. The Dummy slows and backs up slightly before
speeding forward.

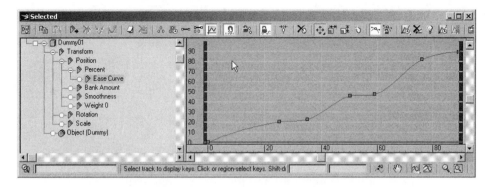

Figure 8.40 An Ease Curve approximates the motion along the roller coaster track. Experiment with adding and moving curves to get the animation the way you like it.

6. Close Track View and save the file. It should already be called Ch8_ANIMATION09.MAX.

You have learned to add and modify an Ease Curve to superimpose velocity changes to an existing animation. You can remove the curve by picking the Delete Ease/Multiplier Curve button in the Track View. This returns you to the base animation you started with.

You have animated Dummy01 moving around the track, but what good does that do if you can never see the Dummy in a rendered image? You will now take advantage of a tool called Hierarchical linking to link the roller coaster car as a Child of the Parent Dummy01. Where the Parent goes, the Child goes too, but the Child can have its own animation.

tip

The number running up the left of the graph is percent along the path, while the numbers left to right on the bottom are frames.

You can also right-click on any selected key on the curve and adjust the tangency on the incoming or outgoing side of the key to fine-tune it.

Because it is the pivot point of the Dummy that is being animated, you will have to align the car to the dummy to match pivot to pivot to ensure the same motion.

In Exercise 8.10 you will align the car to the Dummy and link it as a Child. You will then change some options in the Motion panel for the Path Constraint to cause the car to point straight down the track and bank on the curves.

Exercise 8.10: Basic Hierarchical Linking

1. Open the file called Ch8_ANIMATION09.MAX that you saved in Exercise 8.9 or from the CD-ROM. Save it as Ch8_ANIMATON10.MAX. Right-click in Camera01 viewport to activate it and press W to maximize it. Drag the Frame slider to frame 0. Select the object called BODY, the roller coaster car in front of the structure.

2. In the toolbar, click the Align button, and pick the Dummy01 object in the scene or press H and double-click it in the list. In the Align Selection dialog, check the X Position, Y Position, and Z Position boxes and check Pivot Point in the Current Object column and the Target Object column (see Figure 8.41). Click OK to close the Align Selection dialog. The pivot point of the car is aligned with the pivot point of the Dummy but the car is sideways on the track. You will fix that later.

3. In the toolbar click the Select and Link button at the upper left of the Main toolbar, press H, and double-click Dummy01 in the Select Parent dialog (see Figure 8.42). The Dummy01 is now the Parent of the BODY. Scrub the Frame slider and you will see the car travel sideways around the track with the Dummy.

4. Click the Select button in the toolbar, press H, and double-click Dummy01 to select it. In the Motion panel, Path Parameters rollout, Path Options area, check the Follow option. Play the animation and you will see the car now backs down the track but stays perpendicular to the curves.

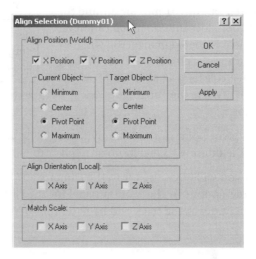

Figure 8.41   With BODY selected, click Align and check all three axis Position options and the Pivot Point option in each column.

Figure 8.42   With BODY selected, click the Link button in the upper left of the Main toolbar, press H, and double-click Dummy01 in the Select Parent dialog to link the car to the Dummy.

5. In the Parameters rollout, Axis area, check the Flip option, and the car now travels forward on the path as you would expect it to. Check the Bank option in the Path Options area. The car now follows and banks on tighter curves of the path in a fairly convincing fashion. Steps 4 and 5 correct the rotation problems seen when the car was first attached to the Dummy01. Without Follow and Bank checked, Dummy01 nor the car rotated at all as they traveled around the path.

6. In the Rendering pull-down menu, choose Make Preview (see Figure 8.43), click the Create button, and click OK to accept the codec. This will render a preview AVI for a shaded animation of the roller coaster that will give you a good idea of what the final rendering would be. Save the file. It should already be called Ch8_ANIMATION10.MAX.

Figure 8.43
In the Rendering pull-down menu, choose Make Preview, click the Create button, and click OK to render a shaded AVI file of the animation for playback. You can also play ROLLER_COASTER.AVI from the CD-ROM.

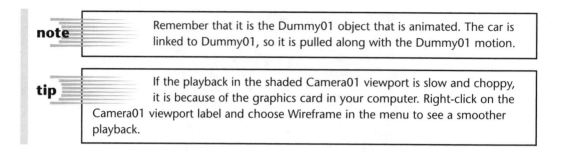

note   Remember that it is the Dummy01 object that is animated. The car is linked to Dummy01, so it is pulled along with the Dummy01 motion.

tip   If the playback in the shaded Camera01 viewport is slow and choppy, it is because of the graphics card in your computer. Right-click on the Camera01 viewport label and choose Wireframe in the menu to see a smoother playback.

Chapter Summary

- **Keyframing**   You have learned the concept of keyframe animation. With the Animate button toggled on and the Frame slider at a frame other than frame 0, almost any change you make to 3ds max 4 becomes animated from the previous key or frame 0 to the current frame.

- **Basic animation calculations**   You have learned some basic calculations for the speed of an object traveling through your scene. Starting with a known speed will make all other timing easier during the animation.

- **Configuring time**   You have learned how to configure time in 3ds max 4 to set the length of a new animation or to change the speed of an existing animation. You can either add or chop frames from an existing animation or expand or compress the total frames.

- **Track Bar and Track View**   You have learned to use the Track Bar and Track View to select and adjust keys to aid in fine-tuning the animation.

- **Tangency controls**   Keys often have tangency information associated with them that allows you to add or remove follow through and anticipation at the keys. You have learned to adjust the tangency at the incoming and outgoing tangency of individual keys.

- **Animation controllers and constraints**   All objects have controllers or constraints when created to define how an object moves. You have learned to change the type of controller or constraint on an object in Motion panel and in Track View.

- **Ease Curves**   You learned to apply basic Ease Curves. You superimposed an Ease Curves on base Path Constraint animation to allow for graphical control of velocity of a roller coaster car on a track. You also learned to hierarchically link a Child object to a Parent object for animation control.

Rendering: Displaying Your Work

In This Chapter

While this will not be a comprehensive tome on all aspects of rendering, you will be introduced to many of the important issues you need to be aware of that will allow you to be productive quickly. Most computer images you will be producing, aside from test renders, will be intended for publication in some form or another. The areas covered in this chapter include:

- **Navigating the Render dialog**   The Render dialog can be intimidating the first time you open it. You will learn to navigate and adjust the essential options to enable you to save and view your work.

- **Rendering efficiency**   Getting the job done on time and on budget is always important. You will learn about the issues that you must be concerned with to make sure you are getting maximum productivity from the render engine.

- **Still image output**   You will learn the fundamentals of rendering still images for viewing or printing. Common file types and appropriate resolution issues will be addressed.

- **Animation image output**   In this chapter you will be introduced to the various animation-rendering processes as well as learn about the basic standards for video- or Web-animation output.

- **Video Post**   A built-in compositing module for overlaying stills or animations on top of each other is provided with 3ds max 4. You will learn the fundamentals of setting up a Video Post render queue.

- **Network rendering**   In this chapter you will be introduced to the processes involved in rendering sequences of images over multiple computers across a network.

Key Terms

Rendering   Rendering shades the design's geometry using the lighting you've set up, the materials you've applied, and environment settings, such as background and atmosphere.

Virtual Frame Buffer   The Virtual Frame Buffer (VFB) is a separate dialog in which the software displays rendered output.

ActiveShade   ActiveShade is a floating dialog similar to the VFB, but it interactively updates to show scene-lighting or material changes without rerendering. It works on the whole scene or on only selected objects.

Resolution   Resolution is simply the number of pixels in width times the number of pixels in height of any image.

Fields   A special method for conveying frame information on a video signal has been developed. This method is called field interlacing. Television monitors display a video signal by separately scanning two portions of each frame called fields. One field contains the odd scan lines of a frame, and the other field contains the even scan lines. Television monitors scan and display the fields of each frame separately. The fields are alternately cycled through every other horizontal line on the screen in a way that they "layer" together to form a single interlaced image.

IFL File   IFL (Image File List) is an ASCII file that lists other single-frame bitmap files to be used for each rendered frame.

NTSC   NTSC (National Television Standards Committee) is the name of the video standard used in North America, most of Central and South America, and Japan. The frame rate is 30 frames per second (fps) or 60 fields per second, with each field accounting for half the interleaved scan lines on a television screen.

PAL   PAL (Phase Alternate Line) is the video standard used in most European countries. The frame rate is 25 frames per second (fps) or 50 fields per second, with each field accounting for half the interleaved scan lines on a television screen.

Codec   Short for compressor/decompressor, codec is an algorithm for compressing and decompressing digital video data and the software that implements that algorithm.

Dithering   Dithering is a method of smoothing the edges between two color regions by mixing their pixels so the edges appear to blend together.

Rendering Fundamentals

You have already performed rendering in previous chapters of this book, either by clicking the Quick Render button or the Render Last button. However, when you close the Virtual Frame Buffer, the rendering is gone and if you close 3ds max 4 and open it again, there is no chance of seeing what any rendering is like without rendering over again.

Rendering, other than test rendering while you are working on a project, usually involves saving the image using one of the file formats that will allow you to view the file at any time from any computer that supports the particular file type you saved.

The process of rendering is often the most time-consuming step of delivering your animation projects to the client, and it is important to develop good habits that will make the process as efficient as possible.

The quality of the rendered images is controlled by several factors that you will learn about in this chapter, including:

- **Image resolution** Both the resolution of the output and the resolution of files used within 3ds max 4 as backgrounds or maps used in materials must be balanced for quality and cost. Images destined for printing must be of a resolution that will result in acceptable quality at acceptable cost.

- **File types** Again, for both output and input, the type of file can affect the quality. Different file types are themselves a compromise of file size versus file quality.

- **Printing or animation playback methods** Images created for one type of printing or animation playback may not be acceptable with other methods.

The Render Scene Dialog

The primary control center for rendering and rendering options is the Render Scene dialog (see Figure 9.1). This is an extensive dialog with many choices that can confuse the new user. In this section you will learn about the most commonly used options that can help increase productivity when you are aware of their functionality. Then you will perform an exercise to render a still image of the finished diner scene used in previous exercises.

This section of the chapter will focus on a still image. The Time Output section in the Common Parameters rollout is set by default to the Single image option. You will address the other options of Time Output in the section on rendering animations.

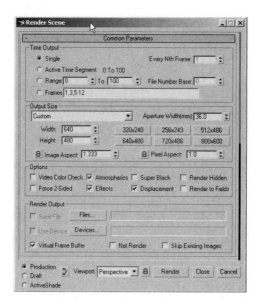

Figure 9.1   The Common Parameters rollout of the Render Scene dialog
is shown.

The Output Size area is where you choose the resolution of the image to render. It is important to set the proper output resolution to make the still image print at the proper size or to make sure animations will fit the display format of the playback device. All renderings done so far in this book have been at the default 640 × 480 pixels. That is a rectangular image 640 pixels wide by 480 pixels tall. This results in an image that is a reasonable size to view on most computer monitors.

The Output Size area has several custom-predefined buttons that you can choose from by picking the button. Before you pick any buttons though, you will learn a little about the Aspect options below the preset buttons. On the left is Image Aspect. This simply reports the aspect ratio of the width in pixels divided by the height in pixels. This can be handy if you know the display aspect you need ahead of time. For example, if you need to render an image that will be projected through a spotlight to cover a wall that is 28 feet wide by 10 feet high, you could render to an Image Aspect of 28 ÷ 10 = 2.8. You set the width resolution to your needs, enter 2.8 in the Image Aspect field, and when you press Enter, the correct height will be calculated.

note

When you enter 2.8, for example, the actual number may round to something else to account for whole numbers in the Width and Height fields.

The Pixel Aspect is more complex in its functionality. Pixel Aspect refers to the width to height ratio for each pixel in the image. It has nothing to do with the Image Aspect. For images that will be printed or displayed on a computer monitor the Pixel Aspect is 1.0. This results in a square pixel output keeping the aspect ratio of the objects in the scene constant in the rendered output. If you change the Pixel Aspect to 2.0 and render an image of a sphere, the sphere will appear distorted. It will be twice as tall as it is wide (see Figure 9.2).

Pixel Aspect settings are designed for video-output devices that perform a process of either overscanning or underscanning to fit the rendered output for viewing on a video monitor or television screen. Each manufacturer of output devices has a different method of correcting the image, so you must check with the owner's manual to get the correct setting. There are three presets common video-output devices, 720×486 resolution with Pixel Aspect of 0.9 for the DPS PVR video-output board, and 512×486 and 256×243 with a Pixel Aspect of 1.266 for the Targa board.

By clicking the Custom field in the Output Size area you can call a list of other standard output sizes for movie, photography, and television industries (see Figure 9.3).

The Options area contains checkboxes for various effects and some options that, when cleared, can save time during test rendering:

- **Video Color Check**   When Video Color Check is checked, 3ds max 4 either corrects illegal video colors or flags those colors with black pixels. There are several options found in the Customize pull-down menu, Preference Settings dialog, Rendering tab, Video Color Check area that describe how illegal colors will be handled. Search on Video Color Check in the Help files for more information on illegal colors.

- **Atmospherics**   Clearing Atmospherics disables effects such as Fog and Combustion effects. This can speed rendering.

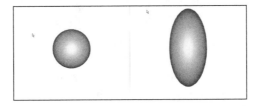

Figure 9.2   The sphere on the left is rendered with a Pixel Aspect of 1.0, the same sphere is seen on the right with a Pixel Aspect of 2.0.

- **Super Black** Checking the Super Black option will ensure that background color will never go below the threshold setting defined in Customize, Preferences, Rendering, Super Black area. This is a setting for television background color.

- **Render Hidden** You can render objects in the scene that has been hidden in the display by checking this option.

- **Force 2-Sided** Faces with the Face Normal point away from the viewer are usually invisible. Checking this option causes 3ds max 4 to show all faces regardless of the direction of the Face Normals. This is good for checking imported mesh objects to see if faces are missing or have just flipped normals. Do not use this for rendering to correct Face Normal problems. Instead use the 2-Sided option in the Material Editor because it is more efficient.

- **Effects** Clearing the Effects option disables lens effects such as Glow and Highlight and effects added to lights. Clearing this option can speed test renders.

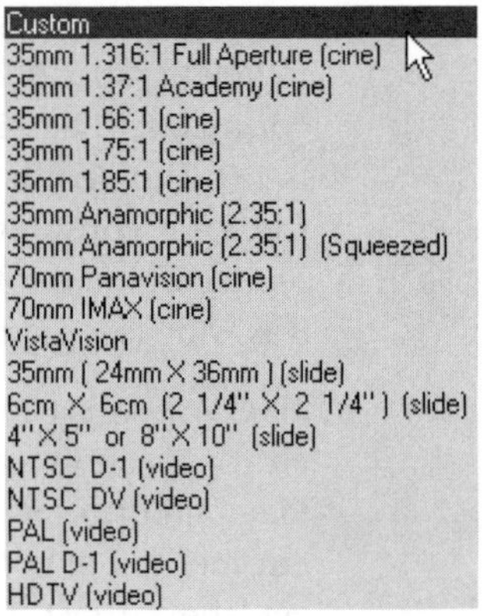

Figure 9.3

Click on the Custom field in the Output Size area of the Render Scene dialog, Common Parameters rollout for a selection of movie, photography, and television preset resolution and Pixel Aspect settings.

- **Displacement** It is possible to create new geometry by using Displacement maps or Displacement modifiers with grayscale images. Clearing this disables the effect during rendering and speeds the process.

- **Render to Fields** Check Render to Fields and the resulting image will contain the even-numbered scan lines from one frame composited with the odd-numbered scan lines from the next image. This can smooth apparent motion when rendering for television or video output.

The Render Output area is where you specify in what file format the rendered images will be saved in. When you click the Files button, you will prompted in the Render Output File dialog for a subdirectory, a filename, and a file type to save to (see Figure 9.4). You can also clear the Virtual Frame Buffer option in this area to render directly to the file without displaying the result on the computer monitor. This can speed the render process, especially when rendering many images for an animation.

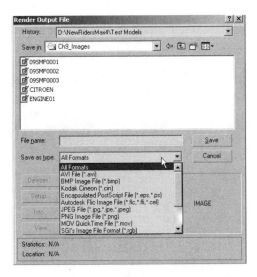

Figure 9.4   The Render Output File dialog allows you to specify a place
and file format for saving your rendered images.

There is also a checkbox to enable Network Rendering to distribute the rendering of
series of still images to various machines on the network. Network rendering will be
covered in more depth later in this chapter.

An option to Skip Existing Images can be handy when rerendering series of animation
files that have been changed. Simply delete the bad files from a subdirectory, tell 3ds
max 4 to render the sequence over, and check this option to have it skip any existing
files in the subdirectory and only render the necessary new files.

The renderer that is used by 3ds max 4 out of the box is called the MAX Scanline A-
Buffer renderer. Several useful options for the new user to be aware of are found here
(see Figure 9.5).

These options include:

- **Mapping**   Clearing this checkbox disables all maps from rendering and that
  can speed test renders. This includes raytrace reflection maps but not raytrace
  material reflections.

- **Shadows**   Clearing Shadows disables shadow calculation for speed and
  computer resource savings while test rendering.

- **Auto-Reflect/Refract and Mirrors**   When this checkbox is clear, no
  Reflect/Refract map effects or Flat Mirror maps effects are calculated. This does
  not affect raytrace map or material reflections or refractions.

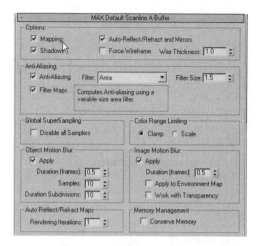

Figure 9.5   The Render Scene dialog, MAX Default Scanline A-Buffer
rollout contains useful options for the new 3ds max 4 user.

- **Force Wireframe**   When checked, this option forces all material assignments
  to be ignored and the mesh objects are rendered with a wireframe material. The
  Wire Thickness setting is in screen pixels.

At the bottom of the Render Scene dialog are options to switch from Production,
Draft, or ActiveShade rendering. These options can be used to speed the production
process. While you are test rendering an animation, for example, you may not need
to see shadows and reflections, but do need to perform color checking to flag illegal
colors with black pixels. You can set a Draft render scheme to reflect these needs and
then choose the Production mode at final render time. The new ActiveShade option
renders to a floating ActiveShade dialog or viewport that automatically reflects the
changes made to lighting or materials in the scene. If objects are selected in the scene
when ActiveShade is invoked, only the changes for those objects are interactively
updated in the windows. This avoids complete scene rerenders when experimenting
with lighting and material tests. When ActiveShade is checked, the options to write
to files are disabled.

There are other rollouts and options in the Render Scene dialog that deal with
antialiasing and filtering of pixels, motion blurring, the new Render Elements
options that will be addressed in Part III of this book. However, those subjects are
beyond the scope of this fundamentals book and are not always essential to good
quality or productive rendering. As with all aspects of 3ds max 4, start simply and
build on existing knowledge to work your way into the more esoteric and complex
areas of rendering.

In Exercise 9.1 you will perform an ActiveShade interactive render on a simple scene first and then make a scene change. Next you will render the scene to a file on your hard drive.

Exercise 9.1: Using ActiveShade and Rendering to Disk

1. Open the file on the CD-ROM called Ch9_CLOCK.MAX. It is a scene with a clock on a table. Save it as Ch9_CLOCK01.MAX. The scene is lit with one Spot light high left behind the camera and one Omni light behind and above the clock (see Figure 9.6). The position of the Omni light causes a specular highlight that is at the left front edge of the clock and is particularly distracting. You will use ActiveShade to reposition the Omni to the back left of the table. The viewer is still aware that the table is wood and somewhat shiny but is not distracted from the main object, the clock.

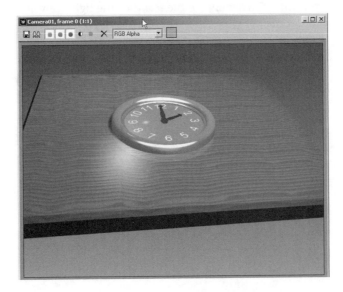

Figure 9.6   A clock sits on a wood table with two lights. The specular highlights at the front left of the clock are distracting.

2. To do a "before and after" comparison, you will first render the Camera01 viewport to the Virtual Frame Buffer and open the result in the RAM Player. In the toolbar, click the Quick Render button. The Camera01 viewport should already be active. Close the Virtual Frame Buffer, and in the Rendering pull-down menu, choose RAM Player. In the Ram Player click the Open Last Rendered Image in Channel A button. Click OK in the RAM Player Configuration dialog to accept the defaults. Minimize the RAM Player.

3. You could change the Omni light in the scene, rerender a test image, maximize the RAM Player, and open the new image into Channel B. If it is not exactly what you want, you could go through the process again. Instead you will use ActiveShade and make several changes that will you be able to see in the ActiveShade viewport. In the toolbar, click the ActiveShade floater button. You will see the Raytrace Engine dialog flash onscreen and the ActiveShade dialog will go black, except for a thin white line that progresses left to right across the top of the image area and then down the right side to show progress. Your image will then appear much as if you were viewing the Virtual Frame Buffer as before.

4. In the Top viewport, select Omni01, click the Select and Move button and move the Omni by picking and dragging on the x transform axis until the light is approximately in the middle of the back edge of the table (see Figure 9.7). The thin white progress line will grow down the right side of the ActiveShade image area and you will immediately see the result of the light move without rerendering the whole scene.

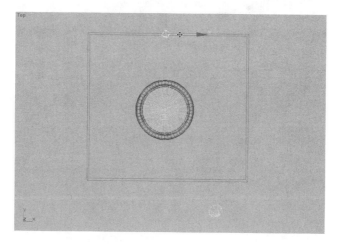

Figure 9.7   In the Top viewport move the Omni01 light to the right to the middle of the top edge of the table. The ActiveShade dialog updates the rendered image in a very short time, compared to a complete rerender of the scene.

5. Press M to call the Material Editor and in the WOOD_TABLE material, which can be found by using the horizontal slider bar at the bottom of the Sample Windows, enter 50 in the Diffuse Color amount field (see Figure 9.8). This shows 50 percent of the diffuse color through the Wood map and the result is shown quickly in the ActiveShade dialog. Close the Material Editor.

tip

Any light type can be positioned with the Place Highlight feature. You must have the light selected and use Place Highlight in a Perspective or Camera viewport.

6. Right-click in the Camera01 viewport to activate it. In the toolbar, click and hold the Align button. In the button flyouts click the Place Highlight button. In the Camera01 viewport, pick and hold on the upper-right corner of the table. You will see a blue Normal Vector appear and the Omni01 light will reposition to place the Specular Highlight at the point of the Normal Vector. While holding the left mouse

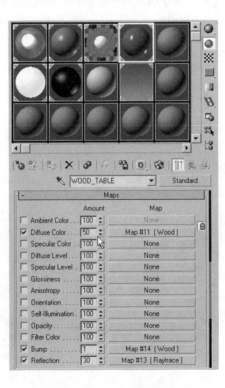

Figure 9.8   Open the Material Editor, and in the WOOD_TABLE material, change the Diffuse Color amount field to 50. The results are seen almost immediately in the ActiveShade dialog.

button, drag the Normal Vector halfway between the clock and the upper-right corner of the table. Release the mouse button and the ActiveShade dialog will update to show the change.

7. Maximize the RAM Player and click the Open Last Rendered Image in Channel B. You will notice that the new image in the ActiveShade dialog is not considered the last rendered image by RAM Player. Right-click on the ActiveShade dialog and choose Render Last in the Render quad menu (see Figure 9.9). This is not the same quad menu you would get if you right-click in the viewports. It has options and tools specifically for ActiveShade. In the RAM Player, click the Open Last Rendered Image in Channel B. You can now use the RAM Player slider to compare the two renderings. Close all the dialogs.

8. Right-click in the Camera01 viewport if it is not already active. In the toolbar, click the Render Scene button. Click the Files button in the Common Parameters rollout, Render Output area (see Figure 9.10). In the Render Output File dialog, choose an appropriate subdirectory, enter CLOCK_TEST01.PNG in the File Name field, and in the Save as type field choose PNG Image File [*.png] (see Figure 9.11). Click the Save button.

tip

You have been using ActiveShade as a floater. By right-clicking on any viewport label, you can choose View and then ActiveShade to make the viewport an ActiveShade viewport.

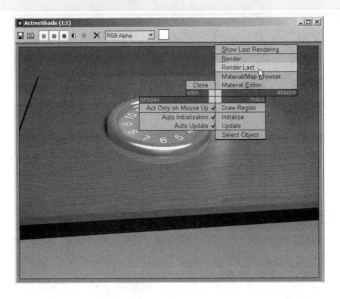

Figure 9.9   Right-click in the ActiveShade dialog and choose Render Last in the Render quad menu. There are other tools and options available only for ActiveShade in this quad menu.

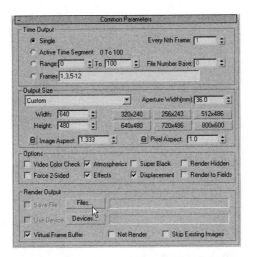

Figure 9.10   In the Render Scene dialog, Common Parameters rollout, Render Output area, click the Files button. The default render settings will be used for this image.

Figure 9.11   Enter CLOCK_TEST01.PNG in the File Name field and choose PNG as the Save as type option.

9. In the PNG Configuration dialog, make sure RGB 24 bit [16.7 Million] is checked and the Alpha channel and Interlaced options are cleared (see Figure 9.12).

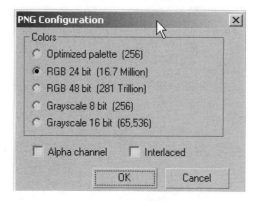

Figure 9.12   In the PNG Configuration dialog, choose RGB 24 bit [16.7 Million] and clear Alpha channel and Interlaced options. Click OK.

Click OK. In the Render Scene dialog, click the Render button. This rerenders the Camera01 viewport and saves the rendered image to the subdirectory and file name you chose in PNG format. It may now be accessed by other users or other software.

10. Close the Render Scene dialog and save the 3ds max 4 file. It should already be called Ch9_CLOCK01.MAX.

You have test rendered a scene and opened it in RAM Player. You have learned to call an ActiveShade floater dialog to see interactive updates of changes to materials and lights in the scene. You then rendered the final image to a file on disk for access by other users and software and compared the final image with the original rendering in the RAM Player.

tip   If you make changes to or transform the objects in the scene, the changes will not be reflected automatically in the ActiveShade dialog. You must right-click on the ActiveShade dialog and choose Initialize in the quad menu.

Rendering Efficiency

In this section of the chapter you will learn about some of the important factors that can affect the length of time it takes to render an image. Very few 3ds max 4 users have the luxury of unlimited time and money budgets, so it is critical that you are not rendering faces or effects that cost either time or money.

For the new user of 3ds max 4, there are three areas of concern that you should focus on in your attempt to cut rendering time:

- **Shadow casting lights** Shadows can be either mathematically expensive or memory intensive.

- **High mesh density** The effect of mesh density on render times is often overlooked by new and experienced users.

- **Bitmap resolutions** High-resolution images, often the result of scanning, can cost computer resources.

These are three issues that, if you become aware of them early, will become second nature to correct as you develop more complex scenes. Ignore these issues early on, and it is very difficult to break bad habits when you are in full production.

In Exercise 9.2 you will open a simple scene that has a coil of garden hose sitting on a poster with the image of a truck. One shadow-casting Spot light is at the upper right and one Omni fill light is low and to the left.

The poster is a flat plane and the garden hose is a twenty-pointed star lofted along a helix. Everything was created using default options and took less than a minute to create.

Two of the issues of concern will be readily apparent: shadow casting and mesh density. You will correct them quickly with noticeable results. The issue of bitmap resolution will only be discussed, and if you have a machine with limited resources, you may see a significant change in render speed by changing bitmaps in the scene.

The image of the truck that is applied to the poster in the scene is a JPG file that is 646KB in size. The same image in uncompressed TGA format is 6135KB or almost 10 times larger. On a machine with limited resources or in a scene with many of these large bitmaps, the paging to the hard drive could occur during rendering, slowing the process to nonproductive levels (see Figure 9.13). Each bitmap used in a scene must be stored in RAM, and if the images are larger than necessary to give the desired results, you

note

As a trainer, the author encounters a surprising number of situations where users have been creating beautiful 3ds max 4 renderings and animations for years but can cut rendering times in half with just a few clicks of the mouse. You must be aware of these simple techniques to make the process more productive.

note

If you have a slow computer the next exercise could take a while due to render times. Bear with the slowness of the first renders to get an idea of how important the information in the exercise is. This is very typical render scenario in terms of time.

Figure 9.13   In this rendered scene of a hose on a poster, render time on a dual Pentium III 650 with 384 megs of RAM is 2 minutes and 15 seconds.

will be using computer resources that might be better applied elsewhere in the render process. Depending on viewed area and output resolution, chances are you would not see any difference between the two images in the final rendering.

Do not throw new hardware at a rendering speed problem until you have gotten your scenes pared down to racing weight. Only then will the new hardware be a cost-effective alternative to increasing productivity.

tip

If the same bitmap is used in multiple locations in the same scene, for example, as a Diffuse Color map and a Bump map and as a Background map, it only has to be loaded into RAM once.

Exercise 9.2: Optimizing for Rendering Productivity

1. Open the file on the CD-ROM called Ch9_HOSE.MAX. Save it as Ch9_HOSE01.MAX. It is the simple scene with a coiled hose, a poster, on shadow casting light, and one fill light. Your task is to improve rendering times. Click the Quick Render button, and when the rendering is finished, read the rendering time in the status bar at the lower left of the display and make a note. A dual 650 Pentium III is 2 minutes 15 seconds for reference.

2. Open the RAM Player and click on Open Last Rendered Image in Channel A. Click OK. Minimize the RAM Player.

3. The scene uses one shadow-casting spot light set to use raytrace shadows. The shadows are often used for outdoor scenes because of the crisp edges. Press H and double-click Spot01 in the Select Objects list. In the Modify panel, Ray Traced Shadow Params rollout, increase the Max Quadtree Depth setting to 10, the maximum (see Figure 9.14). Click the Render Last button.

tip

If you do not see the rendering time because you have done something to cancel it, you can go to Files pull-down menu and choose Summary Info in the menu. This lists the time of the last rendered image, among other things.

note

The quadtree represents the scene from the point of view of the light. Each shadow-casting light ray needs to test intersection with the objects in only one of the leaf nodes of the quadtree. This helps speed up the raytracing process. In general, increasing the maximum quadtree depth can speed up raytracing at a cost of memory.

If you have very limited RAM, setting the Quadtree higher could increase render times.

4. Maximize the RAM Player. Click the Open Last Rendered Image in Channel B button, click OK, and compare the two renderings. There is very little difference. Minimize the RAM Player.

5. In the Shadow Parameters rollout, choose Shadow Map, and in the Shadow Map Params Rollout, enter 1200 in the Size field for a higher-resolution shadow map. Click the Render Last button. On the reference machine this image has took 17 seconds to render.

6. Maximize the RAM Player and click on Open Last Rendered Image in Channel A. Click OK. Comparing the two images will reveal a softer shadow with the Shadow map shadows. Minimize the RAM Player.

7. In the Camera01 viewport, select the HOSE object and then right-click and choose Properties from the menu. This shows that the lofted star on the helix used to make the hose has 58076

tip

By increasing the map size, which is the pixel size of the Shadow map applied at render time, you can sharpen the edge with little increase in overall render times. On machines with minimum RAM, increasing the map size too much can cause paging and longer render times because of the extra RAM needed to store the larger maps.

faces (see Figure 9.15). In the Modify panel, Skin Parameters rollout, check the Optimize Shapes option in the Options area (see Figure 9.16). Close the Properties dialog. This reduces the number of faces by eliminating shape steps in non-curved segments of the loft shape.

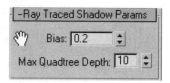

8. Right-click in the viewport and choose Properties again and you will see the face count has dropped to 9676. Close the Properties dialog. Click the Render Last button. The render time on the reference machine has dropped to 7 seconds, a mere 15 percent of the original time with very similar quality of output.

Figure 9.14
Enter 10 in the Max Quadtree Depth field of the Ray Traced Shadow Params dialog. Render the scene again. The dual PIII 650 renders in 34 seconds, about one-quarter the time.

You can now increase the path steps of the lofted hose to remove the segmentation and still keep the same render time. This gives better quality output at 15 percent of the original time.

9. Close all dialogs and save the file. It should already be called Ch9_HOSE.MAX.

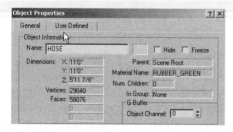

Figure 9.15
Right-click and choose Properties of selected object. The HOSE in the scene has 58076 faces.

Figure 9.16
In Modify panel, Skin Parameters rollout, check Optimize Shapes. This eliminates faces caused by shape steps in segments with no curvature.

You have learned to increase render productivity by controlling shadow type and mesh density. In the heat of deadlines it is very important to watch these items closely. Under certain circumstances, having many maps or very large maps, an increase in productivity can also be realized by changing large bitmaps to a smaller format, JPG or PNG, for example. For this simple still image the difference in noticeable, but if this were a 1000 frame animation, you are talking about a savings of 37.5 hours versus about 2 hours on the reference machine.

There are certainly many other factors that can affect rendering times such as atmospheric effects, lighting effects, or particle systems. However, bitmap size, shadows, and mesh density are often the easiest for the new user to adjust for an increase in productivity.

Rendering for Still Images

In this section of the book you will learn about rendering still images for viewing on the computer or for printing. The major issues for still images are usually these:

- **Resolution** It is often presumed that the greater the resolution, the better quality the image; However, higher resolutions mean larger files.

- **Image Quality** Image quality depends on a few factors including file type and color pixel depth, which will be discussed in more detail later in the chapter.

- **File size** File size becomes more important as the Internet becomes a delivery method of choice to clients. Smaller file sizes transport easier from computer to computer.

You will learn more about these fundamental rendering issues in the following paragraphs. Use this information as a basis to experiment with, not as gospel.

Resolution Issues

As a general rule, higher-resolution still images contain more detail when viewed on computers with larger monitors and the high-resolution images will usually print at higher quality.

However, there is always a price/performance break point that you should be aware of for maximum efficiency. There is no hard-and-fast set of numbers, rather there are rules of thumb that you can use as a starting point for experimentation. Quality is often a very subjective topic that two sides must agree on with compromise on each side.

For example, if you are going to be sending a client still images that they will view solely on the computer and you render those images at a resolution of 4000 × 3000, you will not see the benefit of the higher resolution if the client only has capabilities of viewing at 800 × 600. The extra pixels add time to render and increase file size without much increase in final quality.

The same would be true of rendering an image for printing. If you render to a resolution that is higher than what the printer can output, you might be wasting rendering time. Again there are no hard rules; the process requires experimentation with different resolutions for different output devices.

Printing still images is an art form that requires some experimentation for optimum results. Some of the issues relating to rendering that must be taken into consideration when calculating the resolution for images to be printed include:

- **Printer types**   For example, inkjet printers or others that deposit a certain number of dots of ink on a surface require different resolutions than a continuous tone printer.

- **File types**   Different file types, JPG, BMP, TGA, and so on, have different quality related to color depth and compression ratios.

- **Printer interpolation**   Printers can have software or hardware methods to dither the dots to give the illusion of a higher dot-per-inch count. This allows good quality prints from a lower resolution image.

- **Raster Image Processing**   RIP, as it is often referred to, is a more sophisticated method of dithering that can approach the quality of expensive continuous-tone printers. RIP can be either a software or hardware process.

One term you will hear often in conjunction with printing computer images is *dots per inch*, the number of ink dots in an inch of paper after one pass of the print head. Because of historical reasons, this term is often used inappropriately when referring to computer images.

A computer image is never rendered or viewed in dots per inch, for that is a function of the printer only. Apple Macintosh computers were adopted by the printing community very early on, and because the term was familiar to printers, it became the method of describing what was displayed on the computer monitor. However, the computer monitor displays images in pixels that have nothing to do with the size, in inches, of the monitor. A 15-inch monitor at a resolution of 1024 × 768 displays the same image as a 21-inch monitor at the same resolution. It is just stretched over a larger area.

As an example, Photoshop, a program originally developed for the Macintosh, reports all images, regardless of the resolution at which it was rendered, to be 72 dpi by default.

The following tip is a formula that has become a de facto standard for determining a starting point for display resolution conversion to dots-per-inch printer resolution.

For example, if you want to print a 12 × 8 inch image (horizontal image) on a printer that is rated at 300 dpi you would use:

12 inches × 300 dpi = 3600 for the width in max 4

8 inches × 300 dpi = 2400 for the height in max 4

tip

To calculate the resolution you need to set in 3ds max 4 for printed images, use this formula:

Resolution = print size × dpi rating of the printer

The 12 × 8 would be the actual printer area coverage, not the paper size. This, too, is a rule of thumb. The dithering capabilities of the printer or RIP software can create quality prints at lower resolutions, but if you start here you have some latitude for adjustment.

File Type and Image Quality for Stills

Different file types have different qualities and each file type can have its own levels of quality aside from the resolution. Some of the issues here include:

- **Color depth**   Color depth is the number of possible colors that can be saved within a particular file type, measured in bits, for example 16-bit, 24-bit, or 32-bit color.

- **File compression**   Different file types use different methods of compression for smaller files sizes. Some methods discard information, thus lowering the quality of the image.

Color Depth

Understanding the basics of color depth is important to your choice of file types in many cases. The following is a discussion of the principles of color depth as applied to 3ds max 4 rendering.

The number of colors allowed for a given file type is two to the factor of the color depth, for example:

- 8-bit = 2 to the power of 8 = 256 colors
- 16-bit = 2 to the power of 16 = 65,536 colors
- 24-bit = 2 to the power of 24 = 16,777,216 colors
- 48-bit = 2 to the power of 48 = 281 trillion + colors

The average human's vision can distinguish around 65,000 color shades. However, when an image is rendered with only 256 or even 65,000 total possible colors, subtle shading becomes banded because all the colors have been used elsewhere in the image. This banding effect is often perceived as a low-quality image.

Alpha Channel

You will also see that some of the file types that support 32-bit color depth. That is still only 24 bits of color information with another 8 bits of Alpha channel information attached.

Alpha channel information is transparency information added to a file to allow clean compositing of one image over another and to give smoother edges to images used as Bump, Opacity, or Displacements maps, for example.

note

Many computer games are still rendered as 8-bit or 256 color images. Actually only 236 colors are used in the images; the others are used as the Windows palette.

With careful color planning, stunning images can still be created in 8-bit images, and the low file sizes result in very quick response when played back on the computer.

Computer graphics cards and computer graphics software perform a function called *antialiasing*. Years ago, before antialiasing, a diagonal line drawn on a computer screen resulted in a line with sawtooth edges. Because the computer pixels are single points, a diagonal line has to be represented by offsetting the points causing the stair-stepping or sawtooth effect. Antialiasing smoothes the sawtooth effect by combining primarily line color with a little background color for a few pixels, then combining about 50-50, and then primarily background with some line color. This gives the illusion of a smooth diagonal line.

However, if you have a yellow line on a red background, and then lift the line and composite it onto a white background, the edges are a mess, and the sawtooth effect is made worse with extraneous colors.

32-bit images accomplish the antialiasing, not with color blending, but with 256 levels of transparency. Now when you composite the yellow line onto the white background, there is not a red mix of pixels, rather a variation of transparent yellow. This results in a very clean composite.

See Figure 9.17 for two examples in 3ds max 4 where Alpha channels are explicitly used in both the Materials Editor and in the Video Post dialog.

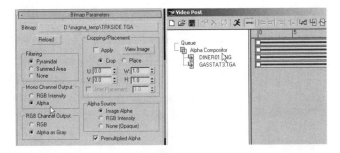

Figure 9.17   The left image shows Alpha Mono Channel Output selected in Material Editor, and the right image shows Alpha Compositor in Video Post.

File Types

3ds max 4 can output to many of the standard file types. The following list gives a short synopsis on some of the more commonly used file formats for rendering still images:

- **Targa**   Targa files usually have the TGA file type. They can be compressed or not and commonly are 24- or 32-bit images. Files can be large.

- **TIFF**   TIFF files have a file ending of TIF and can be compressed or not. They also are often 16-, 24-, or 32-bit images. Files can be large.

- **JPEG**   Files ending in JPG are most commonly 24-bit and do not have Alpha information. They are compressed with a "lossy" algorithm that can cause severe degradation of quality at high-compression rates. File sizes are small.

- **BMP**   BMP files can be 8-bit or 24-bit and contain no Alpha information. Files are moderate to large.

- **EPS**   Encapsulated PostScript files can be adjusted for various PostScript printing device output. Files can be large.

- **PNG**   Portable Network Graphics files are highly compressed with a lossless compression algorithm. They can be from 8-bit grayscale to 48-bit color, most with Alpha channel options. File sizes are small.

- **RPF**   RPF files can be 24- or 48-bit (8- or 16-bits per red, green, and blue channels) with Alpha channel. They may also store a wide variety of optional channels that can be accessed by other software, especially Combustion*, for special effects and editing. RPF files can be enormous, depending on the number of optional channels selected. See Figure 9.18 for the RPF Image File Format dialog.

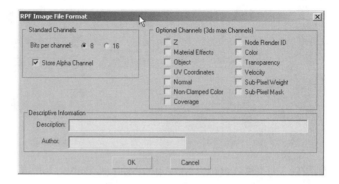

Figure 9.18 In RPF Image File Format dialog, many channels of information can be written and accessed for special effects with programs such as Discreet's Combustion*.

There are other still image formats available in 3ds max 4 that are not so commonly used, including RGB, CEL, and RLA file types. The file type you use will depend on quality needed, importance of file size, and probably most important, whether your client can access the file type you deliver.

Rendering for Animation

Images that are rendered for animations have other criteria that determines the render resolution.

- **Signal converting devices** For animations that will be output to video tape or film recorders, the image must first be processed to the requirements of the particular output device. As mentioned earlier in this chapter, the manufacturer of those devices will specify the resolution and pixel aspect settings that you must render to.

- **Playback media** The performance of the computer on which the animations will play back will affect the resolution you render to. The performance of the computer's playback generally depends on the graphics card and the hard drive performance more than the CPU or amount of RAM in conjunction with the file type rendered to.

tip

There is an old museum rule of thumb that a picture is best viewed from a distance four to five times the length of the diagonal of the image. That is just around 15 feet for a 3 foot × 2 foot image. Large images viewed closely must be very high resolution to be perceived as high quality. However, if you consider this formula, you can still have high-perceived quality images at comfortable viewing distances and much lower resolutions.

Most 3ds max 4 users will be concerned with one of two options, usually video play-back on a television-type device or playback on the computer monitor. Both have very different requirements for cost-effective rendering.

Signal Converters for Video Recording

This section will not cover the pros and cons of specific equipment or conversion methods but will cover the fundamentals of the available options. The quality and price range of video-conversion equipment runs from very inexpensive analog devices to very expensive digital systems. As it stands now, you can usually assume that price directly affects quality. Low-cost devices are incapable of high-quality out-put. The definition of high quality is very dependent on the needs of the viewer, how-ever. Perfectly acceptable quality, when played back on a standard television, can be created for a reasonable price for most users. A range of typical of devices from low cost to expensive include:

- **RGB converters** These are very low-cost devices that may plug into the par-allel port or USB port and convert to a single composite signal. Many laptops come equipped with similar devices today. Prices range from $50 to $200.

- **Mid-range analog and digital converters** These devices output to higher-quality analog component signals as well as the composite signals for bet-ter quality when recorded on S-Video, Hi-8, or Betacam recorders. The newer models often handle Serial Digital (D1) output as well. Costs are several thou-sand dollars and up.

- **High-end uncompressed digital converters** These are very expensive, real-time video output and editing devices. This category includes film recorders for high-resolution feature film output. These are often sold as turn-key systems costing from many thousands to millions of dollars.

Because of the fast-paced changes in the video recording industry, any specific infor-mation would more than likely be outdated by the time this book is printed. When the time comes for you to purchase equipment for production video output, you should search the Internet and attend trade shows such as SIGGRAPH (www.siggraph.org) and the National Association of Broadcasters (www.nab.org) for up-to-date information.

File Type and Image Quality for Animations

Here again, color depth and file compression can be important factors that affect the quality of the output the same as you have for still images. 8- and 16-bit images will show banding, 24-bit images are generally acceptable, and 32-bit images allow for Alpha channel compositing.

Resolution is not such an important factor in animation files because it is determined by either the manufacturer of the converter or the capability of computers to play animations back at an acceptable frame rate. Remember that standard video playback in the U.S. is 30 frames per second, a speed considered to approximate real-time.

Rendering is usually done in one of two manners for animations. You can:

- **Render to an animation file format**   This uses industry standard animation formats known as delta or differential files.
- **Render to still images**   Rendering to sequential still images is a common method of creating animations from 3ds max 4.

The method you choose can depend on the client's need for delivery, animations for video tape or for computer playback. Many users, however, find it useful to use a combination of the methods for convenience and for safety, in case files are damaged or need rerendering.

Rendering to Animation File Format

3ds max 4 has the capability to render to several industry standard file formats that are collectively known as delta or differential file formats. When you render an animation to the hard drive, the first frame is rendered completely. Then the next frame only has the pixels rendered that have changed since the first frame, and so on. Many of the formats also have something called a keyframe, not the same keyframe as in 3ds max 4 itself but a process where approximately every fifteenth frame is rendered completely and the delta process starts again.

File sizes of these delta files are determined by the compression ratio and by the number of pixels that change in each frame. For example, if you have a scene where a small object flies across the screen, the only pixels that change are before and after the object. These files tend to be very small and play back quickly. On the other hand, if you have a scene where the camera pans across the scene, then every pixel changes in every frame. These animations can be extremely large and playback is very choppy.

For images that will be viewed on the computer, either played back from the hard drive, a CD/DVD, or from the Internet, special planning at the storyboard phase to account for the delta process can make the difference between a great reception or disappointment.

Files rendered to a delta format cannot take advantage of the 3ds max 4 ability to render files across a shared network. Because of the difference in the speed of rendering for different machines, there is no way to determine how the delta information should be reassembled.

There are many delta-type file conversion software programs, small files called *codecs*, that you can choose from. File types such as AVI, MOV, and MPEG files can each have many choices that vary in compression rates, color depth, and most importantly, availability. It is critical that you render animations with a codec that is compatible with the codec on the computer on which the file will be played back. This, too, is a fast-changing aspect of computer animation, with new codecs popping up on the Internet practically daily.

caution

When rendering directly to animation file formats, make sure that the codec you are rendering to is available on the computer that will play back the animation.

Animation File Types

3ds max 4 ships with a variety of animation file types and codecs that are considered standards throughout the industry. Using the built-in file types and codecs will insure a reasonable chance that most computers will be able to play back your animations. The commonly used file types include:

- **AVI** Audio-Video Interleaved files in 3ds max 4 include common codecs such as CinePak by Radius, Intel Indeo 3.2, Microsoft Video 1, and Autodesk RLE. AVI files can be rendered in uncompressed form as well. AVI files can have embedded audio tracks.

- **MOV** Apple QuickTime animation format has gained in popularity in recent years. The list of available codecs that ships with 3ds max 4 is impressive. QuickTime MOV files can have audio embedded. See Figure 9.19 for a list of available codecs for MOV files.

- **IFL** Image File List is not an animation file format, but rather an ASCII text file listing single images that can be played back or used within 3ds max 4 as an animation. IFL files do not contain any audio.

Rendering to Still Images for Animation

Rendering to hundreds or thousands of individual still images may not seem to make sense if you are intend to to create an animation to record to video or as computer playback files. However, rendering is a process that adds minimal extra time and offers plenty in the way of safety and flexibility. It's the preferred method of working for many animators.

tip

The RAM Player in 3ds max 4 can play sequential still images or AVI/MOV files back at rates up to 60 frames per second in each channel. The amount of RAM in the computer is the only limitation. Both channels can play animations simultaneously for comparing subtle changes. Sound is not available with the RAM Player.

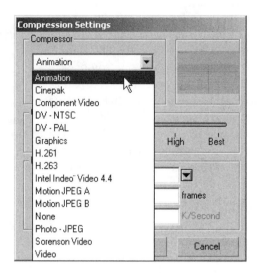

Figure 9.19   MOV file Compression Settings dialog shows codecs
available in 3ds max 4.

A couple of typical scenarios might be, one, that a client tells you that he or she would like an animation that can be played back on the company computers for a few special in-house events. You create a wonderful animation that fits the client's storyboard exactly. You deliver the product and the client tries to play it back on an old 486 laptop and the animation skips large numbers of frames and the quality is terrible.

Or, the client orders the animation for CD-ROM delivery, and it turns out to be a big hit and the client decides to show it at a world-class trade show on a large projector screen.

In both cases you have delivered the wrong format for the situation at hand. The rendering of the animation took two weeks and now you have to render the whole thing again.

Had you rendered the entire animation as a sequentially numbered series of TGA or PNG files, for example, you would have those on disk and could convert them to a new AVI or MOV codec that is more appropriate for the client's computer or copy them directly to a high-end video converter for output to video tape. Both processes that might take a matter of seconds per frame at the most.

The sequential images could also be used in special effects post-processing programs or used back in 3ds max 4 in an IFL file as a Background map or Material map. With the low price of file storage, either on hard drives or on RW CD-ROM, there is little reason not to render to still images and then convert if necessary. You also have the advantage of making changes to the animation, and then rendering only the images that need to be replaced. You cannot insert new information into the middle of an existing AVI or MOV file easily.

In Exercise 9.3 you will render the roller coaster scene as an AVI file, choosing a codec and compression rate. This scene, as you may remember, has the vehicle skidding into place as the roller coaster travels around the track. The rendering process could take a while so plan this exercise accordingly.

> **note**
>
> The reference machine, a dual PIII 650 takes about 17 minutes to render the 90 frames. This file is small enough so the amount of RAM on the computer should not be a significant factor in speed if the machine meets 3ds max 4 minimum requirements as stated in the manual.

Exercise 9.3: Rendering an Animation to a Delta Type Codec

1. Open a file from the CD-ROM called Ch9_ROLLER_COASTER.MAX. Save it as Ch9_ROLLER_COASTER01.MAX. This is the file from Chapter 8 complete with animation. You will render it as an AVI file.

2. Make sure that the Camera02 viewport is active, and in the toolbar, click on the Render Scene dialog. In the Common Parameters rollout, Time Output area, check Active Time Segment. You should see 0 To 89 just after the label indicating it will render the entire 90-frame animation. The default Output Size area resolution of 640 × 480 with a Pixel Aspect of 1.0 will be fine for this animation.

3. In the Common Parameters rollout, Render Output area, click on the Files button. Choose a subdirectory on your hard disk to render to and enter COASTER01.AVI in the File Name field. Choose AVI File (*.avi) in the Save as type list and click the Save button. In the Video Compression dialog, choose Cinepak Codec by Radius, set the Compression Quality slider to 100, and check the Key Frame Every 15 frames (see Figure 9.20). Click OK.

4. In the Render Scene dialog, click the Render button. The animation will render one frame at a time and show each frame in the Virtual Frame Buffer. When the animation is rendered, close the Render Scene dialog and close the Virtual Frame Buffer.

> **note**
>
> If your machine is very slow and will take a long time to render, open COASTER01.AVI from the CD-ROM.

Figure 9.20   In the Video Compression dialog of the AVI render setup, choose CinePak Codec by Radius, set the Compression Quality to 100, and check the Key Frame Every 15 frames option.

5. In the Files pull-down menu, choose View Image File. In the View File dialog, find and click on, COASTER01. This opens Windows Media Player and plays back the animation. Almost any computer should play this animation back at 640 × 480 because the delta information stored in the AVI file is small. Only the vehicle and the coaster are moving in the frames. The file size is just under 4MB.

6. Close all dialogs and save the file. It should already be called Ch9_ROLLER_COASTER01.MAX. You have learned to render a complete animation to AVI format, choosing a codec called CinePak by Radius.

tip

If the file does not play back smoothly on your machine, open RAM Player from the Rendering pull-down menu and open COASTER01.AVI to play it back.

In Exercise 9.4 you will render another scene that has been set up that consists of a flying saucer and a camera. The flying saucer has been animated over 90 frames with movement that corresponds to the objects in Ch9_ROLLER_COASTER.MAX. This time you will render the flying saucer against a black background as a sequentially numbered series of PNG files. The files will be 32-bit images, that is, 24-bits of color with 8-bits of Alpha channel. These images cannot be viewed as an animation with the Media Player. Instead you will have to view them with RAM Player.

Exercise 9.4: Rendering an Animation to Sequential Still Images

1. Open a file from the CD-ROM called Ch9_SAUCER.MAX. It is a very simple scene with only a flying saucer and a camera. Click the Play Animation button to see that the saucer is animated to rise up in the back of the file, set down in the middle, and fly up and off screen over the camera. Click the Play Animation button to stop playback of the Camera02 viewport.

2. With the Camera02 viewport active, click the Render Scene button. In the Common Parameters rollout, Time Output area, check the Active Time Segment option for frames 0 To 89. Again, a resolution of 640 × 480 with a Pixel Aspect of 1.0 will be fine.

3. In the Common Parameters rollout, Render Output area, click the Files button. Go to the same subdirectory you put the last animation file in, enter SAUCER.PNG in the File Name field. Choose PNG Image File (*.png) in the Save as type list, and click the Save button.

4. In the PNG Configuration dialog, check the RGB 24 bit (16.7 Million) option in Colors, and check the Alpha channel option (see Figure 9.21). Click OK in the PNG Configuration dialog and click Render in the Render Scene dialog. Although each frame must be entirely rendered and written to disk, the scene is small and should render quickly. The reference machine took 1 minute 15 seconds for the 90 frames.

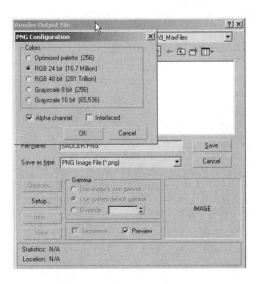

Figure 9.21   In the PNG Configuration dialog, Colors area, choose RGB 24 bit (16.7 Million) option and check the Alpha channel option.

5. In the Rendering pull-down menu, choose RAM Player. In the RAM Player dialog, click the Open Channel A button. In the subdirectory where you saved the rendered files you will see SAUCER0000.PNG through SAUCER0089.PNG, each frame is a separate still image. Choose SAUCER0000.PNG in the list, and at the bottom center of the Open File, Channel A dialog, make sure Sequence is checked (see Figure 9.22). This loads the entire sequence, not just a single image.

6. Click the OK button in the Image File List Control dialog and click OK in the RAM Player Configuration dialog. This loads the sequence in RAM for playback. In the RAM Player, click the Playback Forward button to play the animation of the flying saucer. Close the RAM Player.

7. Close the MAX file. You do not need to save it because you have not made any changes. You have learned to render a sequence of still images to disk and play them back with RAM Player.

tip

If you use Windows Explorer to look in the sub-directory containing the SAUCER sequence of files, you will notice another new file called SAUCER0000.ifl. If you open SAUCER0000.ifl with Windows Notepad or a similar text editor, you will see that it is an ASCII list of all the individual images. You can easily create your own IFL file containing a list of any images, sequential or not, that can be played back or used as a bitmap in the Materials Editor, for example.

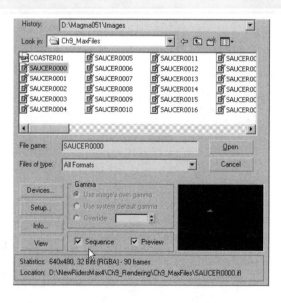

Figure 9.22   Choose SAUCER0000.PNG in the list and check the Sequence option of the Open File, Channel A dialog.

You will use the AVI file and the sequential images in the next section of this chapter on the Video Post module that is included in 3ds max 4.

Video Post

3ds max 4 has a module built into it that is a fairly robust compositing, special effects, and post production tool for assembling and editing animation or still image collages. Video Post offers basic tools for creating more interesting animations including:

- Editing animations and stills with cuts and fades can be done, including Adobe Premier Transition Filters.
- Alpha channel compositing of multiple scenes is possible.
- Scenes can be modified with Adobe Photoshop Filters and Premier Video Filters.
- Contrast and Fade filters can be applied to scenes.
- Lens Effect Glow, Focus, Flare, and Highlights effects can be added to scenes in Video Post.
- Animations can be reversed in Video Post.

Post effects files can be saved as Video Post VPX file types and recalled at a later time for changes or to apply the same effects to different combinations of scenes in the render queue.

Video Post is a linear event processor. You queue a list of events and the scenes or effects get applied in layers from the top of the queue to the bottom. If the hierarchy of events is at the same level, the events are processed one on top of the other. If the event hierarchy is indented in the queue, the indented events are applied only to the last event up the list.

In Exercise 9.5 you will queue the two animations you rendered in Exercise 9.3 and Exercise 9.4. You will then select both events in the queue and apply an Alpha Compositor effect. This overlays one animation over the other using the Alpha information as transparency. Therefore, the AVI file must be first in the queue or the sequence of PNG files will be completely over written by it. With the AVI first and the PNG's second, the transparent Alpha channel will show the underlying scene through it.

Another special effect will be added to the flying saucer layer only to make the specular highlights on the saucer glow.

An output event in the queue will write the composite images out to a new AVI file or sequence of still images.

The process will proceed relatively quickly because the scenes have already been rendered and you will only be applying the compositing and effects.

Exercise 9.5: Video Post Processing

1. Open 3ds max 4 or, in the Files pull-down menu, choose Reset and clear the current session of 3ds max 4. In the Rendering pull-down menu, choose Video Post to call the Video Post dialog. In the Video Post dialog, click the Add Image Input Event button. Click the Files button in the dialog and double-click COASTER01.AVI in the subdirectory where you saved it (see Figure 9.23). Click OK in the Add Image Input Event dialog and the file will be listed in the Video Post Queue.

2. In the Video Post dialog, click the Add Image Input Event button. Click the Files button in the dialog and double-click SAUCER0000.ifl in the subdirectory where you saved it. This loads the list of sequential PNG files of the flying saucer as the second event in the queue. The blue range bars to the right indicate that both files are 90 frames long and both will be processed for the full animation in the order they are in the stack.

Figure 9.23   Double-click on COASTER01.AVI in the Add Image Input Event file list and click OK. This adds the file as the first in the Video Post Queue.

3. In the Video Post Queue, highlight COASTER01.AVI, hold down the Ctrl key, and highlight SAUCER0000.ifl. They should both be highlighted yellow. Click on the Add Image Layer Event button and choose Alpha Compositor in the list. The two animations should be indented below Alpha Compositor in the queue.

note

Entering 200 in the Bright field will cue a glow off pixels that have a brightness of 200 or more onto the flying saucer.

4. In the Video Post Queue, select SAUCER0000.ifl to highlight it yellow (see Figure 9.24). In Video Post, click the Add Image Filter Event. Choose Lens Effects Glow in the Filter Plug-in list, and click the OK button in the Add Image Filter Event dialog to close it. The SAUCER0000.ifl file is now indented below the Lens Effects Glow to show it is the only event affected by the glow.

tip

This would be a good place to use the Online Reference to view the Help file information on Video Post. The Help files are generally more up-to-date than the manuals and contain helpful information.

5. Double-click Lens Effects Glow in the queue and click the Setup button in the Lens Effects Glow dialog. In the Source area, check Whole. In the Filter area, check Bright and enter 200 in the Bright numeric field (see Figure 9.25).

6. In the Lens Effects Glow setup dialog, click the Preferences tab, in the Effects area, enter 4.0 in the Size field. Click OK to save the changes to Lens Effects Glow.

7. Click anywhere in the empty white space of the queue to deselect everything. Click on the Add Image Output Event button. In the Add Image Output Event dialog, click the Files button. In the File Name field enter SAUCER.AVI and choose AVI File (*.avi) in the Save as type list. Click the Save button, click the OK, button, and click the OK button again to accept the Cinepak codec for the output file. Your queue should look like Figure 9.26.

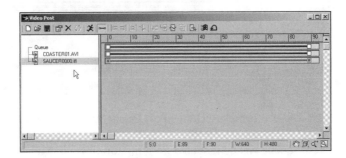

Figure 9.24   Highlight SAUCER0000.ifl in the Video Post Queue to turn it yellow.

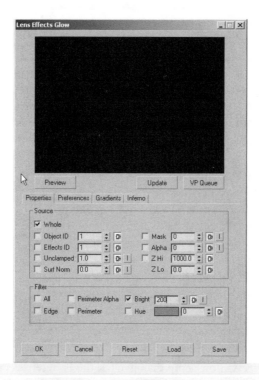

Figure 9.25   In the Lens Effects Glow dialog, Source area, check Whole. In the Filter area check Bright and enter 200 in the numeric field.

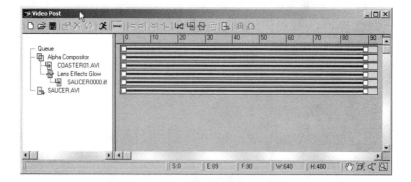

Figure 9.26   In this completed Video Post Queue, the indentations mean the event will be affected by the effect above it only. The queue will be rendered from the top down in a linear fashion. All events take place over 90 frames.

8. In the Video Post dialog, click the Execute Sequence button. In the Execute Video Post dialog, make sure Range is selected and click the Render button. The queue will be processed one event at a time for each frame, ending with the frame being rendered as an AVI file.

tip

If you play back the animation in the RAM Player you can slow the playback to 15 frames per second to better see what the saucer is doing.

9. When the sequence is executed, you can play back the SAUCER.AVI with Media Player or RAM Player to see the result. Close 3ds max 4 without saving any changes.

Because the sequence is executed in a linear manner, the flying saucer and glow effects are applied on top of the roller coaster animation. Complex masking techniques can be used to make the saucer appear to fly from behind the hill and into the structure of the coaster, but that is beyond this lesson.

Network Rendering

Undoubtedly, one of the biggest aids to productivity that is built into 3ds max 4 is the Network Rendering license. The Network Rendering license is the ability to load 3ds max 4 on any number of computers without needing to purchase extra licenses and to render animations across the network. It is simple to set up and easy to manage in a clean network environment. There are a few rules that must be followed:

- One machine must have a legal licensed copy running. An applet known as the Manager is typically run on this machine, but it may also be started on any of the other machines.

- All connected machines, running a Server applet, must have at least a minimal installation of 3ds max 4.

- All machines must meet the minimum requirements to run 3ds max 4 as outlined in the manual.

- All machines must have Microsoft Windows 2000. MS Windows NT 4.0 should work fine but is not officially supported by 3ds max 4.

- All machines must be connected to the network using the TCP/IP protocol.

- Typically, using UNC (Universal Naming Convention) for machines and directories will eliminate confusion with 3ds max 4 finding drives across the network. A UNC name would look like \\sag\d_drive\sub-directory instead of a drive letter. It can also help to set up all path designations in 3ds max 4 (using Customize, Configure Paths, or by editing the 3dsmax.ini file.) to use UNC names.

Starting the Manager Applet

The Manager applet controls the distribution of the rendering to the machines running the Server applets across the network. The Manager must be running for the servers to connect to the Manager.

The Manager may be run as needed or as a Windows 2000 Service in the background where it is always ready. If run as a service, it will be available even after you reboot a machine without the need to restart it.

One way to start the Manager for a rendering session when it is not loaded as a service is to create a Windows Desktop shortcut and load it as needed. When you close a Manager session, it will still be available as a button on the taskbar.

On startup, the Manager dialog reports which machine and subdirectory will share the render jobs and that the Manager has been booted (see Figure 9.27).

You can use the Manager dialog to track the status of aspects of rendering and server assignments and to check error messages while troubleshooting network render problems.

Starting the Server Applet

The Server applet is started in the same manner as the Manager applet, either as it is used or as a service in the operating system.

The Server searches the network and registers itself when it finds the active Manager (see Figure 9.28).

The Server dialog will also track the progress of rendering and error messages for troubleshooting problems you may encounter.

Figure 9.27　Network Rendering Manager dialog is reporting the job share subdirectory and that it has booted.

Figure 9.28   Network Rendering Server dialog is reporting that the Server is started and registered to the TCP/IP address of the Manager.

Starting the QueueManager Applet

Another application included as part of network rendering is the QueueManager. It is not a service, such as the Manager and Server, that enables network transfers but is the control center for monitoring and managing the assignment of network rendering jobs. A shortcut can be created on the Desktop to start QueueManager as needed.

When first started, the QueueManager shows any available servers it finds on the network and lists the Status, Current Job, and Job Status. Because no rendering is in effect as yet, there is minimum information shown (see Figure 9.29).

tip

The most common cause of failure of network rendering seems to be missing maps. Maps may have been deleted or moved to a subdirectory that is not shared by the network rendering system.

Check path configurations and locations of missing maps to correct the problem.

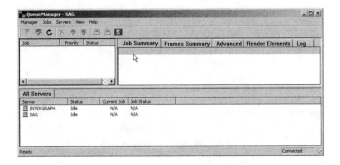

Figure 9.29   QueueManager dialog showing available servers on the network and their status and any assigned render job status.

Rendering to the Network

You set up your scenes as you normally would for any rendering method. When you click on the Render Scene button, you will choose Active Time Segment or a range of files to render, choose the sub-directory and the filename to render to, as usual. You must then check the Net Render option in the Render Scene dialog, Render Output area to tell 3ds max 4 to use the network rendering capabilities (see Figure 9.30).

When you click the Render button of the Render Scene dialog, you will be presented with the Network

Job Assignment dialog. Here you enter a Job Name to identify the project you are rendering and click the Connect button to search for available servers on the network. Valid and available servers will show up in the Server column with a green circle to the left of the server name. Click the Submit button to send the job to the network (see Figure 9.31).

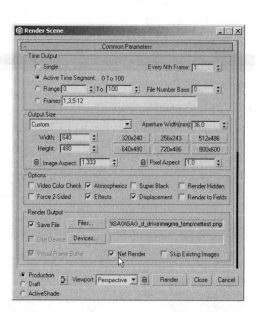

Figure 9.30   In the Render Scene dialog, choose Active Time Segment for a range of frames to render, assign a subdirectory and filename to render to, and check the Net Render option in Render Output area.

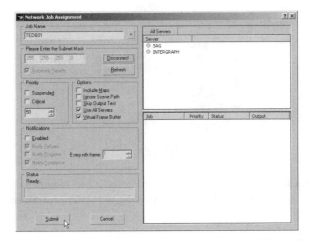

Figure 9.31   In the Network Job Assignment dialog, click the Submit button to send the render job to the servers listed in the upper
right that have green circles to the left of the server name.

After clicking the Submit button, nothing may appear to happen for a few seconds
while the Manager assigns the job to the servers. You should soon see the Render
Scene dialog appear in each server display along with a Virtual Frame Buffer if that
option is turned on.

If you click the Connect button in the QueueManager and choose the Job name,
various information about the rendering progress can be monitored (see Figure 9.32).

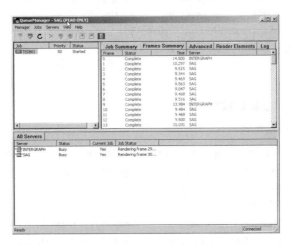

Figure 9.32   Click on the Job Name in the upper left of QueueManager
for reports on the status of the rendering progress and the
status of the assigned servers.

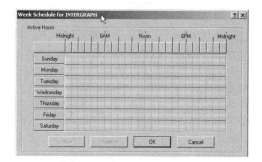

Figure 9.33   A Weekly Schedule can be assigned to servers to avoid scheduled backups or heavy-use periods, for example.

It is possible to suspend, delete, and reprioritize render jobs and to stop or restart servers on the network, among other tasks. Status reports of the progress of the rendering are also available in the QueueManager.

Multiple render jobs can be assigned for overnight rendering and by highlighting and right-clicking on a server name, you can assign a Weekly Schedule to the server to avoid rendering during scheduled backups or during heavy-use times for that Server (see Figure 9.33)

> **tip**
>
> You will probably need the help of a system administrator to ensure that the system will allow access by the network renderer, especially if you have a firewall on your system.

Implementing a network rendering system is generally a straight forward process with few inherent problems. Read the documentation supplied with 3ds max 4 and the readme.txt file that ships with the program before setting up the network rendering system, and then proceed with the setup.

Chapter Summary

In this chapter you have learned about the following:

- **Navigating the Render dialog**   Being comfortable with navigating the Render Scene dialog will help increase productivity by allowing you to quickly choose options that will cut time in the test-rendering or final-rendering process.

- **Rendering efficiency**   You have learned to increase render efficiency by changing shadow parameters, reducing mesh density, and using smaller bitmap file types. Small changes can make enormous gains in productivity.

- **Still image output**   You have learned the fundamentals of rendering still images for viewing or for printing. You learned about different file types and about calculating resolution for a printed image. You learned about the important Alpha channel, too.

- **Animation image output**   You learned that animations can be created by rendering to delta file types or sequential still images. You were also introduced to several of the common animation file types.

- **Video Post**   Here you learned to set up a Video Post queue of animations and special effects. You then executed the queue sequence and rendered the result to a separate file.

- **Network rendering**   In this section you learned the fundamentals of setting up and rendering across a network of compatible computers.

PART III

New and Updated max 4 Features

Modeling: Enhancing Productivity

In This Chapter

In Chapter 10, you will learn about some of the features of 3ds max 4 that will increase productivity and some of the modeling enhancements that have been added to the program.

note
Remember that the most cost-effective method of getting projects done on time and on budget is not to buy new expensive hardware but to utilize all the features built into the program.

tip
As soon as you begin to be comfortable with the 3ds max 4 interface you should investigate the use of the keyboard shortcuts. These one to three key shortcuts are essential to high productivity in the workplace.

You will look at some of the new interface and workflow tools that have been added to the program that help not only while modeling but also while performing other aspects of scene creation. Some of the added features that relate to workflow and the graphical user interface that will be discussed include:

- Quad menus
- Expandable Command panel
- Drag and drop rollouts
- Status line Transform Type-in

- Stack View drag and drop
- Dynamic viewport resizing
- Manipulator mode
- Wire parameters
- Other customization enhancements

By making yourself familiar with these new features and practicing a little on simple scenes, you will quickly incorporate the tools into your daily workflow. Soon the work methods will become second nature, and you will become more productive without really having to learn anything difficult.

Chapter 10 also introduces you to some of the new modeling enhancements added to 3ds max 4. Some of the new tools include new object types while others modify or alter existing objects for more efficient models and workflow. Some of the topics covered include:

tip

By trying the new features on a simple scene you will be able to concentrate better on how the feature works than if you try applying them in large, high-pressure projects.

Breaking old work habits is difficult under deadline stress, but there may be significant increases in productivity once you see how a new feature can be utilized.

- HSDS modifier
- "Turn to" modifiers
- Soft Selection for Editable Spline
- Game tools
- Polygon meshes
- MultiRes modifier
- Cache tools

Again, use these new tools and features on small practice files to get a feel for what they do and how you might blend their usage into your work methods.

Key Terms

Tessellation   The subdivision of surfaces for higher density.

Polygon mesh   A new class of object in 3ds max 4 that uses quads instead of triangles as a sub-object edit level.

HSDS   Hierarchical Sub Division Surface. A new method of subdividing surfaces for multiple levels of higher localized detail.

Border   A new sub-object level within the Polygon mesh object. Edges form a closed interior border.

Point Cache   A file on disk containing the position data for animated sub-object level information. Allows complex animation to play back in real time in the display.

Manipulator   A preprogrammed or customized parameter used to manipulate parameters of objects directly in the viewports.

Workflow Enhancements

You have used some of these new viewport and workflow features if you have performed the exercises in previous chapters of the book. This chapter highlights some of those features if you were paying more attention to the lessons at hand or if you are just focusing on the new features.

Quad Menus

The faster you can access commands without having to remember where a command is located many levels down in a hierarchy of menus, the more productive you will be. Recent versions of 3D Studio MAX have had right-click menus throughout the software. These right-click menus have been augmented with something called Quad menus. Right-clicking in a viewport now accesses a two- to four-panel menu system that places important tools right at your grasp.

Quad menus are named so because a quadrant appears at or near the cursor during a right-click action and the menus grow off these quadrant indicators. (see Figure 10.1).

The actual Quad menu that appears depends very much on what objects are currently selected in the viewport and in what state the object exists, whether it is, for example, a 3D Primitive, a 2D Shape, or an Editable Mesh. The Quad menus will also appear slightly transparent if you are using OpenGL or Direct3D video drivers. This helps view the objects behind the menus when accessing commands.

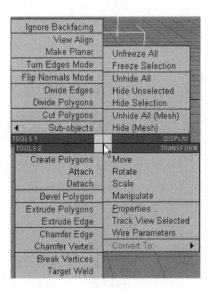

Figure 10.1   Right-clicking in a viewport brings up as many as four Quad menus.

Quad menus are fully customizable in both content of the individual menus and menu appearance upon right-clicking. In the Customize pull-down menu, Customize User Interface dialog, you will see a Quads tab (see Figure 10.2). Within this Quads tab you can change the contents of each Quad menu for the best workflow for your needs.

By clearing the Show All Quads checkbox, only the Quad menu under the cursor will show, making your view of the display clearer. By moving the cursor over another one of the quads, its menu will appear while the other closes.

By accessing the Advanced Quad Menu Options dialog, you can change the look of the Quad menu interface by altering aspects such as the size, color, and fonts used in the menus (see Figure 10.3).

Figure 10.2   In the Customize User Interface dialog, you can choose the Quads tab for customization of the Quad menus.

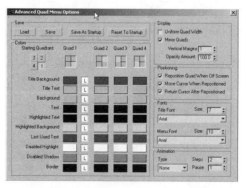

Figure 10.3   More customization of the look of the Quad menus is available in the Advanced Quad Menu Options dialog.

Try right-clicking on various objects and object types in the viewports to get a feel for the capabilities the Quad menus will offer in speeding your access to command levels of 3ds max 4. Remember as you work through exercises or projects to keep trying the right-click options and soon they will become an essential part of your daily routine.

Expandable Command Panel

In previous versions of 3D Studio MAX, it was sometimes very confusing to work with the Command panels that have many options, for example, the Particle Systems Command panel. You could right-click and choose Rollouts to jump to the rollout in the panel, but it is often easier when you can see all the options available at once.

3ds max 4 makes seeing all the options possible with an adjustable Command panel that can be dragged into the viewports for a series of columns showing as many of the rollouts as you need, restricted only by the resolution of your monitor and graphics card.

Clicking and dragging on the left edge of the default Command panel allows you to use as many columns as you need to see all the commands you will be using (see Figure 10.4).

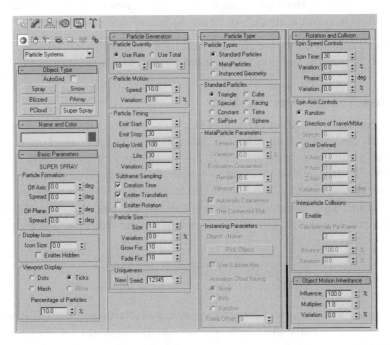

Figure 10.4   The SuperSpray Particle System Command panels expanded on a 1024 × 768 monitor.

By floating the Command panel, you can place it on a second monitor and expand it fully, if your system supports dual monitors.

Drag and Drop Command Panel Rollouts

This is another tool intended to allow you better control over the large unwieldy Command panels. In 3ds max 4 you can reorder the rollouts in the Command panel to bring the rollouts to the top of the panel or just to place them in an order that makes more sense for the task at hand.

In the Command panel you simply click and drag a rollout title bar and drop it higher or lower in the panel. A blue line indicates where the panel will be inserted when dropped. The rollouts can be expanded or closed.

To return the rollouts to their default order in the panel, right-click in an empty space in the panel when you see the hand cursor and choose Reset Rollup Order in the menu (see Figure 10.5).

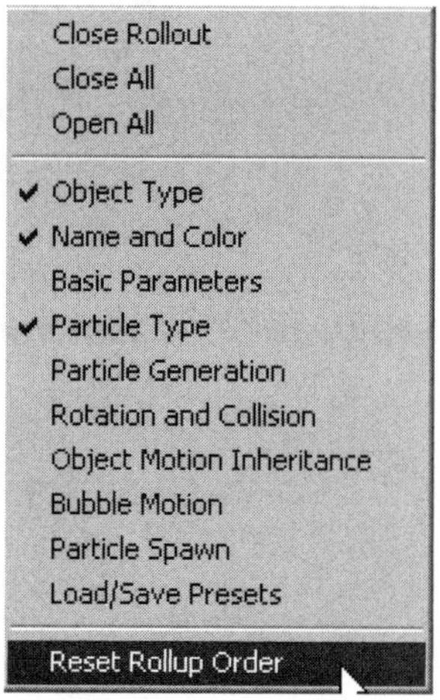

Figure 10.5
Right-clicking in a empty area of the Command panel and choosing Reset Rollup Order in the menu returns the order of the rollouts to the default settings.

The ability to configure the user interface to place most frequently used tools close at hand is invaluable in a production environment.

Status Line Transform Type-In

In previous versions of 3D Studio MAX you have had the ability to select and then right-click on a Transform button: Select and Move, Select and Rotate, and Select and Scale to access a dialog known as the Transform Type-in. It could also be accessed from the Tools pull-down menu or right-click menus. This allows you to type accurate numbers in the Absolute or Relative columns to transform an object a given amount. Those options are still available in 3ds max 4 along with direct entry of numeric data in the Status line coordinate readout fields (see Figure 10.6).

Figure 10.6   You can now enter numeric data directly into the Status line coordinate fields when one of the Transform buttons is active.

In addition, just to the left of the coordinate fields at the center of the Status bar is a Absolute/Relative mode toggle. In Absolute mode the transform happens in absolute World Coordinates. In Relative mode the amount entered in a field is relative to the object's current position, and the axis depends on the current viewport and Reference Coordinate System setting.

note

> In Absolute mode any number entered in the field is added to or subtracted from the total.
>
> In Relative mode the number entered in the field always reverts to 0.0 when you press Enter. This is because the changes in the object are relative to its current state, not from the state it was in before you pressed Enter.
>
> When a Transform button is not selected, the fields report the Absolute coordinate position of the Pivot Point of the current selected object.

Stack View Drag and Drop

Functionality has been added to the editing capabilities within the new Stack View and Modifier List in the Modify panel (see Figure 10.7).

Right-clicking on a modifier in the Stack View offers a menu of choices ranging from renaming and deleting modifiers to temporarily disabling individual modifiers and collapsing part or all of the stack (see Figure 10.8).

You can cut, copy, and paste modifiers with the right-click menu also.

Sub-object editing levels may be selected directly in the Stack View by clicking the plus sign to the left of the stack level and expanding the options (see Figure 10.9).

When a sub-object selection is made in the Stack View, symbols indicating the sub-object level are displayed at the right of the stack.

Modifiers in the Stack View may be reordered, where applicable and valid, by simply dragging and dropping the highlighted modifier or modifiers to a new position higher or lower in the stack.

Modifiers can also be dragged and dropped from the Stack View of one object directly onto another object in the viewport. Dragging a modifier from the stack of

Figure 10.7
The new Stack View and Modifier List in the Modify panel offers functionality and editing capabilities not found in previous versions of 3D Studio MAX.

Figure 10.8
Right-clicking on a modifier
in the Stack View offers easy
editing of the state of the
modifier as well as renaming
to add notation.

Figure 10.9
Click the plus sign to the left
of the object in the Stack
View to expand the item for
sub-object selection levels.
Symbols indicating the
current sub-object level
appear at the right of the
stack.

one object onto another in the scene copies the modifier to the new object. Holding the Ctrl key while dragging and dropping causes the modifier to be instanced and while holding the Shift key moves the modifier from one object to the other.

The names of instanced modifiers are in italic in the Stack View.

Dynamic Viewport Resizing

A feature that has been on the wish list for several versions of 3D Studio MAX is finally available in 3ds max 4: the ability to resize multiple viewports dynamically.

Viewports may be resized at any time by clicking and dragging on the division between two viewports or at the intersection of three or more viewports. (see Figure 10.10.)

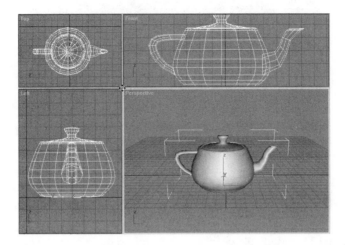

Figure 10.10   Clicking and dragging between two viewports or at the intersection of three or more viewports allows dynamic resizing of the viewports.

To reset the viewports to the default configuration for the number of viewports visible, position the cursor between two viewports, right-click, and choose the Reset Layout option.

Manipulator Mode

There is a new button on the main toolbar called Select and Manipulate or in the Quad menu, Transform, Manipulate. When activated, the Manipulate mode allows editing of objects directly in the viewports by adjusting a Manipulator Gizmo. For example, if you have a Target Spotlight in the scene and you toggle on the Select and Manipulate button, you will see two green Gizmos for the Hotspot and Falloff of the light.

Picking a green Manipulate Gizmo in the viewport highlights it red and allows you to move it to edit the corresponding parameters. A fly-out shows the value of the parameter as you make changes (see Figure 10.11).

Custom manipulators can be created through the Create panel, Helpers panel. You can then use the new Wire parameters to enable a Slider Manipulator to edit the height of a box, for example.

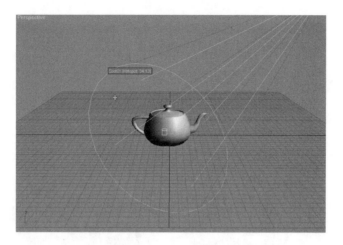

Figure 10.11   Manipulator mode allows you to make edits directly in the viewports while a fly-out shows the parameter settings.

Wire Parameters

The new Wire parameters feature in 3ds max 4 allows you to wire two objects together with relationships that cause a change in one object to affect a parameter of the other. One of those objects can also be a Manipulator Helper mentioned in the previous section.

Wire parameters are applied to one object from the Animation pull-down menu or the Transform Quad menu. Choose a Transform or Object parameter in the pop-up menu that you want to relate to a parameter of another object.

Drag a dashed line to the object you want to wire to and choose either a Transform or parameter of that object. A dialog appears where you can enter an expression that defines a mathematical relationship between the two objects.

Figure 10.12 shows the dialog for a sphere primitive radius parameter being wired with a bidirectional connection to a cylinder height parameter. The expression is Radius*2 (radius times 2). The cylinder's height will always be twice the radius of the sphere. Changing the parameter of one always affects the other and vice versa.

Another example of Wire parameters might be to wire the rotation of a bolt to the Z-axis position of a screwdriver head. As the screwdriver moves down, the screw would rotate clockwise, and as the screwdriver moves up, it rotates counterclockwise for interactive animation.

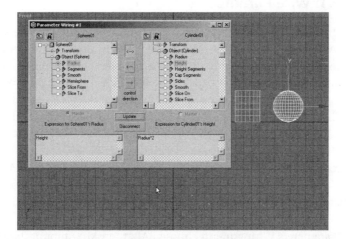

Figure 10.12   Wire parameters can be applied to a sphere and a cylinder so the height of the cylinder is always twice the radius of the sphere, no matter which of the two parameters is changed.

In Exercise 10.1 you will use Wire parameters to associate the color of an object to a specific point in space so that when an object moved into an oven it would glow yellow, as it moved away it would return to gray. The effect is caused by wiring the MixAmount setting of a Blend material to the absolute value of the X-axis coordinate, as measured from 0,0,0 in the World Coordinate System.

note   Exercise 10.1 shows you the process of using Wire parameters. The formula used is for specific points in space, in this case the pivot point of the BAR and 0,0,0 World Coordinate. The formula has to be adjusted for objects in other positions.

tip   The parameters being wired together must be compatible data types. For example, you cannot wire the height of the cylinder with the Bézier Position of the sphere. A single number cannot represent three points in space. You would have to change the Animation Controller to be Euler Position on the sphere to gain access to one axis at a time.

Exercise 10.1: Wire Parameters

1. Open the file called Ch10_WIRING.MAX from the CD-ROM. Save it as Ch10_WIRING01.MAX. The simple scene contains objects representing an oven and a feeder conveyor. As you push the BAR object toward the oven and render the Camera01 viewport, you will see the BAR glow brighter the closer it is to the flame.

2. Right-click in the Camera01 viewport to make sure it is active and render the scene. The BAR is gray at the end of the conveyor, far from the oven flame (see Figure 10.13).

3. Right-click in the Top viewport to activate it and make sure the BAR object is selected in the viewport. In the Animation pull-down menu, choose Wire Parameters, then Wire Parameters again (see Figure 10.14). This calls a menu with all the available parameters of the BAR object.

4. In the Parameters Wiring menu choose BAR, then MixAmount. (see Figure 10.15). Move the cursor and you will see a black dotted line from the Pivot Point of the BAR to the cursor. Pick on the edge of the BAR and choose Transform, then Position, then XPosition in the menus (see Figure 10.16). This wires the MixAmount of the material on the BAR to the XPosition of the BAR itself.

5. In the Parameter Wiring #1 dialog, click the control direction left-pointing arrow button between the upper windows (see Figure 10.17). This creates a one way connection between the parameters with the XPosition controlling the MixAmount parameter. The MixAmount entry in the lower-right window becomes grayed out.

Figure 10.13   Rendering the Camera01 viewport reveals a glowing oven flame and a gray bar at the end of the conveyor.

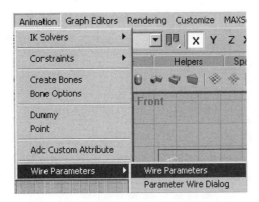

Figure 10.14   From the Animation pull-down menu, choose Wire Parameters, then Wire Parameters again.

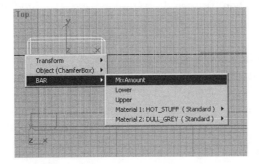

Figure 10.15   In the Parameters Wiring pop-up menu, choose BAR, then MixAmount.

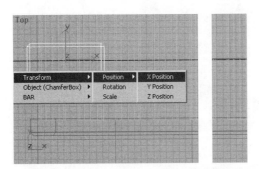

Figure 10.16   Pick the BAR in the Top viewport, then choose, Transform, Position, XPosition from the pop-up menus.

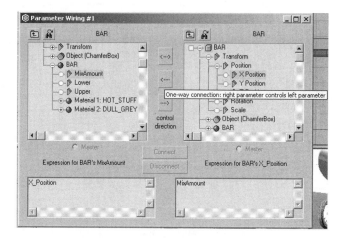

Figure 10.17   Click the left-pointing arrow to create a one-way connection between the XPosition parameter and the MixAmount
parameter. The XPosition controls the MixAmount.

6. In the lower-left window, edit the Expression for BAR's MixAmount formula to
read abs(X_Position/30) (see Figure 10.18). This uses the absolute value of the
XPosition of the BAR Pivot Point to change the MixAmount setting on the Blend
Material. The absolute value is needed because the X coordinate is a negative
number in this case. You divide by 30 to scale the MixAmount number for the
distance from 0,0,0 World Coordinate. Close the Wiring Parameters #1 dialog.

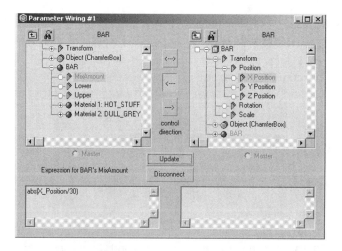

Figure 10.18   In the Expression for BAR's MixAmount window, enter the
formula abs(X_Position/30).

7. In the Camera01 viewport, move the BAR to about halfway between the current position and the oven flame. Click the Quick Render button and you will see that the BAR has changed from gray to a dull yellow.

8. Move the BAR to the edge of the oven flame and render the Camera01 viewport again and you will see that the BAR is a bright self-illuminated yellow. Move the BAR back to the start of the conveyor, render again, and the BAR will be gray.

9. Save the file. It should already be called Ch10_WIRING01.MAX. This is a very specific example of Wire Parameters, but shows the depth that is possible with just a little mathematics knowledge and some planning.

> **note**
>
> While the MixAmount field in the Blend material reads 0 to 100 the internal calculations are based on 0 to 1. Hence, dividing the XPosition by 30 scales the number to work between 0 and 1 in this particular case.

Experiment with some examples of your own wiring. Start with simple steps, perhaps wiring the height of a cylinder to the Radius of a sphere.

Other Customization Enhancements

Many other customization features have been improved or added to make the task of streamlining your workflow even more powerful. Some of the features to increase productivity include:

- **Added keyboard shortcuts**   You can now access many more commands through the Keyboard Shortcut tab of the Customize User Interface menu.

- **Toolbars and menus**   All toolbars and menus can now be customized including pull-down menus.

- **Color customizations**   The Display Color customization tab has been expanded.

- **Track bar**   The Track bar at the bottom of the display is now larger and has ticks showing timing code. You can also display sound tracks below the Track bar.

- **HTML scene summary files**   Through the File pull-down menu you can now save HTML files of scene summaries for publishing directly to Web sites for project management or collaboration.

Take some time to investigate the customization capabilities of 3ds max 4. As you learn more about the program and start to develop work methods, you will be able to set up a workflow that will enable you to get more work done with fewer hassles.

Modeling Enhancements in 3ds max 4

3ds max 4 has not neglected modeling enhancements in this new release. Some of the new features are new methods of modeling like the HSDS modifier, and others are a whole new class of objects such as true Polygon meshes.

There are also new modifiers for optimization of mesh objects and display speed enhancements that should make working with larger mesh objects easier.

Take the time to look through this section of the book and experiment with the new features, again, to get a feel for what they do and how they are different from previous versions of 3D Studio MAX. Once you are comfortable with the feature in its fundamental form you will be able to integrate it into your daily work if it makes sense for you.

HSDS modifier

A new feature that could be significant to many users is the new HSDS modifier. HSDS stands for Hierarchical Sub Division Surfaces, and while it is not used as a primary modeling tool, it allows you to refine a mesh locally with a hierarchy of detail and to have adaptive tessellation of surfaces for more efficiency.

In Exercise 10.2 you will open a file that has a HSDS modifier added to a Patch surface to add some refinement to an eye. It is important that you add detail only where you need it and that you have some flexibility in the editing that allows detail or gross changes. You will move up and down the hierarchy to see where different levels of detail are available. You will not actually need to make any changes in this exercise, it is only to illustrate the use of HSDS modifiers.

Exercise 10.2: HSDS Modifier

1. Open a file from the CD-ROM called Ch10_HSDS01.max. Save the file with the name Ch10_HSDS02.max. The mesh object started as a Patch that was edited at sub-object Vertex into a rough eye shape. For efficiency the Patch was kept at fairly low detail (see Figure 10.19). A HSDS modifier was added and subdivided twice for more detail. In the Front viewport, select the Patch object called EYE.

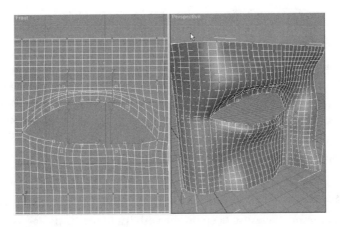

Figure 10.19   The left image is a Patch surface of moderate detail before HSDS modifier is added on the right image.

2. You will notice the HSDS modifier is currently in Vertex mode and a blue selection set of vertices is in the corner of the eye. This is subdivision level 2 of the HSDS modifier. You could transform vertices in this area to form more detail. Try selecting just a few vertices in the inside corner of the eye. In the Modify panel, Soft Selection rollout, check Use Soft Selection and enter 0.2 in the Falloff field. (see Figure 10.20.) This illustrates that you can edit HSDS sub-object level using Soft Selection.

3. In the Modify panel, HSDS Parameters rollout, change the Level of Detail to 1. This is a higher level of vertex editing that surrounds the whole eye. In the HSDS Parameters rollout check and then clear the Only Current Level checkbox. This allows you to hide the parts of the mesh you do not have editing capability on.

4. Drop the Level of Detail to 0 and you have a more global set of vertices available for making larger changes.

5. In the Stack View, choose Vertex sub-object level in the Editable Patch modifier to go to that level. Click Hold/Yes in the Warning dialog. You now have access to very large editing levels using the Editable Patch sub-object tools.

Figure 10.20
Choose the Soft Selection rollout for editing within the HSDS modifier.

6. In the Stack View, click the Vertex level below HSDS and set the Level of Detail to 2. You are back to the fine detail in the corner of the eye. Close the file, you may save any changes you might have made if you like.

With HSDS modifiers you are able to localize the increases in mesh density to fine-tune your models. This can save on computer resources if done on small areas due to the smaller face counts.

Polygon Meshes

Polygon meshes have also been on the wish list of previous versions of 3D Studio MAX and have now been implemented in 3ds max 4. Polygon meshes are very much like Editable Mesh objects, but instead of triangular faces, an extra vertex is added to give you access to true polygon editing. This can help smooth curved surfaces, especially in low polygon models.

An added sub-object level editing option in Editable Poly objects is called Border (see Figure 10.21). A Border is a closed, interior set of images that you can select and modify at sub-object level. The edges that define the eye opening in Exercise 10.1 would be an example of a Border.

Editable Poly objects also have built-in MeshSmooth capabilities and options for weighting or creasing edges or Border selections for smoother or sharper edges.

"Turn To" Modifiers

A new class of modifier called the Turn To modifiers enables you to change the properties of an object from a Mesh to a Patch, for example, within the Modifier Stack. The Turn To modifiers include Turn to Poly, Mesh, and Patch.

This allows you to add specific modifiers that may only pertain to Mesh, Poly, or Patch objects to any object while retaining the ability to control it within the Modifier Stack.

note

You have not changed the topology of the mesh; that is, you have not added or deleted anything at the sub-object level, therefore you can move up and down the stack and ignore the warning.

Figure 10.21

Border is a new sub-object selection level for Polygon Mesh objects that that selects only edges that form a closed interior boundary within a Polygon Mesh.

Converting to a Mesh, Poly, or Patch, on the other hand, is a permanent step that destroys the editing history below the conversion.

In Exercise 10.3 you will open the Patch eye used in Exercise 10.2, without the HSDS modifier. The situation is that you have a Patch object, which you must keep for adjustment purposes, but you also would have an easier time making adjustments around the eye with the Volume Select modifier at Vertex sub-object level. However, in 3ds max 4, a Volume Select modifier operates on the Patch and retains the Patch attributes. You would have better results with your editing if the object were a Mesh object. In 3ds max 4 you can have the best of both worlds with the new Turn to Mesh modifier.

note

In 3D Studio MAX 3, applying a Volume Select modifier to a Patch would automatically convert the whole Patch object to a Mesh object. You would lose the ability to drop down the stack to edit the Patch at this point.

Exercise 10.3: "Turn to Mesh" Modifier

note

Remember, the HSDS modifier is not a modeling tool per se, but a modifier for fine-tuning a surface after the majority of the modeling is finished.

1. Open the file called Ch10_TURNTO.MAX from the CD-ROM. Save it as Ch10_TURNTO01.MAX. It is the mesh used in the previous exercise without the HSDS modifier. The EYE object in the scene is an Editable Patch object, which is ideal for modeling smooth curved surfaces such as faces.

2. In the Stack View, expand the Editable Patch and choose Sub-object Patch in the list. Click the Select button in the main toolbar and, in the Front viewport drag a rectangular selection window over the eyelids. Select should be in the Crossing mode and all the Patch sub-objects forming the eye opening should turn red (see Figure 10.22).

3. In the Modify panel, click the Modifier List and choose Turn To Mesh modifier at the very bottom of the list. Only the selected sub-object Patches are converted to Mesh objects and you still have the opportunity to drop to Editable Patch in the history and make changes at that level.

4. In the Modifier List, Selection Modifiers area, click the Vol.Select modifier. In the Modifier Stack Parameters rollout, check Vertex in the Stack Selection Level area.

5. In the Stack View, choose the Vertex option below Editable Patch. The selected area is passed up the stack and becomes the selected vertices acted on by the Volume Select modifier. You now have all the advantages offered by Volume Select and the capability to edit the eye area as a Patch.

6. Save the file, it should already be named Ch10_TURNTO01.MAX.

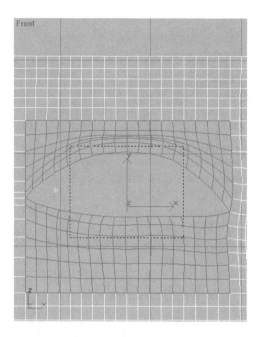

Figure 10.22   Using the Select tool in Crossing mode, select the Patches forming the eye opening.

MultiRes Modifier

MultiRes modifier is, in most cases, a replacement for the Optimize modifier. The Optimize modifier is still available, but MultiRes offers more control and better performance.

In Exercise 10.4 you will apply a MultiRes modifier to a Teapot that has been converted to an Editable Poly object and had the density increased with the built-in MeshSmooth option. With MultiRes you will attempt to reduce the face count of the mesh without destroying the detail.

Exercise 10.4: MultiRes Modifier

1. Open the file from the CD-ROM called Ch10_MultiRes01.max. Save it as Ch10_Multires02.max. It is a teapot primitive that has been converted to Editable Poly and the face count has been increased with the built-in MeshSmooth option. Render the User viewport. From the Rendering pull-down menu, choose RAM Player. In the RAM Player, click the Open Last Rendered Image in Channel A, click OK in the RAM Player Configuration dialog, and minimize the RAM Player. You will compare before and after images.

2. In the Modifier panel, Modifier List, choose MultiRes in the Mesh Editing area. The MultiRes modifier does nothing when first applied. To activate it you must click the Generate button and wait while the original object is cached in memory. You will see a MultiRes cursor appear while the new mesh is being generated.

3. In the MultiRes rollout enter 50 in the Vertex Resolution Percent field and press Enter. The number of faces is reduced to 7945 from 16128 with no noticeable loss of quality. Click the Quick Render button to see the resulting mesh. Maximize the RAM Player and click the Open Last Rendered Image in Channel B button. Click OK in the RAM Player Configuration dialog. Move the small white triangle at the top or bottom of the RAM Player window to compare the teapot before and after optimizing with MultiRes. There is little loss of quality.

4. In the Vertex Count field, enter 2000, and press Enter. The face count drops to 3838 and, if you click the Quick Render button again, you will see just a small amount of distortion at the top edge of the teapot.

5. Enter 10 in the Percent field, press Enter, and notice the face count is only 1548. Render the image and open it in RAM Player Channel B for comparison with the original and you will notice a change in the top edge of the teapot; however, it is not significantly different. The result is far better than the same face reduction with an Optimize modifier on the same object.

One reason MultiRes functions better on the teapot is that it recognizes elements, for example the spout and the handle, and preserves the boundaries between the elements. Optimize treats the object as a single mesh with no distinction at the boundaries.

MultiRes modifier also respects material boundaries better than Optimize, resulting in less distortion of adjacent faces that have different Material IDs assigned.

Soft Selection for Editable Spline

A significant addition to 2D Shape editing is the ability to use Soft Selections on Editable Splines. Soft Selections have been available for Editable Mesh and Vol.Select modifier for a while in previous versions of 3D Studio MAX. The new 3ds max 4 makes it possible to edit 2D shapes with the same control.

Presume you need a map or a mask quickly to create a material that gives the illusion of a fluid dripping down a surface. You do not have any paint software on hand. Exercise 10.5 is a sample file that shows Soft Selection used at the Vertex sub-object level of a

 tip

MultiRes modifier could be used in conjunction with the Wire parameters to create a relationship between the distance of the camera from the teapot to the amount of Vertex Resolution Percent change in the MultiRes.

modified rectangle. The vertices were animated over time and a reference clone was made with a fully white self-illuminated material. All you need to do is render the flat mesh object to an AVI or series of images for your map or mask.

Exercise 10.5: Editable Spline Soft Selection

1. Open a file called Ch10_SoftSelect.max from the CD-ROM. It contains an Editable Spline and a reference clone with a Mesh Select modifier to turn it to a solid plane. The plane has a white material.

2. Scrub the Frame Slider back and forth and you will see that both the 2D shape and the 3D mesh appear to take the form of dripping liquid. (see Figure 10.23.)

3. Pick a vertex or two on the bottom of the 2D shape and see that the Soft Selection allows a weighted effect over several vertices on either side. The color of the vertex indicates how much the vertex will be affected. Red vertices are moved an absolute distance. Orange vertices are affected less, and yellow vertices are affected even less yet. Blue vertices are not affected at all.

4. In the Modify panel, Soft Selection rollout, adjust the Falloff amount up and down to see the effect of increasing or decreasing the radius of influence of the selected vertex.

5. Close the file without saving.

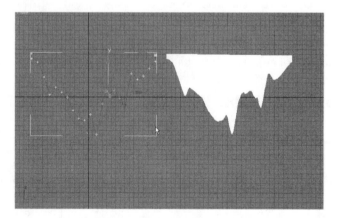

Figure 10.23   Use Editable Spline Soft Selection to create an animated mask or map of dripping fluid.

The process of editing the vertices with a relationship to its neighboring vertices would have required more handwork without the advantage of Soft Selection mode.

Cache Tools

When some modifiers, Flex for example, are applied to objects the mathematical overhead of keeping track of positions of animated vertices during playback can bring even the most powerful computers to its knees.

The Point Cache modifier allows the positions to be written to a file on the hard disk for fast playback.

Exercise 10.6: Point Cache Modifier

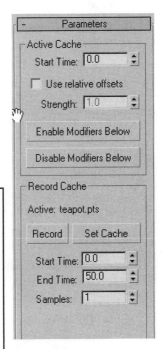

1. Open a file called Ch10_PointCache.max from the CD-ROM. It is a teapot with a Flex modifier set to Soft Body mode. Click the Play Animation button and you should see a very slow, choppy playback.

2. Stop the playback and set the Frame Slider to frame 0. Select the teapot and, in the Modify panel, Modifier List, choose Point Cache (without the leading asterisk) in the Cache Tools area.

> **note** Modifiers that start with an asterisk in the Modifier List indicate a World Space modifier. All the other modifiers are Object Space modifiers.
>
> If you move an object, for example, that has a World Space modifier applied the object passes through space defined by the modifier and changes accordingly. If you move an object that has an Object Space modifier, the modifier's effects are moved along with the object. The movement does not alter the modifier's effect.

Figure 10.24
Clicking the Record button caches the positions of animated vertices and stores them in a file for playback.

3. In the Modify panel, Parameters rollout, click the Record button in the Record Cache area. Enter the name of the .pts file that will be saved on disk and click Save to close the dialog. It may take a while for the cache file to be saved. It will show as the Active .pts file. (See Figure 10.24.)

4. In the Parameters rollout, click the Disable Modifiers Below button so only the point file will be played back.

5. Click the Play Animation button and you will see the flexible teapot animation playing back in real time. The vertex positions are not being calculated and played back live but from the file on disk.

Point Cache modifiers will speed the process of viewing and adjusting animated modifiers that affect sub-object editing of objects in the scene.

Game Tools

A broad range of improvements in 3ds max 4 have been aimed at the computer game market. While aimed at the game market, the improvements can often be taken advantage of by all disciplines of 3ds max 4 users. Some of the improvements include:

- **Interactive multi-texture material in viewports**   This allows the user to view opacity maps and reflection maps in the viewport much as the final game would be rendered. This cuts down on trial-and-error methods of mapping.

- **Viewport vertex illumination and alpha**   This allows color, alpha channel, and illumination vertex editing in the viewports.

- **True transparency features**   Users now see objects in true levels of transparency in the viewports as opposed to the "bug screen" effect in previous versions of 3D Studio MAX.

- **Improved patch modeling**   Soft Selection is available for patch editing. Mapping stays fixed as you edit patches instead of slipping and sliding.

- **Patch Select modifier**   This allows sub-object selections to be passed up to other modifiers. This is more efficient than an Edit Patch modifier, much as Mesh Select works on mesh objects.

- **Custom attributes**   Spinners, sliders, checkboxes, color pickers can be used with Wire parameters to link attributes to parts of the model. For example, a slider in the viewport could be used to adjust the color of an object in the scene.

- **IK limb solver**   This special IK solver type allows game engines to be programmed to use the IK setup directly.

While these are not fundamental topics in the usual sense, become aware of the possibilities in 3ds max 4 early in the learning curve. Review these additions to the program from time to time and see how they might be incorporated into your workflow as you learn 3ds max 4.

Chapter Summary

You have learned topics from workflow improvements to new modeling techniques and methods available in 3ds max 4. Many of the new features fall into both categories by giving you new methods to work with and by helping the workflow as a side benefit.

- **Workflow enhancements**   The ability to customize all menus and to access more commands with keyboard shortcuts can greatly increase the enjoyment of performing repetitive steps by placing the tools where you can get them quickly. The new editing capabilities of the Stack View and expandable Command panels increase this flexibility. The new Manipulator mode allows you to configure objects to be directly edited in the viewports without accessing any menus or panels and Wire parameters lets you set up relationships between object parameters with simple or complex expressions.

- **Modeling improvements**   You have learned about modeling improvements such as Editable Poly objects with built-in MeshSmooth capabilities and about the ability to access and edit the new Border sub-object level. You learned about the new HSDS modifier that allows localized subdivision of surfaces for more detailed editing while leaving the path to higher levels open for more general changes to the mesh. Dense mesh objects may now be optimized with the new MultiRes modifier that respects material and element boundaries for higher optimization with less degradation of quality. Improvements intended for game developers that allow more visual feedback in the viewports of what the game engines will produce is also helpful for the general user of 3ds max 4.

Study the concepts involved in these new features and keep them in mind as you learn the program. As you become more competent with the fundamentals of working with 3ds max 4, incorporate the new features for increased productivity.

Animation: Constraints and Inverse Kinematics

In This Chapter

In Chapter 11 you will learn about some of the new features relating to animation in 3ds max 4. As many of you probably already know from rumors, the Inverse Kinematics (IK) system has been revamped to make it more powerful and easier to use. There are new features for the animation of objects through space, new bones enhancements, and some modifiers have been improved. Some of the things presented in this chapter include:

- **Controllers and constraints** A new paradigm for animating objects
- **Inverse Kinematics** New controls in IK and changes in how bones function.
- **Modifier improvements** Changes in some modifiers add to control and efficiency when animated.

The list of new animation features does not appear to be long, but the changes should allow you to create better animations faster with more control. This frees time that is so critical to the final tweaking that can make the difference between a good animation and a great animation.

This chapter will focus on the highlights of getting started with some of the new animation features. If you are a beginner in 3ds max 4, store this knowledge for later when you become more comfortable with max. More experienced users should investigate applying the concepts and techniques to simple examples. Find out how the options work on a basic model first and then gradually work up to more complex scenes.

Controllers and Constraints

While the heading is "Controllers and Constraints," this section of the chapter is about constraints. The topic of controllers is mentioned because in previous versions of MAX all animation was handled by one controller or another so it is good to know what a controller is.

A default controller is assigned to each object or parameter in 3ds max 4 that can be animated to handle the mathematics of how the animation is applied. Each different type of object can have different types of controllers handling different parameters. For example, if you create a sphere primitive object, its position in space is controlled by a Bézier Position controller that has certain attributes of its own. However, once you apply animation of the radius of the sphere, the default controller handling that is a Bézier Float controller. A Bézier Position controller calculates a value representing the x-, y-, z- axis position of the pivot point of the sphere, while the Bézier Float is a simple floating point value representing the radius.

You, the user, can change the type of controller or, in 3ds max 4, the constraint that changes parameters to calculate those values.

Constraints are different than controllers in that they allow the user to specify several objects in the scene that influence the animation, each with a weighted value that can itself be animated.

Controllers and constraints can be assigned to the transforms in the Motion panel, and to the transforms or object parameters in the Track View.

In this section you will look at several files that show uses for the following new constraints that have been added to 3ds max 4:

- Path constraints
- Position constraints

- Look-At constraints
- Orientation constraints

Look through each exercise and try the suggested changes to see how the constraint can function. Then dissect and disassemble the examples carefully to see the relationship of the components and apply the lessons learned to simple examples of your own.

Path Constraints

In recent previous versions of 3D Studio MAX you could select an object and apply a Path controller to act as an animation path for the object's pivot point. The path you chose had to be an open or closed 2D shape containing one spline only. Animating the object to stray from the actual path required several steps that became a management issue to keep track of when making adjustments.

3ds max 4 now offers a Path constraint. If applied to an object and constrained to a single 2D shape, the constraint would work very much like the Path controller of old. However, in the Path constraint you can select two or more 2D shapes that influence the path of the pivot point over time.

Each of these paths have a weighting value that gives them equal control of the path of the pivot. You can change, animate, or even add a separate controller to the weighting value for some very complex animation that is easy to set up and control.

In Exercise 11.1 you will open a file that contains a chute and a ball. The ball is already animated to rotate on one axis for visualization purposes. You will change from a Bézier controller to a Path constraint to define the position changes for the ball to travel down the chute. You will then make adjustments to make the ball vary its course.

Exercise 11.1: Path Constraints

1. Open a file from the CD-ROM called Ch11_PathConst.max. Save it as Ch11_PathConst01.max. In the file you will see a lofted chute, a sphere, and several 2D shapes. One shape is the loft cross section, and three shapes follow the chute at the bottom center and the two top edges.

2. The Sphere01 should already be the selected object in the scene. In the Motion panel, Assign Controller rollout, choose Position:Bezier Position in the list (see Figure 11.1).

3. Click the Assign Controller button in the Assign Controller rollout, and double-click Path Constraint in the Assign Position Controller dialog (see Figure 11.2).

4. At the top of the Path Parameters rollout, click the Add Path button, press H, and double-click center_path in the Pick Object list. Center_path shows in the Target column with a Weight of 50 (see Figure 11.3). The path is a 2D shape that runs down the bottom center of the chute. The pivot point of the Sphere01 jumped to the path. Scrub the Animation Slider and you will see the sphere move up and down the chute, half in and half out. The path has full control of the position of the pivot point over 100 frames of animation.

5. With the Add Path button still depressed, press H, and double-click left_path in the list. Press H again and double-click right_path in the list. All three 2D shapes are listed under Target each with a Weight of 50. Each has equal influence on the position of the Pivot Point.

6. Scrub the Frame Slider, and then drag it to frame 100. The Sphere01 now hovers equidistant from the three shapes at the end of the chute. In the Path Parameters rollout, highlight center_path in the Target list. Enter 100 in the Weight field and press Enter. The sphere is now weighted toward the center_path shape.

7. Highlight left_path in the Target list, enter 100 in the Weight field and press Enter. The sphere is weighted toward the left edge of the path.

8. Each of the Weight values can be animated over time to cause the sphere to wobble as it travels down the chute. Experiment with various weighting values to familiarize yourself with the influence each can have. Save the file, it should already be called Ch11_PathConst01.max.

Figure 11.1
In the Motion panel, Assign Controller rollout, choose Position: Bezier Position to highlight it.

This animation would probably have been best accomplished with several dummy objects in previous versions of MAX without nearly the control and visual feedback that makes the process quick and easy in 3ds max 4. The paths themselves could also be animated to add even more variation that would be relatively easy to keep track of and adjust.

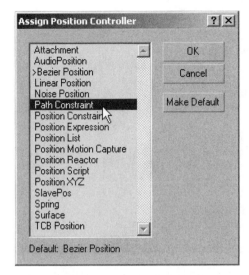

Figure 11.2 Double-click Path Constraint in the Assign Position Controller dialog.

Figure 11.3
Center_path is the target
2D shape that constrains
the position of the
Sphere01 pivot point.

Position Constraints

Where Path constraints use 2D shapes as the constraining elements for the position of the pivot point of objects, Position Constraints use the pivot points of other objects to constrain the position of the given object.

This allows the position of any object to be relative or constant to the position of other objects. For example, if you apply a Position constraint to a sphere and pick two boxes as constraining objects each with a weight of 50, the sphere will always stay equidistant from the two boxes. The sphere moves only if one or both boxes move. Again, everything is based on the pivot point of all objects.

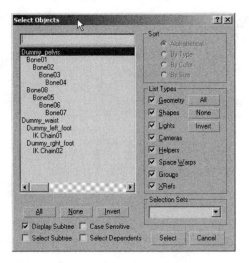

Figure 11.4   The Select Objects list has Display Subtree checked to show hierarchy. Parent objects are to the left, and child objects are indented to the right.

Exercise 11.2 will illustrate a more complex scenario of a bones system of two legs. The legs have an History Independent Solver hierarchy system that you will learn more about later in this chapter.

There are four dummy objects, the left foot, right foot, pelvis, and waist. These are hierarchically linked with the waist as the parent of all dummy objects. See Figure 11.4 for a listing of the hierarchy. Objects to the left are the parent objects. Indentation indicates a child object.

Exercise 11.2: Position Constraints

1. Open a file from the CD-ROM called Ch11_PosConst.max. Save it as Ch11_PosConst01.max. This is a fundamental setup for a bipedal character. The setup uses a Position constraint on the Dummy_pelvis object to position the pelvis equidistant between the dummy objects bound to the feet.

2. In the Perspective viewport, select Dummy_pelvis, the smaller dummy at the top of the leg bones. The large dummy at the top of the leg bones is the waist dummy to which everything is linked. This dummy can be transformed with everything else following and can act as a vertical constraint for the pelvis. If you try to move Dummy_pelvis, you cannot because its position it controlled by the Position constraint.

3. Open Motion panel, Position Constraint rollout to see the assignments of targets (see Figure 11.5.). The Dummy_pelvis is constrained with equal weighting to the waist, right foot, and left foot dummy objects. You will also see that the Keep Initial Offset option is checked to keep the dummies in the same relative position when the targets are assigned.

4. In the Perspective viewport, select Dummy_rght_foot, click Select and Move, and move the dummy up and down in the World Z axis. As you move the dummy, which is linked to the right foot End Effector of the bones system, the leg compresses and the pelvis moves up. The left leg bones also extend to keep a relationship to the pelvis.

Figure 11.5
The Motion panel, Position Con-straints rollout shows the constraint target assignments of the Position constraint assigned to the Dummy_pelvis.

5. In the Perspective viewport, move the Dummy_rght_foot forward and backward in the World Y axis to see that the pelvis stays between the feet in that direction.

6. In the Front viewport, move the Dummy_rght_foot left and right, in the View X axis. The pelvis slides to keep the bones structure in balance (see Figure 11.6). You can tweak the results by adjusting the Weight amounts for each target in the Motion panel, Position Constraint rollout.

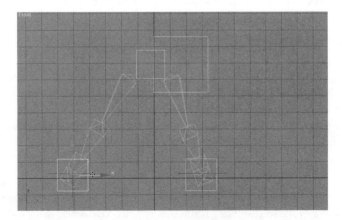

Figure 11.6   Moving the Dummy_rght_foot left and right in the Front viewport causes the Position constraint to hold the pelvis in relationship with the feet, keeping the system balanced.

note To better see what effect the Dummy objects have on the system, try moving the object called IKChain02, the blue Goal crosshair at the end to the right foot HI Solver. This does not use the Position Constraint system and you see that the legs do not keep a relationship with each other and the system appears off balance. Click the Undo button if you actually move the leg and reposition it.

7. Save the file, which should already be called Ch11_PosConst01.max. You should take some time to analyze the hierarchy of the bones structure and try to make the system take a few steps. Previous versions of MAX would have required you to set up mathematical expressions for each of the objects and would not have been easy to tweak.

The Position constraint can be applied to objects to relate their position to that of other objects in the scene. Another use might be to create an atom being held in place by magnetic coils or a squadron of fighters flying in formation.

Orientation Constraints

As a Position constraint handles positional relationships of two or more objects, the Orientation constraint constrains the rotation of an object based on the rotation of its assigned target objects.

In Exercise 11.3 you will see a setup that allows a head to be adjusted to shake a Yes or a No and anything in between by using two dummy objects. The dummy objects have their rotations locked in two of the three axes to make it easy for the animator to shake the head yes or no by quickly rotating the right dummy.

Exercise 11.3: Orientation Constraints

1. Open a file from the CD-ROM called Ch11_OrientConst.max. Save it as Ch11_OrientConst01.max. The file contains the model of a head with the eyes and teeth linked to the head mesh. Two dummies below the face, Dummy_Yes and Dummy_No, have their rotation axes locked in the Hierarchy panel, Link Info, Lock area so that Dummy_Yes can only rotate in the World X axis and Dummy_No can only rotate in the World Z axis.

2. Make sure the HEAD object is selected in the Camera01 viewport. In the Motion panel, you will see that an Orientation constraint has been assigned to the rotation of the head. In the PRS Parameters rollout, check the Rotation button at the bottom of the rollout. In the Orientation Constraint rollout you will notice that the two dummies have been assigned as targets and the Keep Initial Offset has

been checked. Also the Transform Rule is using the World Reference Coordinate System for all objects (see Figure 11.7).

3. Click the Select and Rotate button to activate Rotate Transform, and rotate each dummy in turn in the Camera01 viewport. Because of the locked axis, you can only rotate each in the correct axis to shake the head yes or no. These dummy objects could be anyplace in the scene that is convenient with the same results.

4. In the Motion panel, Orientation Constraint rollout, highlight Dummy_Yes in the Target column and adjust the Weight spinner to see how the orientation can be tweaked toward or away from either dummy.

5. Save the file, which should already be called Ch11_OrientConst01.max. The Orientation constraint gives the animator the advantage of having two remote objects in the scene control the orientation of another object with tweaking capabilities.

The Orientation constraint could be set up to allow dials of gauges to be constraints to the rotation of knobs on a machine or, again, to constrain the rotation of a squadron of fighters to that of the leader.

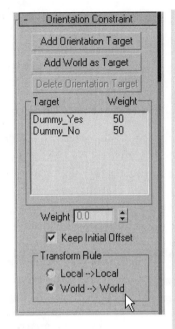

Figure 11.7
An Orientation constraint is assigned to the Rotation Transform of the HEAD object. Dummy_Yes and Dummy_No are assigned as constraints and Keep Initial Offset and World → World are checked.

Look-At Constraints

Previous versions of Max had a Look-At controller that was assigned to the Transform level of an object. It caused the negative z-axis of the always point to the pivot point of a chosen target object.

The new Look-At constraint in 3ds max 4 is assigned directly to the Rotation transform and has many new options for more control. One of the major advantages of the Look-At constraint is the ability to assign an Upnode axis, the axis of the object that points upward. This helps avoid the mathematical situation in previous versions of MAX that caused objects to flip out of control. The Upnode axis was the same as the Look-At axis.

Exercise 11.4 is an example of using a Look-At constraint on the eyes of a character. Each eye is constrained to two dummy objects that, in turn, are linked to the Dummy_HEAD. The results is a system of eye movements that track the dummy objects and can be tweaked for non-human eye effects.

Exercise 11.4: Look-At Constraints

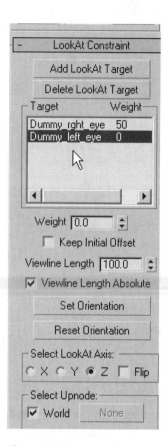

1. Open a file from the CD-ROM called Ch11_LookAtConst.max. Save it as Ch11_LookAtConst01.max. It is a scene with two eyeballs, two eye dummy objects, and a head dummy object. The eyeballs and their dummies are linked to the head so all can be rotated when the head rotates.

2. In the Perspective viewport, select the RIGHT_EYE and click on Motion panel to open it. A Look-At constraint assigned to the Rotation transform of the eye is constrained to each of the eye dummies, for example, the RIGHT_EYE object is set to look at the Dummy_right_eye. The Weight is set so the eye looks straight at its own dummy. The left eye setup is similar.

3. In the Perspective viewport move each eye dummy to see the eye rotate to track the position of the dummy. When you select both eye dummies and move them at the same time, the eyes track in sync with each other.

4. In the Motion panel, LookAt Constraint rollout, high-light Dummy_left_eye in the Target column (see Figure 11.8) and adjust the Weight spinner. The eye can be weighted to look toward one dummy or the other.

Figure 11.8
Adjusting the weighting of an eye to its constrained objects offers fine tuning. This could be useful for the eyes of a lizard tracking two flies, for example.

> **note**
> You will note that each eye has a blue Viewline pointed at the LookAt target. As you change the weight value of the LookAt target in the LookAt Constraint rollout of the modify panel, the Viewline will change white and will reflect the amount of weighting average. Clearing the Viewlength Absolute checkbox causes the Viewlines to extend from the object to the target.

5. In the Perspective viewport, select and rotate the Dummy_HEAD and you will see that the system stays together as the head rotates. Save the file, which should already be called Ch11_LookAtConst01.max.

The new Look-At constraint is applied directly to the Rotation transform of an object and has improved controls over which axis points at the constraint targets and how the Upnode is adjusted to avoid out-of-control situations.

Look-At constraints can also be used to have the back sets of train wheels follow the front wheels around curves on the track or to keep lights trained on actors on a stage.

Inverse Kinematics

Major improvements have been made to the Inverse Kinematics system in 3ds max 4. First, IK is now a controller type known as Solvers. While this has improved the functionality and ease of use for IK, it also leaves the door open for development of new types of IK controllers by Discreet or third-party developers.

Having IK as a controller makes it easier to get rid of any IK animation and allows new bones to be inserted into the middle of a chain, something that required a complete rebuild and setup of the entire chain in previous versions of MAX.

There are now three controllers that can be assigned to bones systems or any hierarchy of linked objects in a scene:

- **HD (History-Dependant) Solver** This replicates the functionality of the old IK system to allow some backward compatibility of files. You would seldom use this in new scenes.

- **HI (History-Independent) Solver** The major feature of this new mathematical algorithm is the fact that you can adjust a Swivel Angle to control the wild fluctuations of bones as they cross the "north pole" of a scene.

- **IK Limb Solver** This new IK controller is specifically designed for two bone systems within special game engines.

This section of the chapter will focus on highlighting some of the attributes of the HI Solver in a straightforward bones system.

The HI Solver controller is much faster than the old History Dependant controller because it doesn't have to keep track of the solutions calculated prior to an given frame. Each frame is calculated only as needed and not referenced back in time.

Another important feature of the HI Solver is the ability to create multiple chains in any system for more local control. An example might be that of a human arm and hand. One solver could run from the shoulder to the finger controlling the whole system, another could run from the wrist to the finger for hand control, and yet another from the wrist to the shoulder for arm control. This allows you to adjust only the chain that makes sense for any given movement.

In Exercise 11.5 you will add a HI Solver to a system of bones representing an arm. The first bone would be the collar bone to hold the arm in position on the body. Bone02 through Bone04 represent the upper arm, forearm, and hand, respectively. Bone05 is the last bone created on mouse-up. You will add a HI Solver and experience the advantages the new Swivel Angle offers in such a system.

Exercise 11.5: HI Solver

1. Open a file called Ch11_HISolver.max from the CD-ROM. Save it as Ch11_HISolver01.max. It contains the bones system described in the previous paragraph. The bones are hierarchically linked with no rotation joint restrictions set in the Hierarchy panel, IK panel.

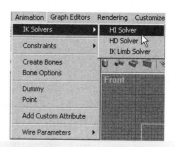

Figure 11.9
In the Animation pull-down menu, IK Solvers menu, choose HI Solver.

2. You will add a HI Solver that will control the chain from Bone05 to Bone02. In the Front viewport, select Bone05 at the end of the hand. In the Animation pull-down menu, IK Solvers menu, choose HI Solver (see Figure 11.9). Move the cursor over Bone02 and click to assign the solver from Bone05 to Bone02 in the Front viewport. A small Goal object will appear at the end of the hand.

3. Select the Goal and, in the Front viewport, click and drag on the XY Transform Gizmo corner and pull the wrist up over the shoulder as if to make a biceps. The arm system rotates strangely around the shoulder and the elbow is bent the wrong way (see Figure 11.10).

4. In the Main toolbar, click the Manipulator button. You will see a green Manipulator handle appear at the end of Bone02. In the Left viewport, place the cursor over the Manipulator handle. A ToolTip will appear indicating the Swivel Angle for the HI Solver.

5. In the Left viewport click the red Manipulator handle and pull the Swivel Angle of the HI Solver so the elbow is in the proper plane. In the Top viewport, move the Goal forward a little. In the Front viewport, pull the Goal to the left a little to place the goal left of the last bone. It should look something like Figure 11.11.

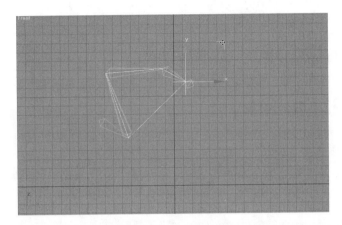

Figure 11.10   Using the XY corner restrict of the Transform Gizmo, move the HI Solver Goal up and toward the shoulder. The elbow bends in the wrong direction.

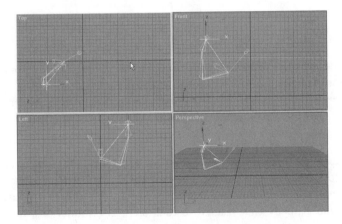

Figure 11.11   Move the Goal forward in the Top viewport and left in the Front viewport to place the Goal as if the hand were in front of an above the face.

6. Save the file. It should already be called Ch11_HISolver01.max. The new ability to adjust a Swivel Angle for a bones system allows new freedom of movement when using IK.

The ability to have multiple chains in a bone system and the advantages of being able to adjust the Swivel Angle of a HI Solver chain should make the entire process of animating characters and machines easier in 3ds max 4. Bones system animation will still require some practice, and you will still encounter unexpected rotations, but you have more tools to recover than ever before.

Animated Modifiers

Two modifiers, while not new to 3ds max 4, have been improved substantially. The two modifiers you will learn about in this section include:

- **Flex** The Flex modifier is a basic form of soft body dynamics modifier. Improvements have been made to the functionality of interaction with Forces and Deflectors.

- **Skin** This modifier allows a mesh surface to interact with a set of bones. There are now Bulge and Angle Deformers.

These modifiers, when animated, can offer a lot of secondary motion in your scenes that add a greater sense of "convinciblity" to the viewer.

tip

> Even small scenes with one seemingly simple Flex modifier can overwhelm even the most powerful computers because of intense calculations.
>
> Once the solution is calculated you can use the new Point Cache modifier to regain real-time playback.

The Flex Modifier

Simulating soft body dynamics on objects can make a simple animation appear much more complex and compelling. For example, a chubby character might seem quite stiff when taking a few steps across the screen but would really come to life with a bit of flex on his belly that reacted to each step. The model of a tree could be greatly enhanced by adding a Flex modifier to the tree and using a Wind SpaceWarp to cause the tree to wave slightly.

In Exercise 11.6 you will use a Flex modifier with the Soft Body Dynamics option to cause a teapot to splatter onto a wall. The scene is set up with the wall and teapot, a Wind force to get the teapot moving, and a Deflector to stop the teapot.

The Flex modifier will cause the teapot to crumple against the wall instead of bounce off.

Exercise 11.6: Flex Modifier

1. Open a file from the CD-ROM called Ch11_Flex.max. Save it as Ch11_Flex01.max. The scene is already set up, and you will add the Flex modifier. The Deflector has been set with a Bounce amount of 0 and a Friction setting of 100 percent. The Wind force is set to a Strength of 0.2. Select the Teapot01 object in the Perspective viewport.

2. In the Modifier panel, click the Modifier List and click Mesh Select in the Selection Modifiers area. Expand Mesh Select in the Stack View and highlight the Vertex option. In the Perspective viewport, select all the vertices of the teapot.

3. In the Modifier List, click Flex in the Animation Modifiers area. Clear the Use Chase Springs and Use Weights checkboxes in the Parameters rollout (see Figure 11.12). Click the Create Simple Soft Body button in the Simple Soft Body rollout.

note   Simple Soft Body creates virtual springs between vertices that cause the vertices to react to the movement of neighboring vertices. Clicking the Create Simple Soft Body button applies spring characteristics based on the Stretch and Stiffness settings found below the button. The Stretch setting sets the elongation of the object while the Stiffness affects the rigidity. The two settings can affect each other to counteract the affect each has.

4. In the Forces area of the Forces and Deflectors rollout, click the Add button, press H, and double-click Wind01 in the Pick Object dialog. You can also pick the Wind01 Gizmo to the right of the box in the Perspective viewport.

5. In the Deflectors area, click the Add button, press H, and double-click Deflector01 or pick the Deflector Gizmo at the front of the box. The rollout should look like Figure 11.13. The Wind force moves the teapot vertices, and the Deflector stops the vertices.

6. In the Modifier List, click Point Cache in the Cache Tools area. Click the Set Cache button and name the file teapot in the Load Points dialog. Click the Open button. In the Record Cache area, click the Record button. You can read the frames as they are recorded at the bottom of the panel.

7. Click the Disable Modifiers Below button in the Active Cache area. Click the Play Animation button, and you will see the teapot slam against the wall and flatten itself. The display plays back quickly because the information is being played from the teapot.pts file, not live.

8. Save the file, which should already be called Ch11_Flex01.max. The Flex modifier is almost always a good candidate for the Point Cache modifier if you want to see the results in the viewports (see Figure 11.14).

Figure 11.12
In the Parameters rollout of
the Flex modifier, clear the
Use Chase Springs and Use
Weights checkboxes.

Figure 11.13
Wind01 is added to Forces
column, and Deflector01 is
added to Deflectors column
in Forces and Deflectors
rollout.

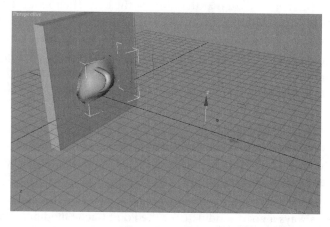

Figure 11.14   The teapot flattens as it hits the wall. Flex and Point Cache
modifiers allow you to play it back in the display.

Used carefully, combinations of Forces and Deflectors used with the Soft Body options of the Flex modifier can give very interesting results.

Skin Modifier

As in previous versions of MAX, the Skin modifier is applied to a mesh object, and a system of bones is linked to groups of vertices. Move the bones, and the mesh follows. There are several improvements in the Skin modifier in 3ds max 4.

In a shaded viewport the influence of the bones is now shown as color information ranging from red to blue to indicate how much the mesh around a vertex is influenced. It is more intuitive to work in a shaded viewport while adjusting the skin of a character, for example, than to work in wireframe.

Angle Deformers are now available in the Skin modifier. These are subsets of vertices that can transform based on the angle of the bone they are attached to. There are Bulge, Joint, and Morph Angle Deformers available in 3ds max 4.

In Exercise 11.7 you will see how a simple bone system that is attached to an arm with the Skin modifier functions. You will add a Bulge Angle Deformer to the forearm bone to cause the biceps to bulge when the forearm is raised.

Exercise 11.7: Skin Modifier

1. Open a file from the CD-ROM called Ch11_Skin.max. Save it as Ch11_Skin01.max. In the Front viewport, pick the HI Solver Goal, the blue cross at the end of the hand bone, and move it up and left to cause the arm to forearm to be vertical. The Skin Modifier assigned to the arm mesh deforms the skin of the arm, but there is no change in dimension (see Figure 11.15). Straighten the arm back near the original position.

2. In the Front viewport, select the ARM mesh. In the Modify panel, Parameters rollout, click the Edit Envelopes button and choose Bone03 in the list. You will see that area of influence of the bone in the shaded viewport (see Figure 11.16).

3. In the Modify panel, Parameters rollout, check the Vertices option in the Filters area.

4. In the Front viewport, drag a selection window around the a few rows of vertices at the biceps area of top of the arm, the area you want to bulge. The selected vertices will turn white. You do not have to be in Select mode; this is a selection for Skin only.

5. In the list of Angle Deformers, at the bottom of the Gizmo Rollout, choose Bulge Angle Deformer. In the Gizmo rollout, click the Add Gizmo button. This relates the angle of Bone03 with the current angle, about 180 degrees.

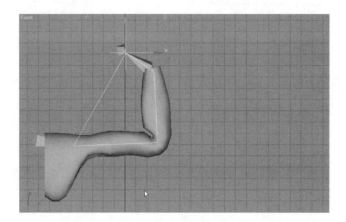

Figure 11.15   Move the Goal of the HI Solver so the forearm is vertical.
The mesh bends but does not change dimension.

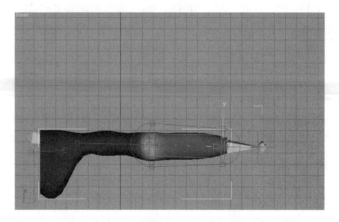

Figure 11.16   The influence area of envelopes shows as colored information in shaded viewport. Red is greatest influence, blue is
no influence.

note   A Bulge Angle Deformer only works on the vertices influenced by the
currently active bone's parent bone. The Joint Angle Deformer functions on the vertices influenced by either the active bone or the parent
bone.

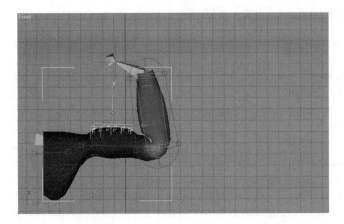

Figure 11.17   In the Deformer Parameters rollout, click Edit Lattice. Select the top two rows of lattice control points and move them upward.

6. In the Stack View, return to the Skin level to exit Envelope mode. In the Front viewport, move the Goal so the forearm is in the vertical position.

7. Select the ARM mesh and choose Envelope level in Stack View. In the Deformer Parameters rollout, check the Edit Lattice button. You will now change the vertices for the new current Bone03 angle.

8. In the Front viewport, select the two top rows of control points for the Bulge Angle Deformer Gizmo and move them up slightly to form a bulging biceps (see Figure 11.17).

> **tip**
>
> The Bulge Angle Gizmo only modifies the vertices that are under the influence of the Parent bone of the bone you change the angle on. Use the Joint Angle Deformer to change the vertices for both the Parent and Child bones.

9. In Stack View, return to the Skin level. In the Front viewport, move the HI Solver Goal to straighten the arm out, and then back to vertical. The biceps should bulge based on the angle of the forearm bone.

10. Save the file. It should already be called Ch11_Skin01.max. The influence ranges in the shaded view makes it easier to adjust the influence of bones and the Angle Deformer options allow for a more convincing look to your animations.

The subtleties that can be created with the Angle Deformers and the new bones enhancements in 3ds max 4 will allow you to create very interesting effects without any add-on software.

As with everything new, start slowly with simple examples and work into more complex scenarios.

Chapter Summary

- **Controllers and constraints** You have learned some aspects of the new constraint system of animation control in 3ds max 4. Constraints like, Path, Position, Look-At, and Orientation have similarities with the old controllers so are not difficult to learn. But they offer much more control by allowing two or more objects to influence the animation created by the constraint. This opens the way for you to create more interesting and complex animations with little more effort.

- **Inverse Kinematics** With a new system of Inverse Kinematics, you learned that setting up and animating a hierarchical linked set of bones or objects is easier to do in 3ds max 4. You now have the control afforded by multiple chains within a bone system and a Swivel Angle manipulator that allows you to direct the direction the bones system functions in.

- **Modifier improvements** You learned about improvements in both the Flex and Skin modifiers. Flex now has better soft body simulation capabilities that allows you to drape cloth or flatten objects onto surfaces, for example. Forces such as Wind or Push or Drag can modify the Soft Body effect within the Flex modifier. Deflectors can also be added to further influence the behavior of the Flex action. The Skin modifier now has the ability to change the mesh based on the angle of bones below or adjacent to the vertices you want to change. This can be used for bulging or morphing effects to give your animations a more organic feel.

Rendering: Interactivity and Layering

In This Chapter

Chapter 12 focuses on some of the new features introduced into 3ds max 4 that deal with rendering and preparing scenes to be rendered. Much of your time involved in the production of a 3D rendered scene is testing rendering images to see changes resulting in some adjustment to file parameters. Other fairly large amounts of time can be spent trying to adjust individual components of a rendered image such as darkening the shadows, coloring the highlights, blurring reflections, and others.

3ds max 4 has added several features that will aid in speeding up the aforementioned situations:

- **ActiveShade** This is an interactive floating window or a viewport showing many elements of the rendered scene. As you make adjustments to lights and materials, the effects show immediately in the ActiveShade view. If you have a slow computer and graphics card, using the ActiveShade option could use valuable resources and could be counter-productive in some cases.

- **Render Elements** Shadows, Specular highlights, Z Depth information, and Self-Illumination are several examples of the types of elements that can be rendered as separate files during the render pass.

- **Render controls** Automatic Exposure controls allow you to adjust overall exposure, color, and chromatic adaptation as part of the render environment.

- **Multi-Pass rendering** Multi-Pass rendering is an improved method of creating Motion Blur and Depth of Field effects in 3ds max 4.

You will learn how to use the ActiveShade feature to cut back on time spent test rendering scenes while adjusting lighting and materials. You will also learn the new methods of rendering individual files containing information that can be modified and composited back to a single image. This can be accomplished in Video Post within 3ds max 4 or, better yet, in a Photoshop or a high-end compositing software like Discreet's Combustion.

Rendering controls are something you will find helpful when making global adjustments to images when sending them to printers or video-output devices. Then you will see how the Multi-Pass feature can give your scenes more punch by adding blurring effects or simulated depth of field.

Key Terms

Render   This process changes vector file information into a 2D format.

Depth of Field   This effect causes objects farther from a camera lens to be more blurred than closer objects.

Motion Blur   This is a blurring effect caused by fast moving objects being recorded on tape or film.

Interactivity Enhancements

There are two new features you will learn about in this section that can help make it easier to view changes affecting rendering. Now 3ds max 4 now supports Microsoft's DirectX 8 and Direct3D 7 and 8 video improvements. With a video card that supports DirectX or Direct3D capabilities, you will be able to view vertex illumination and alpha, true transparency, motion blurring, and particle system effects in the display viewports.

Also, you can use the new ActiveShade feature to render a scene, and then any changes to materials or lighting will update in the ActiveShade window without rerendering the entire scene.

In Exercise 12.1 you will open a file containing three bottles on a table top. You will use ActiveShade to view the effect of lights being turned on in the scene. You will also make some material adjustments to see how the ActiveShade works with selected objects.

note

The features you get and how they are displayed will differ for each card and driver combination.

Exercise 12.1: ActiveShade

1. Open a file called Ch12_ActShade.max on the CD-ROM. Save it as Ch12_ActShade01.max. It is a file with a table top and three green bottles. There are several lights in the scene, but only one light is turned on. Click the ActiveShade button at the far right of the main toolbar. The ActiveShade window appears, and you will see a thin red line progress across the top of the view

area. ActiveShade is initializing. After initialization has taken place, you will see a thin green line progress down the right side of the window. This is updating the viewport. The scene is fairly dark because there is only one low-level Omni light on.

2. In the Top viewport, select Omni03 near the bottom of the viewport, and move it a little to the left. The green line will progress down the right side of the ActiveShade window, and the new lighting effect is updated without rerendering the entire scene.

tip   If you have a slower machine or a large file, setting the render resolution in the Render Scene dialog to 320 × 240 will cause ActiveShade to use that resolution, rendering quicker as a result.

3. In the Lights & Cameras Tab menu, click the Light Lister tool. This button is only found in this Tab menu, not in any other panels or menus. For this scene, the Light Lister shows three other lights in the scene that are not checked on. You will also see the adjustments that can be made to all lights without searching through the scene and selecting the light to adjust it in the Modify panel. There is also a Global Settings rollout that allows you to adjust all lights at once (see Figure 12.1). Move and resize the Light Lister dialog so the Lights rollout and the ActiveShade window are both visible in the display.

4. In the Light Lister dialog, check the On checkboxes for the other three lights in the scene. The green line will update the ActiveShade window, but you will see no changes. This is an action the requires the entire scene to be reinitialized. Right-click in the ActiveShade window and choose Initialize in the Tools quad menu (see Figure 12.2). The red line will appear in viewport and the scene will be rerendered to update the lighting changes. Close the Light Lister dialog.

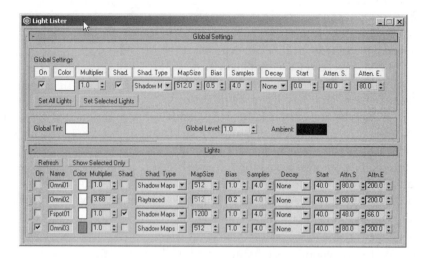

Figure 12.1   This is the Light Lister tool with Global Settings expanded. Omni03 is the only light turned on in the scene.

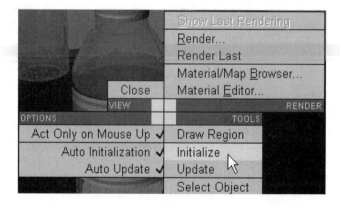

Figure 12.2   Right-click in the ActiveShade window and choose Initialize in the Tools Quad menu.

tip   You can read the progress of the reinitialization and updating in the Status line as well as by viewing the progress of the red and green lines in the ActiveShade window.

note

In ActiveShade, the Initialize Pass must evaluate the geometry in the scene, apply any SpaceWarps, evaluate transforms and clipping, process textures and shade materials, and perform optimization routine, then store the information in a buffer. These are time-consuming steps.

During the Update Pass, the software uses the buffer information and only has to change the pixels that are affected in the image by changing a light or material.

Moving objects in the scene does not update because that step is evaluated by initialization.

Initialize and Update are set to automatic by default, but can be changed to manual to allow you to control when each is performed. This enables you to change several parameters in the scene before updating, for example.

5. Open the Material Editor and click on the LABEL01 sample window. Click the Material/Map Navigator button, and in the Navigator, choose Material 1:LABEL01_BASE [Standard] (see Figure 12.3).

6. In the Material Editor, Multi-Layer Basic Parameters rollout, change the Diffuse color swatch to a bright blue. In the ActiveShade window you will see the Update progress bar, and the labels will change from red to blue without rerendering. Close all dialogs except the Material Editor.

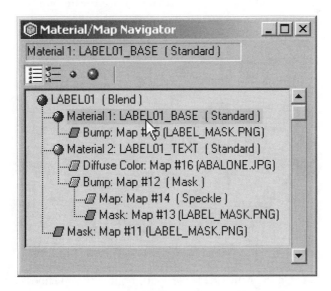

Figure 12.3   In the Material Editor, Material/Map Navigator, choose Material 1:LABEL01_BASE [Standard].

7. Right-click in Camera01 viewport to make sure it is active. Right-click on the Camera01 label, choose Views in the menu, and choose ActiveShade in the next pop-up menu. The Camera01 viewport will turn to an ActiveShade viewport and reinitialize.

8. Right-click in the ActiveShade viewport and choose Draw Region in the Tools quad menu. In the ActiveShade viewport, drag a region around the front label and approximately half the label on the second bottle.

9. In the Material Editor, change the label color to orange. In the ActiveShade viewport, right-click on the dotted line of the region you drew, and in the Tools quad menu, choose Update. The area within the region will update without having to calculate the rest of the scene (see Figure 12.4).

10. Right-click in the ActiveShade viewport and choose Close in the View quad menu. This returns the viewport to a Camera01 viewport.

11. Save the file. It should already be called Ch12_ActShade01.max. You have seen that ActiveShade as a window or viewport can reduce the amount of time you spend rerendering while testing changes in your scenes.

tip

By right-clicking in an ActiveShade viewport, you can choose Select Object and pick an object in the viewport. Now only that object will be initialized or updated. Only one object may be selected at a time.

caution

ActiveShade is not a rendered scene. There are restrictions on the quality and accuracy of the image. You should always do a full test render before committing the scene to a file.

Figure 12.4   In the ActiveShade viewport, right-click and choose Draw Region. In the viewport, drag a region around the front label and half the second label. Right-click on the dotted line of the region and choose Update.

ActiveShade will be very helpful in speeding your day-to-day work. You will soon learn which changes need reinitializing and which will be updated, and your rerender testing will become much less frequent.

Rendering Enhancements

Several features have been included in 3ds max 4 to give you more options while rendering, including:

- Render elements
- Render controls
- Multi-Pass rendering

In this section of the chapter you will perform a few simple exercises that illustrate the functionality and potential of each of the new enhancements.

Most of these rendering changes will be more helpful to those of you who are rendering high-quality, high-resolution images for fields such as television or film, architecture, or advertising. However, many may find the features interesting for making special effects and for tweaking aspects of the rendering.

Render Elements

Render Elements is an option found in the Render Scene dialog that lets you choose various components of an entire rendered scene for rendering to separate files. The separate files can then be manipulated or used in other software for their own purposes or can be composited back into the original rendering. The elements that can be rendered out include:

- **Diffuse**   The diffuse element is the color information.
- **Specular**   This file contains only the specular highlights.
- **Self-Illumination**   This is the self-illumination information.
- **Shadow**   Any shadows in the scene are saved to this file.
- **Reflection**   All reflections are saved here.
- **Refraction**   This element contains refractions.
- **Atmosphere**   Atmospheric effects such as fog and volume lighting are saved here.
- **Z Buffer**   A Z Buffer or Z Depth file is a grayscale image with objects closer to the viewer appearing whiter.

- **Alpha**   An alpha file contains transparency information for matting and masking.

- **Colored Shadow**   Colored shadow files contain only the color differences between shadowed and unshadowed color.

- **Background**   This file contains only the background information.

- **Blend**   Blend saves a combination of the previous elements that you chose.

In Exercise 12.2 you will select several components of the file used in Exercise 12.1 to see the effect of rendering elements.

Exercise 12.2: Render Elements

1. Open a file from the CD-ROM called Ch12_RendElement.max. Save it as Ch12_RendElement01.max. It is the scene with three bottles on a table top. Right-click in the Camera01 viewport to make sure it is active.

2. Click the Render Scene button in the main toolbar. In the Common Parameters rollout, click the Files button and save a file named BOTTLES.PNG in a convenient subdirectory. Expand the Render Elements rollout in the Render Scene dialog (see Figure 12.5).

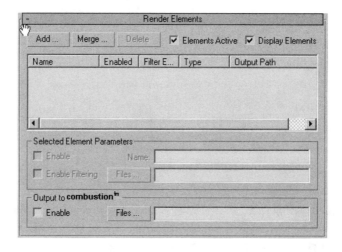

Figure 12.5   In the Render Scene dialog, expand the Render Elements rollout. You can Add or Merge elements to be rendered as separate files within the Render Elements rollout.

3. In the Render Elements rollout, click the Add button. In the Render Elements list, double-click Diffuse (see Figure 12.6) to save the diffuse information to a separate file in the same sub-directory you entered for the BOTTLES.PNG file in Step 2.

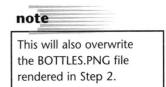

note

This will also overwrite the BOTTLES.PNG file rendered in Step 2.

4. Repeat Step 3 to add Z Depth, Reflections, and Specular elements to the list of rendered elements (see Figure 12.7).

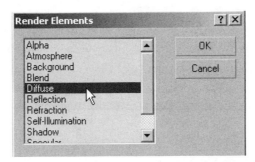

Figure 12.6   In the Render Elements rollout, click the Add button, and then double-click Diffuse in the list of Render Elements available.

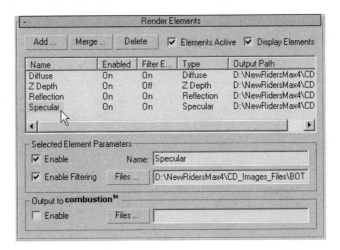

Figure 12.7   The Render Elements list should contain entries for Diffuse, Z Depth, Reflection, and Specular.

5. In the Render Scene dialog, click the Render button. The scene will render normally and the resulting image will be saved to a file. There will also be several quick flashes, and new Virtual Frame Buffer windows will appear with each element. The separate files will be saved with names such as BOTTLES_Specular.png on your hard drive.

6. Close all dialogs and save the file. It should already be called Ch12_RendElement01.max. You may now use the separate files in a program such as Photoshop or Combustion.

If you do not have access to one of the compositing software packages, you could use Video Post to apply Adobe Photoshop or Premier filters or any other available effects to the separate element files, then composite them into a single image file.

Another option in the Render Elements rollout is to render the image as a Discreet Combustion .cws scene. When opened in Combustion, these .cws files contain all the lights and cameras as well as the Z Depth information for fine tuning or special effects.

Automatic Exposure Controls

While not an earth-shaking addition to the program, Automatic Exposure controls can help make global tweaks to the rendered scene easier. Automatic Exposure controls are found in the Rendering pull-down menu, Environment dialog, Automatic Exposure Control Parameters rollout (see Figure 12.8).

The options found in the Automatic Exposure Control Parameters rollout include:

- **Physical Scale**   This is an exposure scale in candelas that affects the brighter areas of the scene more than the darker areas of the scene. It affects the light multiplier values, self-illumination, and some reflection and refraction maps. Upper limits keep the scene from burning completely.

- **Exposure Value**   This affects the brightness in both dark and bright areas.

- **Chromatic Adaptation**   This is a type of color correction. The color in the Color Swatch is essentially subtracted from the scene.

- **Color Differentiation**   This boosts the color information in dark areas of the scene as exposure compensation.

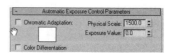

Experiment with the Automatic Exposure controls on a scene with a wide range of brightness values and color information. As with all color correction methods, less is usually better, but again, these features can be used for special effects.

Figure 12.8

In Rendering pull-down, Environment dialog, expand the Automatic Exposure Control Parameters rollout.

Multi-Pass Render Options

As the name Multi-Pass implies, the following options make several render passes to create an effect by building layers in the final image:

- **Depth of Field**   This simulates the distance blurring you will get with a normal camera lens.

- **Motion Blur**   This simulates the blurring effects picked up by film and video cameras of fast-moving objects.

In Exercise 12.3 you will apply both effects to a simple file that contains a trailer in a landscape and some accoutrements found around many trailers: a satellite dish and a lawn ornament. You will use the Depth of Field effect to blur the distant hills. This will focus the viewer's gaze to the foreground elements of the scene.

You will then add the Motion Blur effect to blur the animated wings for the lawn ornament. The Multi-Pass effects are added directly to the camera.

Exercise 12.3: Multi-Pass Rendering Effects

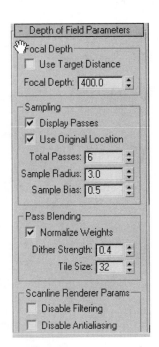

1. Open a file called Ch12_Multipass.max. Save it as Ch12_Multipass01.max. The scene contains a duck, a trailer, a satellite dish, and landscape. Click the Quick Render button in the Main toolbar. In the Rendering pull-down menu, choose RAM Player. In the RAM Player, click Open Last Rendered Image in Channel A and minimize the RAM Player.

2. In the Modify panel, with the Camera01 selected, go to the Multi-Pass Effect area of the Parameters rollout, and make sure Depth of Field is the effect in the list and that the Enable box is checked in the Depth of Field Parameters rollout (see Figure 12.9). The parameters are preset to a Focal Depth of 400 units, Total Passes is set to 6, and a Sample Radius of 3.0 to exaggerate the effect somewhat. All other parameters are default settings.

3. In the Modify panel, Parameters rollout, check the Enable checkbox in the Multi-Pass Effect area. Click the Quick Render button in the main toolbar. The scene will render six times. Each render has a different blur amount and is added to the last rendering pass. The end effect is a graduated blurring of the scene.

Figure 12.9

Select Camera01, and in the Modify panel's Depth of Field Parameters rollout, view the preset values.

4. Maximize the RAM Player and click the Open Last Rendered Image in Channel B button. Compare the two images with and without blurring. Background objects are blurred more than foreground objects.

5. In the Parameters rollout, Multi-Pass Effect area change Depth of Field to Motion Blur (see Figure 12.10). In the Motion Blur Parameters rollout, enter 6 in the Total Passes field.

6. Drag the Frame Slider to set frame 55 as the current frame. Click the Quick Render button. Again, six render passes will be made. This time the fastest-moving objects in the scene are blurred. The wing toward the camera is rotating faster than the other wing (see Figure 12.11).

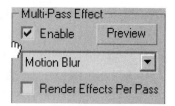

Figure 12.10
In the Parameters rollout, Multi-Pass Effect area, choose Motion Blur.

> tip
>
> For a quick-and-dirty test of the Depth of Field (or Motion Blur) effect in the active viewport, you can click the Preview button in the Parameters rollout, Multi-Pass Effect area. Note that the entire viewport is blurred, Grid Lines, Gizmos, and so on.

Figure 12.11   Frame 55 rendered with Motion Blur Multi-Pass Effect shows the faster-rotating wing with more motion blur.

7. Save the file. It should already be called Ch12_Multipass01.max. Adding blurring effects to scenes, whether it is Depth of Field or Motion Blur can add to the render time significantly. If used judicially, these are powerful tools for composing your scenes and giving a feel of greater movement in animation or stills.

note   Multi-Pass Depth of Field and Motion Blur are relatively fast methods of creating each effect. However, they are mutually exclusive. You cannot have both effects for the same camera. If you need Depth of Field and Motion Blur, set the camera to use Multi-Pass Depth of Field, then use Object Motion Blur in the Rendering pull-down menu, Effects menu. Object Motion Blur is somewhat slower than Multi-Pass Motion Blur.

Chapter Summary

This chapter on display interactivity and render effects has introduced you to the new features that will save test rendering times and create better images by using special effects enhancements, for example:

- **ActiveShade**   You learned that you can now speed the testing process by viewing some light and material changes directly in a window or viewport without rerendering the entire scene. Also, you learned that objects selected in the ActiveShade viewports are reinitialized or updated rather than the changes being applied the whole scene.

- **Render elements**   You learned to render elements such as shadows, specular highlights, Z depth information, and self-illumination as separate files that can be manipulated with other software for fine tuning or special effects.

- **Render controls**   You were introduced to Automatic Exposure controls that allow you to adjust the brightness of the scene and to color correct the scene without adjusting individual lights or materials.

- **Multi-Pass rendering**   Two effects that have been enhanced in 3ds max 4 are Depth of Field and Motion Blurring effects. They can both be added and adjusted in the Camera Modify panel.

Glossary

ActiveShade   ActiveShade is a floating dialog similar to the VFB, but it interactively updates to show scene-lighting or material changes without rerendering. It works on the whole scene or on only selected objects.

Ambient color   Ambient color is the color of the object in the shaded portion or where the object is in the shadow of another object.

Ambient light   Ambient light is the general light that illuminates the entire scene. It has a uniform intensity and is uniformly diffuse. It has no discernible source and no discernible direction

Angle of incidence   The more a surface inclines away from a light source, the less light it receives and the darker it appears. The angle of the surface normal relative to the light source is known as the angle of incidence.

Animation constraint
Constraints are a new form of animation controller in 3ds max 4 that allow multiple weighted objects or parameters to modify animation.

Animation controller   Controllers are plug-ins that handle all the animation tasks in 3ds max 4. All objects have controllers of one form or another by default.

Attenuation   In the real world, light diminishes over distance. Objects far from the light source appear darker; objects near the source appear brighter. This effect is known as attenuation.

Border   A new sub-object level within the Polygon mesh object. Edges form a closed interior border.

Bump maps   Bump maps are maps that use the brightness values of pixels to cause the rendered illusion of raised or depressed areas on objects without generating new geometry.

Codec   Short for compressor/decompressor, codec is an algorithm for compressing and decompressing digital video data and the software that implements that algorithm.

Command panel   Six user-interface panels for accessing most of the modeling and editing tools in 3ds max 4.

Constraints   Constraints are a new form of controller that allows multiple influences on the animation.

Controllers   All animation is calculated by a controller assigned to an object or parameter.

Depth of Field   This effect causes objects farther from a camera lens to be more blurred than closer objects.

Diffuse color   The diffuse color is the color that the object reflects when illuminated by "good lighting," that is, by direct daylight or artificial light that makes the object easy to see.

Direct light   Directional lights cast parallel light rays within a cylinder, as the sun does (for all practical purposes) at the surface of the earth.

Dithering   Dithering is also a method of smoothing the edges between two color regions by mixing their pixels so the edges appear to blend together.

Dummy object   A Dummy helper object is a wireframe cube with a pivot point at its geometric center. It has a name but no parameters, you can't modify it, and it doesn't render. Its only real feature is its pivot, which is used as a center for transforms. The wireframe acts as a reference for transform effects.

Edge   The edge of a 3D face or patch is the boundary of a triangular face that connects two vertices.

Element   An element is a sub-object level collection of faces that is treated as a single entity.

Face Normals   Face Normals are vectors that define the direction a face surface points. If the Face Normal points toward the viewer, the faces are visible in the display and rendered image. Face Normals may be flipped or overridden with 2-sided materials.

Face   A face is a flat triangular plane that is the building block of mesh surfaces.

Fields   A method for conveying frame information on a video signal has been developed. This method is called field interlacing. Television monitors display a video signal by separately scanning two portions of each frame called fields. One field contains the odd scan lines of a frame, and the other field contains the even scan lines. The fields are alternately cycled through every other horizontal line on the screen in a way that they "layer" together to form a single interlaced image.

Forward Kinematics   Forward Kinematics is motion from the top down in a bones system. Moving the hand does not move the upper arm. Move the upper arm and the hand moves.

Glossiness   Glossiness adjusts the size of the specular highlights scattered from the surface.

GUI   Graphical User Interface, what you see in the display.

Hierarchical link   The Select and Link and Unlink buttons on the left side of the toolbar are used to make and break links between objects in your scene. The links are in the form of Parent/Child relationships. The Parent controls the Child.

Home grids   A grid and work plane that defines the default working planes for 3ds max 4.

HSDS   Hierarchical Sub Division Surface. A new method of subdividing surfaces for multiple levels of higher localized detail.

IFL File   IFL (Image File List) is an ASCII file that lists other single-frame bitmap files to be used for each rendered frame.

Inverse Kinematics   Inverse Kinematics is the movement of bones systems controlled from the end back to the parent. The hand moving the upper arm is an example.

Keyboard shortcuts   Combinations of keys that, when pressed, call various commands or options in 3ds max 4. They are fully customizable.

Keyframe   Keyframes record the beginning and end of each transformation of an object or element in the scene. The values at these keyframes are called keys.

Manipulator   A preprogrammed or customized parameter used to manipulate parameters of objects directly in the viewports.

Maps   The images you assign to materials as patterns are called maps. 3ds max 4 provides several different map types. They include standard bitmaps (such as .bmp, .jpg, or .tga files), procedural maps (such as Checker or Marble), and image-processing systems such as compositors and masking systems.

Material Libraries   Material Libraries are files on the hard drive used to store material and map definitions. They can be accessed from any 3ds max 4 file.

Materials   A material is data that you assign to the surface or faces of an object so that it appears a certain way when rendered. Materials affect the color of objects, their shininess, their opacity, and so on.

MAXScript listener   A window at the lower left of the display with a white and a pink field that is used in conjunction with the MAXScript scripting language.

Modifier Stack   The Modifier Stack is a hierarchical list of modifiers that represents the history of changes to an object.

Modifier   A modifier changes an object's geometrical structure, deforming it in some way. Modifiers make changes in the geometry that stay in effect until you adjust or delete the modifier.

Motion Blur   This is a blurring effect caused by fast moving objects being recorded on tape or film.

Multipass rendering effect   A multipass rendering effect uses multiple renderings of the same frame. The multiple passes simulate the blurring that film in a camera would register under certain conditions. Depth of Field and Motion Blur effects are available in 3ds max 4.

NTSC   NTSC (National Television Standards Committee) is the name of the video standard used in North America, most of Central and South America, and Japan. The frame rate is 30 frames per second (fps) or 60 fields per second, with each field accounting for half the interleaved scan lines on a television screen.

Omni light   An Omni light provides a point source of illumination that shoots out in all directions and casts light to infinity.

Opacity   Opacity is the ability of a material to block the passage of light. It is the opposite of transparency.

Opacity maps   Opacity maps use the brightness of pixels to create the illusion of opacity or transparency on surfaces.

PAL   PAL (Phase Alternate Line) is the video standard used in most European countries. The frame rate is 25 frames per second (fps) or 50 fields per second, with each field accounting for half the interleaved scan lines on a television screen.

Point Cache   A file on disk containing the position data for animated sub-object level information. Allows complex animation to play back in real time in the display.

Polygon   A polygon is a collection of triangular faces surrounded by visible edges.

Polygon mesh   A new class of object in 3ds max 4 that uses quads instead of triangles as a sub-object edit level.

Pull-down menus   Menu options at the top of the display that reveal menus when clicked.

Quad menus   A customizable series of menus that appear around the cursor in the display upon right-clicking.

Radiosity   Radiosity is the light bounced from surfaces in the scene onto other surfaces. 3ds max 4 does not calculate radiosity; you must use a program like Lightscape.

Raytrace shadows   Raytraced shadows are generated by tracing the path of rays sampled from a light source. Raytraced shadows are more accurate than shadow-mapped shadows. They always produce a hard edge.

Render   This process changes vector file information into a 2D format.

Rendering   Rendering shades the design's geometry using the lighting you've set up, the materials you've applied, and environment settings, such as background and atmosphere

Resolution   Resolution is simply the number of pixels in width times the number of pixels in height of any image.

Rotoscoping   Rotoscoping is the process of bringing video frames into 3ds max 4 to use as the background for matching objects in a scene.

Segment   A segment is the part of a 2D shape that connects two vertices.

Self-Illumination   Self-Illumination creates the illusion of incandescence by replacing any shadows on the surface with the diffuse color. At 100 percent, the shadows are completely replaced by the diffuse color, creating the illusion of self-illumination.

Shader   A shader is an component of a material that adjusts the shape and edge transition of specular highlights.

Shadow maps   A Shadow map is a bitmap that the renderer generates during a pre-rendering pass of the scene. Shadow maps don't show the color cast by transparent or translucent objects. Shadow maps can have soft-edged shadows.

Shape   A shape is an object made up of one or more splines.

Smoothing   Smoothing is a render effect that causes adjacent faces to appear faceted or smoothed at their shared edge. Smoothing Group Numbers option can be assigned to faces. If two faces share a common number, the edge is smoothed.

Specular color   Specular color is the color scattered off the surface of a material.

Specular level   Specular level is the brightness of the specular highlights, scattered light from a surface.

Spline   A spline is a collection of vertices and connecting segments that form a line.

Spotlight   A spotlight casts a focused beam of light in a cone like a flashlight, a follow spot in a theater, or a headlight.

Status bars   An area of controls and informational windows at the bottom of the display.

Sub-object   Some types of objects let you change to a sub-object level to edit their component parts. For example, editable meshes have Vertex, Edge, Face, Polygon, and Element sub-object levels. NURBS models can have Surface, Curve, Point, Surface CV, Curve CV, and Import sub-object levels. You change the active sub-object level using the Modifier Stack rollout on the Modify panel. The right-click menu provides an alternative way to change the sub-object level.

Tab panel   A row of tabbed toolbars that can be customized by the user.

Tangency   The tangent of a Function Curve affects the interpolated values between keys of an animation. Most animation controllers use fixed tangents to define the Function Curve at a key location. By default, 3ds max 4 assigns smooth tangents to the keys in a Position Function Curve. This is the reason that an animated object moves in smooth curves through the keyframes. 3ds max 4 assigns smooth tangents because they usually provide the most natural motion.

Tessellation   The subdivision of surfaces for higher density.

Tiling   Tiling is an adjustment of maps to vary the repeating patterns.

Time controls   A set of buttons at the lower right of the default display used to configure and control the creation and playback of animations.

Toolbar   A docked or floating collection of command and editing buttons.

Track Bar   The Track Bar provides a timeline below the viewports showing the frame numbers (or appropriate display units). It provides a quick alternative to Track View for moving, copying, and deleting keys and for changing key properties.

Track View   With Track View you can view and edit all the keys that you create. You can also assign animation controllers to interpolate or control all the keys and parameters for the objects in your scene. Some of the functions in Track View, such as moving and deleting keys, are also available on the Track Bar near the time slider. Thirteen Track View layouts can be named and stored in the Track View buffer.

Vertex   A vertex is a nondimensional point in space. Vertices are found in both 2D and 3D objects.

Viewport controls   Navigation tools at the lower right of the display to adjust the viewer's perspective of viewports.

Viewports   A rectangular window to view the 3ds max 4 scene.

Virtual Frame Buffer   The Virtual Frame Buffer (VFB) is a separate dialog in which the software displays rendered output.

What's on the CD-ROM

The accompanying CD-ROM is packed with all sorts of exercise files and products to help you work with this book and with 3ds max 4. The following sections contain detailed descriptions of the CD's contents.

For more information about the use of this CD, please review the ReadMe.txt file in the root directory. This file includes important disclaimer information as well as information about installation, system requirements, troubleshooting, and technical support.

 note

> **Technical Support Issues**
> If you have any difficulties with this CD, you can access our tech support website at http://www.mcp.com/press/CService_form.cfm.

System Requirements

This CD-ROM was configured for use on systems running all Windows (9x and NT) and Macintosh operating systems.

Loading the CD Files

To load the files from the CD, insert the disc into your CD-ROM drive. If autoplay is enabled on your machine, the CD-ROM setup program starts auotmatically the first time you insert the disc. You may copy the files to your hard drive, or use them right off the disc.

 This CD-ROM uses long and mixed-case filenames, requiring the use of a protected mode CD-ROM driver.

Exercise and Figure Files

This CD contains all the files you'll need to complete the exercises in *3ds max 4 Fundamentals*. These files can be found in the root directory's Exercises folder. Please note, however, that you'll not find a folder for Chapter 2 because this chapter does not contain any exercises. Also, each screenshot in this book can be found in full-color in the Figures folder.

Third-Party Programs

This CD also contains several third-party programs and demos from leading industry companies. These programs have been carefully selected to help you strengthen your professional skills in 3ds max 4.

Please note that some of the programs included on this CD-ROM are shareware-"try-before-you-buy"-software. Please support these independent vendors by purchasing or registering any shareware software that you use for more than 30 days. Check with the documentation provided with the software on where and how to register the product.

- **Ultimate MAX Internet Guide (Applied-Ideas)**   Contains a searchable database of over 450 Internet sites. You can search by simple built-in functions like listing all sites that have free tutorials or use a more specific keyword search engine. www.applied-ideas.com

- **Forest Pack Lite (Itoosoft)**   Forest Pack is a package designed to help you create large surfaces of trees and plants. Forest enables you to create a complete forest with thousands of trees. www.itoosoft.com

- **Texporter (Cuneyt Ozdas)**   Texporter is a utility plug-in. Its main purpose is simple mesh painting. If your mesh painting needs are not heavy, then this utility is for you. It unfolds the mesh according to the mapping coordinates and lets you paint whatever you want using your favorite painting program (Photoshop, Fractal Painter, and so on). You can also use this template image to warp an existing image so that it fits perfectly to the mesh when you map it onto the mesh. www.cuneytozdas.com

- **Toy Train (HABWare)**   Toy train is a system plug-in, in which you can define trailers, following an engine at a given distance. www.habware.at

- **Clay Studio Pro (Digimation)**   The best metaballs program for 3ds max just got bigger and better! Clay Studio Pro builds on the interactive foundation laid by Clay Studio, and adds a new creation type to the mix: Clay splines. Clay splines enable you to draw 2D and 3D splines that essentially have the Clay spheres strung along their length. www.digimation.com

- **Texture Lab: Elemental Tools (Digimation)**   Tlab is the first collection of six procedural mapping types representing Fire, Water, Fog, Electrics, Strata, and Noise. These procedurals work in much the same way as the ones that ship with 3ds max, such as Dents or Marble. They can be used in any combination to produce stunning effects[md]everything from animated swirling clouds and water caustics to skin or jittery electricity. www.digimation.com

- **Spray Master (Digimation)**   Do you need to precisely place lots of geometry in your scenes, but find that Scatter was too limiting in its approach? Spray Master is the tool you need. Spray Master enables users to spray geometry, both 2D and 3D, as particles on or around other objects with an easy-to-use freehand brush or spline-based control. If you need lots of particles in one location, simply spray in one spot. www.digimation.com

- **Texture Lab: Tiling Tools (Digimation)**   Texture Lab: Tiling Tools is the sequel to the original Texture Lab: Elemental Tools plug-in. Like the original Texture Lab: Elemental Tools, Texture Lab: Tiling Tools is a collection of material maps for 3ds max and consists of three powerful mapping types. These maps can be applied to any map channel in any material, but are generally used in the Diffuse, Opacity, and/or Bump map channels. www.digimation.com

- **Fractal Mountain Landscape Generator (EffectWare)**   A simple click-and-drag terrain generator, useful if you need to create an impressive landscape in minutes. www.effectware.com

- **EffectWare Stairs (EffectWare)**   Create spiral and straight staircases instantly with this no-fuss, click-and-drag plug-in. www.effectware.com

Index

SYMBOLS

F

H

L

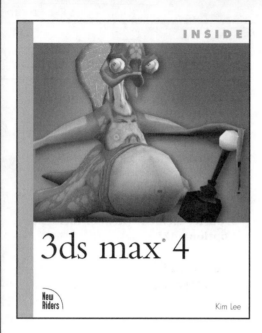

Inside 3ds max 4

Available July 2001

If you enjoyed *3ds max Fundamentals*, be sure to check out New Rider's *Inside 3ds max 4* (ISBN 0-7357-1094-5, $49.99). This latest edition of *Inside 3ds max 4* mirrors an actual production workflow—from concept through output—all the while providing you with best practices and techniques.

Author Kim Lee is recognized as a master teacher in the 3ds max community, and his vision for this project-based reference/tutorial makes it the most useful, real-world look at using this newest version of MAX.

Throughout the following pages, we give you a preview of what this book has to offer.

For more info, stay tuned to www.newriders.com.

Contents

Introduction by Kim Lee

With this new edition of *Inside 3ds max 4*, New Riders Publishing has decided to make some big changes. They wanted a fresh, new approach to the series that would appeal specifically to intermediate and advanced users and go beyond the documentation to help you make the most of your time and effort. Having read many of the past volumes, as well as other works on the subject, I suggested that we put together a book that not only covered the many new features in 3ds max 4 but also focused on real-world use of the tool in production. In order to do that, we needed to involve hands-on artists and technical directors. So, I rounded up a group of fellow post-production artists in the games, broadcast, and film environments and assigned them to write chapters in their areas of expertise. These people, who work day in and day out with 3ds max 4 in production, are in a unique position to bring the much-needed insight into how it really works in a production environment.

The authors have aimed to cover the many new features of 3ds max 4 within the context of a real project. Within these pages you will find many topics that have been merely touched on or even ignored in other publications. However, you may find that certain other topics or techniques have been seemingly left out. The reason for this is simple. The first mandate given to all the authors was "If you don't use it, don't write it." While there are numerous solutions to a given problem in a tool such as 3ds max 4, some are impractical or lack flexibility. This book provides techniques that the authoring artists have found to be the best practical solution in a production environment. They are by no means the only solutions in this ever-changing and evolving field of 3d animation.

I also felt that the book should try to mirror, as closely as was feasible, a real-world production workflow (pipeline for those of you who like catch phrases). For many advanced students and professionals in the field, books on this topic can be and are a major resource for the ever-expanding technical knowledge required by today's computer graphics community. Unfortunately for many readers, myself included, all too often the texts available to the public present tutorials and instruction that, while perhaps technically and theoretically

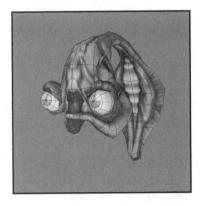

sound, are not practically applicable in a production environment. Being active in the broadcast industry, I, as well as many of my colleagues, have been frustrated by the seemingly constant stream of new animators who have been taught impractical 3d techniques and are unclear of how a full production is completed. Therefore the decision was made to mirror the structure of the book to the process of the production world. And, finally, I felt the book needed to focus on two of the main industries using 3ds max, namely broadcast/film and games/interactive. We concluded that by concentrating on both the broadcast/film and games/interactive industries, we would be able to provide useful information and insights to not only users in those respective fields, but hopefully to users in the many other industries (visualization, corporate design, etc.) that could benefit from the techniques covered.

Kim Lee

Inside 3ds max 4 is brought to you by some of the most-respected professionals in the broadcast, film, and gaming industries. Our authors include: Kim Lee, Brian Austin, Doug Barnard, Neil Blevins, Ian Christie, Brandon Davis, Max Ehrlich, Sean Feely, Mike Hall, Adam Holmes, Dan O'Leary, Mike O'Rourke, Boris Ustaev, and Joseph Yoo.

The New Riders Professional Library

3D Studio MAX 3 Fundamentals
Michael Todd Peterson
0-7357-0049-4

Bert Monroy: Photorealistic Techniques with Photoshop & Illustrator
Bert Monroy
0-7357-0969-6

<designing web graphics.3>
Lynda Weinman
1-56205-949-1

Designing Web Usability
Jakob Nielsen
1-56205-810-x

[digital] Character Animation 2 Volume 1: Essential Techniques
George Maestri
1-56205-930-0

[digital] Lighting & Rendering
Jeremy Birn
1-56205-954-8

E-Volve-or-Die.com
Mitchell Levy
0-7357-1028-7

Flash 5 Magic with ActionScript
David Emberton and J. Scott Hamlin
0-7357-1023-6

Flash Web Design: the v5 remix
Hillman Curtis
0-7357-1098-8

Inside 3D Studio MAX 3: Modeling, Materials, and Rendering
Ted Boardman and Jeremy Hubbell
0-7357-0085-0

Inside Adobe Photoshop 6
Gary David Bouton, et. al
0-7357-1038-4

Inside LightWave6
Dan Ablan
0-7357-0919-x

LightWave 6.5 Magic
Dan Ablan, et. al
0-7357-0996-3

Net Results 2: Best Practices for Web Marketing
Rick Bruner
0-7357-1024-4

Photoshop 5 & 5.5 Artistry
Barry Haynes and Wendy Crumpler
0-7357-0994-7

Photoshop 6 Effects Magic
Rhoda Grossman, et. al
0-7357-1035-x

Photoshop 6 Web Magic
Jeff Foster
0-7357-1036-8

Solutions from experts you know and trust.

www.informit.com

New Riders has partnered with **InformIT.com** to bring technical information to your desktop. Drawing on New Riders authors and reviewers to provide additional information on topics you're interested in, **InformIT.com** has free, in-depth information you won't find anywhere else.

- **Master the skills you need, when you need them**

- **Call on resources from some of the best minds in the industry**

- **Get answers when you need them, using InformIT's comprehensive library or live experts online**

- **Go above and beyond what you find in New Riders books, extending your knowledge**

As an **InformIT** partner, **New Riders** has shared the wisdom and knowledge of our authors with you online. Visit **InformIT.com** to see what you're missing.

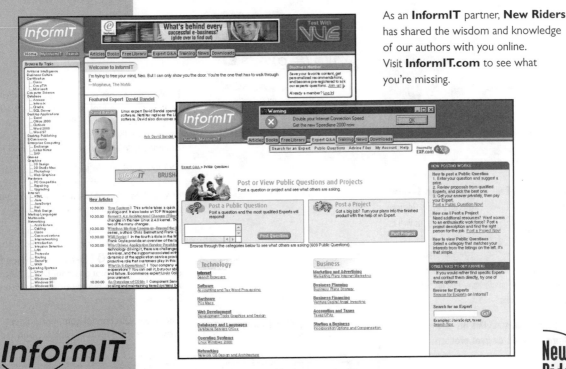

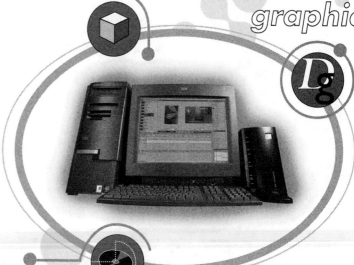

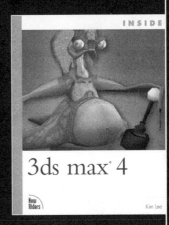

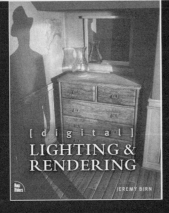

Colophon: *3ds max 4 Fundamentals* was laid out and produced with the help of Microsoft Word, Adobe Acrobat, Adobe Photoshop, Collage Complete, and QuarkXpress on a variety of systems, including a Macintosh G4. With the exception of pages that were printed for proofreading, all files—text, images, and project files—were transferred via email or ftp and edited onscreen.

All body text was set in the Stone Serif family. All headings, figure captions, and cover text were set in the 2 Stone Sans family. The Symbol and Sean's Symbol typefaces were used throughout for special symbols and bullets.

3ds 4 max Fundamentals was printed on 50# Husky Offset Smooth at R.R. Donnelley & Sons in Crawfordsville, Indiana. Prepress consisted of PostScript computer-to-plate technology (filmless process). The cover was printed on 12pt Carolina coated one side at Moore Langen Printing in Terre Haute, Indiana.

The *3ds max 4 Fundamentals* CD

The CD that accompanies this book contains valuable resources for anyone using 3ds 4 max, not the least of which are:

- **Exercise files:** All the example files provided by the author enable you to work through the step-by-step projects.
- **Figure files:** Each figure in this book is provided in full-color in the Figures folder.
- **3ds max 4-related third-party software:** Programs and demos include Forest Pack Lite, Textporter, Clay Studio Pro, and Effectware Stairs.

Accessing the Exercise Files from the CD

The majority of exercises in this book use prebuilt 3ds max 4 files that contain preset parameters, artwork, audio, or other important information you need to work through and build the final project.

We recommend that you copy the exercise files to your hard drive, but this is not absolutely necessary if you don't intend to save the exercise files.

For a complete list of the CD-ROM contents, please see Appendix A, "What's on the CD-ROM"

Read This Before Opening the Software

By opening the CD package, you agree to be bound by the following agreement:

You may not copy or redistribute the entire CD-ROM as a whole. Copying and redistribution of individual software programs on the CD-ROM is governed by terms set by individual copyright holders.

The installer, code, images, actions, and brushes from the author(s) are copyrighted by the publisher and the authors.

This software is sold as-is, without warranty of any kind, either expressed or implied, including but not limited to the implied warranties of merchantability and fitness for a particular purpose. Neither the publisher nor its dealers or distributors assumes any liability for any alleged or actual damages arising from the use of this program. (Some states do not allow for the exclusion of implied warranties, so the exclusion may not apply to you.)